4:50

Ignorance

Manchester University Press

Ignorance
Literature and Agnoiology

Andrew Bennett

Manchester University Press
Manchester and New York
distributed exclusively in the United States exclusively
by Palgrave Macmillan

Copyright © Andrew Bennett 2009

The right of Andrew Bennett to be identified as the author of this work has been asserted by him in accordance with the Copyright, Designs and Patents Act 1988.

Published by Manchester University Press
Oxford Road, Manchester M13 9NR, UK
and Room 400, 175 Fifth Avenue, New York, NY 10010, USA
www.manchesteruniversitypress.co.uk

Distributed in the United States exclusively by
Palgrave Macmillan, 175 Fifth Avenue, New York,
NY 10010, USA

Distributed in Canada exclusively by
UBC Press, University of British Columbia, 2029 West Mall,
Vancouver, BC, Canada V6T 1Z2

British Library Cataloguing-in-Publication Data
A catalogue record for this book is available from the British Library

Library of Congress Cataloging-in-Publication Data applied for

ISBN 978 0 7190 7487 5 *hardback*

First published 2009
18 17 16 15 14 13 12 11 10 09   10 9 8 7 6 5 4 3 2 1

The publisher has no responsibility for the persistence or accuracy of URLs for external or any third-party internet websites referred to in this book, and does not guarantee that any content on such websites is, or will remain, accurate or appropriate.

Typeset
by Florence Production Ltd, Stoodleigh, Devon
Printed in Great Britain
by CPI Antony Rowe, Chippenham, Wiltshire

Contents

	Acknowledgements	*page* vii
	Introduction	1
1	Ignorance and philosophy	9
2	Literary ignorance	33
3	To see as poets do: Romanticism, the sublime and poetic ignorance	55
4	The opposite of epistemology: Keatsian nescience	81
5	Our ignorance of others: *Middlemarch* and *Great Expectations*	100
6	Joseph Conrad's blindness	132
7	Children, death and the enigmatic signifier: Wordsworth and Bowen	154
8	Monsters and trees: epistemelancholia in David Hume and Henry James	176
9	American ignorance: Philip Roth's America trilogy	202
10	The politics of authorial ignorance: contemporary poetry	226
	Index	253

Acknowledgements

My thanks are due to the Arts and Humanities Research Council and to my colleagues in the English Department at the University of Bristol for enabling me to take a period of research leave in order to write this book. A number of chapters have previously been published in earlier forms: Chapter 6 as 'Conrad's Blindness and the Long Short Story', *Oxford Literary Review* 26 (2004): 79–100; Chapter 8 as 'Dendritic', *Oxford Literary Review* 24 (2002), 71–97; part of Chapter 3 as part of 'Poetry and Ignorance', *Angles on the English-Speaking World* 3 (2003), 77–92; Chapter 9 as 'Authorial Ignorance: Philip Roth's American Trilogy', in *Tekijyyden Ulottuvuuksia (Dimensions of Authorship)*, ed. Eeva Haverinen, Erkki Vainikkala and Tuomo Lahdelma (Jyväskylä: Jyväskylän Yliopisto, 2008), pp. 91–114. I would like to thank the editors for permission to reprint this material here.

'Ignorance is not just a blank space on a person's mental map. It has contours and coherence, and for all I know rules of operation as well.' (Thomas Pynchon, Introduction to *Slow Learner*)

'[Y]ou can take interest in what I am doing here only insofar as you would be right to believe that – *somewhere* – I do not know what I am doing.' (Jacques Derrida, *Glas*)

Reading 'demands more ignorance than knowledge'. (Maurice Blanchot, *The Space of Literature*)

'In a manner that is more acute for theoreticians of literature than for theoreticians of the natural or the social world, it can be said that they do not quite know what it is they are talking about, not only in the metaphysical sense that the whatness, the ontology of literature is hard to fathom, but also in the more elusive sense that, whenever one is supposed to speak of literature, one speaks of anything under the sun (including, of course, oneself) except literature.' (Paul de Man, *The Resistance to Theory*)

Introduction

This book concerns the way in which literature, particularly as it is defined at a certain historical moment, is bound up with the question of not knowing. And it concerns the question of what literature knows of ignorance. 'If a narrative is something told', Stanley Cavell speculates very generally in *Disowning Knowledge*, 'and telling is an answer to a claim to knowledge, then perhaps any narrative, however elaborated, may be understood as an answer to some implied question of knowledge, perhaps in the form of some disclaiming of knowledge or avoidance of it'.[1] In this context I will suggest that ignorance may be reconceived as part of the narrative and other force of literature, part of its performativity, and indeed as an important aspect of its thematic focus – what literary texts are 'about'. Concentrating in particular on the Romantic and post-Romantic tradition, I seek to address the question of 'literary ignorance' by attempting to work through some of the consequences of the question of not knowing for our reading of such texts.

The book is also concerned with certain formal, technical, generic and historical questions: with the presentation of both authors and readers as, in their different ways, constitutionally, necessarily ignorant; with the ways in which the formal and indeed linguistic resources of a literary text might resist hermeneutic exegesis (ways in which such a text might resist knowledge, resist our knowing, in that sense); with questions of the novelistic and poetic specificities of ignorance; and with the constitutively literary production of ignorance as a particular kind of historical formation. But it is at the same time concerned with a thematics of ignorance, a thematics that has various dimensions. In this book I explore literary ignorance as having to do with the question of what ignorance feels like, with what it is like to be ignorant. Literary ignorance, for the purposes of this book, involves the question of the ignorance of children or, more precisely, the inability of adults to make themselves understood to children, those beings that they once were, and the fascination that they (adults) have with the ignorance of children. It is concerned with the (philosophical or sceptical) question of other minds and with ways in which the nineteenth-century realist novel in particular might help us to engage with, if not exactly understand, the blank opacities of those other minds, those other people, and indeed therefore to grasp the 'not-knowing by which the subject is inaugurated'.[2] As such, the book is also concerned with the perhaps even more troubling question of the obscurity of our own minds and with the urgent autobiographical and of course psychoanalytical question of how we can know, how we can know about, ourselves. I suggest that this question also plays an important part in the development of the realist tradition in the nineteenth century, as well as being intrinsic to the constitution of modern or post-Romantic lyric poetry. Part of the social and ethical import of the Victorian novel, in other words, is its status as something like a precursor of psychoanalysis, in so much as both discourses present the self as not known – not known, precisely, by the self (that which drives the 'self', the unconscious, being by definition that which that self cannot know). And the book is concerned with the phenomenon, in both poetry and prose, of narrators who can be characterized in terms of their inability to do what their titles should, etymologically, entitle them to do – to know.[3] So that some of the most intriguing and accomplished nineteenth- and twentieth-century narrators present themselves as figures of nescience, as the agnoiological presences that haunt and frame narrative. The book also examines the ways in which, in one of literature's most enduring tropes, its representation of melancholy, depression is articulated as a form of profound ignorance or, coming at it from a different angle, the ways in which radical or philosophical scepticism can be seen as being 'caused by, and causing, a form of melancholy'.[4] And I am concerned finally with the question of ignorance as a political and moral failing, linked even to the violent abnegation that is articulated or enacted in certain forms of twentieth-century terrorism, but also and at the same time with ignorance as a necessary ethical and political ideal, as that which we need to know, even if we do not (cannot) know it, and with the acknowledgement of epistemological fallibility – our own and that of others – as the foundation of the ethical, and constitutive even of democracy, of justice, as well as, therefore, of what one might call the politics of poetry.

In addition to these questions, there are various other aspects of the vast, ungovernable and seemingly infinite topic of human ignorance that the book can do little more than touch on or allude to. These include the history of ignorance, or of literary ignorance, or the literary history of ignorance; knowledge (and therefore ignorance) in the so-called 'Biblical' sense: knowledge of sexuality – along with the many permutations of psychic or social repression or of the censorship or disavowal of sexuality and sexual desire; negative theology or the mystery or mysticism of not knowing in the context of religion or the supernatural; the central literary question in the discourse of philosophical aesthetics of the kinds of knowledge that literature can be said to yield or to resist;[5] the kinds of nescience involved in radical or philosophical scepticism (the claim that we know nothing or that there is nothing that can finally be known); the (de Manian but also more generally the Miltonic and even Homeric) sense of the blindness and insight of authors or critics – the insight that comes from or is created by blindness, literal or metaphorical, or the blindness that is entailed by certain kinds or qualities of insight;[6] questions of 'constructivist' as opposed to 'realist' notions of knowledge;[7] literary representations of the ignorance involved in communities rejecting or denying certain modes of moral or political knowledge, knowledge of the holocaust, for example, or of ethnic cleansing; the (Yeatsian or Foucauldian) question of the relationship between power and knowledge ('Did she put on his knowledge with his power / Before the indifferent beak could let her drop?', asks Yeats, famously, of Leda), and the ways in which political and cultural elites are, anthropologically speaking, defined by their control of the dissemination of what is said to be known or what is said to be possible to know, as well as by their claims to superior or special forms of (religious, political, scientific and other) knowing.

Ignorance is, of course, intrinsic to knowledge: in a non-trivial sense, it is through ignorance that knowledge comes about. In order to learn, one has to understand one's ignorance, to know the limits of one's knowledge.[8] And it is perhaps not too much to claim that, towards the end of the twentieth century, a clearer recognition of the epistemological significance of ignorance began to emerge, not only in the humanities but also in the sciences and in the social sciences. In a book published in 1989, Michael Smithson argued that such fields of investigation had begun to change their approach to ignorance: rather than attempting to eliminate ignorance, Smithson proposed, 'emerging frameworks' of thought had abandoned the idea that it is eliminable and have begun to manage it, to 'understand, tolerate, and even utilize certain kinds of ignorance'.[9] If Smithson is right, this may only be a response to the fact that ignorance is a necessary and irreducible aspect of knowledge, that which knowing cannot do without. As the theoretical physicist David Gross commented in a speech made on accepting the 2004 Nobel Prize for Physics, 'The more we know, the more aware we are of what we know not': in Gross's view, 'the most important product of knowledge is ignorance'. But, as he goes on wryly to declare, 'there is no evidence that we are running out of our most important resource – ignorance'.[10] This is not perhaps the generally held belief or understanding of ignorance, or indeed of science. But as the semiotician Paul Bouissac comments, a discipline that fails to 'generate information', one that 'exhaust[s] its capacity to construct ignorance, would quickly disappear'.[11] Ignorance, which is 'inescapable and an intrinsic element in social organization', should be seen not just as a 'passive or dysfunctional condition', according to the sociologists Wilbert Mount and Melvin Tumin in a 1940 essay, but as 'an active and often positive element in operating structures and relations'.[12] And there is a particular historical dilemma about knowledge and ignorance that has often been pointed out. In a 1920 essay, for example, T.S. Eliot remarked on the 'vast accumulations of knowledge' for which the nineteenth century had been responsible and which had led to 'an equally vast ignorance': 'When there is so much to be known', Eliot argued, 'when there are so many fields of knowledge in which the same words are used with different meanings, when every one knows a little about a great many things, it becomes increasingly difficult for anyone to know whether he knows what he is talking about or not.'[13] The question of ignorance in this respect, as in others, is historically specific and linked in particular to the condition of modernity (the condition associated with the Enlightenment and with the dominance of scientific paradigms of knowledge). It is something of a cliché: the more you know, the more you do not know; or the more you know, the more you know you do not know; or the more that is known (but not to you), the more your ignorance grows.[14] And ignorance is growing, exponentially, as they say, with the extraordinary increase in what is known or understood or what is thought to be known or understood, and with the rapidly increasing availability of information, its worldwide dissemination (through the industrialization of printing, of course, but especially with the recent development of the internet and its instantaneous resources, its instant information).

This book is intended as a contribution to these counter-traditions of thinking about the other of knowledge, ignorance, to the understanding of agnoiology as an important field of investigation, and in particular to an understanding of the relationship between this often overlooked field and developing definitions of literature. The book is not, I hope, so much a contribution to ignorance as a contribution to our knowledge of ignorance, of literary ignorance in particular – an area of investigation in which there have recently been a small number of notable exceptions to a general tendency simply to denounce or ignore or attempt to overcome or reject ignorance. In different ways, recent books by Philip Weinstein and Tim Milnes have come closest to my own concerns (even while they have avoided the loaded term 'ignorance' itself).[15] Weinstein's elegant and intellectually engaging study *Unknowing: The Work of Modernist Fiction* (2006) is one of the few that takes seriously the question of what I call 'literary ignorance'. With immense learning and conceptual panache Weinstein makes a specifically historical argument about the rise of 'unknowing' as motif and metaphor, as trope and condition, in modernist fiction. In looking back to the Enlightenment for a contrasting engagement with knowledge, however, Weinstein overlooks Romanticism – or rather folds it into the Enlightenment condition of knowing. My own book, by contrast, seeks to engage with ignorance as a defining aspect (or figure or trope or theme or practice or technique) of the literary both generally and in particular as it is reconceived in the Romantic and post-Romantic tradition. Tim Milnes makes a rather different point in his subtle and philosophically informed examination of Romanticism's ambivalence with regard to epistemology and philosophical scepticism, *Knowledge and Indifference in English Romantic Prose* (2003). He argues that Romanticism's ambivalent response to David Hume's philosophical scepticism – a kind of despairing 'indifference', as Kant calls it, to knowledge as such – leads stubbornly if at times uncertainly towards an assertion of poetry's epistemological force, towards its conflicted knowing. My own book is centred on thinking about some key moments in Romantic and post-Romantic literary discourse in terms of a privileging of not knowing, of ignorance, in a context in which being concerned with nescience is a very different matter from simply being 'indifferent' to knowledge.

This study focuses in particular on the Romantic period, then, in order to think about the influence of the Romantic conception of literary ignorance in subsequent writing. I argue that while the question of ignorance is undoubtedly an inevitable, unavoidable part of the human condition, of what it means to be human (can an animal be ignorant? Well, perhaps, but what about a tree, or a rock? – the questions seem odd, to say the least), it is also specifically articulated within the definitions of literature that we have largely inherited from the Romantics, and is intrinsic to what we think we know about literature and what, even now, we tend to think literature allows us to know. While I seek to present the question of the framing of literature in relation to the discourse of ignorance as, in the first place, a historical question, I am also interested in the kinds of continuities in thinking about the literary that move beyond the specific historical and material circumstances of a text's production and reception. I argue, in this respect, that the reinvention of literature in the Romantic period around a specific conception of not knowing has had a major impact on literary practice, literary discussion and literary definition ever since, and I do so by tracing different permutations of 'literary ignorance' up to the present. I suggest that this collocation of literature with ignorance is a crucial dimension in certain kinds of contemporary writing, for example, particularly with respect to the ignorance of the author and to the ethical and indeed political value of not knowing. I suggest that contemporary British and Irish poetry on the one hand and the exemplary novels of the American writer Philip Roth on the other hand are in important ways determined by an essentially 'Romantic' conception of the literary in terms of the question of nescience. But I also want to suggest that 'literary ignorance' is embedded within a larger historical schema that the Romantics themselves inherited. I argue that the linking of the literary and the agnoiological in the work of such writers is in fact coded into the discourses of poetics from Plato onwards – and, indeed, especially in Plato. The book begins, therefore, with a discussion of Plato's inaugural and highly influential but in the end anti-Socratic separation of poetry from philosophy precisely around the question of ignorance[16] – around the idea of the knowingness, the knowledge-value, of philosophical discourse, and the sense that its other, the discourse of ignorance, and the acknowledgement of one's own ignorance, should be reserved for the specialist, non-philosophical arena of what the Romantics have taught us to call 'literature'.

Notes

1. Stanley Cavell, *Disowning Knowledge in Six Plays of Shakespeare* (Cambridge: Cambridge University Press, 1987), p. 201.
2. Judith Butler, 'Giving an Account of Oneself', *Diacritics* 31: 4 (2001): 33.
3. Narrator, from Latin *narrare*, to relate or recount, is related, according to the *OED*, to the Greek *gnarus*, 'knowing', or 'skilled'. But it is not just etymology that links the narrator to knowing: both logic and experience would suggest that to fulfil our narratological desires the narrator should be

a person who *knows* something that we do not. See Northrop Frye's comment that 'All the great story-tellers ... have a strong sense of literature as a finished product. The suspense is thrown forward until it reaches the end, and is based on our confidence that the author knows what is coming next' (*Fables of Identity: Studies in Poetic Mythology* (New York: Harcourt, Brace and World, 1963), p. 131.

4 Stanley Cavell, *Philosophy the Day After Tomorrow* (Cambridge, Mass.: Harvard University Press, 2005), p. 40.

5 Paisley Livingston usefully summarizes the three major strands with regard to this tradition as follows: '(1) condemnations of literature as a source of irrationality for author and audience alike ...; (2) defences of literary autonomy based on the idea that knowledge is neither hindered nor advanced by literature because the two move on separate tracks ...; (3) various contentions that literary works do in fact contribute to knowledge' ('Literature and Knowledge', in Jonathan Dancy and Ernest Sosa, eds, *A Companion to Epistemology* (Oxford: Basil Blackwell, 1992), p. 255). As I hope will become clear, however, it is not my concern to attempt to adjudicate between these three positions, or indeed to provide an alternative thinking of this relationship: rather, I consider some of the ways in which the other of knowledge, ignorance, is aroused, enacted and explored in literature – to think about literature, in other words, just in so much as it resists the *question* of knowledge, resists Livingston's question.

6 Let me not be misunderstood, however: this is not a book that proclaims, laughably, the ignorance of the author against the wisdom or knowledge of the reader or critic – as Philip Weinstein puts it, there is something 'comic (not to mention disturbing)' in a critic's assumption of 'the author's total blindness, as opposed to one's own total insight' (*Unknowing: The Work of Modernist Fiction* (Ithaca: Cornell University Press, 2006), p. 81).

7 For an incisive and admirably reasonable account of these debates see Barbara Herrnstein Smith, *Scandalous Knowledge: Science, Truth and the Human* (Durham: Duke University Press, 2006).

8 See Cavell's comment that 'Learning when it is and is not competent to say "I (we) just don't know" is every bit as much a condition of my competence as a knower as learning when to say and when to retract "I am certain"' (*The Claim of Reason: Wittgenstein, Skepticism, Morality, and Tragedy* (1979), new edition (New York: Oxford University Press, 1999), pp. 60–1); and for a brief argument for the pedagogical importance of ignorance and for the 'knowledge of one's own ignorance' see Mark Edmundson, *Why Read?* (New York: Bloomsbury, 2004), pp. 32–5.

9 Michael Smithson, *Ignorance and Uncertainty: Emerging Paradigms* (New York: Springer-Verlag, 1989), p. viii. On 'modern' or 'scientific' ignorance see also Andrew Martin, *The Knowledge of Ignorance: From Genesis to Jules Verne* (Cambridge: Cambridge University Press, 1985), pp. 184–5.

10 David Gross, Nobel prize acceptance speech, January 2005 (http://nobelprize.org/nobel_prizes/physics/laureates/2004/gross-speech-e.html (accessed 15 February 2008)). In the same scientific spirit, see *Science Magazine* special issue on 'What Don't We Know?' (309: 5731 (July 2005): 75); and *The Encyclopaedia of Ignorance*, 2 vols. ed. Ronald F.H. Duncan and M. Weston-Smith (Oxford: Pergamon, 1977).
11 'The Construction of Ignorance and the Evolution of Knowledge', *University of Toronto Quarterly* 61: 4 (1992): 464: as Bouissac suggests, the disciplines are based around their particular 'forms of ignorance', each a separate 'generator of uncertainty'.
12 Wilbert E. Moore and Melvin M. Tumin, 'Some Social Functions of Ignorance', *American Sociological Review* 14: 6 (1949): 788, 795.
13 T.S. Eliot, 'The Perfect Critic', in Frank Kermode, ed., *Selected Prose of T.S. Eliot* (London: Faber and Faber, 1975), p. 55.
14 See Karl Popper, *Conjectures and Refutations* (London: Routledge and Kegan Paul, 1976), p. 28: 'The more we learn about the world, and the deeper our learning, the more conscious, specific, and articulate will be our knowledge of what we do not know, our knowledge of our ignorance. For this, indeed, is the main source of our ignorance – the fact that our knowledge can be only finite, while our ignorance must necessarily be infinite' (quoted in Predrag Cicovacki, *Anamorphosis: Kant on Knowledge and Ignorance* (Lanham: University Press of America, 1997), p. 162).
15 Weinstein, *Unknowing*; Milnes, *Knowledge and Indifference in English Romantic Prose* (Cambridge: Cambridge University Press, 2003). Martin's *The Knowledge of Ignorance* is a rather earlier and geographically and chronologically more expansive study of the significance of ignorance in (Western European) literature. I should also mention here – not least because I fail to make enough of it elsewhere – Paul Fry's *A Defense of Poetry: Reflections on the Occasion of Writing* (Stanford: Stanford University Press, 1995), a book that in many ways may be said, over many years, to have inspired the present book, with its superb and subtle account of the end-stopped, the blank, the 'preconceptual', the 'hum', the 'ostensive' in literature and the (Wordsworthian but also more generally poetic) sense of the 'blank opacity with which the world discloses its being' (p. 7), or the (Dickinsonian but also more generally poetic) sense of the 'disclosure of the insignificant in the very sound of signification' (p. 63). As Fry puts it, 'the suspension of knowledge enabled by ostension can serve to reinvigorate the very quest it interrupts' (p. 201).
16 Plato himself, of course, acknowledges that such a distinction is not his own, referring to what he famously calls the 'ancient quarrel' between poetry and philosophy as part of his justification for excluding poets from his ideal republic (see Plato, *The Republic*, 10: 607B).

1

Ignorance and philosophy

We are ignorant. We are born into and remain in ignorance: this is what we know. And this knowledge of our ignorance is what it means to be human. Socrates, the indigent, know-nothing philosopher who nevertheless promulgated even if he did not invent the oracular dictum 'know thyself', also knows that to be human is not to know.[1] To be human, to have a 'soul', as Socrates has it in the *Phaedo*, is to be confined within the prison of the body and thereby to 'wallow' in the 'mire of every sort of ignorance' – from which it is philosophy's task to free the soul (*Phaedo* 82e).[2] In this regard, the human is a kind of ignorance machine, since its 'apparatus for acquiring knowledge' is, as Friedrich Nietzsche explains *contra* John Locke and others, not 'designed for "knowledge"'.[3] 'Ignorance and fallibility are', as Lorenzo Infantino puts it in a recent book, 'our anthropologic traits'.[4] Even the Bible (a book that is deeply conflicted on the question of ignorance) exhorts or commends human ignorance, not just in the lugubrious declaration in Ecclesiastes that 'in much wisdom is much grief' and that 'he that increaseth knowledge increaseth sorrow' (Ecclesiastes 1: 18) but in its very myth of human origins. Theologically, the purpose of the human has been construed by at least one commentator as that of fulfilling God's omniscience through his or her ignorance: without the ignorance of Adam, God would not be able to *know* nescience and therefore in that sense at least not be omniscient. Human knowledge is prohibited so that God can know everything, even not knowing.[5] Biblically, it is man's function to be ignorant so that God doesn't have to be: we exist *because* we are ignorant; to know is to fall, to be both godlike and mortal, to die. 'I am ignorant', you might say, 'therefore I am'.

Aristotle opens his *Metaphysics* with the declaration that 'All men by nature desire to know'.[6] And yet, to be human, by another, indeed by an earlier reasoning in the Western philosophical as well as the Western theological tradition, is not to know. Or perhaps we should recognize that for Aristotle men may be said to desire to know precisely because they don't. Socrates, for his part, explicitly links the limits of wisdom with the condition of being human. In the *Apology*, he asserts that he may be wise in 'human wisdom' but that he knows nothing of 'wisdom more than human' ('whoever says I do is lying and speaks to slander me', he declares pugnaciously (*Apology* 20d–e)). And he speculates that, in claiming that Socrates is the wisest of men, the Delphic oracle really meant that his kind of wisdom – human wisdom – 'is worth little or nothing': he construes the oracle's statement as meaning that 'This man amongst you, mortals, is wisest who, like Socrates, understands that his wisdom is worthless' (*Apology* 23a–b). Socrates may know more than any other mortal, and know in particular the limits of (his) knowledge, but such knowledge is worth little – worth, indeed, nothing.

But Socrates knows, or says he knows, nothing, not even about knowledge: 'I can't get a proper grasp of what on earth knowledge really is', Socrates comments in *Theaetetus* (146a). And he's not joking. It's a principle that Socrates holds and holds to, even unto death.[7] While Adam and Eve (and following them the whole of humanity) may be said to die because of their desire to know, to die, indeed, in exchange for a certain knowledge, Socrates is prepared to die, and will die, for his ignorance. Socrates is executed – he is forced to drink hemlock – because he has corrupted the youth of Athens through his 'philosophy': in *Euthyphro* we learn that Meletus has accused Socrates of corrupting youth specifically through his 'ignorance' (2 c–d) – through what we might call his philosophy of ignorance. The dialogue ends, indeed, with Socrates lamenting the fact that Euthyphro is leaving without having enlightened him about the nature of piety – in which case Socrates would have been able to 'escape Meletus' indictment', as he puts it, 'by showing him that I had acquired wisdom in divine matters ... and my ignorance would no longer cause me to be careless and inventive about such things' (16a). But Meletus' charge remains: Euthyphro *hasn't* enlightened Socrates, who, by his own account, remains ignorant and insists on continuing to profess his ignorance, and therefore remains guilty as charged. In the *Apology*, however, we learn anyway that one should not fear death because such a fear is itself a form of epistemological vanity: since we do not know what death is, we should not fear it (29a–b). And it is, after all, possible to take literally Socrates' assertion (just before he is sentenced to death for what he sees as living the examined life) that the 'unexamined life is not worth living' (*Apology* 38a): it would be possible to construe it as a serious philosophical argument that one would be better off being dead than not doing philosophy (and to construe doing philosophy, or living the examined life, as a process in which the subject comes to know his own ignorance).[8] Socrates dies, in other words, in defence of his principle of ignorance. One might even link Socrates' death, ultimately caused by his *acknowledgement* of his own ignorance, with Nietzsche's sense that one must embrace ignorance to live: without ignorance, Nietzsche declares, 'life itself would be impossible . . . it is a condition under which alone the living thing can preserve itself and prosper: a great, firm dome of ignorance must encompass you'.[9] Know yourself, then, and know that you don't know. And then die.

This is not, perhaps, as self-contradictory as it might appear: Socrates does know himself in as much as, unlike others, he knows that he doesn't know,[10] and – in an Ancient Greek version of Descartes' certainty only of his own doubt ('I doubt, therefore I am') – he knows that to know is, in the first place (also) not to know. His 'wisdom', indeed, inheres just in this. Unlike the unnamed politician referred to in the *Apology*, Socrates does not think that he 'knows something when he does not': 'when I do not know', he says, 'neither do I think I know; so I am likely to be wiser than he to this small extent, that I do not think I know what I do not know' (*Apology* 21d): it's a small thing, but, for the early Socrates, at least, everything. The conceit of thinking that you know is, according to Socrates' replacement, the Eleatic Stranger in *Sophist*, a type of ignorance that is 'marked off from the others and overshadow[s]' them. 'Thinking that you know' when you don't, according to the Stranger, is what 'causes all the mistakes we make when we think' (*Sophist* 229c). This is what, in the *Laws*, Plato categorizes as 'double ignorance' (*Laws* 863c): it is, as Socrates has it in the *Apology*, the most disgraceful, most 'blameworthy' ignorance (29b). And it is for this reason, no doubt, that in the *Apology*, *Meno*, *Theaetetus*, *Laches*, *Lysis* and other dialogues, especially those specifically concerned with the question of knowledge, Socrates insists on his own ignorance. 'I too speak rather in ignorance', he explains to Meno, 'I only conjecture' (*Meno* 98b).[11] As Richard Kraut puts it, Socrates' claim to wisdom is based on 'his knowledge of how little he knows'.[12] Like a midwife, he is 'barren' – in his case barren of wisdom – he declares (*Theaetetus* 150c). Like the midwife's, his is an inductive rather than productive or creative or procreative art: he induces wisdom – which can (also) mean the recognition of ignorance – in others (see *Theaetetus* 161b). For Socrates, 'wondering' is characteristic of philosophers. Here, in this wonderment, 'is where philosophy begins and nowhere else', he explains (*Theaetetus* 155d; see also 173c–174b). His very method of instruction – the so-called *elenchus*, the strategy of demonstrating the false premises in a philosophical or moral position – is itself the strategy of ignorance. The *elenchus* allows Socrates to demonstrate to his interlocutors through his own denial of knowledge that, rather than knowledgeable, like him they are in fact ignorant. All Socrates can know – and, in the end, all he can teach – is a certain nescience: Theaetetus should not think he knows what he doesn't know, Socrates remarks as he concludes his extended rumination on knowledge and ignorance, and the ignorance of knowledge, that is *Theaetetus*. This assertion of the ignorance of knowledge and this teaching of epistemological modesty 'is all my art can achieve', he says, 'nothing more' (*Theaetetus* 210c). It is a fully consistent position except, of course, in as much as it contains its own paradoxicality: in as much as he knows that he doesn't know, Socrates is wise. But in as much as he is wise, in as much as he *knows* at least that he doesn't know – he is not wise. In which case, he is ignorant – and therefore, because he knows it, wise (and so on).[13]

In one of the most well-known speeches in Plato, as part of his enlightening discussion with Socrates, Meno half-jokingly complains that, although he had started out with a clear sense, in his mind, of what *aretē* (usually translated as 'virtue' or, more generally, 'excellence') means, he has got so confused about it in debating with the master that he is no longer able to speak. Although he is young, Meno is not naive. Socrates' reputation has gone before him: Meno has heard of Socrates' customary habit of protesting his perplexity, and that he tends to perplex others too, but after a dose of the esteemed philosopher's dialectical 'spells and potions' Meno is feeling 'positively mesmeriz[ed]' and 'brimful of perplexity' (*Meno* 80a).[14] Meno had started out, in fact, with no intention of asking about the meaning of *aretē*: he had just asked a simple, practical question about whether it is taught or is learnt through practice. But now he no longer knows what he thought he knew, he no longer knows what *aretē* is, and he feels 'torpid', as if he has had a shock from a torpedo fish. Socrates' wisdom, his philosophy, is like an electric shock to the system. In *Theaetetus*, we learn that Socrates is 'snub-nosed, with eyes that stick out' (*Theaetetus* 143e), and to Meno Socrates is even beginning to *look* like a torpedo fish (Meno is practically hallucinating now). But Socrates agrees with Meno's designation, with certain qualifications. It is not just Meno that's confused, he explains:

> As for me [Socrates comments], if the torpedo fish is torpid itself and that's how it makes other people torpid too, I *am* like it, but not otherwise. For it's not that I myself have the solutions when I make other people perplexed, but that I'm utterly perplexed myself, and that's how I come to make other people perplexed as well. That's how it is with virtue now; I on my side *don't* know what it is, while you on yours *did* know, perhaps, till you came into contact with me, while now you're just like someone who *doesn't* know. (*Meno* 80c)[15]

It's odd. Socrates, the teacher, doesn't know and knows that he doesn't know. Meno, for his part, did know before he spoke to Socrates but now he doesn't, now he's confused, perplexed, in a state of cognitive torpor, like a fish. It's not that Meno *thought* he knew before, mind you: he did know. And now he is *just like* someone who doesn't know – not someone that doesn't know, but *like* that person. So perhaps he still knows, in which case (according to Socrates' impeccable logic) he doesn't know. And that's the point. What Meno is beginning to learn from Socrates is a generally unspoken truth contained within the discourses of knowledge – of education, of scholarship, of philosophy, of science, even: the sciences – the so-called 'human' sciences as much as the 'hard' sciences – are discourses not only of knowledge but also of nescience. Science, knowledge, that is to say, necessarily contains within itself and is in fact produced through and a product of its other, of nescience, ignorance. We should not underestimate the ethical centrality of *knowledge*, of the importance of lacking or curing ignorance, in Socrates or in the Western philosophical or scientific traditions more generally; this, indeed, is the other side of the dialectical or dialogical coin of the Socratic discourse of ignorance. But while Socrates equates virtue with knowledge – or vice with ignorance – in *Meno* and elsewhere, his difficulty in saying what exactly virtue *is* amounts to, and ends up in, a profession of ignorance.[16]

For Plato, of course (as for a certain Socrates, in fact, as for philosophy in general, indeed, and as for most world religions), knowledge is in fact often associated with virtue.[17] Despite Socrates' avowal of his own ignorance, ignorance is repeatedly castigated in the Platonic dialogues: ignorance is a deformity or 'ugliness' of the soul (*Sophist* 228e), a 'disease' (*Timaeus* 86b);[18] ignorance is one of the causes of 'wrongdoing' (*Laws* 10: 863c) and indeed 'no one is wilfully evil' but rather 'becomes evil' as a result of 'an uneducated upbringing' (*Timaeus* 86d–e); poets are to be excluded from the ideal republic because, as imitators (and imitators of imitations at that), they have 'no worthwhile knowledge' of what they imitate (*Republic* 10: 602b). As Thomas Brickhouse and Nicholas Smith put it, *Plato*'s Socrates, at least, sees vice as 'nothing other than moral ignorance'.[19] Ignorance, for philosophy and even for the philosopher called Socrates, is most often figured as that which needs to be resolved. If philosophy begins in ignorance or, as it does for both Socrates and Aristotle, in 'wonder' (*thaumazein*), it is most often presented as that which ends by resolving such perplexity, such ignorance.[20]

In a recent discussion of the question of 'Socratic perplexity' in relation to the question of the 'nature of philosophy', Gareth Matthews suggests that perplexity is at the root of philosophical thinking – that, as he remarks, while being 'seriously perplexed' about why, say, Duchamp's urinal can be seen as a work of art is (part of) what would qualify one to teach philosophical aesthetics, the same level of perplexity over, say, what qualifies as an equilateral triangle would tend to disqualify one from teaching geometry.[21] Philosophical perplexity is a special kind of perplexity, according to Matthews, because it involves a 'paralysis that undermines one's confidence that one even knows how to use the language' (p. 91). But as Matthews points out, *Meno* doesn't end in Socrates' avowal of perplexity in the torpedo-fish exchange: the dialogue goes on to suggest ways in which we can move beyond perplexity towards a sense of resolution. Indeed, Matthews suggests that *Meno* acts as a kind of hinge text, between earlier Socratic dialogues, which seemed to be governed by the figure of aporia – authentic and irresolvable perplexity over ethical and other questions – and later Socratic dialogues in which Plato has the Philosopher express dissatisfaction with aporia and a desire to move beyond it to actually answering the questions that his interlocutors raise.[22] Indeed, in *Meno*, Socrates goes on to attempt to say what knowledge itself is, famously defining it as 'justified true belief' (97e–98a; see Matthews, pp. 71–2). And as Matthews points out, in the middle-period Socratic dialogues, although Socrates induces perplexity in others, he does not admit it in himself. In these dialogues, philosophy can even seem to be 'quite like geometry' in that it seems to have 'theorems, or something like them, that can be argued for and even proved' (p. 72). Thus, Socrates' declaration at the end of the *Republic* 1, that 'the result of the discussion . . . is that I know nothing' (354b–c), should be read not as 'a confession of mind-numbing perplexity' but as a 'stylised gesture, best understood as an admission that the ideas Socrates has thrown out need much more development and defence' – as a form of 'instrumental perplexity', as 'something to be got beyond' (pp. 74–5). Indeed, Matthews locates this change in the shift from the Socratic figure in *Theaetetus* to the Eleatic Stranger in the *Sophist*. And he also argues that since the aporetic dialogues are those that are commonly understood to be the early Socratic dialogues, which in turn are those that are taken to be the most accurate records of the historical Socrates, it is puzzlement, aporia, perplexity that may be said most faithfully to represent the historically authentic Socratic position.[23] Matthews suggests that the standard division in Socrates – between the early aporetic figure and the later, wiser, more knowledgeable, less ignorant one – can be seen to have fundamentally influenced philosophy and may even be said to characterize the institution of Western philosophy as a whole.[24] While philosophers need to 'induce fresh puzzlement' in themselves to keep working, they are also institutionally characterized by the desire for 'philosophical results': they 'seek to turn philosophical perplexity into philosophical problems, or difficulties, that [they] might have some hope of solving' (p. 129). Or as Charles Kahn puts it, the 'aporetic dialogues' of Socrates 'are all also protreptic, urging us on to the practice of philosophy'.[25]

It is in this gap between two versions of Socrates identified by Matthews – to put it crudely, the 'authentic' and the 'Platonic' Socrates – that we might begin to talk about literature. My suggestion is that while literature and philosophy can be combined and contrasted in a variety of ways, the key distinction to be made with regard to ignorance concerns the question of whether or not one moves beyond aporia or perplexity, beyond not knowing. In this sense, the question of Socratic ignorance can help us to think about what I want to call literary ignorance because of the way that, as Kahn, Matthews and others argue, philosophers (the later Socrates, at least, included) seek to go beyond explorations of their own ignorance, to produce 'positive' or 'constructive' knowledge. Indeed, for certain kinds of philosopher, certain 'classical' or 'analytical' or Anglo-American philosophers in particular, the work of philosophy (like, from a certain perspective, the work of science) is precisely to eliminate ignorance. In this respect, Socrates' confessions of ignorance may be seen as having acted as a kind of inaugural inoculation for the now venerable body of (non-sceptical) Western philosophy. In an important sense, literature can be said by contrast to be that discourse which doesn't (or doesn't always or doesn't necessarily) move (or attempt to move, or desire to move) beyond perplexity or aporia, beyond ignorance. Although Socrates doesn't entirely accept Meno's charge that he is like a torpedo fish, a certain thinking of literature – one that, as I shall attempt to demonstrate, became dominant in the period of the institutionalization of literature in Europe in the late eighteenth century

– may be construed in terms of its congruence, in certain respects, with the early and self-perplexing torpedo-fish-philosopher Socrates.

As Plato suggests by his banishment of the poets from his autocratic Republic, in some respects and according to some accounts, the 'disease' of ignorance may be said to constitute the very condition of poetry, of literature. In an important sense, in other words – a sense that I wish to probe in this book – the disease of ignorance, this monster or deformity,[26] is most fully explored and indeed enacted within a certain conception of the discourse of literature. Literature, in this respect, is the discourse or institution that is above all others, and in some senses against philosophy, allied with ignorance. One might of course object that philosophy itself is founded on (early) Socratic assertions of the philosopher's own ignorance and on Socrates' claim that that is the one thing that he does for certain know. Certainly, the French philosopher Jacques Derrida, for one, has argued that philosophy involves an 'essential and mandatory incompetence, a structural nonknowledge': as Derrida comments, the philosopher 'gives himself the right (even if he does not always take it, in fact) to incompetence in all the domains of the encyclopaedia, all of the departments of the University'. But, as Derrida argues, such incompetence is generally claimed in order to assert a larger, meta-epistemic or legislative right, the right, as Derrida puts it, 'to pronounce the law about the totality of these knowledges and about the essence of knowledge in general'.[27] And Socrates, for his part, at least in Plato's account, eventually moves beyond ignorance. Philosophy, by this argument, can be seen as the discourse, before all others, that in the end and because it knows ignorance, because it knows its own ignorance, can *repudiate* ignorance, defend against it and expose it, thereby curing it. This, indeed is the double force of Socrates' sense of ignorance: he both admits it, confesses to it and exposes it in others – exposes others' sense of knowledge as in fact their ignorance of their own ignorance – thereby freeing or hoping to free them from it.

But while the dialogues of Socrates may be said to constitute a preliminary investigation of the field, philosophy in general has lacked a theory of ignorance. A vast area of philosophy is designated as epistemology, the theory of knowledge, but still there is no, or only a little, agnoiology, only a little anepistemology.[28] This is perhaps surprising in view of the fact that the Scottish rationalist philosopher James Ferrier, who coined the term 'epistemology', also invented 'agnoiology' in his 1856 *Institutes of Metaphysic*. Optimistically determined to put an end to 'all scepticism' and to all 'vacillation, or indecision of opinion on philosophical topics', Ferrier divided philosophy into epistemology, agnoiology and ontology.[29] In some respects, agnoiology takes prime place: 'our ignorance is excessive', Ferrier declares, since it is 'far more extensive than our knowledge' (p. 50); 'The fact of our extreme ignorance' is, he says, 'undeniable' (p. 407). It is therefore necessary, he reasons, to 'examine and fix what ignorance is – what we are, and can be, ignorant of'; we need to embark upon 'an entirely new research, constituting an intermediate section of philosophy which we term the AGNOIOLOGY . . . the theory of true ignorance' (pp. 50–1). As Ferrier comments, while there have been 'many enquiries into the nature of knowledge' there has been 'no inquiry into the nature of ignorance' (p. 406): his investigation is therefore 'an entire novelty in philosophy', he says (ibid.). The fact that Ferrier himself devotes only 44 pages to his 'Theory of Ignorance', by contrast with the 323 pages on the 'Theory of Knowledge', is indeed indicative (the lack of a history of agnoiology accounts for the 'fewness and brevity of the accompanying annotations', as he puts it (ibid.)). But Ferrier makes two important points about ignorance: firstly, he defines it as a 'deprivation of knowledge' and therefore as 'an intellectual defect, imperfection, privation, or shortcoming' (p. 405); secondly, he proposes that 'we can be ignorant only of what can possibly be known' (p. 412), thus distinguishing the question of ignorance from the simple unknown and from mystery: he suggests, indeed, that 'nescience of that which it would contradict the nature of all intelligence to know' is not a defect but rather 'the very strength or perfection of reason' (p. 414).

But in spite of Ferrier's efforts, the word 'agnoiology' is now more likely to be used in dismissive contexts, such as when A.C. Grayling suggests that 'it is a mistake to think of skepticism as consisting in an agnoiology, that is a thesis to the effect that we are ignorant either globally or in some region of inquiry', since any such claim is self-defeating (because you are saying that you know something about that which you claim not to know).[30] Nevertheless, it would not in fact be unreasonable to see epistemology itself – recently defined, for example, by Jonathan Kvanvig as centring on 'the difficult questions of whether knowledge is possible and, if it is, how much of it there is'[31] – as something like a theory of ignorance, since the question of whether (any) knowledge is possible concerns, even if only implicitly, what we don't know (and must logically include, indeed, the possibility that we don't know anything). Moreover the inherently related, indeed inseparable but uneasily marginalized field of philosophical scepticism (in short, the claim that 'We do not know anything', or 'we do not know what we think we know')[32] does itself, *pace* Grayling, come close at times to a theory of ignorance. And it comes as no surprise, therefore, that one of the remarkable things about philosophical scepticism is its paradoxical place in Western European and especially Anglo-American philosophy generally – as the discourse that is both central to and, at the same time, the other of those traditions. Steven Luper's recent collection of essays on scepticism, *The Skeptics* (2003), is exemplary in this respect: in this volume almost all of the nineteen contributors engage with philosophical scepticism by seeking to refute it, suggesting that there is a sense in which one could think of scepticism as the other of epistemology, the other of philosophy, even. The assertion that one knows nothing is or might seem 'preposterous', according to Peter Klein; to doubt that we have knowledge is 'absurd', David Lewis argues; the idea (for example) that I am deceived in seeing a computer monitor before me is a variant of 'science fiction' Keith Lehrer suggests.[33] These and even more extreme charges against scepticism are indeed widespread in philosophical discourse. Scepticism can be conceived of as something like an act of intellectual terrorism, like an anonymous letter sent to blow up in the face of the philosopher.[34] If it was true, scepticism would be catastrophic.[35] Scepticism is 'outrageous', a form of hysteria.[36] It hypnotizes, mesmerizes us.[37] Scepticism is a form of 'perversity', 'irrational', 'the recoil of a demonic reason',[38] an incurable 'malady',[39] an infection.[40] The sceptic 'bamboozles' us with her 'unreal question[s]'.[41] Scepticism is the 'mongrel brother' of philosophy;[42] it is the skeleton in the closet of 'western rationalism'.[43] More soberly, perhaps, scepticism is 'some species of intellectual tragedy, or folly', a 'stumbling block' which 'run[s] us up against the incredible' and which 'interfer[es] with' the philosopher's 'intellectual conscience', as Stanley Cavell has it, a 'paradoxical presence within our very possession of language' which tells us that 'there is something fundamental to or in our existence that we do not know'.[44] Perhaps the most insulting charge against the sceptic (insulting, that is, if the sceptic can be said to have a self that can be insulted) is the charge simply that the sceptic does not, cannot, exist: 'outside of the study or the classroom', John Greco argues after David Hume, there are simply 'no skeptics to be debated or persuaded'.[45] And when Greco talks about the outside of the study or classroom he means to denote reality: in reality, in real life, he means, there are no sceptics; no one is (since no one logically can be) a sceptic. What could be more offensive, for the sceptic? – assuming, as I say, that the sceptic is the kind of person that can be said to take offence, or indeed to be a person at all.

As this would suggest, there seems to be a sense in which, for philosophy, the sceptic's paradoxical confession of ignorance – 'I *know* that I don't know and I know that you don't know either' – *must* be rejected, abjected. Scepticism is the 'threat', the 'irreducible threat' that must be denied, outmanoeuvred.[46] It may be of 'central significance in epistemology', that which 'keeps the theory of knowledge going', and 'the opening gesture of modern philosophy',[47] but the imperative of certain kinds of philosophy is to refute, deny, destroy it. And the contemporary rejections of scepticism echo centuries of philosophical abuse. For Kant, writing in the Preface to the second edition of the *Critique of Pure Reason* in 1787 scepticism (or 'idealism', as he calls it) is 'a scandal to philosophy and to human reason in general'.[48] Twentieth-century linguistic or analytical philosophy tends to see scepticism as 'little more than a mess of false analogies, definite errors, and even identifiable fallacies which had bewitched the intelligence of earlier philosophers', as Barry Stroud puts it.[49] Stanley Cavell, the philosopher who has most interestingly brought scepticism and literature together in recent years, comments that 'Everyone knows that *something* is mad in the skeptic's fantastic quest for certainty' (*Disowning Knowledge*, p. 8). Scepticism, according to Cavell, is 'inherently unstable': 'no one simply wants to be a . . . skeptic' (ibid., p. 198).[50] Not only does nobody want to be a sceptic, but it is questionable whether (*pace* Luper et al.) academic philosophy can even be bothered to refute it any more. 'It is still widely felt', remarks Barry Stroud, writing in 1984, 'that scepticism is not really worth taking seriously', since it consists in 'paradox, absurdity, dilemma, and difficulty'.[51] As Stroud comments, while scepticism has long been seen as a 'constant and profound threat' and while 'the urge to understand precisely how it is to be avoided was a motivating force in philosophy', this is no longer the case, since philosophers no longer 'take scepticism seriously, or seriously enough'.[52] After all, as Stroud comments, 'almost nobody thinks for a moment that scepticism could be correct'.[53]

And yet there remains the paradox that philosophical scepticism does still need to be refuted – or to put it differently, that philosophy does still feel the need to attempt to refute it. As Richard Foley comments, epistemologists are 'prone to say that radical skeptical hypotheses are not worthy of serious philosophical attention' while, at the same time, they 'cannot help but try their hand at refuting them'.[54] According to Cavell, indeed, scepticism 'remains active in the conflicts between traditional philosophers and their ordinary language critics, and it inhabits the void of comprehension between Continental ontology and Anglo-American analysis as a whole' (*Disowning Knowledge*, p. 94). Indeed, Michael Williams goes so far as to suggest that what he calls the 'New Scepticism' (in the work of, most notably, Barry Stroud, Thomas Nagel and P.F. Strawson) is 'one of the most important movements in contemporary philosophy'.[55] This may be because, as Stroud has it, scepticism 'appeals to something deep in our nature and seems to raise a real problem about the human condition. It is natural to feel either that we must accept the literal truth of the conclusion that we can know nothing about the world around us, or else we must somehow show that it is not true.'[56] For Cavell, indeed, scepticism is – in an argument that seems to take pleasure in its own paradoxicality – part of being human. Scepticism, for Cavell, is the place where 'the human wish to deny the condition of human existence is expressed'; but that denial is itself 'essential to what we think of as human'. The 'threat' of scepticism, indeed, is 'a natural or inevitable presentiment of the human mind'.[57] As Michael Williams comments, scepticism 'points to a profound, albeit normally incredible, truth about the human condition'. Scepticism, he suggests, might just be the 'inevitable outcome of questions that, to creatures like us, come naturally': the sceptic is no 'literary invention', in other words, but 'all of us in our philosophical moments'. Scepticism is 'the legacy of the attempt to philosophize'.[58] The 'truth' of scepticism, according to Cavell, is that 'the human creature's basis in the world as a whole, its relation to the world as such, is not that of knowing, anyway not what we think of as knowing'.[59]

If it is possible to see philosophical scepticism as engaged with or part of a theory of ignorance, then, it would seem to follow from the repeated attempts to reject or refute it that ignorance, the avowal or performance of nescience, is the 'other' of Western academic philosophy – that it is both implicit in or central to philosophy and, at the same time, that which philosophy (or at least epistemology) is designed to alleviate or eliminate or cure. Indeed, the sceptic is not some well-armed and external 'adversary': as Williams comments, scepticism, the 'enemy', is *us*.[60] If ignorance is the abjected of philosophy, it is also, like the Freudian repressed (itself fundamentally a form of not knowing, or ignorance), that which returns, that which is uncomfortably retained within philosophical discourse – fundamental, central, indeed, to it. 'Philosophy is not separable from scepticism', Emmanuel Levinas comments, which is like a 'shadow' that philosophy 'drives off by refuting it', only to find it 'once again on its footsteps': 'skepticism is refutable, but it returns'.[61]

'How do we learn that what we need is not more knowledge but the willingness to forgo knowing?', Stanley Cavell asks. As he comments, this might sound like a plea for irrationality or superstition. But while scepticism is usually taken to mean that 'we cannot know the world exists' and therefore that 'perhaps there isn't one', Cavell suggests that a different way of thinking about scepticism would be to see that it is making a claim that 'since we cannot know the world exists, its presentness to us cannot be a function of knowing': the world, therefore, is simply 'to be *accepted*' (*Disowning Knowledge*, p. 95). The 'point of forgoing knowledge', Cavell suggests, is in fact 'to know' (ibid., p. 96). Scepticism, it turns out, may be seen as an expression of the rage for knowledge, as part of the rage for the order of certainty – just as its other, epistemology, can be construed in terms of the philosopher being racked with doubt, with not knowing, with *not* being certain that one can know, or how. Cavell links the question of scepticism with a brilliant and properly influential reading of Shakesperean tragedy in which, he suggests, 'it is the thing we do not know that can save us' (ibid., p. 97). A 'radical necessity haunts every story of tragedy', he remarks:

> It is the enveloping of contingency and necessity by one another, the entropy of their mixture, which produces events we call tragic. Or rather, it is why the death which ends a tragedy strikes one as *inexplicable*: necessary, but we do not know why; avoidable, but we do not know how; wrapped in meaning, but the meaning has not come out, and so wrapped in mystery. (Ibid., p. 112)[62]

Cavell links the 'disowning' of knowledge that exists in a certain thinking of philosophical scepticism with literature, then, suggesting that what we respond to in Shakespearean tragedy is what philosophy has 'intellectualised as scepticism' (ibid., p. 170). For Cavell, scepticism amounts to 'a relation to the world, and to others, and to myself, and to language, that is known to what you might call literature, or anyway responded to in literature'.[63] And in this sense, without simply aligning it with or defining it as scepticism, literature may be said more generally to be bound up with philosophy's essential other, or at least with a certain will to, or interest in the nature of, ignorance, nescience, not knowing – in knowing what it is like not to know. After all, literature has been, from the first – from Plato onwards – not only designated as the realm of ignorance but designed as that mode of writing in which paradoxical, self-refuting or 'impossible' statements such as the confession of ignorance ('I know that I am ignorant'; 'We are all ignorant'; 'I know that nothing can be known') are seen simply not as self-contradictory (and therefore paradoxical, absurd, nonsensical, scandalous, a threat to rationality or reason, to good sense, a tragedy or folly, hysterical) but also as *possible* – and possible to take seriously. The position of ignorance, indeed, may be said to drive literature or a certain thinking or certain traditions of thinking of literature. Plato, the poet or ex-poet,[64] is of course peculiarly insistent about the ignorance that constitutes poetry, not least in his influential descriptions of the poet. Lyric poets are 'not in their right minds' when they make poems, he says; the poet is 'an airy thing, winged and holy, and he is not able to make poetry until he becomes inspired and goes out of his mind and his intellect is no longer in him' (*Ion* 534a–b). Anyone coming to the 'gates of poetry' under the illusion that they can compose 'without the Muses' madness' is mistaken (*Phaedrus* 245a). The poet has 'neither knowledge nor right opinion about whether the things he makes are fine or bad' (*Republic* 10: 602a). Poetry, like music, produces 'a certain harmoniousness, not knowledge' (*Republic* 7: 522a). Like soothsayers and prophets, poets 'have no knowledge of what they are saying' (*Meno* 99d). Socrates explains in the *Apology* that he has visited the poets, trying to 'catch myself being more ignorant than they', but when he asks them what their poems mean he finds that they cannot tell him: 'I soon realised that poets do not compose their poems with knowledge, but by some inborn talent and by inspiration, like seers and prophets who also say many fine things without any understanding of what they say' (*Apology* 22b–c). Plato is insistent: he can hardly mention poetry without referring to what he sees as poets' constitutive ignorance. As Julius Elias comments, the 'principal themes' of Plato's attack on poets are their 'ignorance, incoherence, irresponsibility, and madness'.[65]

Philosophy, then, as knowledge, as science – and literature as its other, as what science is not.[66] The way in which poets are to be distinguished from philosophers (and the way that a certain kind of philosopher – Cavell? Nietzsche? Kierkegaard? Heidegger? Derrida? – may be distinguished from their more conventional or indeed 'analytical' colleagues) has to do with a certain nescience, a refusal or inability regarding what they can know. But it is also possible to construe poetry or literature more generally as the place where ignorance can be entertained, explored, enacted. Literature may be conceived of as the space that can, unlike many forms of philosophy, accommodate, for example, self-contradiction, permanent perplexity, aporia; literature, in effect, may be seen as beyond the law of non-contradiction, as the space in which contradiction somehow – perhaps as an aspect of our 'willing suspension of disbelief'

– *works*, and is put to work. Like the unconscious, in which, according to Freud, there are no negatives, literature may be conceived as that space in which there is no contradiction – or *only* contradiction. *This is the author speaking*, the text asserts, *but not the author; this is true*, it implies, *but it is not true; these are people*, it proposes, *but not people; this involves a particular use of language, can only be expressed by these words, in this order, but it has or strives for general, universal, timeless significance*. And literature may therefore be seen as the space in which the paradoxical assertion 'I know that I know nothing' can be put to work, engaged, explored, performed. Literature is, after all, the space of imagination, of dreams, of bewitchment, of the unconscious: if, as Wittgenstein declares, 'Philosophy is a battle *against* the bewitchment [*die Verhexung*] of our intelligence by means of language',[67] then literature might be seen as an engagement with bewitchment, even *as* bewitchment by and in language, an acknowledgement just that language is bewitching and that we cannot escape it.

Scepticism declares (however paradoxically): there is nothing I know of this world, nothing with certainty I can claim to know; there is nothing I know of others, of other minds (even whether or not others *have* minds); there is nothing I know, finally know, of myself (even whether or not there is a 'myself', whether or not I am, whether I have what is called a 'mind', rather than, say, what seems to be only an infinitely complex system of synapses and neurotransmitters, of infinitesimal electrical charges and chemical changes). If the institution of literature involves not simply or as such a form of scepticism, we can perhaps at least say that it tends to involve openness to these ways of not knowing, these ways of being in, of living with (or 'acknowledging', in Cavell's formulation), what I am calling 'ignorance'.[68]

'What would it mean ... to conceive of an experience that is constituted by the very way it escapes or resists comprehension?', Cathy Caruth asks, in an enquiry that seems in some ways to encapsulate the experience of reading.[69] Beginning in this space between philosophy and literature, or this apprehension of literature by philosophy (the apprehension of literature as conceptually innocent, nescient, ignorant), we might begin to seek to clarify the relationship between literature and agnoiology. For it is in literature, as I say, that ignorance is most clearly encompassed, articulated and performed. If, as Michael Smithson remarks, we are currently undergoing an 'ignorance explosion',[70] this book involves an attempt to think through, or at least think about, the implications of such an explosion in one area of the 'human sciences', literature – an area of discourse that has, after all, from Plato onwards, been designated as constituting the realm of ignorance.

Notes

1 On Socrates' indigence see *Apology* 23b: 'I live in great poverty because of my service to the god' (unless otherwise stated, quotations from Plato are taken from *Plato: Complete Works*, ed. John M. Cooper (Indianapolis: Hackett, 1997)). The question of whether or not Socrates was in fact claiming to know anything is one of the more controversial in contemporary assessments of the philosopher. Two related questions arise: (1) how much did Socrates in fact claim not to know? and (2) in his declarations of ignorance, does he mean what he says (or is he lying, insincere, joking, provoking, are his claims ironical, a sham, a ruse, a trick, or a trap)? With regard to the idea that the claim of ignorance is a ruse, the popular image of Socrates is constituted by a sense of his disingenuousness: 'Socratic irony' *means* insincerity with regard to what one knows, as the *OED* makes clear ('Irony', sb.3): 'In etymological sense: Dissimulation, pretence; esp. in reference to the dissimulation of ignorance practised by Socrates as a means of confuting an adversary (Socratic irony)'; and see the *OED*'s citation from Thomas Stanley's 1655 *History of Philosophy*: 'The whole confirmation of the Cause, even the whole Life seems to carry an Irony, such was the Life of Socrates, who was for that reason called εἴρων; that is, one that personates an unlearned Man, and is an admirer of others as Wise'. But as Thomas C. Brickhouse and Nicholas D. Smith comment, 'Socrates himself never admits to being an ironist; only his annoyed interlocutors make that charge against him'. As they remark, 'recent scholarship rejects this solution' to the problem of the 'paradox' that Socrates confesses his own ignorance while also claiming to know certain things – including just that he is ignorant (*Plato's Socrates* (New York: Oxford University Press, 1994), p. 32); see also Hugh Benson, *Socratic Wisdom: The Model of Knowledge in Plato's Early Dialogues* (New York: Oxford University Press, 2000), p. 179n. In other words, Socrates' declaration of ignorance should (contrary to tradition and indeed to popular belief) be taken seriously. With regard to the idea that Socrates is sincere in his claims to ignorance, as Brickhouse and Smith make clear contemporary commentators are generally agreed that Socrates did not in fact claim to have *no* knowledge. Critics offer various solutions to the 'Socratic paradox': J.H. Lesher argues that Socrates simply claimed to have no knowledge of particular cases or subjects ('Socrates' Disavowal of Knowledge', in William Prior, ed., *Socrates: Critical Assessments, Volume 1: The Socratic Problem and Socratic Ignorance* (London: Routledge, 1996), pp. 261–74); Gregory Vlastos suggests that Socrates distinguishes between different senses of 'knowledge', infallible certainty on the one hand and knowledge that is constituted by

'justified true belief' on the other ('Socrates' Disavowal of Knowledge', in ibid., pp. 231–60); while Brickhouse and Smith argue that Socrates' claim is that he has 'knowledge without wisdom' in the sense that he knows *that* certain things are the case but not *how* or *why* (*Plato's Socrates*, p. 41; see also p. 42). Brickhouse and Smith also point out that Socrates is not interested in epistemological questions in the modern sense – he is not interested in 'propositional' knowledge for its own sake – but is concerned above all, or even exclusively, with ethics (p. 43). For a useful discussion of these points see Benson, *Socratic Wisdom*, ch. 8. Benson argues that Socrates's claims to ignorance are sincere and that he is a sceptic, but that his scepticism is limited (he doesn't argue that knowledge is in principle not possible or even give reasons for not knowing, and he doesn't suggest that knowledge is beyond human capabilities). 'Socrates's professions of ignorance are pervasive, sincere, and broad-ranging', Benson comments, however, and to this extent he is 'a genuinely skeptical philosopher' (p. 187).

2 *The Dialogues of Plato*, trans. B. Jowett, 4 vols. 4th edn (Oxford: Clarendon, 1953), 1: 438.

3 Friedrich Nietzsche, *The Will to Power*, trans. Walter Kaufmann and R.J. Hollingdale (New York: Random House, 1968), 496 (p. 273); quoted in Alexander Nehamas, 'Will to Knowledge, Will to Ignorance, and Will to Power in *Beyond Good and Evil*', in Yirmiyahu Yovel, ed., *Nietzsche as Affirmative Thinker* (Dordrecht: Martinus Nijhoff, 1986), p. 96. For Nehamas, Nietzsche's notion of the 'will to ignorance' involves the idea that 'every effort to understand something is . . . a refusal to understand something else': the 'will to knowledge' and the 'will to ignorance' are therefore not, as they might seem to be, opposed (p. 98). See John Locke's assertion that 'we cannot act any thing, but by our Faculties; nor talk of Knowledge it self, but by the help of those Faculties, which are fitted to apprehend even what Knowledge is' (*An Essay Concerning Human Understanding*, ed. Peter H. Nidditch (Oxford: Clarendon, 1975), 4.11.3 (p. 631)). As Barry Stroud puts the problem, 'speaking "anthropologically", we can say that human beings gain knowledge of the world through sense-perception. And when we look more closely into how sense-perception works . . . it can become difficult to see how perceptual knowledge of the world is possible. It can be made to look as if it is not possible': but for philosophy, as Stroud puts it, 'that is absurd, or paradoxical' (*Understanding Human Knowledge: Philosophical Essays* (Oxford: Oxford University Press, 2000), p. 123).

4 Lorenzo Infantino, *Ignorance and Liberty* (London: Routledge, 2003), p. 1.

5 See Andrew Martin's suggestive commentary on the Book of Genesis in these terms in *The Knowledge of Ignorance: From Genesis to Jules Verne* (Cambridge: Cambridge University Press, 1985), pp. 10–23: 'man', Martin comments, is, by this reasoning, 'a device for discovering and experiencing the condition of ignorance' (p. 19). Since, as Theodore Ziolkowski points out, the Christian

tradition from Paul to Milton and beyond emphasizes the *disobedience* of the act of eating the fruit, and downplays the question of knowledge, one might even see ignorance as the repressed in the cultural reception of the Fall narrative: see *The Sin of Knowledge* (Princeton: Princeton University Press, 2000), p. 17. See also pp. 17–18 on the importance of knowledge and ignorance in the Christian Fall myth in particular and in contrast to other mythologies: 'Why should it have been a tree of *knowledge* through which sin was introduced into the world?', asks Ziolkowski (p. 18). The Christian Fall narrative, according to Ziolkowski, is essentially one in which 'man' is divided from nature through the 'sin of knowledge'. Ziolkowski's book concerns variations on a theme of epistemological transgression, the ways in which the three mythic heroes, Adam, Prometheus and Faust, 'violate divine prohibitions' against knowledge (p. 69).

6 Aristotle, *Metaphysics*, trans. W.D. Ross, in *The Complete Works of Aristotle*, ed. Jonathan Barnes, 2 vols. (Princeton: Princeton University Press, 1984), 2: 1552.
7 Hugh Benson notes that eleven of the fourteen 'early' dialogues end in Socrates' profession of ignorance (*Socratic Wisdom*, p. 178); and see his comment that for Socrates 'one who lives in ignorance of the most important things is better off dead', but that 'this is the condition that mortals find themselves in' (188).
8 For an elaboration of this point see Brickhouse and Smith, *Plato's Socrates*, pp. 206–12.
9 Nietzsche, *The Will to Power* 609 (p. 328): as Nehamas glosses this passage, 'The will to ignorance must therefore turn upon itself and become a will to ignore the fact that one is not coming to know many things in coming to know about one, to ignore the fact that one is merely producing an interpretation' (Nehamas, 'Will to Knowledge', p. 105).
10 Or, as Hugh Benson puts it, he 'recognizes that he fails to know what he fails to know' (*Socratic Wisdom*, p. 170).
11 Jowett translation (*Dialogues* 1: 298). Socrates goes on to affirm that it is no 'conjecture' with him that 'knowledge differs from true opinion': 'There are not many things which I profess to know, but this is most certainly one of them', he asserts (ibid.).
12 Richard Kraut, *Socrates and the State* (Princeton: Princeton University Press, 1984), p. 273.
13 However, as Hugh Benson points out, there is still a sense in which Socrates is ignorant about his ignorance since unlike, 'ordinary' sceptics, he 'provides no indication at all regarding what grounds his profession of ignorance' (*Socratic Wisdom*, p. 184).
14 Quotations from *Meno* in this section are from Jane Day's translation in *Plato's 'Meno' in Focus*, ed. Jane M. Day (London: Routledge, 1994).
15 Although it is seldom remarked upon by commentators, it is no doubt significant that the torpedo fish or electric ray was used by the Ancient Greeks

as a cure for certain conditions, including gout and headaches: it seems likely, therefore, that Plato is in part alluding to this curative sense of the torpidity produced by Socratian ECT.
16 Virtue, Socrates concludes, doesn't come by 'nature' or by 'teaching' but instead 'by divine dispensation without thought' (*Meno* 99e).
17 For a digest of comments on the relationship between evil and ignorance in the world's major religions see www.unification.net/ws/theme049.htm (accessed 5 February 2008). This is not of course to say that the Old Testament, for example, is not as ambivalent on the matter as Socrates/Plato – as the narrative of the Fall suggests (and see also 1 Corinthians 3: 18: 'If any man among you seemeth to be wise in this world, let him become a fool, that he may be wise').
18 'It must be granted, surely, that mindlessness is the disease of the soul, and of mindlessness there are two kinds. One is madness, and the other is ignorance. And so if a man suffers from a condition that brings on either one or the other, that condition must be declared a disease' (*Timaeus* 86b). The important distinction is of course between what we might call 'necessary' or unavoidable ignorance (ignorance of that which cannot be known or that we cannot know), on the one hand, and 'culpable' ignorance (ignorance of that which we can or should know), on the other – a distinction that is often central to ethical and religious conceptions of ignorance (see, for example, the entry for 'Ignorance' in *The Catholic Encyclpaedia* (www.newadvent.org/cathen/07648a.htm (accessed 5 February 2008)).
19 Brickhouse and Smith, *Plato's Socrates*, p. 125; for Plato's Socrates, they suggest, 'no one does evil knowingly, for to do evil is necessarily to do harm to oneself . . . All evil, then, is some kind of ignorance' (p. 207); see also Charles H. Kahn, *Plato and the Socratic Dialogue: The Philosophical Use of a Literary Form* (Cambridge: Cambridge University Press, 1996), pp. 72–4, 92–3.
20 See Aristotle, *Metaphysics* 982b (*Works* 2: 1554): 'For it was owing to their wonder that men both now begin and at first began to philosophize.' As Aristotle goes on to say, 'a man who is puzzled and wonders thinks himself ignorant (whence even the lover of myth is in a sense a lover of wisdom, for myth is composed of wonders)'; men began to philosophise, he says, to 'escape from ignorance'. See also, from two millennia later, Ludwig Wittgenstein's remark that 'A philosophical problem has the form: "I don't know my way about"' (*Philosophical Investigations*, trans. G.E.M. Anscombe, 2nd edn. (Oxford: Blackwell, 1958), 123 (p. 49e)). For a discussion of these comments see Gareth B. Matthews, *Socratic Perplexity and the Nature of Philosophy* (Oxford: Oxford University Press, 1999), pp. 13–14, 30.
21 Matthews, *Socratic Perplexity*, p. 69 (hereafter cited in the text).
22 The point is also made by Kahn, *Plato and the Socratic Dialogue*, p. 99: according to Kahn, in both *Meno* and the *Sophist*, 'Plato recognizes the negative elenchus as a necessary preliminary, preparing but not constituting the constructive search for knowledge'.

23 See Matthews, *Socratic Perplexity*, p. 121 and ch. 10.
24 For a statement of and challenge to this model see Kahn *Plato*, pp. 3, 40–2, and passim: Kahn argues for a 'unified' Socrates, a 'literary' figure carefully constructed and gradually developed by Plato. While he doesn't state it, though, Matthew's model is in some ways exemplified by Kahn's argument: Kahn argues for a 'unified' Socratic figure who lays the ground for the later, 'mature', dialogues by the aporiai of the earlier dialogues – he even suggests that the puzzling or enigmatic moments in the earlier dialogues are resolved or eliminated by later dialogues (ibid., pp. 60, 65). Plato reinterprets the Socratic *elenchus*, Kahn proposes, 'as the preparation for constructive philosophy' (ibid., p. 100).
25 Kahn, *Plato*, p. 180.
26 On the Renaissance attacks on 'monstrous ignorance' see Ian D. McFarlane, *Renaissance France, 1470–1589* (London: E. Benn, 1974); more generally, the collocation of 'monstrous' with 'ignorance' is of course as alive today as it was in the Renaissance.
27 Jacques Derrida, *Who's Afraid of Philosophy?*, trans. Jans Plug (Stanford: Stanford University Press, 2002), pp. 61–2.
28 The word 'anepistemology' is not in the *OED* but is used (and coined?) by Andrew Martin in *The Knowledge of Ignorance*, p. 10. Martin refers to the theory of ignorance as a 'systematic anepistemology', and suggests that what he sees as the philosophical 'indifference' to such a theory is a consequence of 'an enduring Platonic disposition to confuse knowledge with virtue' (ibid.). On the idea that there is little theory of ignorance see Michael Smithson's comment that 'theories of knowledge far outnumber those of ignorance' (*Ignorance and Uncertainty: Emerging Paradigms* (New York: Springer-Verlag, 1989), p. 2).
29 James Ferrier, *Institutes of Metaphysic*, 3rd edn (1875), ed. John Haldane (Bristol: Thoemmes Press, 2001), p. 45 (further references are cited in the text).
30 A.C. Grayling, 'Skepticism and Justification', in Steven Luper, ed., *The Skeptics: Contemporary Essays* (Aldershot: Ashgate, 2003), p. 29.
31 Jonathan L. Kvanvig, *Value of Knowledge and the Pursuit of Understanding* (Cambridge: Cambridge University Press, 2003), p. ix.
32 Keith Lehrer, 'Skepticism, Fallibility and Circularity', in Luper, ed., *The Skeptics*, p. 95; Stroud, *Understanding Human Knowledge*, p. 177. Compare Peter Unger's attempts at a definition of scepticism: 'no one ever *knows* anything about anything', or 'Everybody is always *ignorant of everything* (*Ignorance: A Case for Scepticism* (Oxford: Clarendon, 1975), pp. 1, 94); and see Stanley Cavell's useful definition of scepticism as not 'the discovery of an incapacity in human knowing' but as 'an insufficiency in acknowledging what in my world I think of as beyond me, or my senses' (*Philosophy the Day After Tomorrow* (Cambridge, Mass.: Harvard University Press, 2005), p. 12);

Ignorance and philosophy 29

see also Stroud's sense that scepticism 'says that nobody knows anything, or that nobody has good reason to believe anything' (although Stroud also suggests that it can also be construed as relating to particular areas of knowledge, and that it is in fact 'most illuminating' when taken in that sense (*Understanding Human Knowledge*, p. 139)). With regard to scepticism as a theory of ignorance, Lehrer does in fact at least *ask* if philosophers shouldn't 'turn from constructing a theory of knowledge, epistemology, to constructing a theory of ignorance, agnoiology' (p. 95).

33 See Lehrer, ed., *The Skeptics*, pp. 77, 119, 89.
34 See Richard H. Popkin, 'Skepticism', in *The Encyclopaedia of Philosophy*, ed. Paul Edwards, vol. 7 (New York: Macmillan, 1967), p. 459: scepticism 'has been like an anonymous letter received by a dogmatic philosopher who does hold a position. The letter raises fundamental problems for the recipient by questioning whether he had adequate grounds for his assertions and assumptions' (quoted in Ewa Płonowska Ziarek, *The Rhetoric of Failure: Deconstruction of Skepticism, Reinvention of Modernism* (Albany: State University of New York Press, 1996), p. 5.
35 Michael Williams, *Unnatural Doubts: Epistemological Realism and the Basis of Scepticism* (Princeton: Princeton University Press, 1996), p. 9).
36 Bryan Frances, *Scepticism Comes Alive* (Oxford: Clarendon Press, 2005), p. 73; Stanley Cavell, *Disowning Knowledge in Six Plays of Shakespeare* (Cambridge: Cambridge University Press, 1987), p. 94 (hereafter cited in the text).
37 See Frances, *Scepticism Comes Alive*, p. 203: 'There is something simple, clean, hypnotizing, and beautiful about the classic arguments for radical scepticism. They can mesmerize just about anyone . . .'
38 Stanley Cavell, *In Quest of the Ordinary: Lines of Skepticism and Romanticism* (Chicago: University of Chicago Press, 1988), p. 138.
39 David Hume, *A Treatise of Human Nature*, ed. David Fate Norton and Mary J. Norton (Oxford: Oxford University Press, 2000), Book 1, part 4, section 2 (p. 144): 'this sceptical doubt . . . is a malady, which can never be radically cur'd'.
40 Cavell, *The Claim of Reason: Wittgenstein, Skepticism, Morality, and Tragedy* (1979) new edition (New York: Oxford University Press, 1999), p. 59.
41 J.L. Austin, *Sense and Sensibilia* (Oxford: Oxford University Press, 1962), p. 142.
42 José Ortega y Gasset, *The Idea of Principle in Leibnitz and the Evolution of Deductive Theory*, trans. Mildred Adams (New York: Norton, 1971), p. 271.
43 Michael Williams, *Problems of Knowledge: A Critical Introduction to Epistemology* (Oxford: Oxford University Press, 2001), p. 5.
44 Cavell, *Philosophy the Day After Tomorrow*, pp. 12, 133.
45 John Greco, *Putting Skeptics in their Place: The Nature of Skeptical Arguments and their Role in Philosophical Inquiry* (Cambridge: Cambridge University Press, 2000), p. 64.

46 On scepticism as an 'irreducible threat' see Cavell, *Philosophy the Day After Tomorrow*, p. 138; as a threat, see pp. 1, 3, 134, 139; and see Stroud, *Understanding*, pp. 139, 140, 141.
47 Stroud, *Understanding*, pp. 139, 141; Cavell, *Philosophy the Day After Tomorrow*, p. 1; see also the assertion by Shaun Nichols, Stephen Stich and Jonathan M. Weinberg that 'Arguments for scepticism have occupied a central place in western philosophy' ('Meta-skepticism: Meditations in Ethno-epistemology', in Luper, ed., *The Skeptics*, p. 246); and Grayling's comment that 'The study of scepticism might be said to define epistemology' ('Skepticism and Justification', ibid., p. 29).
48 Immanuel Kant, *Critique of Pure Reason*, trans. Norman Kemp Smith, 2nd impression (Basingstoke: Macmillan, 1933), p. 34n. For Kant, the scandal lies in the fact that reason is unable to refute such a position; Heidegger retorts in *Being and Time* that the scandal lies in the fact that 'such proofs are expected and attempted again and again' (quoted in Cavell, *Philosophy the Day After Tomorrow*, p. 133).
49 Stroud, *Understanding Human Knowledge*, p. 38.
50 See also Cavell, *Quest*, p. 44: 'No one wants to be a skeptic; to be gripped by its threat is to wish to overcome it.'
51 Stroud, *Understanding Human Knowledge*, p. 1. See also p. 124: his and Michael Williams's appreciation of the 'depth' and 'difficulty' of enquiring into the very possibility of human knowledge, he remarks, 'does not appear to be widely held in philosophy today'.
52 Ibid., p. 38.
53 Ibid., p. 100.
54 Richard Foley, 'Three Attempts to Refute Skepticism and Why They Fail', in Luper, ed., *The Skeptics*, p. 62.
55 Williams, *Unnatural Doubts*, p. xiv. For Williams, in fact, the problem is not that scepticism has not been refuted, but that it has been refuted 'too often': 'Theoretical defences of human knowledge encourage scepticism as much as sceptical attacks on it' (pp. 10, 6).
56 Barry Stroud, *The Significance of Philosophical Skepticism* (Oxford: Clarendon, 1984), p. 39. See also Frances, *Scepticism Comes Alive*, pp. 66–9 and passim, for a defence of the importance to contemporary philosophy of sceptical arguments.
57 Cavell, *Quest*, pp. 5, 48.
58 Williams, *Unnatural Doubts*, pp. xiii, xv, 9. Williams's position, however, is that in order to circumvent or resist scepticism we must refute the claim that scepticism is just the condition of being human: he argues that the 'Humean [i.e. sceptical] condition and the human condition are not the same' (p. 359) – a claim which itself, he argues, undermines the tenacious grasp of scepticism.
59 Cavell, *The Claim of Reason*, p. 241.

60 Williams, *Unnatural Doubts*, p. 12.
61 Emmanuel Levinas, *Otherwise than Being or Beyond Essence*, trans. Alphonso Lingis (The Hague: Martinus Nijhoff, 1981), p. 168 (translation modified).
62 For a rather different take on the link between tragedy and ignorance see Slavoj Žižek's *Did Somebody Say Totalitarianism? Five Interventions in the (Mis)use of a Notion* (London: Verso, 2001), p. 12, on the idea that tragedy is 'based on some misrecognition or ignorance' (by contrast with melodrama, which 'always involves some unexpected and excessive knowledge possessed not by the hero but by his or her other', knowledge which is revealed to the hero at the end of the narrative). But see Aristotle's *Poetics*, in which tragic narrative plotting is said to hinge around a moment that involves the end of ignorance, of *anagnorisis*.
63 Cavell, *Quest*, pp. 154–5.
64 According to Nietzsche, 'the first thing the youthful tragedian Plato did' in order to become Socrates' pupil 'was to burn his poetry' (*The Birth of Tragedy and Other Writings*, ed. Raymond Guess and Ronald Speirs (Cambridge: Cambridge University Press, 1999), p. 68; see also Shelley's comments in his 'A Defence of Poetry' on Plato as 'essentially a poet' on the grounds that 'the truth and splendour of his imagery and the melody of his language is the most intense that it is possible to conceive' (*Shelley's Poetry and Prose*, ed. Donald H. Reiman and Sharon B. Powers (New York: Norton, 1977), p. 484). Plato as much as admits this himself in *Republic* Book 10 where he says that he is 'well aware of the charm' that poetry exercises and that in banning poetry he is acting like a lover who forces himself to stay away from an inappropriate object of desire (607c–e).
65 Julius A. Elias, *Plato's Defence of Poetry* (London: Macmillan, 1984), p. 5. Although he excludes the productions of 'the pleasure giving Muse' from his Republic, Plato does allow that 'hymns to the gods and eulogies to the good people' should be admitted, and he concedes that poetry would be allowed to enter the city if it can successfully defend itself (*Republic* 10: 607a–d). Elias defends Plato's attack on poets by suggesting that what he means by 'poet' is a rather more expansive category than it is today, and that it can be said to include physicists, cosmologists, moralists, legislators, politicians, religious leaders and patriots, and that Plato's point was that poets 'promote ignorance' by 'surrounding falsehood with an aura of piety' (modern poets, as Elias comments, are just not important enough for the authorities to bother banning or censoring, on the whole and outside of certain totalitarian states); and he suggests that the modern 'rhetors' are 'lawyers, journalists, politicians, admen . . . lobbyists' (pp. 213–14): Elias suggests that if we believe (1) that people can be educated/manipulated, and (2) that some myths are false, then 'we shall want to limit public access to the proponents of false myths' and that that is all Plato is asking for (p. 221).

66 'May we think as follows?', asks Cavell: 'If philosophy of science can be taken to be what philosophy is, that is because philosophy is, and is content to be, recognizable, or practicable, as (a chapter of) science; whereas were philosophy of art to make of itself a chapter of one or more of the arts, it would no longer be recognizable as philosophy' (*Philosophy the Day After Tomorrow*, p. 14).

67 Wittgenstein, *Philosophical Investigations* 109 (p. 47e; italics added); see also *The Blue and Brown Books* (New York: Harper Torch Books, 1965), p. 27: 'Philosophy, as we use the word, is a fight against the fascination which forms of expression exert upon us'. It should be noted, though, that Wittgenstein also suggests that 'It is the business of philosophy, not to resolve a contradiction by means of a mathematical or logico-mathematical discovery, but to make it possible for us to get a clear view of . . . the state of affairs *before* the contradiction is resolved' (*Philosophical Investigations* 125 (p. 50e)).

68 Philip Weinstein also fruitfully invokes the notion of acknowledgement, in *Unknowing: The Work of Modernist Fiction* (Ithaca: Cornell University Press, 2006), although curiously without acknowledging Cavell.

69 Cathy Caruth, 'Introduction: The Insistence of Reference', in Caruth and Deborah Esch, eds, *Critical Encounters: Reference and Responsibility in Deconstructive Writing* (New Brunswick: Rutgers University Press, 1995), p. 1.

70 Smithson, *Ignorance and Uncertainty*, p. 4; see also, for a very different take on the alleged virtues of such an 'explosion', Julius Lukasiewicz, *The Ignorance Explosion* (Ottawa: Carleton University Press, 1994).

2

Literary ignorance

'Be quick when you switch on the light / and you'll see the dark / was how my father put it', John Burnside remarks in 'Otherlife', Part IV of 'Fields' in *The Asylum Dance* (2000): 'catch / the otherlife of things', he goes on, 'before a look / immerses them'.[1] It is this 'otherlife' of things that is the large topic, the *topos*, of poetry – of ancient as much as of contemporary poetry. The clear implication of Burnside's lines is that it is this 'otherlife' of things that poetry enables us to see – to see and not see, as you might 'see the dark' as (but when? – well, that's why you have to be quick) you switch on the light. And that not seeing is as important as seeing.

This section of Burnside's poem, 'Otherlife', concerns the death of the poet's father. Burnside remembers burying his father's clothes in a 'disused lair' in a field, waiting or hoping for something to change, for some sign, as he sits by the lair with the clothes. And it is about the way that nothing happened on that day except a sense of something 'half-seen' and of the 'pull of the withheld':

> but all I found in there was mould and spoor
> where something had crept away
>   to feed
>   or die
> or all I can tell
>   though for years I have sat up late
> and thought of something more
>   some half-seen thing
> the pull of the withheld
>   the foreign joy
> I tasted that one afternoon
>   and left behind
> when I made my way back down the hill
> with the known world about me.[2]

The poem is about the 'pull of the withheld' in relation to the 'known world' that surrounds us, about 'something more', something 'half-seen' that is not seen. It's not only, of course, that the poem is *about* what is not known, not only that it tells a story in which nothing becomes known, but that it expresses that half-knowledge in a language of half-knowledge – somewhat vague, syntactically ordered by the spatial and linear and syntactical disorder, the interruptions, the lurch, in its lines.

Emily Dickinson does something, or talks about something, similar in many of her poems (the difference between doing something and saying something itself constitutes part of the specificity, the point, of literature). 'There's a certain Slant of light' is both famous and instructive:

> There's a certain Slant of light,
> Winter Afternoons –
> That oppresses, like the Heft
> Of Cathedral Tunes –
>
> Heavenly Hurt, it gives us –
> We can find no scar,
> But internal difference,
> Where the Meanings, are –
>
> None may teach it – Any –
> 'Tis the Seal Despair –
> An imperial affliction
> Sent us of the Air –
>
> When it comes, the Landscape listens –
> Shadows – hold their breath –
> When it goes, 'tis like the Distance
> On the look of Death – [3]

Among the many difficulties of this poem is the comma in line 8 that divides 'Meanings' from 'are'. The comma is often left out in reproductions of the poem, because without it the line makes sense, although it is less good – less powerful, less provocative, less breath taking – as poetry. Without it, indeed, the line becomes banal: the meanings are there (where? just there, where there is internal difference, where there is heavenly hurt but with no scar, that no-place of hurt). Add a comma, and the line becomes more difficult, more resistant to immediate and reassuring sense-making, more productive of a certain kind of 'ignorance' – bafflement, conceptual blankness, uncertainty – that I am aligning with literature, or poetry, and therefore with the experience of reading. The internal difference produced by the comma within the line forces a kind of blank indifference to sense, forces our ignorance. It can't be taught, a poem like this – another effect of or consequence of a certain thinking of poetry and, or as, ignorance – and the poem doesn't seem to teach, to teach much, to teach anything. The comma, indeed, constitutes, in itself, something like the 'internal difference' referred to in the previous line, makes the grammar of the line different, internally different, from itself and from what we might expect, from what we can read, in a gesture that we can define as, that we can call, poetry.

In the first place, then, the question of literary ignorance is a question of reading. It is no doubt a truism – something that nobody can fail to recognize – to say that we are, by definition, or that we should be, ignorant as we begin a poem or story. T.S. Eliot suggests that ignorance is the proper condition for reading: 'In my own experience of the appreciation of poetry', he remarks, 'I have always found that the less I knew about the poet and his work, before I began to read it, the better'.[4] In one respect, we just are, or should be, ignorant as we start to read: we don't know what will happen in a narrative, or how the words of a poem will collect and congregate, mesh and interweave. Indeed, reading may be said to be driven by such narrative or hermeneutic ignorance. Reading tends to begin with curiosity, with the desire to know just *because* we don't. Even rereading may be said to be undertaken on the premise of ignorance: we reread in order to remember what we have forgotten (and in that sense don't know), or to get a clearer sense of the text or to discover what we missed earlier (and in *that* sense don't know).

This is perhaps self-evident, but it connects with what is a rather less prominently acknowledged question of reading, the idea that we are not only ignorant as we start to read a text, but ignorant, properly speaking, of *how* to read anyway, and ignorant if we are reading properly, reading well, at the end. 'Genuine poetry can communicate before it is understood', to cite T.S. Eliot again.[5] But for some commentators, genuine poetry would be that which communicates without ever being 'understood'. For some, the ignorance of the reader, her ignorance of how to read, amounts indeed to the proper condition of reading. Eliot himself seems to make this point in another essay when he comments that 'there is, in all great poetry, something which must *remain* unaccountable however complete might be our knowledge of the poet'.[6] That most eminent of twentieth-century French readers, Maurice Blanchot, is perhaps most direct, most forthright on this point. What most 'threatens' reading, he argues, is 'a man who knows in general how to read'. What threatens reading for Blanchot is the reader's 'reality', his 'personality, his immodesty, his stubborn insistence upon remaining himself in the face of what he reads'.[7] Or as Wallace Stevens more caustically if ambiguously puts it, 'The poem reveals itself only to the ignorant man'.[8] It is not just the text that we do not or should not presume to know but ourselves too. Reading, Blanchot argues, 'demands more ignorance than knowledge'; it requires 'knowledge endowed with an immense ignorance', he suggests, knowledge which has 'each time to be received and acquired in forgetfulness of it'.[9]

In his own way, Paul de Man has also called for a theory – and a practice – of reading that acknowledges, at the same time, the impossibility of reading, or the impossibility of a theory of reading. For de Man, the 'grammatical decoding' of a literary text necessarily leaves 'a residue of indetermination' since no such reading could 'claim to reach the determining figural dimensions of a text'.[10] As de Man puts it, in his characteristically arcane way, reading is 'a negative process in which the grammatical cognition is undone, at all times, by its rhetorical displacement' – a 'negative process' that may be said to amount to or result in a hermeneutics of uncertainty, undecidability or ignorance.[11] To read, de Man comments in an essay on Shelley's *The Triumph of Life*, is 'to understand, to question, to know, to forget, to erase, to deface, to repeat': 'No degree of knowledge can ever stop this madness', he comments of Shelley's poem but also more generally of reading poetry, 'for it is the madness of words'.[12]

Literary ignorance, then, is in the first place the ignorance of reading, the ignorance that is reading. Reading begins in ignorance, in the search for enlightenment. But readers – certain kinds of readers, responding to or reading certain kinds of text – may be said to seek out, to desire, the enigma without resolution, the conundrum without revelation, the secret without content, desiring not (or not only) knowledge, enlightenment, meaning, understanding, but also in the end nescience. This reticence is what we learn, or what we can learn, from books – not to know, not to desire knowledge. Or to 'know', rather, a book's opacity, or what Paul Fry calls the 'ostension' of the poem – the way that, like some lines of poetry, a poem can be 'end stopped', can lead, cognitively, just nowhere.[13] In this regard, epistemophilia, the desire or drive to know, which itself drives reading and structures narratives may be said to be shadowed by its other, by what we might call anepistemophilia or even by epistemophobia, by the desire not to know – or by the desire to know, to take cognisance of, nescience. And what Eliot and Blanchot and de Man suggest through their different vocabularies is that in a certain way readers, in reading, after reading, at least if they are reading well, reading properly, go on not knowing, remain in doubt, in ignorance, and go on not knowing how to read.

But literary ignorance is not only, of course, a question of reading. As Plato suggests, it is also the condition of a certain conception of writing, of authorship. One way to approach literary agnoiology would be to consider the importance, in the history of aesthetics more generally, of the separation of art from truth because of its divorce from cognition and reason. Undoubtedly the most influential expression of such 'aesthetic alienation'[14] is Immanuel Kant's conception of art as autonomous and as involving 'purposefulness without purpose'. In his discussion of genius in the *Critique of Judgement* (1790), Kant responds to the notion of aesthetic experience – put forward by Alexander Baumgarten in particular – as 'confused cognition'.[15] Reacting against such a notion, against, that is, aesthetic judgement as a form of cognition *per se*, Kant proposes a conception of art as pleasure without a concept. As Kai Hammermeister argues, in fact, the 'status of art can only be raised if the connection between art and cognition is severed': the 'aim' of the *Critique of Judgement* is therefore 'to establish our pronouncements on art and beauty not as an inferior version of our judgments on truth or morality, but as independent of both'.[16] As Kant remarks at the beginning of the *Critique of Judgement*, to decide whether or not something is beautiful 'we do not use understanding to refer the presentation to the object so as to give rise to cognition': therefore the 'judgement of taste is not a cognitive judgement . . . but an aesthetic one, by which we mean a judgment whose determining basis *cannot be other* than *subjective*'.[17] In his discussion of the origin of this conception of 'art', Kant therefore argues that 'Genius is the talent (natural endowment) that gives the rule to art' and that genius is defined as 'the innate mental predisposition *through which* nature gives the rule to art', meaning that the author or artist cannot know 'how he came by the ideas' for his work: it is *nature*'s work, not his.[18]

While Kant may be said to have brought the notion of art to philosophical attention and to have crystallized an important eighteenth-century concern within the new discourse of aesthetics, he can by no means be said to have originated the connection between authorship and not knowing – which, as we have seen, can be found expressed in rather different ways (in terms of a *positive* authorial nescience, ignorance as a condition of a certain sense of authorship, rather than in terms of a distinction between authorship and cognition) in classical notions of inspiration, most clearly expressed in Plato's *Ion* (see especially 534a–b). What we can say is that the Platonic notion of poetic mania, of the poet being out of his head, beside himself, not in his right mind in the act of literary creation, had enormous influence in the era in which the very institution of the aesthetic in general and literature in particular – literature as a new or newly conceived cultural institution – was being instantiated: in other words, the later eighteenth and early nineteenth century, the era normally designated under the catch-all term 'Romanticism'. With the Romantics, I suggest, the question of authorial ignorance became central to literary and other aesthetics. This point is perhaps most succinctly put by Stanley Cavell in a rhetorical question that seems to go to the heart of the problem of authorship: 'Is authoring the obliteration or the apotheosis of the writer?'[19] This question is intrinsic to the new institution of literature (that 'strange institution', as Jacques Derrida puts it, strange not least just because of this question).[20] And there is a sense in which we might say that it is precisely the uncertainty of this question that accounts for much of the interest in reading itself.

This tradition continues to influence contemporary engagements with questions of authorship and contemporary poetics (it is prominent, for example, as I will argue in Chapter 10, below, in descriptions by poets of their acts of composition). And it is therefore no coincidence that Derrida, one of the most influential twentieth-century theorists of literature (amongst much else), repeatedly returns to the question of authorial ignorance. In *Glas*, for example, that most authorially alert, most literary and most textually aleatory of philosophical works, Derrida tellingly remarks that 'you can take interest in what I am doing here only insofar as you would be right to believe that – *somewhere* – I do not know what I am doing'.[21] The remark has large implications for our understanding of the modern literary institution. We are dealing here with what E.D. Hirsch calls the 'commonplace' that 'an author often does not really know what he means'.[22] Hirsch quotes Kant (in the *Critique of Pure Reason*) on Plato: 'it is by no means unusual . . . to find that we understand [an author] better than he has understood himself' (quoted p. 219). Hirsch rejects this 'commonplace', and argues that 'by claiming to perceive implications of which the author was not conscious, we may sometimes distort and falsify the meaning of which he was conscious, which is not "better understanding" but simply misunderstanding of the author's meaning' (p. 21). For Hirsch, such a 'misunderstanding' involves a confusion of the distinction between 'meaning' and 'subject matter'. But he does allow circumstances where an interpretation has 'made explicit certain aspects of an author's undoubted meaning of which the author was unconscious' (p. 22). Hirsch's answer to this apparent inconsistency in his position is that 'It is not possible to mean what one does not mean, though it is very possible to mean what one is not conscious of meaning'. 'That', he goes on, 'is the entire issue in the argument based on authorial ignorance' (p. 22). But, he declares, 'No example of the author's ignorance with respect to his meaning could legitimately show that his intended meaning and the meaning of his text are two different things' (p. 22). What I am trying to suggest in this book is that we should try to open up – rather than to close down – this 'commonplace' idea of 'authorial ignorance', to suggest that the very institution of poetry or literature as it is conceived within a certain tradition may be said to be constituted in relation to it.

Hirsch's engagement with the unconscious is symptomatic of his approach. On the one hand he allows 'unconscious' meanings in so much as they are 'willed', in so much as they are 'present in another region of [the author's] mind' (p. 52). On the other hand, he excludes them from 'meaning' in so much as they are 'symptomatic' and therefore part of 'significance': 'Symptomatic, involuntary meaning is part of a text's significance, just as its value or its present relevance is', he remarks. For Hirsch, significance belongs to the provenance of criticism rather than interpretation. Interpretation, for Hirsch, has as its exclusive object the text's 'verbal meaning' (p. 57). But from another perspective it is in this that reading (what Blanchot would call 'real reading') may be said to begin – in this surprise, in this *authorial* ignorance 'somewhere' of what is being said. Derrida's work, by contrast with that of Hirsch, is pervasively engaged with the apparent paradox that an author can always say 'more, less, or something other than what he *would mean* [*voudrait dire*]'.[23] As he remarks in 'The Time of a Thesis', 'this is what I hold and what in turn holds me in its grip, the aleatory strategy of someone who admits that he does not know where he is going'.[24] And as he comments in *Of Grammatology*, reading 'must always aim at a certain relationship, unperceived by the writer, between what he commands and what he does not command of the patterns of the language that he uses'.[25] What is interesting for us, as readers, is in fact precisely this aspect of authorial ignorance, precisely that of which we can conceive the author to be incognisant, nescient. (But how *can* we conceive of it, if we do not know, really know, how to read? Well, perhaps it is in this productive tension that the interest of reading lies – in this tension between our sense of an author's ignorance and our sense of our own.) Derrida is concerned about all authors, any author, of course, and not just those authors that we might define as 'literary' – novelists, poets, playwrights, short-story writers, essayists. But it is in literature that the question of authorial ignorance – of knowledge and nescience – is emphasized and even celebrated. One might even argue – as critics such as Avital Ronell, Stathis Gougouris and Marjorie Garber have recently done – that the literary can be *defined* in terms of this uncertainty or undecidability, this aporia, with respect to cognition;[26] and Derrida's career-long interest in literature, in the 'strange institution' of literature, and in the constitution of the literary, may be accounted for, at least in part, by the fact that literary texts are concerned to explore the paradoxical authority of authorial ignorance. It is, in other words, just this sense of a fundamental or constitutive uncertainty of authorial intention that may be said to distinguish literature itself (and in particular the self-conception of Romantic and post-Romantic literature) from other discourses (from a certain thinking of philosophy in particular).

One of the problems raised by such a conception of the literary involves its challenge to conventional notions of authorial intention. E.D. Hirsch, whose work on intentionality has now spanned four decades, is, as we have seen, an important and influential advocate for an intentionalist approach to reading and for the intentionality of the literary act. His two books, *Validity in Interpretation* and *The Aims of Interpretation* from 1967 and 1976 respectively, have been followed by two essays, 'Meaning and Significance Reinterpreted' from 1984 and 'Transhistorical Intentions and the Persistence of Allegory' from 1994. Both of the essays are concerned with a problem that was touched upon but not, to Hirsch's mind at least, satisfactorily resolved in the earlier books – the problem of how a text will be read in an ungovernable, unpredictable future. As Hirsch argues, a certain kind of writing – including writing that since the Romantic period we have tended to call 'literature' – 'typically intends to convey meaning beyond its immediate occasion into a future context which is very different from that of its production'.[27] In his *Intentionalist Interpretation: A Philosophical Explanation and Defense* (1999), William Irwin usefully elaborates this idea by addressing the conventional idea that literary texts are supposed to be 'universal' or 'timeless'. On the face of it, this might seem to work against the intentionalist position that the meaning of a text is synonymous with what the author intended by it, since when we talk about the 'timelessness' of, say, a Shakespeare sonnet, for example, what we usually want to say is that such a text can be interpreted *differently* at *different* times. If this was not the case, rather than being 'timeless' the sonnet would be time-bound and its interest ultimately limited or finite. For Irwin, this is where criticism comes in. 'Criticism', Irwin remarks, 'is an essential operation in keeping literary texts fresh, alive, and read with each passing generation and era': criticism therefore has the 'vital task' of 'demonstrating the relevance of the text to our own time – showing that what Shakespeare wrote was indeed timeless'.[28] But Irwin goes on to argue that this 'need not be at odds with the meaning the author intends':

> As Hirsch says of Shakespeare's Sonnet 55 . . . 'The author's intention in this poem (and this is characteristic of literature, law, and religion) includes an intention to communicate effectively in the future'. This underscores the point that authors of literary texts may have intentions of various types . . . An author's intention may be specific or vague, firmly grounded in the present or open to future applications, productive of logical reasoning or of aesthetic experience. The possibilities are nearly endless . . . Whatever the author intended to communicate is . . . the meaning of the text'.[29]

Hirsch is right, I think, to say that Shakespeare's sonnet appears to include 'an intention to communicate effectively in the future'. But it is significant that in both his 1984 and his 1994 essays he chooses to focus on this particular poem, one that takes as its subject matter precisely the idea (and the difficulty) of communicating effectively (or indeed at all) with or into the future (but how else can one communicate, what else is there to communicate with?). In Sonnet 55, it is precisely the nature of such a future which is at stake:

> Not marble, nor the gilded monuments
> Of princes shall outlive this pow'rful rhyme,
> But you shall shine more bright in these contents
> Than unswept stone besmearched with sluttish time.
> When wasteful war shall statues overturn,
> And broils root out the work of masonry,
> Nor Mars his sword, nor war's quick fire shall burn
> The living record of your memory.
> 'Gainst death, and all oblivious enmity
> Shall you pace forth, your praise shall still find room,
> Even in the eyes of all posterity

>   That wear this world out to the ending doom.
>   So, till the judgement that yourself arise,
>   You live in this, and dwell in lovers' eyes.[30]

I want to suggest that the success of the poem's 'communication' with the future is a function of the fact that the intention to last, to live on, *conflicts with* the intention to communicate, with the intention to 'communicate effectively', and indeed that in this respect poetry may be conceived precisely in terms of the production of *and* the resistance to, the suspension of, 'communication'. But what happens to Irwin's declaration (a gloss, in effect, on Hirsch and one that seems to accord uncannily well with a similar but supposedly *anti-*intentionalist claim by Wimsatt and Beardsley in their 1946 essay on the 'Intentional Fallacy') that 'Whatever the author intended to communicate is . . . the meaning of the text'[31] – what happens to this claim if what the author intends to communicate is the *resistance* to communication? While we might speculate that certain traditions within the discourses of law or religion or philosophy have it as their purpose, their 'intention', to 'communicate effectively' in the future, it may be that what makes a poem a poem, and what indeed makes it last, is just the way in which it disturbs 'effective communication'. In the end, I want to suggest, this links with our concern with ignorance, the author's and the reader's. But before I get to this point, it might be helpful to look more closely at Shakespeare's sonnet.

The force of Shakespeare's 'powerful rhyme' is constituted, at least in part, by an aporia, by the figure of non-interpretability – of unreadability, to use Paul de Man's term – by the figure of the resistance to communication. Shakespeare's poem, I think, is exemplary just in as much as it presents an opacity, a blockage or barrier to interpretation in relation to its presentation of temporality, in its striving to 'communicate effectively into the future'. The argument of the poem is that 'you' – the young man who appears to be the addressee of the first 126 of the sonnets – will 'live in this', will live on in this poem beyond the young man's and presumably the author's own death but also, more importantly, beyond the lifespan of 'marble' and 'gilded monuments' since, as material artefacts, these are necessarily subject to decay and destruction, necessarily subject to 'sluttish time'. And yet, in a familiar irony, the addressee, the 'you', of the poem does not 'live' in the poem, even metaphorically, *except* in this address, in this 'you', since the poem is not concerned to describe the young man or to list his qualities but rather to describe his survival in words, to figure him in language, substituting his life, his survival, for the poem's – indeed for the poem's argument *about* his survival. What lasts is not the young man but the poem, this 'powerful rhyme', and its powerful arguments concerning the survival not so much of young men but of poems. It is only to the extent that the poem lives on that the young man will, and then only by association, only tangentially, incidentally – only indeed as the subject of a deictic gesture of reference. This, as I say, is a familiar irony, as is the fact that, at the same time, memorializing the young man means, in effect, killing him, figuring his death, representing his being dead: 'you live in this', declares the speaker but only, implicitly, to the extent that 'you' are text, *only* in this – only in this 'this' or in this 'you', this word 'you', this 'you' that is and cannot be you. As the double deixis reveals in its gesture of concealment of this fact, the young man lives only to the extent that he is *not* present, only to the extent that he is constitutionally, fundamentally absent, only to the extent that this 'this' and this 'you' is language. But such a reading of the sonnet, such an interpretation of Shakespeare's intention, works against that other reading, works against our understanding that the poem is about the intention to effect the young man's survival, the sense that the performative address, the apostrophic 'you', allows the young man to live, to live on, to live now. On a very basic level, then, Shakespeare's sonnet 'communicates' (at least) two contradictory senses, senses that work against each other and resist the imputation of effective communication. Hirsch's point is that the sonnet 'includes an intention to communicate effectively in the future' and that in writing it Shakespeare intended that 'his future meaning should *not* be restricted to his own moment'.[32] What I want to suggest, as I say, is that the poem communicates effectively precisely to the extent that it *fails* to communicate effectively: for the poem to succeed, for the poem both to 'communicate' and to 'live' or to survive, to go on being read, the reader must remain in a state of uncertainty, of communicative suspense, must remain in a state of what I am calling ignorance. Beyond the numerous questions of verbal and rhetorical detail that have vexed Shakespeare's commentators on this sonnet, there are a number of overarching questions: is the young man represented as alive or dead? what is it exactly in this regard that the poem is attempting to communicate? These are, of course, questions that may be subsumed within another urgent, unanswerable question: what, finally, does the author intend? Does he intend to celebrate the young man's survival, or his death and the poem's superior, more powerful, more enduring life? Does he know, indeed, what he intends? Is this what intending means? Knowing? Or might one at once intend something and be ignorant of it (as Freud proposes in his theory of the unconscious and as Hirsch seems to accept)? Paradoxically, of course, it is precisely the difficulty in answering such questions, precisely this resistance to interpretation, to communication, that enables us, that forces us even, to go on reading the poem, that makes it 'timeless' in Hirsch's sense of that term, as I say (which must surely mean something like 'timely', of and in time, operating over time and through time, working within different historical, political and cultural contexts and discursive frameworks): the uncertainty of what (or indeed whether or how) Shakespeare intends is what makes the poem 'timeless'.

Hirsch himself concedes some of this in his 1984 essay, 'Meaning and Significance Reinterpreted'. As we have seen, for Hirsch, Shakespeare's intention 'includes an intention to communicate effectively in the future'. By allowing for this future communication, Hirsch also allows for the possibility that such communication includes elements unforeseen by the author himself, he allows that the author may be communicating something that he didn't intend, he allows for what he calls the 'provisionality' of the intention. But Hirsch still argues for the coherence and 'self-identity' of authorially intended meaning, for the author's 'self-same meaning' even while admitting that 'minor conceptual adjustments' will be produced by historical variations in understanding. By contrast, I want to suggest that what we mean by poetry – what we mean by the word because this is what the Romantics have perhaps unwittingly programmed us to mean by the word – involves a certain programmed unprogrammability, a resistance to the understanding, coherence, self-identity, that for Hirsch makes meaning. It is precisely this incalculability, this unprogrammability, that Derrida points to in his announcement in *Glas* that we take an 'interest' in his work because we correctly believe that at some level he *doesn't* know what he is doing. According to the strong intentionalist case – that of Hirsch and Irwin – my reading of the poem is valid only in so much as it coincides, somewhere, with the intention of the poem's author, allowing for that intention to include a certain 'tolerance', certain minor semantic or hermeneutic perturbations over the centuries. But I want to suggest that such a coincidence of intention and interpretation is written out of this poem. Or, to put it more accurately, the poem (also) resists such a coincidence. If I have properly analysed Shakespeare's intention, if I have accurately interpreted the text as including the intention at once to communicate effectively and to resist communicating effectively, then he will have failed in his intention, or at least in part of it, in his intention to resist effective communication. If my reading is right it is wrong, in other words, but this can only mean that communication has failed, which means, in another, poetic sense, succeeded.

In his edition of the sonnets, Colin Burrow allows himself a certain levity in wittily understating that the sonnets are 'not easy poems'. But if they 'thwart readers' desires to know', he goes on, they 'do so artfully and with a systematic elusiveness'.[33] While we might agree that the poems thwart readers' desires to know, we might at the same time question the terms of this thwarting, the implied exclusiveness of its artfulness and systematization. What Burrow's formulation fails to allow for is a Keatsian sense that Shakespeare's sonnets are 'full of fine things said unintentionally', or a Laplanchean sense that the one who sends a message is other to himself and 'does not entirely know what he is saying',[34] or a Derridean sense that we might take an interest in a text just in so far as we are right to believe that 'somewhere' the author doesn't know what he is saying. This is not of course to argue simply for the rejection of authorial intention in acts of interpretation. My intention (I promise you) is rather to suggest that the very project that Hirsch is involved in, the ascription of 'meaning' to a poem, itself begs the question of authorial ignorance (the idea of 'authorial ignorance' – which is Hirsch's own phrase, after all – being a 'commonplace' for Hirsch, and an assumption that will 'distort' or 'falsify' the text). There is much, too much, we don't know about Shakespeare and about his poetry. What I want to suggest, however, is that in reading Sonnet 55 we are dealing not only with our ignorance of Shakespeare's intentions but with a form of ignorance that is integral to literary speech acts themselves, to the poem as conceived in particular (but not exclusively) by Romantic and post-Romantic poets, critics and theorists. Shakespeare's sonnet is constituted in and by exemplary ignorance, ignorance that amounts to a certain unprogrammability: the poem's future of reading, the poem's future reading, is the unknown, unknowable axis of its meaning. Readers and writers are caught up – properly, productively caught up – in a dance, a play of nescience.

The other major question that a study of literary ignorance must address is the ancient question of the knowledge that literary texts allow. Venerable as it is, the question continues to be asked – as if there is something about literature (and about art more generally) that prevents us from answering the question, that stops us knowing what kinds of knowledge we get and, indeed, knowing whether we can, whether we should, know anything from a poem. In a recent account of twentieth-century approaches to the question of 'Art and Knowledge', the philosopher Berys Gaut suggests that the 'cognitivist' arguments for art as providing knowledge (or 'truth') are more compelling than the 'anti-cognitivist' arguments that it does not. According to Gaut, there are really two separate questions involved in the claim that art produces knowledge: firstly, there is the 'epistemic' question of whether art 'can give genuine knowledge'; secondly, there is the 'aesthetic' question of whether a work's 'capacity to give such knowledge is an aesthetic merit'.[35] Gaut alludes briefly to the famous tagline about beauty and truth from Keats's 'Ode on a Grecian Urn', in the course of a discussion of the idea – put forward by Peter Lamarque and Stein Haugom Olsen – that no truth claim made by a literary work is relevant to its literary value. Lamarque and Olsen's position is part of what Gaut dubs the 'institutional argument', since it relies on an assumption that, as Gaut puts it, literature is 'constituted as an institutional practice, specified by a set of conventions, and not by the intentions of individual authors', and that these conventions include the fact that, by contrast with philosophy, say, while 'there are branches of literary study devoted to the study of narrative techniques and motifs, there is none devoted to the study of the truth or falsity of the implicit claims advanced by literary works'.[36] According to Gaut, though, Lamarque and Olsen exaggerate the difference between philosophical and literary study since 'critics do debate the truth of some literary claims (for instance Keats' equation of truth with beauty), and the discussion of the truthfulness of the portrayal of certain classes of persons, including women, blacks, and the poor, is a mainstay of much contemporary criticism'.[37]

One way to engage with this discussion would be to focus on the parenthesis on Keats in Gaut's sentence, since I think it is incorrect, or since I think it represents a misrepresentation of the institutional nature and (currently) dominant practices, as I understand it, of literary studies. A brief discussion of this point might help us to come closer to what I want to argue is the intimate relationship between literature and ignorance. There is no doubt that some critics – and some philosophers – might be tempted to discuss the validity of the equation of beauty with truth. But discussing the truth value of *Keats's* equation of beauty and truth in the final lines of 'Ode on a Grecian Urn' is likely to seem – from the institutional perspective of at least twentieth- and twenty-first-century Anglo-American literary studies – to miss the point, or to be attending to far less than the full point of the lines.[38] And I say this for two reasons. In the first place, the equation of beauty with truth is not original: it is an 'equation' that Keats had made at least twice before in his letters,[39] and it is in fact almost a cliché of early nineteenth-century aesthetics.

The identification of beauty with truth was, as John Barnard comments, 'a widespread topic in the eighteenth century, and was a common Romantic concern'.[40] In as much as it is something like a cliché, I suggest, the phrase 'Beauty is truth' tells us what we already know. It is, indeed, part of the *function* of the statement that it is not new, that it is not designed in that sense to convey new information, to institute or to yield knowledge. It works precisely in relation to the already known: we already know that beauty is truth, and the force of the phrase, its 'literariness', inheres in its relation to a certain intertextuality or 'citationality' as well as to certain rhetorical effects, a certain rhetoricity. It is, indeed, with regard to this lack of originality – to the intertextuality of the phrase – that literary critics or readers of the poem tend to respond, rather than in relation to its alleged truth value. The point in this sense is not that Keats is *making* a claim but that he is *repeating* it. Unlike philosophers or theorists of aesthetics, literary critics (in as much as they are literary critics, in an institutional sense, and therefore necessarily not at the same time philosophers or aestheticians) tend not to be interested in the truth or otherwise of the statement. What they do tend to discuss – and this is my second reason for challenging Gaut's view – are a series of questions that are not primarily concerned with the truth value of the statement: what is the provenance of Keats's sources for the assertion and the nature of the assertion's intertextual resonance?; to what extent is the assertion 'ironical'?; what are the generic conditions under which the statement is made?; what kinds of formal restraints (such as rhythm, rhyme, assonance, alliteration, stanza form and so on) are at work in the line?; what is the dramatic force of the statement?; according to the textual evidence, who is saying this ('Beauty is truth, truth beauty') and to whom?; what is the impact and significance of the tropological dimensions of the assertion (of its chiastic repetition, in particular: the poem doesn't just say 'Beauty is truth' but 'Beauty is truth, Truth Beauty' – a rhetorically very different statement or series of statements)?; what are the effects of poetic 'voice', narratorial identity, and authorship in this ending?; how is it possible to conceive of the rhetorical coherence of the lines within the context of the poem as a whole? In fact, I would go so far as to say that it would seem rather strange, even professionally inept, for a critic *simply* to talk about whether or not the poem's statement that 'beauty is truth' is true (unless she was the kind of critic that was interested not so much in Keats's poem in itself but in questions of beauty and truth – of aesthetics – more generally and thus, as Gaut is, simply using the poem as an example of a poem). Such a critic would just seem to be missing the point of the poem – or missing the point that it is a poem and therefore singular and not just exemplary. And this is the point: what a poem does with knowledge is to complicate it, perplex it, frustrate it by embedding it, irreducibly and emphatically, in language, by drawing attention to its linguisticity, to its specificity or singularity as a speech act, by drawing attention to the way in which it is presented by these words in this order. When we extract the statement 'Beauty is truth' from Keats's poem, when we deal with it in isolation (or when we say that it is the 'same' as Boileau's 'Rien n'est beau que le vrai' or Shaftesbury's '*all* Beauty is TRUTH')[41] we are no longer dealing with Keats's poem (it's no more *his* statement, after all, than it is mine). We are now dealing instead with a general philosophical or aesthetic statement about a general or 'universal' truth (or alleged truth) rather than a poem. In as much as we are concerned with a poem, with Keats's poem, we cannot *just* be concerned with the validity or otherwise of the statement. This is what we mean when we talk about the singularity of a literary text, or about its exemplarity singularity.[42] That is to say that, while the poem may be said to include truth statements or epistemic assertions, these are fundamentally complicated (in ways that certain kinds of philosophers wish philosophical or analytical statements not to be, even though they always are) by language, by rhetoric. And it is to say, indeed, that to the extent that things are not complicated or perplexed by language, by linguistic context or by a particular way of saying, of talking or writing, we are not dealing with a *poem*. In the case of Keats's 'Ode on a Grecian Urn', then, what critics talk about is more typically how the statement should be read, how it should be understood – which is not exactly the question of whether it is true, but the question of how it can be seen to be coherent in the context of the poem as a whole. It is a rhetorical or linguistic concern (which is to say only that it is a 'literary' or poetic concern) rather than one that involves simply the validity or 'truth' of the statement.

One way to think about this is to think about the way in which Keats's poem mixes up the specific instance of saying something – saying that beauty is the same as truth in this particular way – with the general or (so-called) 'universal' statement itself (this is why literature may be said always in some sense to be 'performative', or from a different perspective 'exemplary'). What the philosopher wants to talk about is whether it can be said, in general, that beauty is truth. What the poet and the critic are (institutionally) interested in talking about is how such a statement can possibly work or what it can possibly be doing, what its effects might be, in this particular context, in this particular saying, this formulation. It is important, of course, that the line is engaging in one of the perennial issues in poetics and aesthetics, crucial, indeed, for our understanding (or our non-understanding) of Keats's poem, important that it is making a truth statement. That it appears to be presenting a universal truth is precisely the point of the line, and an integral part of its force in this poem. But it is only in the specific context(s) of the poem itself (which include the unlimited contexts of literary history, aesthetics, biography, early nineteenth-century social, class, gender, economic and political history, imperial conquest and the appropriation of classical antiquities) that the line can be said to work and only through the particular linguistic formulation, through these words in this order – only, that is to say, as part of this poem.[43]

Gilles Deleuze has proposed that literary language 'seems to be seized by a delirium, which forces it out of its usual furrows'.[44] I want to end this chapter with some brief comments that might help to illustrate this thought and connect it to ignorance by referring again to Keats but also to Wordsworth. Both poets present us with famously strange moments of poetic communication that also involve ignorance, not knowing. It is well known that in Book 5 of *The Prelude* Wordsworth recounts a dream told to him by his friend in which his friend meets an Arab holding a stone and a shell. The stone represents geometry or mathematics, while the shell represents poetry. The poet[45] holds the shell to his ear and hears

> ... that instant in an unknown tongue,
> Which yet I understood, articulate sounds,
> A loud prophetic blast of harmony,
> An ode in passion uttered ...[46]

The 'articulate sounds' of the ode are, impossibly, both understood and in an 'unknown tongue': the passage presents poetry as both the subject of understanding and the subject of ignorance. It is poetry because it is both.

There is no coincidence, I think, in the fact that a similar but here highly eroticized effect is encountered in Keats's 'La Belle Dame sans Merci', where the speaker declares that the gorgeous, deadly woman he encounters speaks to him in a language which is at the same time 'strange' *and* translatable:

> And sure in language strange she said –
>   'I love thee true'. (lines 27–8)

The language is strange, foreign, other, but understood. And the translation is framed by an uncertain knowing, a knowing uncertainty. 'Sure' denotes both the poet's certainty that this is what the woman said and the woman's sense of security in speaking a strange language. But at the same time the word includes the possibility of *uncertainty*, 'sure' as suggesting that the poet has doubts: *surely* she said that, *surely* I have understood . . .[47]

This is poetry, then, and reading: a certain uncertainty, the state of being 'sure', *surely*, that one reads aright this language strange, this unknown tongue, these particular words. It's an effect in effect of ignorance, of not knowing (quite) what one is reading, because of the determination of poetry by a certain nescience, because of language, the language strange that is poetry, and because of our certainty that poets are people like us, that, bewitched as they are by the strangeness of poetic language (the strangeness of language, that is to say), poets – somewhere – do not know what they are doing.

Notes

1 John Burnside, *The Asylum Dance* (London: Jonathan Cape, 2000), p. 42.
2 Ibid., pp. 43–4.
3 *The Complete Poems of Emily Dickinson* (Boston: Little, Brown, 1960), no. 258.
4 T.S. Eliot, 'Dante', in Frank Kermode, ed., *Selected Prose of T.S. Eliot* (London: Faber and Faber, 1975), p. 205.
5 Ibid., p. 206.
6 Eliot, 'The Frontiers of Criticism', in *On Poetry and Poets* (London: Faber and Faber, 1957), p. 109 (italics added).
7 Maurice Blanchot, *The Space of Literature*, trans. Ann Smock (Lincoln: University of Nebraska Press, 1982), p. 198.
8 'Selections from "Adagio"', in James Scully, ed., *Modern Poets on Modern Poetry* (London: Fontana,1966), p. 154.
9 Blanchot, *Space*, pp. 198, 192. In this sense, reading may be said to respond to what Derrida conceives of as the 'singularity' of literature: see Derek Attridge, *The Singularity of Literature* (London: Routledge, 2004), and Timothy Clark, *The Poetics of Singularity: The Counter-Culturalist Turn in Heidegger, Derrida, Blanchot and the later Gadamer* (Edinburgh: Edinburgh University Press, 2005).
10 Paul de Man, 'The Resistance to Theory', in *The Resistance to Theory* (Manchester: Manchester University Press, 1986), p. 15.
11 Ibid., p. 17.
12 Paul de Man, 'Shelley Disfigured', in *The Rhetoric of Romanticism* (New York: Columbia University Press, 1984), p. 122.

13 Paul Fry, *A Defense of Poetry: Reflections on the Occasion of Writing* (Stanford: Stanford University Press, 1995).
14 See J.M. Bernstein, *The Fate of Art: Aesthetic Alienation from Kant to Derrida and Adorno* (Cambridge: Polity, 1992), p. 4.
15 See Kai Hammermeister, *The German Aesthetic Tradition* (Cambridge: Cambridge University Press, 2002), pp. 6ff. For the idea of the distinction between knowledge as either obscure or clear, and of 'clear' knowledge as either 'confused' or 'distinct', see Gottfried Wilhelm Leibniz, 'Meditations on Knowledge, Truth, and Ideas' (1684), in *Philosophical Papers and Letters: A Selection*, trans. Leroy E. Loemker, 2nd edn (Dordrecht: D. Reidel, 1969), p. 291. Leibniz remarks that artists 'are often unable to give a reason for their judgment but tell the inquirer that the work which displeases them lacks "something, I know not what"' (ibid.). On the significance of the *je ne sais quoi* in seventeenth- and eighteenth-century aesthetics and proto-aesthetics see Jeffrey Barnouw, 'The Beginnings of "Aesthetics" and the Leibnizian Conception of Sensation', in *Eighteenth-Century Aesthetics and the Reconstruction of Art* ed., Paul Mattick, Jr, (Cambridge: Cambridge University Press, 1993), pp. 63–4. See also Richard Scholar's full-length study *The Je Ne Sais Quoi in Early Modern Europe: Encounters with a Certain Something* (Oxford: Oxford University Press, 2005).
16 Kai Hammermeister, *The German Aesthetic Tradition*, p. 23.
17 Immanuel Kant, *Critique of Judgment*, trans. Werner S. Pluhar (Indianapolis: Hackett, 1987), p. 44. This may (and perhaps should) of course be construed in terms of the *irrelevance* of ignorance (because of the irrelevance of cognition and therefore knowledge) to the discourse of aesthetics (see, for example, Predrag Cicovacki, *Anamorphosis: Kant on Knowledge and Ignorance* (Lanham: University Press of America, 1997), p. 33: aesthetics is another kind of discourse, separate from both knowledge and ignorance. But I would want to assert the discursive pertinence of not knowing to the discourse of aesthetics, to assert that Kant's conception of the aesthetic as being separate from cognition means that that discourse is bound up in the condition that we call 'ignorance', *not* knowing. The kind of aesthetic statement that Cicovacki gives as an example of the aesthetic ('This rose is beautiful') clearly differs, cognitively, from an 'epistemological' statement ('This is a rose') (p. 34). But literature presents us with other kinds of sentences, which present certain kinds of cognitive interruption. If we exchange 'This rose is beautiful' for 'My Luve's like a red, red rose', we come across a form of cognitive disturbance in the figure of the simile, in 'like': our 'ignorance' involves an uncertainty over the nature of the relationship, between, as Paul de Man would put it, grammar and rhetoric, or as others would put it, between the tenor and the vehicle of the metaphor (how is she like a rose? In what sense can she said to be 'red'? but also, more outlandishly, should we read 'read' in the first 'red', so she is like a 'read, red rose'?, and so on).

18 Ibid., pp. 174–5.
19 Cavell, *In Quest of the Ordinary: Lines of Skepticism and Romanticism* (Chicago: University of Chicago Press, 1988), p. 126; see also his comment on 'romanticism as working out a crisis of knowledge' (p. 52); and see his suggestion that 'skepticism is what romantic writers are locked in a struggle against' (*Disowning Knowledge in Six Plays of Shakespeare* (Cambridge: Cambridge University Press, 1987), p. 8).
20 See '"This Strange Institution called Literature": An Interview with Jacques Derrida', in Jacques Derrida, *Acts of Literature*, ed. Derek Attridge (London: Routledge, 1992), pp. 33–75.
21 Jacques Derrida, *Glas*, trans. John P. Leavey and Richard Rand (Lincoln: University of Nebraska Press, 1986), p. 64R.
22 E.D. Hirsch, Jr, *Validity in Interpretation* (New Haven: Yale University Press, 1967), p. 19: hereafter cited in the text.
23 Derrida, *Of Grammatology*, trans. Gayatri Chakravorty Spivak (Baltimore: The Johns Hopkins University Press, 1976), p. 158.
24 Derrida, 'The Time of a Thesis: Punctuations', in Alan Montefiore ed., *Philosophy in France Today* (Cambridge: Cambridge University Press, 1983), p. 50.
25 Derrida, *Of Grammatology*, pp. 157–8.
26 See Avital Ronell's comment that the 'failure of cognition is the province of literary language' (*Stupidity* (Urbana: University of Illinois Press, 2002), p. 6); Stathis Gourgouris's remarks on 'the way that literature thinks casts into all sorts of turbulence the status of the act of thinking, if not the actual notion of thought itself' (*Does Literature Think? Literature as Theory for an Antimythical Era* (Stanford: Stanford University Press, 2003), p. 1); and Marjorie Garber's proposal that literature can be defined as 'the discourse in which the knowledge of the discontinuity of thought is made fleetingly available' (*A Manifesto for Literary Studies* (Seattle: University of Washington Press, 2003), p. 66).
27 E.D. Hirsch, Jr, 'Transhistorical Intentions and the Persistence of Allegory', *New Literary History* 25 (1994): 552.
28 William Irwin, *Intentionalist Interpretation: A Philosophical Explanation and Defense* (Westport, Conn.: Greenwood Press, 1999), pp. 116–17.
29 Ibid., p. 117; quoting Hirsch 'Meaning and Significance Reinterpreted', *Critical Inquiry* 11 (1984): 205.
30 Colin Burrow, ed., William Shakespeare, *The Complete Sonnets and Poems* (Oxford: Oxford University Press, 2002), p. 491.
31 'One must ask how a critic expects to get an answer to the question about intention. How is he to find out what the poet tried to do? If the poet succeeded in doing it, then the poem shows itself what he was trying to do' (W.K. Wimsatt and Monroe C. Beardsley, 'The Intentional Fallacy', in W.K. Wimsatt, *The Verbal Icon: Studies in the Meaning of Poetry* (Lexington: University of Kentucky Press, 1954), p. 4).

32 Hirsch, 'Meaning and Significance', 205–6.
33 Burrow, ed., *Complete Sonnets and Poems*, p. 138.
34 John Keats, *The Letters of John Keats, 1814–1821*, ed. Hyder Edward Rollins, 2 vols (Cambridge, Mass.: Harvard University Press, 1958), 1: 188; Jean Laplanche, 'Transference: Its Provocation by the Analyst', in *Essays on Otherness* (London: Routledge, 1999), p. 229: for more on Laplanche's sense of the importance of ignorance in psychoanalysis see pp. 156–8 below.
35 Berys Gaut, 'Art and Knowledge', in Jerrold Levinson, ed., *The Oxford Handbook of Aesthetics* (Oxford: Oxford University Press, 2003), p. 449.
36 Ibid., p. 448. See Peter Lamarque and Stein Haugom Olsen, *Truth, Fiction and Literature: A Philosophical Perspective* (Oxford: Clarendon, 1994), ch. 13.
37 Gaut, 'Art and Knowledge', p. 448. Gaut does not provide evidence for the claim about literary critics' interest in truth claims about 'women, blacks and the poor' but instead refers to M.W. Rowe's 'Lamarque and Olsen on Literature and Truth', in *Philosophical Quarterly* 47 (1997): 322–41. It is in fact not clear that the *truthfulness* – rather than the ideological force or adequacy – of such portrayals is quite the point, or all of the point, of much feminist, Marxist or postcolonial criticism. On the knowledge that literature affords see also Michael Wood's subtle and elegant consideration, *Literature and the Taste of Knowledge* (Cambridge: Cambridge University Press, 2005): Wood explores what he calls 'the unsettling of direct knowledge by other knowledges [in literature]; and the return of knowledge after its suspension' (p. 7). For a bracing – and to my mind largely persuasive – account of the reason for rejecting the view that literature produces or offers knowledge see Jerome Stolnitz, 'On the Cognitive Triviality of Art' (1992), reprinted in Eileen John and Dominic McIver Lopes, eds, *Philosophy of Literature: Contemporary and Classic Readings, An Anthology* (Oxford: Blackwell, 2004), pp. 317–23. Alarm over such arguments (and over the resistance of literary scholars to the methodologies of the sciences and the social sciences, their resistance to empirical verification and to any contribution to such knowledge) has recently been expressed by, among others, Paisley Livingston, *Literary Knowledge: Hermeneutic Inquiry and the Philosophy of Science* (Ithaca: Cornell University Press, 1988); John Guillory, 'The Sokal Affair and the History of Criticism', *Critical Inquiry* 28: 2 (2002): 470–508; and Peter Swirski, *Of Literary Knowledge: Explorations in Narrative Thought Experiments, Evolution, and Game Theory* (London: Routledge, 2007).
38 Rowe states that 'a great deal' of the discussion of the lines 'centres on whether the lines are true' ('Lamarque and Olsen': 326) but gives only one somewhat tendentious example. The point is – my position is – that, even if you refute the proposition that 'Beauty is truth', that refutation does not invalidate the poem as a poem in the way that such a refutation would invalidate an argument in (say) aesthetic theory.
39 See Keats, *Letters*, 1: 184, 192.

40 John Barnard, ed., *John Keats: The Complete Poems*, 3rd edn (London: Penguin, 2003), p. 676.
41 Barnard cites both phrases as possible sources for the phrase (ibid.).
42 See Attridge, *The Singularity of Literature* and Clark, *The Poetics of Singularity*; and see Catherine Belsey's remark that knowledge 'deals in universals' and 'negates' particularity (*Culture and the Real: Theorizing Cultural Criticism* (London: Routledge, 2005), p. 27).
43 The point about the 'exemplarity' of the literary text is one that I discuss briefly in *The Author* (London : Routledge, 2005), pp. 123–7, particularly in relation to 'Ode on a Grecian Urn'. For more on this poem see pp. 90–1, below.
44 Gilles Deleuze, 'Literature and Life', *Critical Inquiry* 23 (1997): 229.
45 In 1850, the subject of the dream, the dreamer, is explicitly figured as the poet himself.
46 William Wordsworth, *The Prelude, 1799, 1805, 1850*, ed. Jonathan Wordsworth, M.H. Abrams and Stephen Gill (New York: Norton, 1979), p. 156: Book 5 (1805), lines 94–7.
47 See my *Keats, Narrative and Audience: The Posthumous Life of Writing* (Cambridge: Cambridge University Press, 1994), pp. 114–15.

3

To see as poets do: Romanticism, the sublime and poetic ignorance

The quintessential text for a certain conception of Romanticism, and for the Romantic sublime in particular, is Wordsworth's apostrophe to the Imagination in Book 6 of *The Prelude*. The declaration of ignorance, of bafflement or cognitive loss, follows on from and is indeed produced in response to the so-called 'Simplon Pass' episode in which Wordsworth records a moment of geographical bafflement, a moment at which the poet comes to the uncanny realization that he has already passed the crossing-point that he is, however, still seeking. As is typical in a certain configuration of the sublime that inhabits Wordsworth's poetry, the poet moves from a sense of loss, of being lost, to a sense that he is in a different sense (still) lost; it moves from loss to loss. But what is particularly striking about this famous passage is the way that it conflates being lost in a geographical sense with being lost in a spiritual or intellectual or indeed metaphysical sense; and the way that it conflates the moment of the experience of physical loss with the loss that is constituted by writing itself:

> Imagination! – lifting up itself
> Before the eye and progress of my song
> Like an unfathered vapour, here that power,
> In all the might of its endowments, came
> Athwart me. I was lost as in a cloud,
> Halted without a struggle to break through,
> And now, recovering, to my soul I say
> 'I recognise thy glory'. In such strength
> Of usurpation, in such visitings
> Of awful promise, when the light of sense
> Goes out in flashes that have shewn to us
> The invisible world, doth greatness make abode,
> There harbours whether we be young or old.[1]

What we encounter here may be taken to be paradigmatic not only for the Wordsworthian sublime but for the Romantic sublime more generally; and not only for the sublime, indeed, but for the whole project or discourse of Romanticism and, in a certain sense, therefore, for our own, our 'modern' conception of poetry itself. What characterizes Romanticism – and therefore what characterizes a certain tradition of poetry or literature and certain traditions of thinking about, conceptualizing, poetry or literature – is the moment of bafflement or obscurity, the 'rift', as Maureen McLane puts it, between poetry and knowledge, this 'particularly volatile cultural faultline'.[2] This moment in *The Prelude*, then, marks the sublime moment of canonical Romanticism, the 'apotheosis', as Samuel Monk has it, of the eighteenth-century sublime, the 'very type', for Thomas Weiskel, of 'Romantic transcendence'.[3] The sublime, in other words, is fundamentally a discourse of ignorance. Edmund Burke is unequivocal on this point: 'It is our ignorance of things that causes all our admiration, and chiefly excites our passions', he claims as he attempts to define the sublime at the beginning of Part 2 of his *Philosophical Enquiry*.[4] As Weiskel comments, within the Simplon Pass episode there 'lurks perplexity which seems to resist the light of interpretation'.[5] This is part of a larger project, which Tim Milnes has described as the Romantic attempt to 'refashion the poetic as a supracognitive sphere',[6] the problem with knowledge being, as Gerald Bruns puts it, that it is a 'condition of separation': in knowing the world we are somehow disengaged, as knowing subject, from the world.[7]

Wordsworth's apostrophe to the Imagination has two notable characteristics. In the first place, as critics have pointed out, at this moment it is impossible to tell whether the poet is speaking of the original experience itself or of the repetition or recreation of that experience in poetry. The grammar, indeed, is ambiguous: the participle 'lifting' in the first line could refer to the past of experience or the present of writing; 'here' seems to denote the place of writing, but can also refer to the Simplon Pass; 'came' seems to refer back in time to the poet's experience in the Simplon Pass, but could also refer to the moment, just now, when the memory came back to him and stopped him in his compositional tracks; 'I was lost' and 'Halted' again seem to refer back to the experience on the mountain, although since he is '*as* in a cloud' rather than 'in a cloud' it could also be a reference to writing; 'And now' and 'I say' seem explicitly to refer to the 'now' of writing but could involve the narrative present of a 'now' that is 'then'. In other words, as well as recording a certain experience of the natural sublime, this moment of bafflement is itself the moment at which that experience is remembered or recalled or written. The second, related point that I want to make is that this is a moment of loss – a moment in which poetry, poetic composition, is constituted *as* cognitive loss: the subject is lost, halted; he is 'visited' by 'strength of usurpation', and 'visited' therefore in this moment of loss by sublime poetry.

In this context, it is significant that the passage also contains its own interpretative moment of nescience, readerly nescience, generated by a certain visual occlusion. In an equivocation or 'trick' of language that William Empson remarked on half a century ago in *The Structure of Complex Words*, Wordsworth suggests both that the 'light of sense' 'Goes out' and that it 'Goes out in flashes that have shewn to us/The invisible world'.[8] The 'light of sense' both illuminates and is obliterated; it illuminates *as* it is obliterated. The equivocation between light going out, being extinguished, and going out in flashes to illuminate (going outwards, in other words) is clarified, in fact, in the 1850 text, which presents more clearly the paradox involved: 'when the light of sense/Goes out, but with a flash that has revealed/The invisible world' (*The Prelude* (1850) 5: 600–2). Here, the light is explicitly figured as being extinguished in a singular, non-repeatable act. The 1850 text, in other words, unambiguously aligns the sublime moment with – after a flash of cognition or apprehension – darkness and ignorance, with the sense that it is finally the absence of sense, of knowledge and of visual perception that constitutes the sublime and revelation. In the 1805 text, by contrast, there is a momentary hesitation – a flash of sense – as we read from 'Goes out' to 'in flashes that have shewn to us'. But, as Empson remarks, the 'verbal ambiguity in the first version only drives home the paradox which [Wordsworth] retained in the later one' (p. 295), since even here, in 1805, the flash of recognition or revelation is enough to suggest the possibility of darkness and nescience. There is a sense, indeed, in which the 1805 equivocation itself *performs* something like a flash of recognition, a hermeneutic or readerly flickering between revelation and obscurity. This equivocation is emphasized by the image itself, by 'flashes' – by the fact that, although the light of sense illuminates, it does so only sporadically or momentarily. Enlightenment, light as knowledge, in other words, is sporadic or momentary, figured as both light and darkness, as both knowledge *and* ignorance.

In an influential essay originally published in 1962, 'Romanticism and Anti-Self-Consciousness', Geoffrey Hartman confronts head-on the question of Romantic ignorance by engaging with the question of consciousness and self-consciousness.[9] Elaborating a conception of Romanticism that will later, rather differently, be explored by M.H. Abrams in terms of a secularized version of the Biblical Fall, Hartman argues that the Romantics typically explore the 'dangerous passageways of maturation' in which the subject comes into the state of self-consciousness and begins to suffer from the '"strong disease" of self-analysis'.[10] Hartman suggests that one remedy for the 'disease' of self-consciousness is 'almost coterminous with art itself in the Romantic period': the 'remedy' seeks to 'draw the antidote to self-consciousness from consciousness itself'. What the Romantics seek is not to 'escape from or limit knowledge', he suggests, but rather a way to 'convert it into an energy finer than intellectual'. In other words, the cure to self-consciousness involves the idea of 'a return, via knowledge, to naïveté – to a second naïveté',[11] a return, in a specific sense, to ignorance (ignorance as innocence, as lack of judgement or experience or wisdom). For Hartman, indeed, it is with the Romantics that poetry 'begins to be valued in contra-distinction to directly analytic or purely conceptual modes of thought': for the Romantics, the intelligence is conceived as a 'perverse though necessary specialization of the whole soul of man', and art is seen as a 'means to resist the intelligence intelligently'.[12] Self-consciousness – which in the end can just mean knowledge, a certain way of knowing, of knowing the self – is, as Wordsworth recognizes (according to Hartman), 'at once necessary and opposed to poetry'.[13] And it is not only, of course, in poems like *The Prelude* or in sections of *The Prelude* like the Simplon Pass episode that this poetic logic, this literary agnoiology or anepistemology, is played out. As I have argued elsewhere, the attractions of childhood in, say, 'We Are Seven' or 'Anecdote for Fathers' (and the attractions of such ignorant narrators as those in 'The Thorn' or 'The Idiot Boy', neither of whom can 'tell', in both senses) have to do with the possibility of certain kinds of ignorance or naivete, certain forms of nescience indeed that cannot, however, be reduced simply to not knowing.[14]

As Wordsworth's apostrophe to the Imagination suggests, the sublime itself is bound up in unknowing. Edmund Burke is very clear about this, about 'our ignorance of things' and about the relationship between such ignorance and the experience of the sublime. As I have indicated, Burke broaches the topic at the beginning of Part 2 of his *Philosophical Enquiry*, just as he is finally getting round to coming up with something like a definition of the sublime, and as he considers astonishment as one of the effects or qualities of sublime experience: 'The passion caused by the great and sublime in *nature*, when those causes operate most powerfully', he declares, is 'Astonishment'. Astonishment, he goes on, is 'that state of the soul, in which all its motions are suspended, with some degree of horror'. 'No passion so effectually robs the mind of all its powers of acting and reasoning', he asserts, 'as fear' (p. 53). This is what Andrew Ashfield and Peter de Bolla refer to variously as a 'blinking' or 'pulsation' or 'suspension' of consciousness:[15] the moment of the sublime as the moment of cognitive distension, dysfunction, distress, dissolution.

When Wordsworth develops Burke's conception of the sublime in 'Lines Written a few Miles Above Tintern Abbey', he all but excises terror, which is associated instead, as it regularly is in *The Prelude*, with the younger man, with the poet as a young man or boy, who is then figured as 'like a man/Flying from something that he dreads', and who is said to have experienced 'aching joys' and 'dizzy raptures'.[16] Nevertheless, Wordsworth does retain Burke's sense of cognitive suspension. In something like a direct allusion to Burke's discussion of the sublime, Wordsworth tries to define the 'gift' that he 'owes' (l. 37) to the 'forms of beauty' of nature in the Wye Valley, and attempts to explain the 'aspect more sublime' (l. 38), as he puts it, to which he responds on his return to that place. The poem may be read as, amongst other things, a meditation on the nature of sublime experience, as an attempt, after Burke, just to define the sublime. The gift that the poet declares he 'owes' to nature, that 'aspect more sublime', involves

> that blessed mood,
> In which the burden of the mystery,
> In which the heavy and the weary weight
> Of all this unintelligible world,
> Is lighten'd ... (ll. 38–42)

It is a mood in which the 'motion of our human blood' is 'almost suspended', Wordsworth says, and in which 'we are laid asleep' (ll. 45–6). For both Burke and Wordsworth, then, at least part of what goes to make up the sublime, to produce the apprehension or experience of the sublime, involves a 'suspension' of certain 'motions', both intellectual and physical. For Wordsworth this 'blessed mood' that is 'of aspect more sublime' involves a 'lightening' of the 'burden of the mystery', a lightening of the 'weight' of 'all this unintelligible world'. It is important to note, I think, that the burden is lightened not because we are finally able to understand the world – it remains, after all, unintelligible – nor because we are finally able to penetrate to the centre of the mystery, to dissolve or resolve it, but precisely because we no longer need to, want to or try to. Instead, we are 'laid asleep', Wordsworth declares, and with our eye 'made quiet by the power/Of harmony' we are able to 'see', as he puts it, 'into the life of things' (ll. 46–50). But this is a seeing that would seem specifically to exclude seeing *things*, seeing things themselves, and even to exclude seeing the 'life of things', whatever that would mean (whether it would be a visual apprehension or something other). The phrase can be read in more than one way, of course, but, just as the poem as a whole famously argues for an understanding of nature that involves an appreciation of what the eye and ear 'half create,/And what perceive' (ll. 107–8), I would suggest that we might take these lines as in fact quasi-Kantian in their rejection of our knowledge of things, of the possibility of knowing things in themselves ('We have no insight whatsoever into the intrinsic nature of things', declares Kant in the *Critique of Pure Reason*).[17] It is not the 'life of things', in other words, but an ability to see *into* them, to see beyond their phenomenal surface, their appearance, their visual aspect, to see beyond them, not indeed to see them, that the sublime moment allows or produces. If the sublime allows us to 'see into the life of things', I am suggesting, it does not allow us to see things as they are, in their 'intrinsic nature'. The poet is precisely not seeing things because it's a form of seeing that goes beyond, sees through, transcends, things. This seeing is a seeing without seeing, it seems, since the eye – that pesky organ, the most 'despotic', the most 'tyrannical', of the 'outward sense[s]', as Wordsworth has it in *The Prelude* (1805; Book 11, ll. 173, 179, 187) – since the visual organ is, for once, 'made quiet'.[18] This is the condition of the poet, the condition of 'blindness to the external world', as Geoffrey Hartman has it, which is 'the tragic, pervasive, and necessary condition of the mature poet'.[19] It is an experience of seeing without sight, and by implication, I would suggest, therefore an experience of knowledge without knowingness, knowledge without our knowing.

Burke's word for such nescience at the beginning of Part 2 of his *Philosophical Enquiry* is, as I have noted, 'astonishment' – astonishment as 'the effect of the sublime in its highest degree' (p. 53), as he puts it. Astonishment, then, the state, as the *OED* has it, of insensibility, paralysis, numbness, deadness; a state in which one is said to lose one's 'presence of mind' – perhaps even to lose one's mind – a state of 'dismay, consternation, dread'; a state in which wonder is said temporarily to overpower the senses, in which one is stunned or bewildered, dismayed, mentally or intellectually 'deadened', in which one is stupefied, made stupid (to denote astonishment, 'The Romans used the verb *stupeo*', Burke remarks (p. 54)). The state of astonishment can be distinguished from its near synonym, 'surprise', in that surprise seems to denote access to a new understanding or new knowledge: we are surprised because *now* we know what *then* we didn't. But the experience of the sublime is a state in which we no longer *know*. It is a state that can be terrifying, appalling, in Burke's formulation, or one that is indeed that of terror, but one that can also, at least for Wordsworth, involve an easing of the 'burden' of consciousness. In both cases, though, astonishment, the experience of the sublime, is an effect of, or is itself a form of ignorance, of not knowing. As James Usher has it in *Clio; or a Discourse on Taste* (1769), the object that the 'mind labours with' in its apprehension of the sublime is 'different from any thing we know'.[20] Astonishment – the experience of the sublime – is an ignorance effect, is bound up in nescience, in agnoiology, in our ignorance of things; the sublime is, philosophically speaking, anepistemological.

Here, then, is how Burke presents the idea of sublime ignorance, or of certain forms of ignorance as themselves sublime: 'poetry with all its obscurity', he says,

> has a more general as well as a more powerful dominion over the passions than the other art [painting]. And I think there are reasons in nature why the obscure idea, when properly conveyed, should be more affecting than the clear. It is our ignorance of things that causes all our admiration, and chiefly excites our passions. Knowledge and acquaintance make the most striking causes affect but little ... The ideas of eternity, and infinity, are among the most affecting we have, and yet perhaps there is nothing of which we really understand so little, as of infinity and eternity (p. 57)

'A clear idea', he famously declares in the next paragraph, is 'another name for a little idea' (p. 58). Obscurity, then, both cognitive and visual, is what defines the sublime for Burke, which is to say that visual occlusion and cognitive nescience, our ignorance of things, is what the sublime produces and is that through which the sublime is generated: ignorance is constitutive of the sublime, how it is experienced.

Despite the differences between the Burkean and the Kantian sublime and between the English and German traditions, it is possible to see that for Kant the sublime also partakes of an aspect of Burke's 'ignorance of things'. This is clearest, I think, in relation to his account of the mathematical sublime. For Kant, the sublime involves a 'feeling of displeasure' which 'arises from the imagination's inadequacy' as one apprehends the absolute enormity or magnitude of the object, along with a simultaneous pleasure that is said paradoxically to 'arise' from the realisation that 'this very judgment' of the 'inadequacy' of one's 'sensibility' in this situation is a function of one's reasoning.[21] Or to put it more simply, Kant argues that the sublime is produced through a simultaneous 'ignorance' of or inability to 'understand' the object, and an acknowledgement that this apprehension of ignorance is produced precisely through our reason: we *know* that we are ignorant, unable to 'understand' or indeed to 'imagine' the infinite size of the universe, for example, and this knowledge, since it includes a reasoned apprehension of the infinite, is itself sublime. The 'subject's own inability uncovers in him the consciousness of an unlimited ability which is also his', as Kant puts it. The mind 'can judge this ability aesthetically only by that inability' (p. 116). As Paul Hamilton comments, the Romantic sublime 'recasts failures of understanding as the successful symbolic expression of something greater than understanding'.[22] Kant expresses the point most succinctly if most paradoxically when he comments in the 'Analytic of the Sublime' that the sublime is 'an object (of nature) *the presentation of which determines the mind to think of nature's inability to attain to an exhibition of ideas*' (p. 127). It is, in other words, an 'exhibition' of ideas – a form of knowing – that does not, in fact, involve the apprehension of ideas, that is not a form of knowing. More generally, art, for Kant, is to be distinguished from the knowledge, the knowableness, the knowingness, of science: 'Art in general', he declares, should be 'distinguished from *science* ([i.e., we distinguish] *can* from *know*)', and for that reason we 'refrain from calling anything art that we *can* do the moment we *know* what is to be done' (p. 170): only if 'even the most thorough acquaintance' with something doesn't allow us to create it 'then to that extent it belongs to art' (p. 171).[23] Indeed, for Kant, aesthetic judgement in general is not cognitive: as Kai Hamermeister puts it, for Kant 'matters of art and matters of knowledge must not be confused'.[24]

For Kant the experience of the sublime in particular is directly linked to the kind of apprehension of an object that is associated with 'poetic' apprehension, which in turn is specifically conceived in opposition to knowledge. In a passage that Paul de Man worries at in at least two essays from the early 1980s,[25] Kant declares that the apprehension of the sublime is possible only if we see the ocean, for example, 'as poets do': we should not 'judge the sight of the ocean ... on the basis of how we *think* it, enriched with all sorts of knowledge which we possess, ... e.g., as a vast realm of aquatic creatures, or as the great reservoir supplying the water for the vapors that impregnate the air with clouds for the benefit of the land', and so on, since such knowing apprehension leads only to teleological rather than aesthetic judgement (p. 130). Instead, Kant says, 'we must be able to view the ocean as poets do, merely in terms of what manifests itself to the eye' (ibid.). But to see as the poets do, to see only according to 'what manifests itself to the eye', as we know from the *Critique of Pure Reason*, would therefore be to not know, since, as he comments there, 'we have no insight whatsoever into the intrinsic nature of things': we are ignorant, in other words, of 'things as they are'.[26] This is what de Man terms Kant's 'material' vision, a vision that is 'emphatically not tropological'.[27] The eye, including especially the poet's eye, when 'left to itself', as de Man puts it, 'entirely ignores understanding'.[28]

The Romantic conception of the sublime, then, in both poetry and philosophy, in both the English and the German traditions, is concerned with cognitive dysfunction and with the oxymoron of anepistemological apprehension. Ignorance, in other words, is central to the Romantic conception of the sublime. And in this sense, ignorance is also central, more generally, to Romantic poetry and poetics. A striking and strikingly common pattern in canonical Romantic narrative illustrates this point. The subject or protagonist of the poem – often the poet or poet-manqué – comes upon or is guided towards a site of knowing, of knowledge. But the knowledge that the poet-figure seeks or desires is resisted, refused or denied; or it is encountered as in some way troubling, even as terrifying or traumatic. At this point, the poet-figure either retreats or the poem just ends or is abandoned without knowledge being achieved or allowed; or the results of knowing are shown to be in some way catastrophic, or deadly. Notable examples of catastrophic encounters with sites of knowledge occur in various religious traditions, featuring specifically in the Biblical account of the 'Fall of man' as well as in literary texts at least as far back as Sophocles' *Oedipus Rex*. While seriously doubting, doubting himself, his own sense and his own senses, Shakespeare's Hamlet may be said to suffer from knowing or thinking that he knows. And the dangers of excessive knowing are fundamental to the Faust narrative, as articulated in Marlowe's seventeenth-century drama or in Goethe's early nineteenth-century reworking of the story – as they are in the tradition of the Prometheus myth, which culminates in a novel about the seductions and dangers of hubristic scientific discovery in Mary Shelley's *Frankenstein*. And such an anxiety of knowing is central to the larger gothic tradition that is exemplified, for example, in the epistemophobic orientalism of William Beckford's *Vathek* (1780), or, rather differently, in the structurally perverse anti-sublime empiricism of Ann Radcliffe's rationalized or explained supernatural. But the narrative of epistemological recoil that I am referring to is particularly notable in canonical poems of the Romantic period – appearing as it does in Byron's *Manfred* and in his *Cain*, for example, in Keats's 'Hyperion' poems, and in Shelley's *The Triumph of Life*. Indeed, in the Romantic period the recurrence of this figure – the figure of the fateful and fated seeker after knowledge, the figure through which knowledge is finally resisted – may be seen as part of a wider problematic: in Romanticism (the literary movement that Stanley Cavell characterizes as suffering from or as involved in a 'crisis of knowledge')[29] the idea of ignorance, of not knowing, comes to be embedded, structurally embedded, in literary culture. In some ways, ignorance comes to define the new institution of literature.[30]

The problem of knowledge, of traumatizing knowledge, then, is thematized in numerous works of the period. Byron's Manfred, for example, is unequivocal about knowledge, declaring in the opening speech of the verse-drama that takes his name that 'Sorrow is knowledge': 'they who know the most', Manfred asserts, 'Must mourn the deepest o'er the fatal truth' since 'The Tree of Knowledge is not that of Life' (*Manfred* 1.1.10–12).[31] What Manfred desires above all is 'Forgetfulness' and 'Oblivion, self-oblivion' (1.1.136, 145): in particular, he yearns to forget the unnamed 'crime' that he has committed with his erotic double, Astarte. Manfred's chronic, melancholy condition is, in fact, directly related to his desire for knowledge. He has 'pass'd/The nights of years in sciences untaught' (2.2.83–4), he has made his 'eyes familiar with Eternity' (2.2.90), and with his studies his 'thirst of knowledge' has in fact, and somehow paradoxically, increased (2.2.95). Raging against his fate, therefore, he finally rejects knowledge, claiming to know that philosophy is 'of all our vanities the motliest,/The merest word that ever fool'd the ear' (3.1.10–11). When it comes to it, when he is offered it, Manfred refuses to take up the offer of godlike knowledge, resisting the Faustian temptations of gnosis: 'thou dost forgo/The gifts of our great knowledge', the Witch of the Alps declares, and instead 'shrink'st back/To recreant mortality' (2.2.125–6). Byron's melancholic, misanthropic and theologically disillusioned hero has no doubts about the futility of knowing. What Manfred must understand, the first Destiny explains, is that

>   knowledge is not happiness, and science
>   But an exchange of ignorance for that
>   Which is another kind of ignorance. (2.4.61–3)

This position, which Manfred does not deny, seems to insist that knowledge itself is ignorance.[32] And the point is not *simply* paradoxical: there is an impeccable logic in claiming that knowledge or 'science' involves the exchange of one form of ignorance for another. The more you know, the more you do not know, the cliché goes – or at least the more you know you do not know, since in knowing more you understand more about the limits of your knowledge.

Manfred is described as having a 'brotherhood' with the hero of Byron's later verse-drama, Cain (*Manfred* 1.1.249), and *Cain* is, if anything, even more forthright in its exploration of the vanity of human knowing. *Cain* may be read as a minimally displaced critique of the Biblical creation narrative, of the myth of humankind's accession to knowledge and subsequent fall. While the verse-drama is unmistakably 'blasphemous' (despite Byron's protestations against such a reading), at the same time it reinforces the Biblical ideology of knowledge suggested by the story of the tree of knowledge in as much as it suggests that knowing is unendurable, fatal – in Cain's case fatal but necessary. The play's ambivalence with regard to knowledge – its bitter epistemological irony – is most clearly expressed by Lucifer's description of the prelapsarian condition as 'A Paradise of Ignorance' from which 'Knowledge was barr'd as poison' (*Cain* 2.2.101–2).[33]

The central action of the play is not so much Cain's murder of Abel, indeed, as his journey with Lucifer, the enlightenment man, the enlightener, light-bearer, to the underworld, where, in a final, climactic speech, Lucifer explains that the 'fatal apple' has at least given Cain – and humankind more generally – 'one good gift', that of 'reason': 'let it not be over-sway'd / By tyrannous threats to force you into faith', he urges, ''Gainst all external sense and inward feeling' (2.2.459–62). What drives Cain, from the start of the drama in fact, is his sense of the paradox, the theological dilemma, that 'knowledge is good' but designated by God as 'evil' (1.1.36–7). As if to confirm *God's* view, however, the knowledge that Cain gains is just that of the nothingness of human life. '[T]o what end have I beheld these things?', he asks Lucifer at the end of his sojourn in the underworld (2.2.417), to which Lucifer explains in true Socratic fashion that Cain has learnt to 'know thyself' (2.2.420). 'Alas! I seem / Nothing', replies Cain, to which Lucifer answers like some latter-day French existentialist:

> And this should be the human sum
> Of knowledge, to know mortal nature's nothingness;
> Bequeath that science to thy children, and
> 'Twill spare them many tortures (2.2.421–4)

Lucifer's demand, therefore, is that Cain should know nothingness, know, really know, nothing, know what nothing is and know 'mortal nature's nothingness'. If, as was commonly assumed in Byron's day, the verse-drama involves a blasphemous attack on institutional Christianity, that attack is severely vexed, ambivalent, torn. For the choice with which Cain seems to be presented is that between the ignorance demanded by God and the knowledge of nothing, of nothingness, nature's nothingness, demanded by Lucifer.

Keats's 'Hyperion' poems and Shelley's *The Triumph of Life* repeat, in some ways, the Dantesque model of traumatic or interrupted knowing presented in Byron's *Cain*. All three poems share an engagement with knowledge, in particular the knowledge that a poet needs, that is articulated most succinctly in their abruptly interrupted endings. Put very simply, like *Cain*, all three poems present narratives in which the poet-figure meets a superhuman being who offers to allow him access to a certain ultimate and indeed non-human knowledge. In each case, the poet-figure within the poem fails, finally, to gain that knowledge because the poet without fails to complete the poem. In other words, each poem stages the struggle of poetic nescience, the conflicted and contested presentation of the poet as epistemologically searching but finally, necessarily and constitutively, ignorant. And it is the latter point – that the poet is *constitutively* rather than occasionally or contingently ignorant – that, I suggest, marks out or characterizes the figure of the Romantic poet as it is presented in such works. The poet in each case comes up against the limits of human knowing, is constituted as a poet by his engagement with or apprehension of his own ignorance.[34]

Shelley's *The Triumph of Life* involves what Paul de Man calls a 'trajectory from erased self-knowledge to disfiguration'.[35] The poem ends, is interrupted (on account of Shelley's death), by the Poet's ultimate question: 'Then, what is Life?'[36] There is no answer to the question, and not, we might surmise, just because of Shelley's untimely death. The poem, more generally, is *about* there being no answer to the question. When the poet asks about the significance of the 'Triumph', the *Trionfo* or pageant (but also, and here in bitter irony, the victory or conquest of Life over, precisely, life or the living), he is answered by the figure of Rousseau (a figure that, in a perhaps distorted echo of the Biblical Fall, he had mistaken for a tree), with one word: 'Life' (l. 180). Rousseau then presents a 350-line monologue aimed at 'abating' the poet's 'thirst of knowledge' (l. 194), before the poet, unabated, asks his crucial and unanswerable question, 'What is life?' De Man alerts us to the central rhetorical and narrative question in this poem when he argues that 'the structure of the text is not one of question and answer, but of a question whose meaning, as question, is effaced from the moment it is asked'. The answer to the question of what the Triumph signifies is another question, which asks why the question has been asked, 'thus receding ever further from the original query'.[37] And the series of questions is governed by forgetting. 'Each of the episodes', de Man asserts, 'forgets the knowledge achieved by the forgetting that precedes it'.[38] For de Man, this condition of forgetting is transferred to the interpretation of the poem, a poem in which 'knowledge, oblivion, and desire hang suspended' in a sequence that 'demands' – but resists – interpretation.[39]

While these large Dantesque epics of traumatic knowledge play out most clearly Romanticism's aversion to knowing, shorter canonical lyric or ballad-like poems of the period can also be read in terms of such a concern. Coleridge's poetry evinces this most clearly, perhaps. 'Kubla Khan', for example, is based around the poet's ignorance of his own poem, the nescience that constitutes it, the poem that he says he could have but cannot now write.[40] The Preface to the poem explains that the 'fragment' that remains is a testament to a forgotten 'vision in a dream', one that witnesses, before all else, what the poet and reader cannot know. Rather differently, Coleridge's conversation poems are structured around constitutionally ignorant – because sleeping, absent, silent, young or female – interlocutors. The fantasy of communication – of 'conversation' – around which the poems are structured, is compromised by the fact that the addressee in each case does not know what the speaker is saying: in effect, this interlocutorial ignorance is what generates the emotional power of the poems, their sense of loss of and longing for community. In 'Christabel', more dramatically, it is our, and, more permanently, more completely, Christabel's ignorance – and her naive insouciance – concerning Geraldine's reality that drives the narrative forward: the poem is in fact structured around the discrepancy between the knowledge of Roland de Vaux and the ignorance of his daughter as to the lamia-like nature of their guest.

Most notable in this context, though, is 'The Rime of the Ancient Mariner', which engages directly with the question of the relationship between ignorance and the experience of the sublime. The poem, indeed, can be read as being constituted by the discourse of ignorance, structured by it – by the ignorance of its characters, by that of its narrator, by that of its interlocutor, by that of its reader. In the 1817 version of the poem Coleridge makes it clear that ignorance is a central theme of the poem by including a Latin epigraph from Thomas Burnet's 1692 *Archaeologiae Philosophicae*, in which Burnet declares that 'there are more invisible than visible Natures in the universe' and that the 'human mind has always sought the knowledge of these things, but never attained it'.[41] Nescience, sublime ignorance, is evoked most clearly on the level of the frame-narrative to Coleridge's poem, in which, after hearing the Mariner's tale, the Wedding Guest experiences something of the cognitive, if not bodily, disintegration that the Mariner himself has recorded a few stanzas earlier. On its approach to land, the Mariner's ship sinks with, or because of, the sound that 'smites' both 'sky and ocean', and he loses consciousness: he is 'Stunned by that loud and dreadful sound' (l. 550). If the Mariner is 'stunned' by an unearthly, sublime sound,[42] the Wedding Guest is in turn stunned by the unearthly, sublime sound of the Mariner's narrative, by, in effect, the Mariner's 'strange power of speech' (l. 587), by the sound of the narrative that Coleridge has written and made the Mariner speak. At the end of the Mariner's tale, the Wedding Guest is reported to leave 'like one that hath been stunned' (l. 622). Although he is allegedly a 'wiser man', he is nevertheless 'of sense forlorn' – wiser perhaps just *because* he has lost his sense, in the Socratic sense that the wiser the man the more he *knows* that he doesn't know. The effect of poetry, of narrative, the effect indeed of the sublime (a phenomenon with which Coleridge's poem is everywhere engaged) is to stun – to deprive one of consciousness, as the *OED* puts it, to make one lose one's sense, to make one amazed or astounded or astonished, to daze or bewilder (for example with noise), to put one, in short, in a state of cognitive stupor, of nescience. And the conclusion that the Wedding Guest leaves sadder if wiser cannot disguise the fact that we, readers, are left epistemologically bereft with regard to various questions – questions of ethics, emplotment, causality – by the ending of the poem: why does the Mariner kill the albatross? why is he later redeemed? what does the poem mean or foretell? What are we to make of it? How should we read it?

If ignorance is the burden of much canonical Romantic poetry, it is also an important aspect of Romantic poetics, as is evinced in particular by two of the most influential statements of poetic theory of the period, Wordsworth's 1800/1802 Preface to the *Lyrical Ballads* and Shelley's 1821

'Defence of Poetry'.[43] But it is also famously encapsulated in Thomas De Quincey's influential distinction between the literature of 'power' and the literature of 'knowledge'. De Quincey first broaches the topic in five articles published in 1823 in the *London Magazine* entitled 'Letters to a Young Man Whose Education has been Neglected'. It is in the third letter that the distinction is fully explained. The 'philosophical' use of the word 'literature', De Quincey argues, signifies 'the direct and adequate antithesis of books of knowledge'. Excluded, therefore, from 'literature' are factual books such as dictionaries, grammar books, almanacs and so on. Even books of 'much higher pretensions' such as travel narratives should be excluded on the principle that they are works in which 'the matter to be communicated is paramount to the manner or form of its communication' (*Works* 3: 69–70).[44] Here is the foundation of the new institution – the strange institution – of literature, a certain relation of 'matter' to 'manner' or 'form', in which there is what Derrida will call a 'suspension' of the 'thetic relation to meaning and referent'.[45] But De Quincey goes on to locate literature in its relationship to 'power': appealing to the classical, Horatian formulation of poetry as the combination of pleasure and instruction, De Quincey attempts radically to transform this definition by suggesting that the 'antithesis' to knowledge is not pleasure but power (*Works* 3: 70). In this manoeuvre, De Quincey displaces the classical distinction *internal* to poetry, between knowledge or 'instruction' on the one hand and pleasure (translated by De Quincey as 'power') on the other, to a distinction between that which is not literature (i.e. knowledge) and that which is (i.e. pleasure/power).[46] 'All, that is literature', De Quincey famously declares, 'seeks to communicate power; all, that is not literature, to communicate knowledge'. When he says that Milton's *Paradise Lost* 'communicates power', De Quincey explains, he means to suggest that the communication of power is 'a pretension far above all communication of knowledge' (p. 71). 'Henceforth', De Quincey concludes, 'I shall use the antithesis power and knowledge as the most philosophical expression for literature (i.e. Literae Humaniores) and anti-literature (i.e. Literae didacticae – Παιδεια)' (p. 71). Literature, in other words, is not knowledge, because it is power.

The distinction is developed and refined but also qualified and compromised twenty years later in De Quincey's 1847 review of George Gilfillan's eight-volume edition of the works of Pope. In this review, rather than opposing literature, De Quincey seems to make the power/knowledge distinction internal to the category of literature itself. 'In that great social organ, which collectively we call literature', De Quincey explains, 'there may be distinguished two separate offices that may blend and often *do* so, but [are] capable severally of a severe insulation, and naturally fitted for reciprocal repulsion' (*Works* 16: 336). He then goes on to elaborate the distinction:

> There is first the literature of *knowledge*, and secondly, the literature of *power*. The function of the first is – to *teach*; the function of the second is – to *move*: the first is a rudder, the second an oar or a sail. The first speaks to the *mere* discursive understanding; the second speaks ultimately it may happen to the higher understanding or reason, but always *through* affections of pleasure and sympathy . . . What do you learn from Paradise Lost? Nothing at all. What do you learn from a cookery-book? Something new, something that you did not know before, in every paragraph. But would you therefore put the wretched cookery-book on a higher level of estimation than the divine poem? What you owe to Milton is not any knowledge, of which a million separate items are still but a million of advancing steps on the same earthly level; what you owe – is *power*, that is, exercise and expansion to your own latent capacity of sympathy with the infinite . . . (ibid., pp. 336–7)

Jonathan Bate and others have argued that in the later presentation of an opposition between a literature of power and a literature of knowledge, De Quincey may be seen to be backsliding with regard to defining knowledge as outside of, alien to, the discourse of literature.[47] But if literature is or involves knowledge or if it is a 'discourse of knowledge' – and it is a highly contested, highly dubious 'if' (what we owe to Milton, after all, is '*not* any knowledge') – then it is also clear that it involves a mediated knowledge, knowledge mediated by 'affection and pleasure and sympathy', knowledge that is in fact therefore constituted primarily in terms of its other, by 'power'.

In 'A Defence of Poetry', Shelley makes extraordinary claims for the kind of knowledge that is associated with or constituted by poetry (poetry in the 'restricted sense', as opposed to the more general discourse of lawmakers, institutors of civil society, founders of religion, painters, musicians, and so on).[48] A poem, Shelley declares, is 'the very image of life expressed in its eternal truth' (p. 485); it 'awakens and enlarges the mind itself by rendering it the receptacle of a thousand unapprehended combinations of thought' (p. 487). But as it does for De Quincey after him and for Wordsworth before him, for Shelley poetry also has an anepistemological force. In his 'Defence' Shelley responds to and half-agrees with Peacock's provocation in 'The Four Ages of Poetry' (1820) concerning modern poets' intellectual and moral degradation – their 'wallowing', as Peacock puts it, in 'ignorance'.[49] For Shelley, the possibility that poetry can function without the reader or the poet quite understanding is a central dimension of poetry. Poetry acts 'in a divine and unapprehended manner, beyond and above consciousness', Shelley declares (p. 486), and it is for this reason that neither the poet nor his contemporaries can know the value of a poem or its true effects. In 'lift[ing] the veil from the hidden beauty of the world' poetry 'makes familiar objects be as if they were not familiar' (p. 487), he continues, suggesting that part of the force of poetry is to make us ignorant of what we thought we knew. Poetry both exposes or reveals, and *resists* revelation: 'Veil after veil may be undrawn, and the inmost naked beauty of the meaning never exposed' (p. 500), Shelley explains. For Shelley, poetry is fundamentally historical in the sense that its 'meanings' are discerned only within specific historical occasions – which means, in turn, that it is a fundamentally nescient discourse:

> A great Poem is a fountain for ever overflowing with the waters of wisdom and delight; and after one person and one age has exhausted all its divine effluence which their peculiar relations enable them to share, another and yet another succeeds, and new relations are ever developed, the source of an unforeseen and an unconceived delight. (p. 500)

What is remarkable here is the insistence on the unforeseeability of poetry – which can be translated in terms of the claim that the *poet*, in fact, cannot foresee the poem or its effects, cannot know it in advance – and its resistance to being 'conceived'. But whether it is the poet or the poet's audience that lacks foresight, what is clear is that poetry is a discourse mired in nescience. While one might exhaust a poem's meanings, within the terms or the limitations of one's own historical context, Shelley seems to be saying, the poem itself remains inexhaustible.

Shelley is insistent on this point, on the point that poetry is not consciously 'foreseen' and in a sense not consciously 'seen' or fully apprehended, either by the poet or by the reader. Poetry is not, Shelley declares, 'like reasoning', not 'a power to be exerted according to the determination of the will' (p. 503). Instead, it works through inspiration, and the poet is 'unprophetic' of its approach or departure (p. 504): Milton is right to describe his 'song' as 'unpremeditated' in *Paradise Lost* (9: 24), Shelley suggests, since the 'poetic faculty' works through 'instinct and intuition' (p. 504). Poetry, he says, 'differs from logic' since it is 'not subject to the controul of the active powers of the mind': it has 'no necessary connexion with consciousness or will' (p. 506). And Shelley famously ends the 'Defence' with the resounding claim that poets are 'perhaps the most sincerely astonished' at the poems they write since the poem is not a 'manifestation' of the poet's 'spirit' but of the 'spirit of the age'. Poets are therefore

> the hierophants of an unapprehended inspiration, the mirrors of the gigantic shadows which futurity casts upon the present, the words which express what they understand not; the trumpets which sing to battle, and feel not what they inspire; the influence which is moved not, but moves. (p. 508)

Despite the slippage between poet and poem here, from the subjectivity of an author to a system of language, each metaphor triumphantly declares the absence of agency, and of thought, of consciousness, and finally of knowledge. The one thing that the poet does not, cannot do, as poet, is finally and fully to know.

In fact Shelley's sense of the relationship between poetry and knowledge amounts to what in the context of the prose writings of other Romantics Tim Milnes terms 'ambivalence', but what one might more accurately call 'aporia'. In either case, what Shelley is articulating can be understood to be largely a function of imagination. Imagination both is and is not a form of knowing, for Shelley. Or to put it the other way round, imagination both is and is not a form of ignorance. Poetry, Shelley tells us, 'enlarges the circumference of the imagination' and thus 'strengthens that faculty which is the organ of the moral nature of man' (p. 488). Moreover, for Shelley, knowledge requires imagination even as imagination – or poetry – is not, not quite knowledge. Shelley argues against the utilitarian application of knowledge, suggesting that knowledge needs to be tempered or indeed applied through imagination, through poetry:

> We have more moral, political and historical wisdom, than we know how to reduce into practise; we have more scientific and œconomical knowledge than can be accommodated to the just distribution of the produce which it multiplies. The poetry in these systems of thought, is concealed by the accumulation of facts and calculating processes. There is no want of knowledge respecting what is wisest and best in morals, government, and political œconomy, or at least, what is wiser and better than what men now practise and endure. But we . . . want the creative faculty to imagine that which we know; we want the generous impulse to act that which we imagine; we want the poetry of life: our calculations have outrun conception; we have eaten more than we can digest. The cultivation of

those sciences which have enlarged the limits of the empire of man over the external world, has, for want of the poetical faculty, proportionally circumscribed those of the internal world; and man, having enslaved the elements, remains himself a slave. (pp. 502–3)

Shelley is making several separate but interlinked points here. The primary idea is that, since we have more knowledge than we know how to use, we require imagination in order to utilize it. Secondly, though, and as a corollary to the first point, he suggests that the overabundance of knowledge itself veils or disguises or conceals the 'poetry' that lies at its heart. Thirdly, Shelley proposes that in order to fully exploit our knowledge we must 'imagine that which we know', we must gain access to and implement our knowledge through poetry. And the final point is that our obsession with the ability of science to harness the natural world has led to a neglect of the 'internal world'. The argument, or series of arguments, is not of course in any simple sense an argument for ignorance: Shelley is not suggesting that we should reject, ignore or forget what we know. But it is an argument that positions the imagination generally and poetry in particular by the side of knowledge, suggesting that poetry is, in a sense, not knowledge and even that it is the other of knowledge.[50] When in the next paragraph he goes on to declare (ambiguously) that poetry 'creates new materials of knowledge' (suggesting both that it creates new forms of knowledge and that it creates new materials from knowledge), and when in the paragraph after that he claims that poetry is 'at once the centre and circumference of knowledge', that which 'comprehends all science' and that to which 'all science must be referred' (p. 503), Shelley both affirms the centrality of knowledge to poetry and of poetry to knowledge and displaces this relation. Poetry is both the centre *and* the circumference, both at the heart and outside, demarcating the limits of knowledge. Taking 'science' in its most general, and indeed etymological sense (from the Latin *scientia*), taking it, in other words, as knowledge,[51] we can see that poetry is here being defined as not knowledge (since to say that x 'comprehends' y, and that x must be 'referred' to y, can only mean that $x \neq y$, even when y can be a subset of x). The 'creative faculty' is, then, 'the basis of all knowledge' (p. 503), but is not knowledge itself (again, to formalize the proposition: if x is the 'basis' of all y, then $x \neq y$).

This rather abstract argument is explained in more concrete terms in a telling passage on the defamiliarization of poetry, on its intrinsic articulation of the uncanny. Through poetry, Shelley suggests, we can escape that which 'binds' us to the present and to the 'accident of surrounding impressions' (p. 505). Poetry 'creates for us', he declares, 'a being within our being':

> It makes us the inhabitants of a world to which the familiar world is a chaos. It reproduces the common universe of which we are portions and percipients, and it purges from our inward sight the film of familiarity which obscures from us the wonder of our being. It compels us to feel that which we perceive, and to imagine that which we know. It creates anew the universe after it has been annihilated in our minds by the recurrence of impressions blunted by reiteration. (pp. 505–6)

If we can associate 'familiarity' with knowledge of something, Shelley would seem to be suggesting that knowing *itself* prevents (true) knowledge. Knowing something, knowing it too well, knowing it habitually, interferes with our (true) knowledge of it. But what poetry offers is not so much more knowledge or even a different kind of knowledge. Instead it offers 'chaos' or 'wonder', or it offers something (a universe) made 'anew'. If the universe is made 'anew' – and this is the point of the claim – it will be new to us, unfamiliar, *not* known. Poetry doesn't so much produce knowledge as make us aware that we don't know what we think we know, what we know or think we know only too well. And another way to talk about this is to talk about ignorance: poetry offers us ignorance of the world we (thought we) knew, so that we can know it again as if it was new to us, know it as a new, unknown, world of wonder. Poetry doesn't just begin in wonder, as Aristotelian philosophy does, but ends there, it ends up, if we are to see as poets do, in or with our ignorance of things.

Notes

1 William Wordsworth, *The Prelude, 1799, 1808, 1850*, ed. Jonathan Wordsworth, M.H. Abrams and Stephen Gill (New York: Norton, 1979), p. 216: Book 5 (1805), ll. 525–37.
2 Maureen N. McLane, *Romanticism and the Human Sciences: Poetry, Population, and the Discourse of the Species* (Cambridge: Cambridge University Press, 2000), p. 4.
3 Samuel Monk, *The Sublime: A Study of Critical Theories in Eighteenth-Century England* (1935; rpt, Ann Arbor: University of Michigan Press, 1960), p. 231; quoted in Neil Hertz, 'The Notion of Blockage in the Literature of the Sublime', in Cynthia Chase, ed., *Romanticism* (Harlow: Longman, 1993), p. 83; Thomas Weiskel, *The Romantic Sublime: Studies in the Structure and Psychology of Transcendence* (Baltimore: The John Hopkins University Press, 1976), p. 195.

4 Edmund Burke, *A Philosophical Enquiry into the Origin of our Ideas of the Sublime and Beautiful*, ed. Adam Phillips (Oxford: Oxford University Press, 1990), p. 57: further references are cited in the text. Compare Philip Shaw's comment that ignorance is a 'crucial component of the sublime' (*The Sublime* (London: Routledge, 2006), p. 51).
5 Weiskel, *The Romantic Sublime*, p. 195.
6 Tim Milnes, *Knowledge and Indifference in English Romantic Prose* (Cambridge: Cambridge University Press, 2003), p. 13.
7 Gerald L. Bruns, 'Poetic Knowledge: Geoffrey Hartman's Romantic Poetics', in Helen Regueiro Elam and Frances Ferguson, eds, *The Wordsworthian Enlightenment: Romantic Poetry and the Ecology of Reading* (Baltimore: The Johns Hopkins University Press, 2005), p. 113: Bruns is referring here to a tradition of thinking about poetry that was prominent in the mid-twentieth century (and developed by such critics as Robert Langbaum and Jacques Maritain), where poetry is 'prior to writing, the experience of things (and of others) in their proximity and singularity as if they were part of ourselves' (pp. 113–14).
8 William Empson declares his reluctance to attribute 'ambiguity' to Wordsworth, on the grounds that his style 'in general . . . does not want any concentrated piece of trickery' and that Wordsworth is 'trying to state his position, even if he fails'. But Empson nevertheless suggests that there is a 'trick' of language here, one that 'is as glorious as such a thing could be', since the poet is saying two things at once (*The Structure of Complex Words*, new edn (London: Hogarth, 1995), p. 294).
9 Cynthia Chase summarizes Geoffrey Hartman on Wordsworth's 'fundamental experience' as a 'passage from sense-experience, to an obliterating self-consciousness' or 'apocalypse' (Chase, 'Introduction', in *Romanticism*, p. 6).
10 Geoffrey H. Hartman, 'Romanticism and Anti-Self-Consciousness' (1962), reprinted in Chase, ed., *Romanticism*, pp. 45, 44; see also M.H. Abrams, *Natural Supernaturalism: Tradition and Revolution in Romantic Literature* (London: Oxford University Press, 1971).
11 Hartman, 'Romanticism and Anti-Self-Consciousness', p. 45.
12 Ibid., p. 47. See Robert Langbaum's comment on the 'specifically romantic contribution to literature' as being the ability to 'give facts from within, to derive meaning that is from the poetic material itself rather than from an external standard of judgment' and that 'sympathy or projectiveness, what the Germans call *Einfühlung*, is the specifically romantic way of knowing' – knowing, we might infer, as a kind of unknowing (*The Poetry of Experience: The Dramatic Monologue in Modern Literary Tradition* (New York: W.W. Norton, 1963), pp. 78–9).
13 Hartman, 'Romanticism and Anti-Self-Consciousness', p. 49.
14 'Wordsworth's Poetic Ignorance', in Stefan Hoesel-Uhlig and Alex Regier, eds, *Wordsworth's Theory of Poetry* (Basingstoke: Palgrave, 2009); for a

reading of Wordsworth's autobiographical poems in terms of not knowing (specifically in terms of forgetting) see my *Wordsworth Writing* (Cambridge: Cambridge University Press, 2007), ch. 8.

15 Andrew Ashfield and Peter de Bolla, eds, *The Sublime: A Reader in British Eighteenth-Century Aesthetic Theory* (Cambridge: Cambridge University Press, 1996), p. 130. As Hertz notes, the Kantian category of the 'mathematical' sublime involves or is generated through 'sheer cognitive exhaustion', the mind being 'blocked' before there is a positive 'compensatory movement' in which the mind 'exults' in 'its own rational faculties' ('The Notion of Blockage', p. 79).

16 *'Lyrical Ballads' and Other Poems, 1797–1800*, ed. James Butler and Karen Green (Ithaca: Cornell University Press, 1992): 'Tintern Abbey', ll. 71–2, 85, 86.

17 Immanuel Kant, *Critique of Pure Reason*, trans. and ed. Paul Guyer and Allen W. Wood (Cambridge: Cambridge University Press, 1998), A277/B333.

18 On the idea of the 'tyranny of the eye' in Wordsworth see William H. Galperin, *The Return of the Visible in British Romanticism* (Baltimore: The Johns Hopkins University Press, 1993), pp. 211–13.

19 Hartman, *Wordsworth's Poetry, 1787–1814* (New Haven: Yale University Press, 1964), p. 41.

20 Ashfield and de Bolla, eds, *The Sublime*, p. 151.

21 Immanuel Kant, *Critique of Judgment*, trans. Werner S. Pluhar (Indianpolis: Hackett, 1987), pp. 114–15: further references are cited in the text.

22 Paul Hamilton, *Metaromanticism: Aesthetics, Literature, Theory* (Chicago: University of Chicago Press, 2003), p. 231; see also Rudolph Makkreel, 'Imagination and Temporality in Kant's Theory of the Sublime', in *Immanuel Kant: Critical Assessments, Vol. 4, Kant's Critique of Judgement*, ed. Ruth F. Chadwick and Clive Cazeux (London: Routledge, 1992), p. 388.

23 James Creed Meredith's translation of the final point is slightly clearer: 'To art that alone belongs for which the possession of the most complete knowledge does not involve one's having then and there the skill to do it' (Immanuel Kant, *The Critique of Judgement* (Oxford: Clarendon, 1952), p. 163.

24 Kai Hammermeister, *The German Aesthetic Tradition* (Cambridge: Cambridge University Press, 2002), p. 40.

25 Paul de Man, 'Phenomenality and Materiality in Kant' and 'Kant's Materialism', both in *Aesthetic Ideology*, ed. Andrej Warminski (Minneapolis: University of Minnesota Press, 1996).

26 Kant, *Critique of Pure Reason*, A277/B333; see Rae Langton, *Kantian Humility: Our Ignorance of Things in Themselves* (Oxford: Clarendon, 1998), p. 2.

27 De Man, *Aesthetic Ideology*, p. 87; see also pp. 127–8.

28 Ibid., p. 127.

29 Stanley Cavell, *In Quest of the Ordinary: Lines of Skepticism and Romanticism* (Chicago: University of Chicago Press, 1988), p. 52.

30 In *Knowledge and Indifference in English Romantic Prose*, Tim Milnes describes this rather differently, as a sense of 'indifference' to knowledge, suggesting that 'Romantic discourse develops an alternating pattern of engagement with, and abstention from philosophical argument' (p. 3). According to Milnes, later eighteenth-century thought was 'burdened' by the sense that it may be impossible to argue against the logic of Humean scepticism but that to accept this position would be to accept that 'there can be no science nor knowledge of any kind', as Lord Monboddo puts it (quoted p. 6: the claim is from Monboddo's 1789 *Antient Metaphysics*). 'The anti-philosophical turn in English Romanticism', Milnes argues, was 'itself sustained by a deep epistemological anxiety' – the anxiety that the condition of scepticism is in fact irredeemable, irresolvable (p. 7). Only with Romanticism, Milnes claims, 'does one find the idea that aesthetic creativeness might be paradigmatic for human knowledge' in the sense that, as Richard Rorty puts it, 'truth is made rather than found' (p. 8: quoting Rorty, *Contingency, Irony, Solidarity* (Cambridge: Cambridge University Press, 1989), p. 7). According to Milnes, English Romanticism 'comes to define itself' by 'oscillation and indecision' between knowledge as discovery and truth as creative, 'prizing indifference and "negative capability" above argument to the point where the literal articulation of its ideal is itself superseded by its metaphoric presentation, its enactment in poetry' (p. 9). The present book, and the present chapter in particular, owes much to Milnes's study but differs in several key respects: Milnes's book is concerned with the specificity of a certain prose of the eighteenth-century and Romantic period, and it explicitly ignores poetry; his book is concerned with a certain 'indifference' towards knowledge and the relation of such indifference or ambivalence with regard to philosophy or knowledge, rather than with what I suggest is a more active or positive drive for or towards nescience; his book is concerned with an eighteenth- and early nineteenth-century philosophical tradition rather than with a Romantic and post-Romantic literary tradition; and his book is not concerned, as mine is (this, indeed, is its main burden), to explore the relationship between ignorance or not knowing and the literary as such.
31 Quotation from Byron's poetry are from Jerome J. McGann, ed., *Byron: The Oxford Authors* (Oxford: Oxford University Press, 1986). Compare Lucifer's comment in *Cain* that the 'eternal sorrow' that Cain and mankind gained from the tree of knowledge is *itself* 'knowledge' (1.1.354).
32 Compare Byron's brusque take on Socratic ignorance in *Don Juan*, canto 7, stanza 5: 'Socrates said, our only knowledge was / "To know that nothing could be known"'.
33 But see also Lucifer's comment that 'ignorance of evil doth not save / From evil; it must still roll on the same, / A part of things' (2.2.235–7).
34 For a further consideration of Keats's 'Hyperion' poems see Chapter 4, below.

35 Paul de Man, *The Rhetoric of Romanticism* (New York: Columbia University Press, 1984) p. 100: as de Man comments, 'Each of the episodes forgets the knowledge achieved by the forgetting that precedes it' (p. 119).
36 *Shelley's Poetry and Prose*, ed. Donald H. Reiman and Sharon B. Powers (New York: Norton, 1977), p. 470 (l. 544).
37 De Man, *The Rhetoric of Romanticism*, p. 98.
38 Ibid., p. 119.
39 Ibid., pp. 106–7.
40 The importance of ignorance for Coleridge's poetics is made clear in the first of his 1811–12 lectures on Shakespeare, where he explains the various causes of 'false criticism', the first 'Permanent' cause being 'The greater delight in being reminded of one's knowledge than of ones ignorance' – the implication being that for Coleridge, as for Maurice Blanchot, true criticism would involve an acknowledgement of one's one ignorance (R.A. Foakes, ed., *The Collected Works of Samuel Taylor Coleridge: Lectures 1809–1819 on Literature* (London: Routledge and Kegan Paul, 1987), p. 187; see also pp. 191–2 (I am indebted to Jane Wright for pointing me to this reference).
41 Samuel Taylor Coleridge, *The Complete Poems*, ed. William Keach (London: Penguin, 1997), p. 504.
42 As Burke remarks, 'Excessive loudness is sufficient to overpower the soul, to suspend its action, and to fill it with terror' (*A Philosophical Enquiry*, p. 75).
43 On Shelley's 'Defence' see below, pp. 70–4; for Wordsworth's 'Preface' see my 'Wordsworth's Poetic Ignorance'.
44 *The Works of Thomas De Quincey*, 21 vols. ed. Grevel Lindop et al. (London: Pickering and Chatto, 2000–3), 3: 69–70 (hereafter cited in the text); see also letter 1, in which De Quincey defines *Belles Lettres* as 'exclud[ing] all *science* whatsoever' (3: 43), and letter 4, where De Quincey refers to 'the proper sense of the word literature as a body of creative art' (3: 82). For a useful discussion of Hazlitt's parallel conception of the relationship between power and knowledge (or his 'ambivalence' towards knowledge) see Milnes, *Knowledge and Indifference*, ch. 3. This may in fact be a reasonably conventional distinction by this time. Richard Terry points out that half a century earlier, in William Enfield's *The Speaker* (1774), the word 'literature' is discriminated from what are classified as 'works of knowledge' (*Poetry and the Making of the English Literary Past, 1660–1781* (Oxford: Oxford University Press, 2001), pp. 18–19 (quoting Enfield's *The Speaker or Miscellaneous Pieces Selected from the Best English Writers* (1774), p. xxix).
45 Jacques Derrida, *Acts of Literature*, ed. Derek Attridge (London: Routledge, 1992), pp. 45. See Brian McGrath, 'Thomas De Quincey and the Language of Literature: Or, On the Necessity of Ignorance' (*Studies in English Literature* 47: 4 (2007): 847–62), on De Quincey's establishment of literature as the discourse of letters as opposed to knowledge and as involved in a resistance to referential language.

46 It is significant that in replacing pleasure with power De Quincey also displaces his own authority to speak of literature by referring to the authority of William Wordsworth: in a footnote, he records that he is indebted to 'many years' of conversation with Wordsworth and refers to Wordsworth's 'rhetorical' use of the word 'power' in relation to poetry in 1798 (*Works* 3: 70). In fact, Wordsworth does not use the term in the 1798 Advertisement to *Lyrical Ballads*; the term does however make a notable appearance in the 1815 'Essay, Supplementary to the Preface': a poet 'has to call forth and to communicate *power*'; 'to create taste is to call forth and bestow power, of which knowledge is the effect', he says, 'and *there* lies the true difficulty' (*Shorter Poems, 1807–1820*, ed. Carl H. Ketcham (Ithaca: Cornell University Press, 1989), p. 655).

47 See Jonathan Bate's discussion of the way that the distinction in the letters between literature as an 'aesthetic' category that involves 'power' as distinguished from other forms of discourse which involve 'knowledge' is itself complicated and compromised in the more famous distinction in the Pope review-essay between the 'literature of knowledge' and the 'literature of power' – a distinction *within* the category of literature. According to Bate, the Pope essay 'shifts the ground of the discussion of power from the affective to the ethical' ('The Literature of Power: Coleridge and De Quincey', in Tim Fulford and Morton D. Paley, eds, *Coleridge's Visionary Languages: Essays in Honour of J.B. Beer* (Cambridge: D.S. Brewer, 1993), p. 149); see also McGrath, 'Thomas De Quincey and the Language of Literature'. In fact, though, in the Pope essay, De Quincey still insists, more than once, that the 'power' of literature is affective; and it might be argued that the later distinction is a justified refinement on the original distinction, a recognition that a purified realm of literature is a fantasy, that literary ignorance is always, necessarily 'contaminated', as it were, by knowledge (see *Works* 16: 336). On De Quincey's distinction see also Frederick Berwick, *Thomas De Quincey: Knowledge and Power* (Basingstoke: Palgrave, 2005), especially ch. 1.

48 Shelley, 'Defence of Poetry', in *Shelley's Poetry and Prose*, p. 483: references to this essay are hereafter cited in the text.

49 Thomas Love Peacock, 'The Four Ages of Poetry', in David Bromwich, ed., *Romantic Critical Essays* (Cambridge: Cambridge University Press, 1987), p. 208. Peacock seems to be directly alluding to *Phaedo* 82e here (see p. 9, above).

50 William Hazlitt seems to be saying something comparable in his slightly earlier lecture, 'On Poetry in General' (1818): 'poetry is one part of the history of the human mind, though it is neither science nor philosophy ... the progress of knowledge and refinement has a tendency to circumscribe the limits of the imagination, and to clip the wings of poetry. The province of the imagination is principally visionary, the unknown and undefined: the understanding restores things to their natural boundaries, and strips them

of their fanciful pretensions ... we can only fancy what we do not know' (*The Selected Writings of William Hazlitt, Volume Two: The Round Table and Lectures on the English Poets*, ed. Duncan Wu (London: Pickering and Chatto, 1998), p. 172.

51 The date first entry in the *OED* for the most common contemporary sense of 'science' – as denoting the natural or physical sciences – is 1867; science as just knowledge, the *OED*'s 'The state or fact of knowing', and 'knowledge acquired by study' (definitions 1a and 2a), is current in the early nineteenth century.

4

The opposite of epistemology: Keatsian nescience

It feels odd, this question, the question that poems often seem to be asking – 'What is it like to be ignorant?', or 'What is not knowing like?' It feels odd because we hardly need a poem or novel to tell us what it is like, mired as we are in ignorance, stymied at every turn by things we don't know, things that we don't even know we don't know. But from a different perspective we might think it not so strange, we might think that in fact poetry is anyway everywhere concerned with such questions – questions of the ordinary, the obvious, the everyday. We might think that poetry, indeed, just is those kinds of questions. Poetry asks about the so-called 'everyday' as if it doesn't, or we don't, know what the everyday is like. What is it like to be in love or to wake in the morning?, a poem might ask. What is it like to talk, or to sleep, or to smell a flower? What is thinking like, or knowing? What happens when you read *King Lear* for a second or third or fourth time? What does a nightingale's song sound like? How does a field of stubble seem when you look at it? Poems, at least in the Romantic and post-Romantic traditions are everywhere concerned with the 'everyday', and it may even be somewhat 'everyday', something of a cliché, to say that within these traditions poems are concerned, not least, with making strange or making new those everyday experiences. Poems are concerned with asking the ordinary question, or asking questions of the ordinary. And poems are also concerned with the extraordinary, the unfamiliar, with things we don't know: they act as if such things, such unknown things, can be known. 'What is it like to fall in love with the moon or to be left forlorn on a hillside by a mysterious, spectral woman?', a different kind of poem might ask, indicating by representing such things that such things just sometimes happen. What is it like to be a god that has lost his power? What would I see if I could see inside my own head? What happens when a man secretly watches a woman undressing and then merges into what seems to be her dream?

What happens when we dream, or when we don't know whether or not we are dreaming? Or when a man falls for a snake transformed into a beautiful woman? What would an ancient Greek urn say to us if it spoke? Can the experience of reading a poem be likened to the hush of wonder at discovering a new continent?[1]

So asking what it is like to be ignorant is perhaps not so odd for a poem, or we shouldn't think it so odd, since poems often seek out the unknown in what we (think we) know so well, or they explore ways in which the miraculous, the unimaginable, the unknown, can be imagined or conceived. In both ways, contrary as they are, poems explore our ignorance: the act of 'making new', of 'defamiliarizing', whether it is achieved in terms of the familiar being made strange or the strange made familiar (a shorthand way of talking about it would be to talk about the 'uncanny'), is a way of engaging in, and engaging, our ignorance.

John Keats, from whose poems these examples come, might be thought to be exemplary of the kind of poet who is concerned in particular with asking about what ignorance feels like. 'What creates the intense pleasure of not knowing?' he asks in a marginal annotation in his copy of *Paradise Lost*. Keats thinks he knows the answer to this question: 'A sense of independence, of power, from the fancy's creating a world of its own by the sense of probabilities'.[2] The answer raises as many questions as it resolves: what is the relationship between ignorance and probability? How do we 'sense' a probability if we don't know it? How does the 'fancy' create this world? And what is the 'fancy', anyway? The comment is nevertheless a striking and compelling assertion of the power of ignorance. We may be stymied by our ignorance, 'wallowing' as we are in the 'mire of every sort of ignorance',[3] but for Keats it is knowledge itself that may be said to stymie, to limit or compromise poetry. And Keats's letters are in fact full of the appreciation and evocation of poetic ignorance, of the powers of compositional nescience – most famously perhaps in his laconic declaration that what goes into forming a 'Man of Achievement' is 'Negative Capability', a capacity for 'being in uncertainties, Mysteries, doubts, without any irritable reaching after fact & reason';[4] or in his equally famous though perhaps more oblique assertions that he is 'certain of nothing but of the holiness of the Heart's affections and the truth of Imagination', and that 'What the Imagination seizes as Beauty must be truth' ('O for a Life of Sensations rather than of Thoughts!', he declares) (*LJK* 1: 184–5). From one perspective at least, 'negative capability' can be understood as a resistance to a fixed position

– or as a sceptical position concerning the value of such fixities (except, arguably, that of its own scepticism). 'We hate poetry that has a palpable design upon us', Keats says, thinking of Wordsworth, not least (*LJK* 1: 224). And then, again with regard to Wordsworth (and his poem 'Gipsies'), Keats writes in October 1817 to Benjamin Bailey referring to a recently (re)published essay by William Hazlitt in *The Round Table* in which Hazlitt criticizes Wordsworth's lack of sympathy for the gypsies' 'indolence': 'I think he [Wordsworth] is right and yet I think Hazlitt is right and yet I think Wordsworth is rightest.' This doesn't end the matter, however: 'if Wordsworth had thought a little deeper', Keats goes on, 'he would not have written the Poem at all' – which suggests in fact that Hazlitt is 'rightest'. But then it might also be said, he says, that 'had Hazlitt thought a little deeper and been in a good temper he would never have spied an imaginary fault there' (*LJK* 1: 173–4). The mood of 'negative capability' is also associated in Keats with what he refers to, in a letter of February 1818 to J.H. Reynolds, as his own 'delicious diligent indolence': rather than reading, rather than 'hurrying about and collecting honey-bee like', Keats suggests that there is value in being 'passive and receptive'. And he includes a sonnet for Reynolds's indolent delectation ('O thou whose face hath felt the Winter's wind'), which urges, not once but twice, 'O fret not after knowledge – I have none' (ll. 9, 11). Keats says that he is 'sensible' that 'all this' – the poem and the comments in the letter – is 'a mere sophistication': 'It is no matter whether I am right or wrong', he says (*LJK* 1: 231–3). It is, indeed, a continual belief, almost a permanent position, for Keats: he has no constant opinions, no fixed beliefs. 'Now my dear fellow', he tells Benjamin Bailey in March, 'I must once for all tell you I have not one Idea of the truth of any of my speculations' (*LJK* 1: 243). 'What a happy thing it would be if we could settle our thoughts, make our minds up on any matter in five Minutes and remain content', he remarks to James Rice a few weeks later (admitting, however, the impossibility of such contentment) (*LJK* 1: 254). 'I am . . . young writing at random – straining at particles of light in the midst of a great darkness – without knowing the bearing of any one assertion of any one opinion', he writes to his brother and sister-in-law George and Georgiana Keats in the spring of 1819 (*LJK* 2: 80). And he complains to the same couple a few months later that his friend Charles Dilke 'cannot feel he has a personal identity unless he has made up his Mind about every-thing', while Keats for his own part believes, by contrast, that 'The only means of strengthening one's intellect is to make up one's mind about nothing' (*LJK* 2: 213). Most famously, of course, there is the letter on the 'camelion

Poet' from October 1818 in which Keats describes the poet as having no identity and therefore no fixed opinions – even about having no fixed opinions: 'But even now I am perhaps not speaking from myself', he ends the letter, 'but from some character in whose soul I now live' (*LJK* 1: 388).

This is not, of course, the whole story: if it had been, it would itself have been, in its fixedness and determination, paradoxical or self-contradictory – and, in the sense that I am attempting to establish in this chapter, un-Keatsian. Keats also often yearns after knowledge. In April 1818, for example, he tells John Taylor that he is hoping to travel 'over the north' during the summer but that he may be prevented by one fact: 'I know nothing', he says, 'I have read nothing and I mean to follow Solomon's directions of "get Wisdom – get understanding"'. His 'cavalier days' are gone, he tells Taylor, and he can have 'no enjoyment in the World but continual drinking of Knowledge'. He says that he has been 'hovering for some time between an exquisite sense of the luxurious and a love for Philosophy' but that as he is not 'calculated' for the former, he will 'turn all my soul to the latter' (*LJK* 1: 271). A month later, Keats is still extolling the virtues of knowledge: 'Every department of knowledge', he writes to Reynolds, 'we see excellent and calculated towards a great whole'. He is therefore thankful, he affirms, that he has not given away his medical books:[5] 'An extensive knowledge is needful to thinking people' he writes, 'it takes away the heat and fever and helps, by widening speculation, to ease the Burden of the Mystery' (*LJK* 1: 277).

Even in his celebrations of knowledge, though, ignorance has a part, an important part, to play: knowledge aids 'speculation', Keats explains to Reynolds, and it eases our sense of 'mystery'. In both cases, that which is not knowledge – speculation or mystery – remains. Keats wouldn't do without speculation, just as he wouldn't do without 'mystery' – and just as he wouldn't do without poetry. And in the end, he says, it is 'impossible to know how far knowledge will console us for the death of a friend and the ill "that flesh is heir to"' – which might mean that it will console us, but might equally mean that it won't (*LJK* 1: 278). The letter meanders from one perspective on or valuation of knowledge to another, and a page or two later things are seen from a different aspect. '[A]xioms in philosophy', says Keats, 'are not axioms until they are proved upon the pulses', which leads to the thought that 'Until we are sick, we understand not', and immediately, if inconsequentially, to some epigrammatic thoughts on knowledge and wisdom: 'in fine, as Byron says, "Knowledge is Sorrow";[6] and I go on to say that "Sorrow is Wisdom" – and further

– for aught we can know for certainty! "Wisdom is folly"' (*LJK* 2: 279).⁷ It is in this letter that Keats works up his renowned metaphor of life being like a 'Mansion of Many Apartments', a metaphor which is itself concerned with the question of knowledge and ignorance: he suggests that life begins in the 'infant or thoughtless Chamber' where we remain while we 'do not think'. The second chamber is the 'Chamber of Maiden-Thought' in which one's vision is 'sharpened' and where one sees that 'the World is full of Misery and Heartbreak, Pain, Sickness and oppression' – but where one also *doesn't* see, where one is in a state of ignorance:

> This Chamber of Maiden Thought becomes gradually darken'd and at the same time on all side of it many doors are set open – but all dark – all leading to dark passages – We see not the ballance of good and evil. We are in a Mist. *We* are now in that state – We feel the 'burden of the Mystery'. (*LJK* 1: 280–1)

Although Keats then goes on to provide an optimistic account of the general 'advance of human intellect' in a summary of the intellectual and scientific advances made by the Enlightenment in Europe, and thereby explains how or why Wordsworth is 'deeper than Milton', he gives a clear sense here that the human condition – at least the human condition in May 1818 – involves darkness, blindness, ignorance.⁸

Like its accompaniment, the mood of indolence, ignorance is associated for Keats with poetic composition. In the summer of 1820 Richard Woodhouse recorded some detailed and telling comments that Keats made on his own compositional methods, methods that clearly link inspiration with not knowing:

> He has said, that he has often not been aware of the beauty of some thought or expression until after he has composed & written it down – It has then struck him with astonishment – & seemed rather the production of another person than his own – He has wondered how he came to hit upon it . . . It seems scarcely his own; & he feels that he could never imitate it or hit upon it again: & he cannot conceive how it came to him – Such Keats said was his Sensation of astonishment & pleasure when he had produced the lines 'His white melodious &c' – It seemed to come by chance or magic – to be as it were something given to him. –⁹

As we will see, 'His white melodious throat' is from Book 3 of 'Hyperion', where Apollo, god of poetry and knowledge, is himself inspired to pronounce the name of Mnemosyne unwittingly, without knowing how, or why. Keats's comments suggest that the poem is 'other' to the author, that the poet is aware of the 'beauty of some thought or expression' only after he has written it down. The expression strikes him with 'astonishment', and as work not his own: he 'cannot conceive how he came upon it', he cannot conceive, that is to say, how he conceived it, this chance or magic of poetry, of composition that comes upon him. Poetry, poetic writing, composition, in other words, is produced in an expression of ignorance.

Perhaps we know Keats's poetry too well, or think we do, so that we can too easily forget, too easily fail to see that not knowing is one of his poetry's keenest pleasures, that ignorance is celebrated in his verse – in his sonnet 'To Homer', for example, where the poet's own 'giant ignorance' is likened to the 'triple sighted' blindness of Homer, the archetypal unseeing and therefore at least metaphorically unknowing (but therefore knowing) poet.[10] Keats's poetry often luxuriates in the indulgence of not knowing – and not caring about knowing, as in 'Sleep and Poetry': 'What is more tranquil than a musk-rose blowing', he asks, 'In a green island, far from all men's knowing?' (ll. 5–6) – which means in secret, away from other men, unknown, of course, but which might also suggest the fancy of being in a place where the poet is apart from the knowing of *all* men, from *all* knowing, including his own. In Keats's well-known odes in particular, not knowing, mistaking, misunderstanding, neglecting, disregarding, ignoring are crucial concerns. This may be conceived of as *the* major theme in the odes, indeed, connected as it is to the epistemological question of whether the subject, the knower, wakes or sleeps. 'Surely I dreamt to-day, or did I see / The wingèd Psyche with awaken'd eyes?' (ll. 5–6), the speaker in 'Ode to Psyche' asks, with a peculiar, vexing semantic uncertainty over 'sure' or 'surely', the word that should denote epistemological certainty but can also always unground it. 'I see, and sing', he says, 'by my own eyes inspired': awake or asleep it is the eyes – the eyes as well as the I and even the vocalised /ai/ within 'inspired' – that inspire, as if I and the eye and inspiration are all somehow one, and all conditioned by an uncertainty over sight, over specular knowledge.

And 'Ode to Psyche' is, of course, all about the I, about the sceptic's questions: how can I know myself? how can I know my own mind, my soul, my psyche? It gives us an answer, of sorts, one that might at least (begin to) satisfy a certain kind of (ex-)medical student, one who has had the privilege of viewing the human brain in medical illustrations and perhaps in cadavers and who has, through such sights, begun to imagine them. To know my self, my soul, my mind – to know my 'psyche' – the poem seems to assert, I can look inside my head and, through metaphors, see my working brain, my brain figured as

> some untrodden region of my mind,
> Where branchèd thoughts, new grown with pleasant pain,
>   Instead of pines shall murmur in the wind:
> Far, far around shall those dark-cluster'd trees
>   Fledge the wild-ridgèd mountains steep by steep;
> And there by zephyrs, streams, and birds, and bees,
>   The moss-lain Dryads shall be lull'd to sleep;
> And in the midst of this wide quietness
>   A rosy sanctuary will I dress
> With the wreath'd trellis of a working brain,
>   With buds, and bells, and stars without a name,
>   With all the gardener Fancy e'er could feign,
>   Who, breeding flowers, will never breed the same.
>
>   (ll. 51–63)

Looking inside my own head: in such shadowy thought I must be dreaming, dreaming a landscape of the mind, dreaming what I do not, cannot know, dreaming the very seat of knowledge and not knowing.

'Ode to a Nightingale' repeats the sceptic's question 'Do I wake or sleep?', at the end of a poem that is even more fully concerned with not knowing, with ignorance and forgetting and with the question of inspiration as *loss* of eyesight, of vision, of empirical knowledge. 'Ode to a Nightingale', indeed, is concerned with, is articulated by, a poet who wishes to disappear into a state of self-abnegation, in which, crucially, nothing is *known* because nothing is seen (sight being the epistemologist's instrument, above all others, of certainty): the speaker desires, he says, to 'Fade far away, dissolve, and quite forget' what the bird 'among the leaves has never known' (ll. 21–2), indicating that part of the attraction of the nightingale is that it does not know. Knowing is not knowing in this ornithological ode. The speaker seeks to fly 'to thee', to the bird, on the 'viewless wings of Poesy' (ll. 31, 33) – on a personified or ornithomorphic if invisible poetry, certainly, but also perhaps (owing to an inevitable ambiguity in or indeed pun on, 'viewless') on or by means of sightless, blind poetry, poetry that cannot 'see'. As well as echoing blind John Milton,[11] the line recalls Byron's *Manfred* (the poem that Keats (mis)quotes in a letter from May 1818 with respect to sorrow and knowledge), a poem itself centrally concerned with the problem of knowledge – with the fate of the subject that knows. Hearing the 'natural music of the mountain reed' (a shepherd playing on a pipe) Manfred wishes to *be* the music, just as Keats's speaker wishes to *be* the nightingale's song:

> Oh, that I were
> The viewless spirit of a lovely sound,
> A living voice, a breathing harmony,
> A bodiless enjoyment . . . (*Manfred* 1.2.48, 52–5)

The explicit verbal link with Byron's poem is, of course, the word 'viewless' – a not uncommon word in the poetry of the early nineteenth century, certainly,[12] but in the context here there is enough to alert us to the similarity of desire in the two poems. The word denotes invisibility, as I say, but it also suggests anepistemology or agnoiology in the punning sense that the subject cannot see and cannot therefore know: in this respect, for Keats and Byron music, poetry, art is desired – and the poet/tragic hero desires to *be* art – because of its epistemological weakness, its 'ignorance'. It is, after all, what the nightingale *doesn't* know – 'the weariness, the fever, and the fret' – that is important for Keats's speaker. What the speaker wants is to be in a state of ignorance, to be in a state in which 'the dull brain perplexes and retards': the dulling and perplexing of the poet's brain is a small price to pay, it would seem, for forgetting, for not knowing. Better, it is the price you must pay, might wish to pay, for such delightful nescience. By the time we come to stanza five of Keats's 'nightingale' ode, the speaker's desire appears to have been achieved, and the speaker relishes the sensory deprivation of poetic composition: 'I cannot see what flowers are at my feet', he complains, or rejoices, 'Nor' – he goes on in a kind of insentient innocence, a skewing, of the senses in something like a nonsense of sensory dysfunction – 'Nor what soft incense hangs upon the boughs' (ll. 41–2) and instead has to 'guess' (l. 43) at his surroundings.

The speaker in this poem, I want to suggest, is what he so often is in Keats, whether in letters or in poems: the opposite of an epistemologist. I don't think that this really means that he is a sceptic (someone who is defined as a kind of crazed or morbid or hysterical or mesmerized or self-deceived, or error-ridden epistemologist – at least by the epistemologists). Rather, I think that it has to do with the speaker being the kind of person that wants to know what not knowing is like, to experience it fully and without the encumbrances of memory, self-consciousness and of course (it goes without saying) knowledge. Such a desire, such a programme, is far from straightforward, since however mired in ignorance we might be, we are also – even if deceived – never, if we are conscious, in a state of total ignorance, or at least never without the sense that we are experiencing *some* knowledge, about *something*, even if it is our own ignorance (that must be part, at least, of what being conscious means, after all – as Pascal notes when he remarks that he can 'easily imagine a man without hands, feet, head', but that he 'cannot imagine a man without thought').[13] And this is one of the difficulties of ignorance theory, of agnoiology: we cannot finally know what the state of ignorance, of proper ignorance, total ignorance, is like, since knowing such a state would allow there to be *something*, at least, that the subject knows. If I know what ignorance is like, I at least know *that*, so that my ignorance is not unalloyed, is impure, lacking. In a sense, the curse of consciousness is just that while we can in principle know anything else, we cannot know ignorance.[14] It is not just God that cannot know ignorance, it seems: at some level, we too are ignorant of ignorance. We can 'be' ignorant, for sure, just as we can be happy or 'have' an unconscious. But being (or having) ignorance is not the same as knowing it. And this perhaps is why Keats wants to know what such a state is like, what ignorance is like, and why he has to write poems about it (perhaps, he might lead us to think, that is what poems are for).

And what *is* ignorance like? Well, it's like hearing a bird's song, or reading or writing a poem, or being inspired, or waking from a dream.

In this respect, all of the spring odes can, in their different ways, be read in terms of epistemological abnegation, of anepistemology: all can, to a greater or lesser degree, be read in terms of the (impossible) desire to know what not knowing is like. In 'Ode on Indolence', a kind of companion poem to 'Ode to a Nightingale', the speaker is knowledgeable, but knowledgeable in the wrong classical discipline, and is therefore ignorant: despite being deep versed in 'Phidian lore' and knowledgeable therefore about the Elgin Marbles, the vase that he gazes on – one presumably from a different age and expressing different traditions or 'lore' – is 'strange' to him (ll. 9–10). So again the poem is punctuated by questions: 'How is it, Shadows! that I knew ye not? / How came ye muffled in so hush a masque?', the poet asks (ll. 11–12). Here, as in many others poems, 'hush', silence, is a metaphor for ignorance, for what is not known. And as in 'Ode to a Nightingale', the speaker desires the kinds of sensory deprivation that would intensify his ignorance: his eyes are 'Benumbed' by indolence so that 'Pain ha[s] no sting' (ll. 17–18). His desire, his one desire, is not to feel, is for the 'feel of not to feel it', as Keats puts it in 'In drear nighted December' (l. 21): he desires the sense of not sensing, and by that token (since the senses are a primary route by which we can be said to gain knowledge), the knowledge of not knowing. 'Why did ye not melt', the speaker asks in 'Ode on Indolence', 'and leave my sense / Unhaunted quite of all but – nothingness?' (ll. 19–20). The third time the figures on the urn pass, or the third time they are turned towards him as he gazes in idle curiosity, he identifies them as Love, Ambition and 'my demon Poesy' (l. 30). But this is not a welcome knowledge and he rejects each of the figures: 'What is love? and where is it?', he asks; ambition is no more than a 'short fever-fit' (l. 34); and poetry lacks the 'joy' of 'drowsy noons, / And evenings steeped in honeyed indolence' (ll. 35–6), reminding him as it does of temporality and his own mortality. The speaker would prefer never to know 'how change the moons, / Or hear the voice of busy common-sense!', he says (ll. 39–40). So in this poem, this poem of the end of poetry, Keats suggests that even poetry – the very realm, in another sense, of ignorance – is unwelcome because of its epistemological potentiality, because of what it offers us of a possible knowledge. Even poetry, for the poet of indolence, of ignorance, can be too knowing.

In 'Ode on a Grecian Urn' the speaker's rapt contemplation on the urn is itself structured by his ignorance of the ancient symbolism inscribed on or around it. The increasingly frantic questions in stanzas one and four ('What leaf-fringed legend . . .? What men or gods . . .? What maidens loth . . .? What mad pursuit? What struggle to escape? / What pipes and timbrels? What wild ecstasy?' (ll. 5–10); and 'Who are these coming . . .? To what green altar . . .? What little town . . .?' (ll. 31–5)) offer few answers – as befits a poem that ends in a statement of inhuman knowledge, of knowing that also firmly declares the poet's and our own ignorance, that declares the limits of our knowledge, in a statement that has baffled readers and critics ever since. We know it, only too well:

> Beauty is truth, – Truth Beauty, – that is all
>   Ye know on Earth, and all ye need to know.

or

> Beauty is Truth, Truth Beauty. – That is all
>   Ye know on Earth, and all ye need to know.

or

> 'Beauty is truth, truth beauty', – that is all
>   Ye know on earth, and all ye need to know.

or

> 'Beauty is truth, truth beauty, – that is all
> Ye know on earth, and all ye need to know'.

It's all about ignorance, this strangely troubling, gnomically knowing ending (or series of endings), and in that sense it's about the limits of human knowledge. The urn or poet knows at least something, even if what it or he knows is our, our human, ignorance. By defining what we *do* know, the urn or the poet also alludes to what we do not – or, in another reading, what the urn does not – know. That is *all* we know or all the urn knows, apparently – that beauty is truth and (rather differently) that truth is beauty. But the lines themselves have famously generated their own forms of readerly ignorance or uncertainty or confusion already figured, in fact, in the speaker's questions to the urn. And it all turns on the question of who speaks, of 'who says what to whom' at the end of the ode, an uncertainty generated in part by the variable punctuation in the four different versions reproduced above – as it appears in two surviving manuscript transcriptions (but in hands other than Keats's own); as it appears in the poem's first publication, in the *Annals of the Fine Arts*, in January 1820; as it appears in book form, in Keats's 1820 *Lamia* volume (a volume overseen not by Keats himself, who was too ill, but by his publisher); and as it appears in modern editorial versions of the latter (in this case, John Barnard's Penguin edition). The variable punctuation itself leads to multiple theories of the lines' possible meanings. Barnard lists five possible readings:

1 The urn is speaking both lines to the reader (or to humankind) in general.
2 The poet is speaking both lines to the urn.
3 The poet is addressing the figures on the urn.
4 The inverted commas included in the book version indicate that the urn is speaking the first five words but that the poet is speaking the remainder of the lines to his readers.
5 The urn articulates the 'motto', as in (4), but the poet then addresses the urn rather than humankind.[15]

The point is that these multiple possibilities entail an irreducible readerly engagement in the experience of ignorance: we may believe that we know what the lines mean but we cannot know that we know it. The urn, the 'sylvan historian' is, or seems, like any art object, a container of knowledge. Indeed, as Susan Wolfson points out, 'historian' ultimately derives from the Greek 'learning or knowing by inquiry'.[16] By contrast with the urn, however, it may be said that we, we readers, are denied even the possibility of the deferred knowledge provided by the historian's inquiry: we are able to speculate, but not to know. We cannot finally know the meaning of these lines since, in a sense, there *is* nothing to know, finally know. We may feel like historians, literary historians of this poem, and may indeed be readers of the legend that haunts about it – a legend that haunts us, telling us, amongst other things, that we must die – but like the figures on the urn we remain in a state of suspended animation, in a state of something like hermeneutic inanimation, in at least that kind of ignorance that we call uncertainty. We are left in doubt, doubting the sense of the poem's final lines and therefore its proper or final sense – as if in homage to the impulse towards ignorance that may be said to define the Keatsian poetic.

Keats's narrative and longer poems, and the 'Hyperion' poems in particular, are also concerned with ignorance and may indeed be construed as being about the way in which poetry is bound up with the question of knowledge and with the failure of knowing in particular. 'La Belle Dame sans Merci' famously involves narrative and therefore hermeneutic circularity, since the opening question of why the knight loiters in this place, is 'answered' in the final stanza only by an echo of the first. The answer is no answer and we are left, like the knight, in a kind of interpretative limbo. 'Lamia' is also of course strikingly concerned with ignorance – with, in this case, wilful ignorance, with fantasy or wish-fulfilment and with antagonism towards certain forms of knowledge or knowingness. One of the alterations that Keats made to Burton's brief recounting of the tale of Lycius and the lamia in his *Anatomy of Melancholy* concerns the transfer of the name 'philosopher' from Lycius himself in Burton to Apollonius in Keats: whereas Burton refers to Lycius as 'a young man, a philosopher', Keats gives the epithet, or job-description, to Apollonius, the 'bald-head philosopher' (2: 245), the one who destroys Lycius's luxuriant, erotic dream of uxoriousness by revealing Lamia's true identity. Lycius doesn't want, doesn't really need, to know And knowing, he dies; he dies because he knows.

Most importantly, though, the question of knowledge and the fiction of knowing is central to the 'Hyperion' poems, both of which concern the overthrow of Hyperion by Apollo, the sun-god and god of poetry, of music, and of prophecy – which means, in effect, of a certain knowledge.

As critics have pointed out, Keats appears to be more interested in the fall, the failure, of the Titans, than in Apollo's accession to godhead and to knowledge. The god of poetry and knowledge never, in fact, succeeds Hyperion, since both poems end before – or with 'Hyperion' just as – he becomes a god. It is in Book 3 of 'Hyperion' in particular that Keats explores the ignorance that is involved in literary composition, through the dialogue between Apollo and Mnemosyne. Mnemosyne, mother of the muses, named after memory, is herself centrally linked with knowledge, as Lemprière, one of Keats's probable sources, points out: 'the poets have rightly called memory the mother of the muses because it is to that mental endowment that mankind are indebted for their progress in science'.[17] Mnemosyne *is*, in a sense, an embodied or personified representation of knowledge. What Keats emphasizes, as Mnemosyne appears to Apollo in 'Hyperion', is the fact that Apollo's sense of her identity, his knowledge of 'memory', of, indeed, knowledge itself, is severely limited: he tries to figure out memory 'with eager eyes' and begins to 'read' her face, but to 'read / Perplexed . . .' (3: 48–9). So he asks her a series of questions about her presence, including the formal philosophico-epistemological question that so insistently characterizes Keats's verse: does he wake or sleep?

> 'How cam'st thou over the unfooted sea?
> Or hath that antique mien and robèd form
> Moved in these vales invisible till now?
> Sure I have heard those vestments sweeping o'er
> The fallen leaves, when I have sat alone
> In cool mid-forest. Surely I have traced
> The rustle of those ample skirts about
> These grassy solitudes, and seen the flowers
> Lift up their heads, as still the whisper passed.
> Goddess! I have beheld those eyes before,
> And their eternal calm, and all that face,
> Or I have dreamed.'
>
> (ll. 50–61)

Sure, again, surely: the Keatsian word of uncertainty. He is sure, in other words, but he may have been dreaming (there's an epistemological bathos to this passage, so certain it seems until the delayed, controlled epistemological explosion of the final half-line). As in 'Ode to Psyche', and as indeed in 'La Belle Dame sans Merci', Keats plays on the epistemological crux of 'Sure'/'Surely', to suggest the insecurity of knowledge within the certainty of 'sure': 'I am sure I have heard the rustle of those vestments' means also, of course, that I am *not* sure; 'surely I have traced that sound' means that I may *not* have done so. And the uncertainty is emphasized by the possibility of dreaming, of having dreamt all this. Apollo doesn't know, doesn't remember memory, the goddess of memory, the very goddess that provokes or instils or allows knowledge – what knowledge there is – that enables poetry to happen in the first place. Apollo, the god of knowledge and foresight – or the figure, at least, who is about to be that god – is defined at this point in his meeting with memory and poetry by, precisely, his ignorance. And in Keats's poems he hardly gets beyond that state.

In an odd moment of anamnesis that might remind us of Keats's own account of poetic composition in his 1820 letter to Richard Woodhouse, Apollo then remembers memory's name, remembering her name without remembering it, or without knowing how he remembers:

> Apollo then,
> With sudden scrutiny and gloomless eyes,
> Thus answered, while his white melodious throat
> Throbbed with syllables: 'Mnemosyne!
> Thy name is on my tongue, I know not how.'
>
> (3: 79–83)

What is here enacted is a sublime moment of inspiration, of access to knowledge that Apollo doesn't know that he has. Mired in the state of ignorant melancholy – in the condition of what we will come to call epistemelancholia,[18] the condition of being melancholy just *because* one doesn't know why one is melancholy (such ignorance being the very definition of melancholia) – Apollo goes on to ask a series of unanswered questions:

> 'Why should I tell thee what thou so well seest?
> Why should I strive to show what from thy lips
> Would come no mystery? For me, dark, dark,
> And painful vile oblivion seals my eyes:
> I strive to search wherefore I am so sad,
> Until a melancholy numbs my limbs;
> And then upon the grass I sit, and moan,
> Like one who once had wings. O why should I
> Feel cursed and thwarted, when the liegeless air
> Yields to my step aspirant? Why should I
> Spurn the green turf as hateful to my feet?
> Goddess benign, point forth some unknown thing:

Are there not other regions than this isle?
What are the stars?'

(3: 84–97)

Apollo's state, therefore, his natural, undeified state, is of ignorance, of melancholy ignorance: he sits 'idle' on the 'shores' (itself perhaps an ironic, teasing pun on his *lack* of certainty, his not being 'sure') in 'aching ignorance' (ll. 106–7). But as he 'reads' Mnemosyne's face he begins to understand, to know, 'Names, deeds, grey legends, dire events, rebellions' and so on (l. 114), and is thereby beginning to be 'deified' (l. 118): 'Knowledge enormous', he declares, 'makes a God of me' (l. 113). But there it ends: the deification doesn't happen:

At length
Apollo shrieked – and lo! from all his limbs
Celestial . . . (3: 134–6)

The abrupt ending of the first 'Hyperion' here (the second doesn't even get to this point) suggests the impossibility of poetic creativity, or of the realization of poetry in and as knowledge. What is striking about the passage, about the ending to 'Hyperion', its representation of Apollo's non-passage to knowledge, is the way in which it seems to enact a struggle within the poet between knowledge and ignorance (a struggle that will again be played out in the new 'induction' to 'The Fall of Hyperion') and the way in which it seems to suggest the impossibility of poetic knowledge – or at least the sense that the poet-figure, the very representation of the poet, is likely to remain (1) human and (therefore) (2) ignorant.

What can we make of this Keatsian urge towards anepistemology, the poet's apparent *desire* for ignorance, his resistance to the epistemophilic drive? Keats's poems certainly enact the concern with agnoiology that his letters express so clearly, characteristically concerned as they are with states of ignorance. Indeed, Keats's characteristic question, on which hinge, as we have seen, several of his poems (notably 'Ode to Psyche', 'Ode to a Nightingale', 'Hyperion' as well as, to a greater or lesser extent and with greater or lesser explicitness, *Endymion*, 'O thou whose face hath felt the winter's wind', 'Ode on a Grecian Urn', 'La Belle Dame sans Merci', 'The Eve of St Agnes', and 'Lamia'), is the epistemologist's question of whether we can know if we are awake or asleep. And Keats's poetic dream of hypnological uncertainty is even expressed in an apparently wakeful state in at least one of his letters: 'Shall I awake and find all this a dream?', Keats writes plaintively to Charles Brown as he embarks on his final voyage to Rome in September 1820 (*LJK* 2: 346), as if in remembrance of his poetry and as if, in the desperation of mortal sickness and the loss of his beloved Fanny Brawne, he would will the philosophical sceptic's hypothesis – that we might in fact be dreaming everything that we think we know – somehow to be true. But if this is the epistemologist's question, in fact, as I have indicated, Keats presents the poet as more like what we might conceive to be the opposite of the epistemologist. If we can say that one way of knowing what it is that an epistemologist is, or wants to be, is to say that she is the kind of person that seeks to know, really to know, what it is like to know, what it is like really to know, and in particular to know that one can know, then we might say that what Keats is, or wants to be, is the sort of person (there are perhaps not that many of them, and they might, some of them at least, be called poets) who wants to know, really know, what it is like not to know. There's the possibility of a kind of paradoxical certainty in that too, of course, in not knowing, in knowing that you don't know (that, after all, has always been the charge against those epistemologists that are called sceptics), but it's a certainty that Keats never really seems to reach, or that when he does reach or approach – in the heat of 'Ode to a Nightingale', say, as he blindly apprehends the flowers around him, or in the intense agonies of a poet's new accession to the world's sorrows that begins 'The Fall of Hyperion' – he immediately veers away or wakes from or just stops, as he re-achieves a state of doubt, uncertainty, perplexity. But there is anyway in Keats this interest, this perplexed fascination, this wanting to know about what it is like not to know. This is not to say that Keats is an epistemologist, and still less, I think, that he is (necessarily, as might be supposed, by virtue, for example, of his trade or craft) a philosophical sceptic. The difference is, perhaps, contained in that 'like': while the epistemologist may be said to want to know, and to want to know that and how we can know, and while the sceptic may be said (paradoxically) to know or at least to believe that we cannot know anything, or cannot at least know *this* (that this is my hand or body, that a table, these my thoughts, that you are or have a mind, and so on), the poet is not so much interested in the question of *whether* we can or cannot know, as he is in the (ordinary, after all, the everyday, but also the exotic, the unknown) experience of knowing what not knowing is like. And it is not just, I think, a question of what Tim Milnes analyses as the Romantic 'indifference' to knowledge since in fact the poet called John Keats seems to value very highly, to passionately value, the experience of not knowing, and suggests, I think, that it might be related somehow to poetry – to the experience of both reading and writing poetry. Instead, it has to do with the suggestion that poetry's embodiment or enactment of a certain ignorance may in fact be, in part at least, just what we value in poetry: that this, this nescient force of poetry, is what we read poetry for and part of the reason why, in the end, we read it, if we do, at all.

Notes

1 We might be reminded of Coleridge's comment on 'Christabel' as 'in direct opposition to the very purpose for which the *Lyrical Ballads* were published, viz an experiment to see how far those passions, which alone give any value to extraordinary Incidents, were capable of interesting, in & for themselves, in the incidents of common Life' (*Collected Letters of Samuel Taylor Coleridge*, ed. Earl Leslie Griggs, 6 vols. (Oxford: Oxford University Press, 1956–71), 1: 631), or of the rather fuller account of *Lyrical Ballads* that he gives in *Biographia Literaria* (see *Biographia Literaria*, eds James Engell and W. Jackson Bate, 2 vols (London: Routledge and Kegan Paul, 1983), 2: 6–7). This form of question – 'what is it like . . .?' – leads to the kind of knowledge that Dorothy Walsh argues pertains to literature (*Literature and Knowledge* (Middletown, Conn.: Wesleyan University Press, 1969). But see Peter Lamarque and Stein Hougon Olsen's riposte that such 'experiential' knowledge is both 'specifically literary' and 'unique', so that the suggestion amounts to 'the near tautology that reading literature extends our knowledge of the kind of subjective experience offered by literary works' (*Truth, Fiction, and Literature: A Philosophical Perspective* (Oxford: Clarendon Press, 1994), p. 378.
2 John Keats, *The Complete Poems*, ed. John Barnard, 3rd edn (London: Penguin, 2003), p. 521. All quotations from Keats's poems are from this edition.
3 *The Dialogues of Plato*, trans. B. Jowett, 4 vols. 4th edn (Oxford: Clarendon, 1953), 1: 438.
4 *The Letters of John Keats, 1814–1821*, ed. Hyder Edward Rollins, 2 vols. (Cambridge, Mass.: Harvard University Press, 1958), 1: 193: further references are cited in the text as *LJK*.
5 Compare his advice to his sister Fanny, after her legal guardian Richard Abbey took her out of school in December 1818, to 'keep up all that you know and to learn more by yourself however little' (*LJK* 2: 38).
6 Keats is confusing Byron with Ecclesiastes 1: 18 here: Byron's dictum is in fact that 'Sorrow is Knowledge', see *Manfred* 1: 1.10.
7 Compare the flippant close of another letter, to Benjamin Bailey, later in the month, where Keats hopes to meet up with Bailey so that they can see whether 'a little more knowledge has not made us more ignorant' (*LJK* 1: 288).
8 Compare a letter of July 1818, in which, on contemplating the poverty of the rural Scotch and Irish and the power of the church in both countries,

Keats concludes that 'We live in a barbarous age' and that the 'present state of society' is one in which 'the world is very young and in a verry ignorant state' (*LJK* 1: 320). Very differently, ignorance even has an erotic charge for Keats, it being one of the words that he uses to describe Fanny Brawne as he falls for her in the winter of 1818–19: 'she is not seventeen – but she is ignorant – monstrous in her behaviour flying out in all directions, calling people such names – that I was forced lately to make use of the term *Minx*', he writes, appalled and fascinated at the same time (*LJK* 2: 13). Less ambivalent – and entirely unerotic – is his furious description of Mrs Abbey's talk to Fanny Keats as 'unfeeling and ignorant gabble' (*LJK* 2: 41). Above all, knowledge for Keats is troublesome: 'The more we know the more inadequacy we discover in the world to satisfy us', he remarks to George and Georgiana Keats in November 1818 (*LJK* 2: 18).

9 *The Keats Circle*, 2nd edn, 2 vols. ed. Hyder Edward Rollins (Cambridge, Mass.: Harvard University Press, 1965), 1: 129 (cancelled readings and contractions omitted).

10 Compare a note to *Paradise Lost* where Keats ponders that 'One of the most mysterious of semi-speculations is . . . that of one Mind's imagining into another . . . A Poet can seldom have justice done to his imagination – for men are as distinct in their conceptions of material shadowings as they are in matters of spiritual understanding: it can scarcely be conceived how Milton's Blindness might here ade [for 'aid'] the magnitude of his conceptions as a bat in a large gothic vault' (Barnard, ed., *John Keats: The Complete Poems*, p. 518).

11 See John Hollander, *The Figure of Echo: A Mode of Allusion in Milton and After* (Berkeley: University of California Press, 1981), p. 94: Hollander comments that 'viewless' echoes Milton's 'bad poem' 'The Passion' ('thence hurried on viewless wing'), as well as *Comus* – which itself echoes *Measure for Measure* 3.1 ('viewless winds'). See also Cynthia Chase, '"Viewless Wings": Intertextual Interpretation of Keats's "Ode to a Nightingale"', in Chavia Hosek, Patricia Parker and Jonathan Arac, eds, *Lyric Poetry: Beyond New Criticism* (Ithaca: Cornell University Press, 1985), pp. 208–25.

12 A search on the Literature Online online database, for example, displays 170 hits in poems published in the years 1790–1819 (see http: //lion.chadwyck.co.uk).

13 Blaise Pascal, *Pensées*, trans. Martin Turnell (London: Harvill, 1962), p. 162. See also David Hume, *A Treatise of Human Nature*, ed. L.A. Selby-Bigge, 2nd edn, revised by P H. Nidditch (Oxford: Oxford University Press, 1978), p. 183: 'Nature, by an absolute uncontrollable necessity has determin'd us to judge as well as to breathe and feel' (quoted in Tim Milnes, *Knowledge and Indifference in English Romantic Prose* (Cambridge: Cambridge University Press, 2003), p. 3).

14 See Andrew Martin, *The Knowledge of Ignorance: From Genesis to Jules Verne* (Cambridge: Cambridge University Press, 1985), p. 10: 'nothing is quite so unknowable as knowledge, unless it be the entire absence of knowledge'.
15 See Barnard, ed., *John Keats: The Complete Poems*, p. 652.
16 Susan J. Wolfson, 'The Know of Not to Know It: My Returns to Reading and Teaching Keats's "Ode on a Grecian Urn"', in *'Ode on a Grecian Urn': Hypercanonicity and Pedagogy*, ed. James O'Rourke, *Romantic Circles Praxis Series* (2003) (www.rc.umd.edu/praxis/grecianurn/contributorsessays/grecianurnwolfson.html (accessed 15 February 2008)), para. 8. The derivation itself contains its own sense of ignorance (hence the need for 'inquiry') within knowledge: the historian in this sense is one who does not know but who needs to inquire, or one who is in the process of gaining knowledge by inquiry.
17 Quoted in Barnard, ed., *John Keats: The Complete Poems*, pp. 734–5; see, however, Keats's complicating of the identification of memory with knowledge in an aside in a letter to J.H. Reynolds, of February 1818: 'Memory should not be called knowledge', he declares (*LJK* 1: 231).
18 See Chapter 8, below.

5

Our ignorance of others: *Middlemarch* and *Great Expectations*

How do you get hold of other people conceptually, how do you know them, grasp them?[1] It is often said, and more often, I suppose, just thought or assumed, that the point of literature, part of its point at least, and the point in particular of novels and especially the classic nineteenth-century realist novel, is to allow us to understand and therefore to know, to grasp, others.[2] Structurally, that is to say, the tradition of the classic realist novel, in particular, can be conceived as a vast network of textuality with just one purpose: to comfort the bewildered reader with a sense – wholly illegitimate, the philosophic sceptic would say, wholly without warrant, an illusion – not only that there are other minds but that we can know them. The novel and particularly the Victorian novel has, in this regard, an intimate relationship with a certain branch of epistemology, that which has to do with the question of other minds – of whether there are any, and of whether we can approach or access or apprehend them. Behind or within its dignified analytical reserve, certain forms of epistemology, like certain kinds of realist novels, constitute a project of reassurance: both involve attempts to resist the desperate sense or intuition, intrinsic to Western notions of subjectivity and selfhood, that we cannot finally know whether or not there are in fact other minds – and the sense that our knowledge of these minds, if they exist, may be irredeemably obscure, fragile or faulty. It is from this concern about our ignorance of other minds, one might say, that both epistemology and the classic realist novel are designed to save us.[3]

The philosophical question of others' minds, then, might be thought of in literary terms in the context of the question of genre. Lyric poetry, to take pretty much the opposite of the nineteenth-century classic realist novel, might also be seen as a vast project of epistemological salvation, but one that invokes a very different solution. Poetry, lyric poetry in particular, is typically structured around the fiction or illusion of unmediated access to the subjectivity of the speaker or the poet. The point has recently been voiced once again (for it is a pervasive point in at least Romantic and post-Romantic poetics) by Robert Pinsky, in *Democracy, Culture and the Voice of Poetry* (2002). Poetry, Pinsky says,

> has roots in the moment when a voice makes us alert to the presence of another or others. It has affinities with all the ways a solitary voice, actual or virtual, imitates the presence of others. Yet as a form of art it is deeply embedded in the single human voice, in the solitary state that hears the other and sometimes recreates that other. Poetry is a vocal imagining, ultimately social but essentially individual and inward.[4]

The role of the lyric poem, for Pinsky, has to do with this apparently paradoxical combination of inwardness and individuality with an orientation towards the social and the other. In this respect, lyric poetry in particular is seen as allowing us an inward sense of another person, of that person as, in a sense, oneself: one knows him or her as one knows oneself – or perhaps one knows him or her even better, since the lyric 'I' is able to articulate things that the individual is hardly able to know or to express of itself. In fact, the apparently unmediated subjectivity of the lyric poet's 'I' may be said to perform a rather complex trick, the result of which is that, despite it being *another*'s subjectivity, the effect of this other subjectivity is to allow an identificatory reading that seduces you into the sense that this other consciousness is in fact your own: it is not only Coleridge but also somehow the reader that experiences this vaguely melancholy sense of pensive solitude as one contemplates one's friends walking on the Quantock hills nearby; it is not only Emily Dickinson but also somehow the reader that watches a bird walk down a path and quietly fly away; it is not only W.H. Auden but also somehow the reader that wonders at the old masters' sense of the indifference of the world to human suffering; it is not only Derek Walcott but also somehow the reader that contemplates this frigate bird sail on cruciform wing over these foam-topped Atlantic breakers, feels this breeze, sees this white sand on this island shore.

By contrast, the novel seems to present us with a way of coming to know the *otherness* of others, of knowing others *as* others, of knowing anyway the otherness of people in books. The novel – the Victorian 'classic realist' novel and its subsequent traditions, in particular – may be characterized in terms of its ability to present *other* people through the multiplicity of subjectivities required by its plotting, since the presentation of what might be taken as a 'realistic' vision of a society requires the evocation of multiple individuals: no man or woman is an island in industrialized, urbanized nineteenth-century Britain, even if he or she might seem to be elsewhere and at other times (the fact that one of the earliest English novels, Daniel Defoe's *Robinson Crusoe*, is based *on* an island and on an individual's attempt to recreate a micro-society from what is available to him – including, especially, the man he calls Friday – may be seen perhaps paradoxically or counter-intuitively to confirm the importance of the social to this emerging literary form). The novel – the genre that in the nineteenth century is brought to fruition through the developing technologies of narrative perspective, including, in particular, free indirect discourse and, later on, stream of consciousness – is based on the possibility (and therefore on the problem, the difficulty) of knowing others. Even first-person narrators tend willingly to compromise their own apparently isolated subjectivity through their concern with what might almost be said to be the definition of the realist novel – the representation of the consciousness of other people. And third-person narrators – especially those misnamed 'omniscient'[5] – are of course specifically engineered (specifically invented, one might say) to at least offer the possibility of exposing the inner workings of the minds of other people to the curiously inward but public gaze of readers,[6] a technique that may be said to take the place of that other mechanism of paradoxical interiority, the theatrical soliloquy, and one that complements that other nineteenth-century invention, the monodrama or dramatic monologue. That, in particular, is the significance of the invention and refinement of free indirect discourse in the early nineteenth century, a new narrative technology that above all others drives the development of the post-Romantic novel.[7]

The matters raised here involve complex issues in literary history, particularly with respect to narrators and characters and the new technologies of nineteenth-century narrative fiction. In this chapter, though, I will confine myself to a discussion of two of the most fully achieved and most commonly discussed English novels from the mid-nineteenth century, Charles Dickens's *Great Expectations* (1860–61) and George Eliot's *Middlemarch* (1871–72). And I will focus my discussion further by grounding it in an observation that Stanley Cavell has recently made on what might seem to be the self-evident fact that we know others through what he calls the 'subtler movements of the body', including those of the face in particular but also, 'as documentary filmmakers insist', the hands.[8] As it happens, just such a strategy is put into effect in these two novels – novels which, in their (differently complex, layered and self-consciously or self-reflexively compromised or constructed) 'realism' may be said to be indirectly related to the contemporary documentary at key points: both *Great Expectations* and *Middlemarch* substitute or supplement talk about the minds of other people with talk of those people's hands.[9] In this chapter I will briefly try to indicate the contrasting ways in which hands act as signifiers of personhood in the two novels, and examine what this might tell us not so much about the saving knowledge of others (and therefore of the self) that the realist novel purports to provide but rather about the ineluctable ignorance of others that it in fact offers. For the third-person 'omniscient' narrator of *Middlemarch*, the otherness of others involves the question of the minds of other people. For the first-person, fictionally autobiographical narrator of *Great Expectations*, the otherness is perhaps even stranger, since it also involves the otherness of oneself.

Writing to Grace Norton in March 1873 after drafting a review of *Middlemarch*, Henry James commented that his brother William had said that he was 'aghast' at the 'intellectual power' of George Eliot's new novel, and that for his own part he was certain that 'a marvellous *mind* throbs in every page'.[10] In the review itself, James commented on the 'constant presence of thought, of generalizing instinct, of *brain*' in the novel, which is at times, he wryly remarked, 'too clever by half'.[11] One of the things that marks George Eliot out as a writer for James, in other words, is her knowingness, and one of the things that characterizes this knowingness is her command of what goes on in people's minds. *Middlemarch* in particular is centrally concerned with and based on knowledge, on knowing, not least on knowing others.[12] 'No other Victorian novelist – no other novelist anywhere or perhaps at any time – was as well equipped as Eliot to undertake a task of this magnitude', comments Felicia Bonaparte in her 1997 Introduction to the Oxford World's Classics edition of the novel,[13] on Eliot's attempt to establish, against Victorian philosophical, theological and scientific scepticism, that there is finally 'something we must believe in and do' (*Middlemarch*, p. 225). Eliot is qualified, according to Bonaparte, because 'No one had a better mind or as extensive a body of knowledge' than her, and because she brings her 'massive knowledge' to the task of writing the novel (pp. xi, xxxv): it was Eliot's 'exceptional mind and knowledge' that began her career (p. x); her 'moral vision' is 'among the glories' of the novel, which is in part an indictment of 'the ignorance of the world in which young women were allowed, and even encouraged, to grow up' (p. xiii);[14] her 'admiration for science is not for a moment in doubt', Bonaparte opines (p. xv). And for a critic like Bonaparte, what Eliot knows above all is other people. As Bonaparte puts it, Eliot is 'responsive' to the 'philosophic questions that had reference to human nature'; she is the 'first true psychological novelist' (p. xxiii). Bonaparte suggests that while the ironical stance of her narrators remind us that 'few things are as certain as they seem', nevertheless Eliot also 'assures us we have the power, if we trust our imaginations, to perceive and to interpret, to conceive and to create': what Eliot allows us to understand is others, other people, since she has 'a genius for imagining' their 'inner lives' (p. xxii).[15] As Eliot herself puts it in 'The Natural History of German Life' (1856), 'Art . . . is a mode of amplifying experience and extending our contact with our fellow-men beyond the bounds of our personal lot'.[16]

From its first publication, however, critics have identified one major weakness in *Middlemarch* – the character of Ladislaw and his marriage with Dorothea. An anonymous reviewer in the *Saturday Review* (7 December 1872) was one of the first to notice this: Ladislaw is 'a great favourite with the author', the reviewer remarks, but 'we scarcely know on what grounds' he is so.[17] Rather differently, in the *Fortnightly Review* (19 January 1873), Sidney Colvin sees the culmination of the Dorothea–Ladislaw relationship as an aesthetic flaw: the fact that Dorothea ends up marrying a man who is 'hardly worthy of her', he suggests, leads to 'that feeling of uncertainty and unsatisfiedness as to the whole fable and its impression which remains with the reader when all is done'.[18] Henry James was troubled more generally by the figure of Ladislaw, as he makes clear in his review of the novel: 'Our dissatisfaction . . . is provoked in great measure by the insubstantial character of the hero. The figure of Will Ladislaw is a beautiful attempt, with many finely completed points; but on the whole it seems to us a failure . . . the only eminent failure in the book.'[19] This nineteenth-century sense of Ladislaw as a failure was indeed almost universally acknowledged in criticism of the following century, becoming something of an accepted fact for mid-twentieth-century readings: Ladislaw is 'mere pasteboard' (Oliver Elton in 1920), a victim of George Eliot's 'highmindedness' (V.S. Pritchett in 1947), an 'artistic failure' (Arnold Kettle in 1951), 'the weakest of the major characters' and the scenes he shares with Dorothea 'full of high-flown nonsense' (Quentin Anderson in 1958);[20] his relationship with Dorothea constitutes 'the psychological and structural flaw' in the novel so that 'the weakness of the novel, and the weakness of Will Ladislaw, are located in his relationship with Dorothea' (Barbara Hardy in 1964).[21]

The point is confirmed in W.J. Harvey's Introduction to the widely circulated Penguin paperback edition of the novel, published in the mid-1960s and reprinted regularly for almost forty years until superseded by a new edition introduced by Rosemary Ashton in 2003. Harvey argues that the novel exemplifies what he calls George Eliot's 'poised' moral vision, in particular by the deployment of the omniscient narrator (or 'omniscient author', as Harvey calls her in what might seem to be an odd kind of tautology) who 'sometimes act[s] as a guide, sometimes as an unobtrusive chorus'. According to Harvey, however, this 'adult' voice 'falters' at just one point in the novel, in 'the culmination of the Dorothea–Ladislaw relationship'.[22] Harvey is referring, in particular, to chapter 83, where, in a scene of high, if expressively muted passion, Ladislaw returns to Lowick and finally declares his love to Dorothea – who reciprocates as they finally agree (without any real asking) to take each other's hand in marriage.[23] For Harvey, the scene falters specifically with regard to the poised, unobtrusive but controlling 'omniscient' narrator:

> This *is* a flaw which no critic can satisfactorily excuse; for whatever reason, George Eliot cannot adequately handle the intensities of romantic love. But even this is not so much a positive fault, an ugly blotch; rather it is a blur on a canvas so impressively crowded as to divert our attention elsewhere.[24]

Harvey treats the 'blur' as if it is in accordance with the principle of the exception that proves the rule. Just *because* we can identify this faltering in the narrator's adult voice, we are therefore able to see the force of that voice's habitually poised, disinterested wisdom. And Harvey makes it very clear that what is at stake here is, precisely, knowledge, knowledge of others:

> The moral vision embodied in *Middlemarch* creates a corresponding response in the reader. By her method of interweaving concurrent stories, by the proliferation of characters, by the complicated structure of parallels and contrasts, George Eliot bestows upon the reader a wide variety of viewpoints, of changing perspectives, which enlarge our understanding both of the fictional world and of the real world. In this process we constantly revise our judgements and alter the balance of our feelings; we are involved in the protagonists and yet – because of our wider view – we know more than any of them can, so that our sympathies are checked and controlled by our perception or their limitations and blind spots . . . Any tendency to idealize Dorothea is checked by a cool flow of ironic and qualifying comment.[25]

The paragraph is illuminating from a number of perspectives. In the first place it allows us to understand what is wrong, for Harvey, with chapter 83: it lacks the 'cool flow of ironic and qualifying comment' that allows Eliot to 'check' any tendency to 'idealize' Dorothea. But the passage also gives us a clear sense of what is at stake for Harvey in this novel and in the nineteenth-century novel more generally: what is at stake is the possibility precisely of knowing a person – a character – and of knowing that person, indeed, better than the person can know herself. Finally, there is a discreet interchange between author and reader: the author knows and transmits this knowledge to the reader, who then becomes more knowledgeable both about particular characters and about life or morality more generally, and gains, in reading, something of the 'moral vision' of the author. But for Harvey, the emotional climax of Eliot's novel, the scene of romantic fulfilment that is presented in chapter 83, fails to provide such moral vision, or fails to sustain it.

I want to suggest that what happens in chapter 83 in fact exposes the difficulty of knowing other people that Harvey, Bonaparte and others register (that, indeed, it is registered by the institutional reception of the novel more generally, as evinced by its distaste for the Dorothea–Ladislaw narrative settlement). I will argue that the movement of hands in the chapter itself expresses or gestures towards the difficulty of such knowledge, and that it is no coincidence that it is just at the point where the two characters tentatively reveal their true 'selves' to each other, the truth about their sincere feelings, that Eliot's model of knowing falters or fails. Since – so the argument will go – knowing other people may be understood to be difficult or even impossible, and since the rhetorical or literary fiction that we can do so may be just that – a fiction or illusion – there is a certain logic in the fact that at the moment of most intense self-exposure, of subjective clarity, such a novel will come undone, and the paradoxical nature of the strategy will be revealed. Not only does the narrator fail to remain ironically 'detached' from her characters at this point but her very ability to know them comes unstuck. Novels – nineteenth-century realist novels in particular – show us how we can come to know other people. But they also show us the limits of that knowledge and the beginning of our ignorance of others.[26]

I want to suggest that we can begin to grasp all this by looking at the ways in which hands are manipulated – touched or touching, held or grasped, displayed, in motion, stilled – in chapter 83. There is of course a heavily overdetermined thematic context for the representation of hands in this chapter that concerns, above all, the problem of hands in two legal senses. In the first place, there is the idea of giving one's 'hand in marriage'. As certain kinds of readers might have registered only too well for much of the last 82 chapters, there can be only one resolution to *Middlemarch* – the resolution involved in Dorothea finally marrying Will Ladislaw. However unsatisfactory the match might seem, and however unsatisfactory its culminating representation turns out to be in this chapter, there can be only one resolution to the question of Dorothea's desire within the terms of this novel. Casaubon must die. Dorothea must marry Ladislaw. And it is in chapter 83 that this revelation finally comes about: over the course of a passionate and melodramatically torturous conversation, Dorothea and Will finally decide that they can after all marry, that they can join their hands in matrimony. The second legal and therefore metaphorical 'hand' that the chapter evokes is of course the 'dead hand' of Casaubon (a figure already emphasized, not to say overdetermined, by its use as the title to Book 5 of the novel): a major part of the narrative drive of the last 33 chapters and the reason why Dorothea cannot, for much of the novel and even for most of chapter 83, conceive of marrying Will Ladislaw, is the legal 'dead-hand' that Casaubon has inserted into his will: if she accepts Will, Dorothea will be disinherited. It is, in effect – and indeed without ambiguity – a battle of 'wills', a battle between the dead hand of Casaubon's legal grasp on Dorothea, his last will and testament, and the implicit but literal – physical as well as figurative – offer by Will Ladislaw of his living hand in marriage.

The question of the hand is, therefore, over determined, symbolically, thematically and conceptually by the time we get to chapter 83, and it is perhaps not surprising therefore that hands themselves are emphasized in this chapter. In fact, as Daniel Karlin has shown, hands are a topic of significant interest throughout the novel.[27] And there is no doubt that it is by means of hands that Eliot expresses the emotions, thoughts, desires of the two characters: she plays out the emotions and desires of the two characters by focusing in particular on the conscious and (in fact mainly) unconscious actions of their hands. The hands in this chapter seem to link volition with unconscious desire and indeed with the inexpressible – the hand presenting that which cannot otherwise be presented. The hand constitutes a kind of hinge, or handle, on or between what is not known and inexpressible and what is desired. The hand articulates, in particular, what the characters do not know not only about each other but about themselves.

The words 'hand' and 'hands' are used seventeen times in this relatively short chapter[28] and it is by grasping these hands that we can track the intense romantic drama of the liaison.[29] Dorothea is restlessly alone at Lowick, attempting to catch her 'vagrant mind' and 'arrest her wandering thoughts' by dutifully studying a map of Asia Minor, occasionally breaking off to put her hands 'on each side of her face' and exclaim 'Oh dear! Oh dear!' (pp. 756–7). She is interrupted by Miss Noble, whose hand she presses and who tells her that Will Ladislaw has come to see her. As Dorothea waits for Ladislaw to enter the room, she stands, unconscious of her body

> with her hands falling clasped before her[.] (p. 758)

Will arrives and she seems to have a spell on her that

> hinder[s] her from unclasping her hands[.] (ibid.)

She does not put out her hand in greeting as she usually does, the absence of which action causes Will some confusion. As he begins to speak, referring to the 'painful story about my parentage', Dorothea moves slightly:

> she unclasped her hands but immediately folded them over each other. (pp. 758–9)

The conversation revolves around what Dorothea had known of Ladislaw – whether she had trusted him or lost trust or respect for him – around the question, in other words, of Dorothea's knowledge of this other person. Will declares that his sense that Dorothea no longer trusted him meant that for him 'there was nothing to try for – only things to endure' (p. 759), which brings a strong – and therefore strongly manual – response from Dorothea:

> 'I don't doubt you any longer', said Dorothea, putting out her hand; a vague fear for him impelling her unutterable affection. (p. 760)

The action brings an equally strong and equally strongly manual response from Will:

> He took her *hand* and raised it to his lips with something like a sob. But he stood with his hat and gloves in the other *hand*, and might have done for the portrait of a Royalist. Still it was difficult to loose the *hand*, and Dorothea, withdrawing it in a confusion that distressed her, looked and moved away. (ibid.; italics added)

Everything here focuses on the hand: one of Will's hands is raised to the lips while his other, as if resisting the significance of this gesture keeps grasp of those items which indicate (1) where he has come from and (2) where, at this point, it is known that he must go (i.e. in both cases outside, away). And this focus on the hand also suggests a stiff, formal, unemotional, artificial and purely 'external' pose, the pose of an individual standing for a certain kind of portrait. The passive voice in the second sentence blurs the question of agency, the question of whether it is Dorothea or Will that finds it difficult to 'loose the hand', as well as emphasizing Will's passivity (a pattern of passivity followed by a sudden, seemingly instinctual, almost unconscious rush of action, is emphasized throughout the chapter). But then, as Will insists on speaking 'without disguise' (declaring that, since he must leave, Dorothea should think of him as 'on the brink of the grave'), there arrives the novel's most emotionally melodramatic moment, evoked through a kind of manual ballet:

> While he was speaking there came a vivid flash of lightning which lit each of them up for the other – and the light seemed to be the terror of a hopeless love. Dorothea darted instantaneously from the window; Will followed her, seizing *her hand* with a spasmodic movement; and so they stood, with *their hands* clasped, like two children, looking out on the storm, while the thunder gave a tremendous crack and roll above them, and the rain began to pour down. Then they turned their faces towards each other, with the memory of his last words in them, and they did not loose *each other's hands*. (p. 761; italics added)

Will's seizing of Dorothea's hand 'with a spasmodic movement', and the action of standing 'with their hands clasped', register what is increasingly emphasized, through hands, in this chapter – that the couple act without thinking, unconsciously, unpremeditatedly. It is not just that they have trouble deciphering what the other is feeling or thinking, but that they cannot decipher their own emotions and impulses. And that is the problem with knowing others, or not knowing them: that our ignorance of others is merely an effect, a signifier, of our ignorance of ourselves. Dorothea and Will remain indecipherable to each other, then, and their hands act not only as signs of inner turmoil but *as* that turmoil. They don't know what they are doing or are going to do, in other words, and they are in a sense governed by their hands. It is the hands of the characters, and more generally their bodies, that act.[30] Significantly, it is within the rhetorical context of the so-called 'pathetic fallacy' that this helpless sense of characterological nescience occurs. The pathetic fallacy is the possibility of animism – and here in particular it suggests the truly terrifying possibility that the natural world knows more about us, is more in touch with us, with our feelings or our selves, than other people are.[31] In this instance, there is a sense that in their desperation to know each other, now, in their desire finally to know what the other is thinking, feeling, to achieve a longed-for decipherability of the always enigmatic other (the 'enigmatic signifier' – to coin a pun[32] – that the other person always remains to us), consciousness is transferred on to nature, projected on to and as a storm. But it is not of course the characters, the fictional people, who effect this transformation, this projection: it is Eliot herself. The projection of emotion on to the landscape may be read as, in effect, a desperate attempt by Eliot to overcome the indecipherability of her own characters, the people that she invents, these fictional others – and, as such therefore, to overcome the irreducible indecipherability of people in general (for what, as I say, are realist novels if not formal, controlled experiments in attempting to know others?).[33]

It is my suggestion, then, that what Stanley Cavell points to as the documentary film-maker's signifier of the other's obscurity, the hand, is in fact powerfully at work in this precursor of such cultural artefacts, in *Middlemarch* (the novel is a vast nineteenth-century precursor of modern-day television soaps, of course, but it is also, in some respects, something like a precursor of television reality shows or docudramas, a kind of prose documentation, almost a fictionalized documentary, in its attempted fidelity towards a certain idea of the complex interactive 'reality' of community life). But hands in this chapter do not so much reveal the subjectivity of the characters as expose the obscurity of that subjectivity, its indecipherability, both to the other and indeed to the self. The hand signifies the impulsive nature of the characters' acts, the way in which they don't know what they are doing until they have done it. The body moves first, then the mind. It is, indeed, as if there is no subjectivity, nothing to know, only the body (including the hand) itself, moved and moving of its own irrational and unpredictable volition. In the novel's most intensely emotional, most subjectively intense chapter, Eliot's art of consciousness fails. In a sense, you could say, what the general cultural reception of this novel, what W.J. Harvey and others want, is not available. Even in our most psychologically knowledgeable, most fully knowing, novelist, there is a blank, there is ignorance, ignorance concerning subjectivity or consciousness, concerning the very stuff of people, the very stuff indeed of the classic realist novel.

For George Eliot, much of an individual's 'inward life' is 'made up of the thoughts he believes other men to have about him' (*Middlemarch*, p. 647):

'there is no creature whose inward being is so strong', Eliot remarks at the end of her novel of ethics, the individual, and society, 'that it is not greatly determined by what lies outside it' (p. 784–5). Such questions have recently been taken up in a powerful and in some ways rather moving essay on the possibility of ethics or accountability within the context of a presumed 'opacity' of the subject by Judith Butler. Butler builds on Hegelian and Lacanian notions of the other and on reflections on subjectivity by Hannah Arendt and Adriana Caverero to argue that it is 'precisely by virtue of its relations to others' that the subject is 'opaque to itself'.[34] The subject is constituted, Butler suggests, is identified as or identifies itself, grants itself an identity, in relation and only in relation to others – by virtue, indeed, of the recognition or acknowledgement of others. But this recognition itself constitutes a 'transformation' in or of identity, a kind of ineluctable narration of identity: 'recognition becomes the process by which I become other than what I was and, therefore, also, the process by which I cease to be able to return to what I was' (p. 23). This involves the temporality of a certain autobiographicity, according to which one becomes what one was not, by virtue of the recognition of others, by external 'mediation':

> I find that the only way to know myself is precisely through a mediation that takes place outside of me, exterior to me, in a convention or a norm that I did not make, in which I cannot discern myself as an author or an agent of its making . . . The possibility of the 'I', of speaking and knowing the 'I', resides in a perspective that dislocates the first-person perspective whose very condition it supplies. (p. 23)

In other words, one cannot know the 'I' except through the other, but this kind of knowledge is itself a kind of nescience. And to put it crudely, this means that, in effect, the problem of other minds is not just the problem of *other* minds, but also the problem of my own mind, of the mind that I reputedly 'own': my mind is itself other to itself.[35]

The problematic of the subject that Butler is addressing is intimately linked to autobiographical writing since it is in 'giving an account' of myself that I establish myself, my identity, or subjectivity: I make myself 'recognizable' or indeed 'understandable' – to myself in the first place – through a narration or telling of myself. But this narration is necessarily 'disorientated by what is not mine, or what is not mine alone' (p. 26). Indeed, giving an account of myself in autobiography, narrating myself, involves talking about what I do not know: according to Butler, it involves, in the first place, 'bearing witness to a state of affairs to which

[I] could not have been present, prior to [my] own becoming'. So autobiography involves 'narrating that which [I] cannot know' (p. 26). 'There is that in me', Butler asserts, 'and of me for which I can give no account' (p. 27).

Butler is particularly concerned about the ethical aspects of accounting for oneself, and interested in the question of how, given one's 'opacity' to oneself, the subject can be held accountable, can account for, itself. Her suggestion is that, rather than the 'violence' of the demand that the other 'manifest and maintain self-identity at all times' (p. 27), it is in fact necessary to accept the position of 'humility' or 'generosity' whereby I can be 'forgiven for what I cannot fully know' and, by the same logic, be 'under a similar obligation to offer forgiveness to others who are also constituted in partial opacity to themselves' (p. 28). Ethics, in other words, *begins* where knowledge (knowledge of self, of others) stops. Nescience is intrinsic to the ethical. And it is just such nescience, in fact, that for Butler constitutes 'life' itself – it is 'that which exceeds any account we may try to give of it' (p. 28):

> If letting the Other live is part of a new definition of recognition, then this version of recognition would be one that is based less on knowledge than on an apprehension of its limits. In a sense, the ethical stance consists in asking the question, 'Who are you?', and continuing to ask the question without any expectation of a full or final answer. This Other to whom I pose this question will not be captured by any answer that might arrive to satisfy the question. So if there is, in the question, a desire for recognition, this will be a desire which is under an obligation to keep itself alive as desire, and not to resolve itself through satisfaction. (p. 28)

Butler is concerned, as I say, with the ethics of this presentation of identity, and with the legal, social, political and other ramifications of ethical judgement, with judgement, condemnation, denunciation – precisely those dimensions of social life that the Victorian realist novel is concerned to unfold or expose (one of the great pleasures of reading Victorian and other realist novels is, after all, seeing the hero or heroine's enemies get their just deserts, their punishment after proper (including proper readerly) judgement). But for Butler, condemnation works against self-knowledge, however limited self-knowledge must ultimately be, since it seeks to 'purge and externalise one's own opacity', and it therefore fails to 'own its own limitations': it allows for no possibility of a 'reciprocal recognition of human beings as constitutively limited' (p. 31). In other words, we are back to the question of Plato's double ignorance and the Socratic valorization of nescience: what Butler calls 'condemnation' asserts the possibility of ultimate or absolute or unequivocal knowledge (of the other, and of the self), a position that is doubly ignorant, since it ignores, it blithely denies the ineluctable opacity of both self and other.

I want to suggest in this context that, like Dickens's other novels, *Great Expectations* is based around the irretrievably stubborn, recalcitrant otherness of others – others as stubbornly other and as resistant to one's own will, indeed resistant to one's condemnation, recalcitrant in their resistance to one's own sense of order and reason: that is what characterizes other people for Dickens and that is why his novels are full of so-called 'characters', characters who often indeed amount to little more than caricatures (as George Eliot herself points out).[36] But, at the same time, it is others, for Dickens, that make you, it is others around whom your identity, your sense of self congregates. Dickens's novels seem to register the fact that you are determined in relation to others, and determined by how others see you. And *Great Expectations* seems to register the fact that in writing your autobiography you inevitably write as Pip accuses Estella of speaking: 'You speak of yourself as if you were some one else', he tells her (p. 262). The structure of autobiography – the fundamental structure of the older subject looking back at himself as a younger subject – involves just such 'speaking', involves speaking of myself as if I was another.

And once again I want to suggest that this otherness – the otherness of the (autobiographical) self – is marked in *Great Expectations*, as it is in *Middlemarch*, by the discourse of hands. Critics have not failed to notice that hands are prominently at work in Dickens's *Great Expectations*. By contrast with *Middlemarch*, though, in *Great Expectations* it is within the generic and structural terms of (fictional) autobiographical narrative (that other great nineteenth-century tradition of the realist novel) that hands operate. And here's the problem, the question, of the other, the self as other that, I suggest, *Great Expectations* attempts to resolve – or at least to grasp – with its concentration on characters' hands (and here I will try to augment Butler's brilliant analysis of the ethics of the subject giving an account of herself): on the one hand (as it were), I am the best person to know about me. On the other hand, I am also the person that knows least about me, cannot know me, and, even if I could, cannot *allow* myself to know me. This has at least two aspects. In the first place, in order to maintain the illusion of self, as well as the illusion of the particular self that I hold, I have to repress, deny, negate, disavow certain aspects of myself (my greed, vanity, egotism, for example, certain kinds of desires, longings, repulsions and so on, including those that I can hardly, hardly bear to, guess at). Secondly, the interminable (Western, modern, liberal, humanist) project of knowing myself must involve knowing who or how I am in relation to others, must involve seeing myself as others see me. But I cannot see myself as others see me or know myself as others know me (I cannot 'know' myself, therefore) except in distorting representations – in reflections, in photographs or portraits, in others' reports or their overheard gossip, or in my imagining of what it is that they might be saying about me, or not saying about me, when I am not present. Others' perceptions of me are opaque, just as opaque as I already am to my own perception of my self. And anyway, since these representations are necessarily partial or distorted versions of how others see me and since of course there are a potentially infinite number of ways in which the seemingly infinite number of people whom I meet might see me, such a project is bound in principle to fail.

As an autobiographical writer, however, I have a strategy to combat this failure of self-cognition. In order to know about, to grasp, my self, to overcome my own otherness, I will write about myself (I write about myself, therefore I am (me)), and I will write about myself as other to myself. This is not to say that knowing myself is my only reason for writing about my self (I write to confess, justify, excuse, explain, valorize, publicize myself, for example, or to gain vengeance, respect, love, sex, money, religious salvation, status, influence and so on). But it is structurally part of autobiography, part of the autobiographical contract or pact, that in writing about myself I not only communicate information about myself but I also come to 'know' myself.[37] In fact, however, this strategy results only in a further conundrum of autobiographical writing: to echo Derrida, in *Glas*, we might say that you can take an interest in me, in my writing about myself to be sure, but also just in me, in what I do or say or how I behave, to the extent that you believe that what you know about me is, at the same time and at some level, what I don't know about myself. That is what makes you my friend, my enemy, my lover, my therapist, my confessor, my ally, my collaborator, my interlocutor or auditor, my reader . . . To the extent that you take an interest in me, my ignorance of myself is part of what makes you do so. It is what I *don't* know, or tell (what I 'cannot tell', in both senses) about myself that you find interesting and even – dare I say it, hope it? – attractive. It is this ignorance, indeed, that allows you to acknowledge me, to acknowledge me as other and therefore to ascribe to me the political, ethical and indeed metaphysical autonomy that I require, that I need to become a 'subject'.

By the same token, what interests you in my writings about myself is what I cannot tell you or, more properly, what I don't know that I am telling you. If my autobiographical writing is based on a doubleness in me – me knowing now about the necessarily unknowing me then – it is not just in this epistemological gap that the interest lies: rather, the reason you read my autobiographical story or listen to my tale about myself is to discern what I *still* don't know, can't tell of myself, my 'unconscious', my otherness to myself – 'that which I cannot own', that which cannot be 'mine', and that which 'threatens us with an insupportable unintelligibility',[38] even if (or precisely because) at some level this nescience remains obscure to you too. That's what gets you and what you get in reading, in reading me.

In *Great Expectations* Pip has an acute sense of others; he is, indeed, defined by others, even potentially in death. Towards the end of the novel, Orlick threatens to kill Pip in the sluice-house. The older Pip remarks that 'The death close before me was terrible, but far more terrible than death was the dread of being misremembered after death. And so quick were my thoughts', he goes on, 'that I saw myself despised by unborn generations – Estella's children, and their children – while the wretch's words were yet on his lips' (p. 420). Being misremembered: a fate worse than death. As this suggests, Pip has a particularly acute sense of the otherness of his own identity – otherness with regard to the way that he is conditioned by others, by how others see him. One way to observe this sense of otherness is to attend briefly to the almost obsessive attention that the novel pays to hands. As I have indicated, critics have not been slow to point out that hands play a prominent role in *Great Expectations*. In 1961, for example, developing a hint from J. Hillis Miller in his 1958 book on Dickens, Charles Forker argued that 'human hands' are a 'recurring feature of the narrative'. Forker suggests that Dickens is 'the most theatrical of the great Victorian writers' and that he therefore pays particular attention to hands and gestures as 'an indispensable shorthand for individualizing character and dramatizing action and response': in *Great Expectations*, Forker asserts, hands are 'almost an obsession'.[39] Forker argues that in *Great Expectations*, 'as in no other of Dickens's novels', hands

> serve as a *leitmotif* of plot and theme – a kind of unifying symbol or natural metaphor for the book's complex of human interrelationships and the values and attitudes that motivate them. Dickens not only reveals character through gesture, he makes hands a crucial element of the plot, a means of

clarifying the structure of the novel by helping to define the hero's relations with all the major characters, and a device for ordering such diverse themes as guilt, pursuit, crime, greed, education, materialism, enslavement . . . friendship, romantic love, forgiveness, and redemption.[40]

Hand imagery in *Great Expectations*, according to Forker, 'helps to knit together a fabric of many threads': it helps us to understand the novel's characters as well as its plot.[41]

In recent years, the insights of Forker and others on hands in the novel have been most fully and indeed most controversially developed by William Cohen, in a 1993 essay on the ways in which hands in *Great Expectations* signify homoeroticism and masturbation (the novel 'relegates' 'unutterable instances' of autoeroticism 'to the commonplace, benign, and unblushing representation of characters' hands', Cohen maintains).[42] Cohen's essay is, in a sense, all too knowing (the charge that I also make of Eve Kosofsky Sedgwick's homosocial reading of Henry James, in Chapter 8, below): I am not – the present book is not – simply resistant to the force of such sexualized, such homosocial or homoerotic readings of classic Victorian authors;[43] but there would necessarily be, in ignorance theory, a scepticism towards the hermeneutic certainties of such accounts.[44] The homosocial reading would, by its own definition, be in a sense *too* knowing. This is also, of course, the charge often laid at the door of critics in general, the charge against all criticism, interpretation, reading even: its knowingness, a knowingness that knows not its own nescience. That, in a sense, is the fate or at least the risk of criticism – to know more than the author (or to think it does), and in that sense to know too much, or to consider itself all-knowing. Criticism wants to know even the author's ignorance – even while it is precisely that ignorance (and, in a sense, our ignorance of it) that, at some level, impels us to read. Cohen's reading – to take a now notorious example – urges us in fact to stop reading since we can *know* now what Pip or what Dickens is up to. Ignorance theory, by contrast, would at least guard against such knowingness, would value a certain authorial reserve, a narratorial nescience, indeed, without necessarily trying to know it – as would any critic who took seriously Blanchot's asseveration that reading 'demands more ignorance than knowledge'.[45]

Trying to understand how the work of a writer with such a 'coarse' mind could have achieved the status of 'real and acknowledged classic', A.O.J. Cockshut echoes and reinforces a certain tradition of thinking about Dickensian-authorial ignorance as he enumerates the 'handicaps' that he maintains are 'inherent' in Dickens's mind, including the fact that 'to the end of his days, he never came to understand himself or his own motives very well'.[46] My suggestion, though, is this: as critics have noted, *Great Expectations* is, from the very opening paragraph, concerned with the question of identity, the central question of the classic Victorian orphan narrative, in a sense its *only* question: who am I?[47] And – to put it crudely – who Pip *is* is determined in various ways by his own as well as by others' hands. Hands in *Great Expectations* are signifiers not so much of inner states – emotions, consciousness – but of culturally or socially negotiated identity: as Forker and others have noted, you can tell *who* someone is by looking at their hands (Pip's hands are, to his embarrassment and shame, 'coarse' (pp. 61, 63, 64); Jaggers's hands, which he compulsively cleans, are 'large', and his pockets contain secrets (pp. 81, 238); Miss Havisham's hands are, like her soul and her body, 'withered' (p. 82); Molly's hands are preternaturally 'strong', built as they might have been for murder by strangulation (p. 212); Estella's hands mark a genetic identity with her mother (p. 387); Joe's hands of course are 'blackened' – a sign of vocation rather than character as such, one which may be seen to work indeed in ironic opposition to his pure, un-'blackened' moral character (p. 281); Magwitch has 'large brown veinous hands' in accordance with his unnerving and vaguely repellent physical presence (p. 311)).

Despite their intensive concentration on hands in the novel, however, both Forker and Cohen refer only glancingly to what I take to be one of the most significant turns on, or with, hands: Matthew Pocket's renaming of Pip as 'Handel' – as if Pocket wants to put his friend 'in' himself, his Hand(el) in his Pocket.[48] There is a certain paronomastic logic of identity here and in the novel more generally that needs unpacking. Hands-in-pockets in fact occur in two other quite prominent ways in the novel – in ways, indeed, that might help to explain the narrative dream-logic of this renaming of Pip. Both occurrences have to do with the central question of Pip's ontology, the question of his personal identity. In the first place, in the famous opening scene Pip figures his siblings as having their hands permanently in their pockets (after death). He deciphers the characters of his family by the 'turn of the inscription' on their tombstones:

> To five little stone lozenges, each about a foot and a half long, which were arranged in a neat row beside their grave, and were sacred to the memory of five little brothers of mine – who gave up trying to get a living, exceedingly early in that universal struggle – I am indebted for a belief I religiously entertained that they had all been born on their backs with

their hands in their trousers-pockets, and had never taken them out in this state of existence. (p. 3)

Pip is addressing the question of his sense of self, of personal identity, in this opening scene (after moving out in a proto-cinematically panning description of the landscape, the third paragraph of the novel suddenly zooms in to conclude the opening soliloquacious meditation with the remark that 'the small bundle of shivers growing afraid of it all and beginning to cry, was Pip' (p. 4)), and he is preparing the way for a narrative which is all about attempts to figure (out) who he is. It is therefore clear that his sense of identity is at least partly determined by his controlling fantasy of the 'character' of members of his family. There is a kind of crooked logic – a form of what we can call narrative dream-logic – to the fact that in order perhaps to lay hold of or influence or grasp him, his friend, Pocket, later gives Pip the handle 'Handel',[49] with its pun on 'hand': Pip almost *becomes* what marks the character of his five brothers, a hand in a pocket (a Hand(el) within (the conception of) a Pocket).

The second example of the motif of hands-in-pockets also works through another kind of dream-logic to achieve a (perverse) sense for Pip of personal identity. In this case, it is a question of Pip's enemy, his nemesis, Orlick, who is described as habitually having his hands in his pockets (see pp. 110, 116). The link here to Pip's personal identity, his sense of self, comes through the question of whether Pip is able, finally, to know that he is *not* (like) Orlick, even that Orlick is not, finally, Pip.[50] The need to determine that he is *not* Orlick is a result of the fact that he might be since there are disturbing similarities between the two. In the first place, Orlick's name has a status very similar to Pip's. As Joe has it, 'Pip' is neither a Christian name nor a surname, but 'a kind of family name what he gave himself when a infant, and is called by' (p. 75). Orlick has a similarly fictitious name: 'he pretended that his Christian name was Dolge – a clear impossibility', the narrator (Pip) remarks (p. 110): both Orlick's and Pip's names are invented, impossible.[51] Furthermore, we learn that when Pip becomes Joe's apprentice, Orlick 'was perhaps confirmed in some suspicion that I should displace him' (p. 110), a comment that confirms the putative or potential identification of Orlick with Pip. But the identification is perhaps confirmed by Pip himself with regard to the attack on his sister. According to Pip's dream-logic – the dream-logic of the novel as a whole, indeed – it is not clear that Pip is not responsible for it. The attack apparently happens while Pip is listening to Wopsle reading the 'affecting tragedy of George Barnwell'

(p. 114). Although this act of enforced listening gives Pip an alibi for the attack, it also (paradoxically and counter-factually) implicates him in it. The tragedy that Wopsle insists on reading out (with the help of Pumblechook) concerns an apprentice (like Pip) who robs his employer and murders his own uncle. Pip's reaction to the reading is to associate himself with the murderer: 'What stung me', he comments, 'was the identification of the whole affair with my unoffending self . . . At once ferocious and maudlin, I was made to murder my uncle with no extenuating circumstances whatever' (p. 115). This is no doubt an internalization of the charge made by Wopsle and especially Pumblechook, who clearly identifies Pip with the murderous apprentice: '"Take warning, boy, take warning!"', Pumblechook warns, 'as if it were a well-known fact that I contemplated murdering a near relation' (p. 115). On his return home (accompanied by Orlick) Pip finds that his sister has been beaten 'by some unknown hand' (p. 117) in a 'murderous attack' (p. 129) and immediately blames himself:

> With my head full of George Barnwell, I was at first disposed to believe that *I* must have had some hand in the attack upon my sister, or at all events that as her near relation, popularly known to be under obligations to her, I was a more legitimate object of suspicion than any one else. (p. 117)

And this indeed is the charge that Orlick himself makes in an extension or playing out of the novel's dream-logic when he traps Pip in the sluice-house – that it is Pip's 'doing': 'It was you as did for your shrew sister . . . it was your doing . . . it was done through you . . . it warn't Old Orlick as did it; it was you' (p. 421). (Orlick's logic is that Pip was 'favoured' while Orlick was 'bullied and beat' (p. 421), a logic that in fact overlooks another parallel between the two: as Pip repeatedly insists, he was 'brought up by hand', a process that is remarkably similar to Orlick's experience of being 'bullied and beat'.)[52] Finally, Pip is like Orlick in that, while Orlick 'pursues' Biddy (p. 280), Biddy is the woman that Pip could have but (due to his 'great expectations') *failed* to pursue[53] – until it is too late.[54] The point here – the point of recalling these similarities between Pip and Orlick – is to suggest that the identificatory dream-logic of the novel involves the possibility that one's sense of self is constituted in relation to others both by opposition and by similarity. Orlick *is*, in a sense, Pip, another Pip. He expresses, as Julian Moynahan, Hilary M. Schor and others have argued, Pip's repressed desires and (or for) veiled or disavowed violence. And the fact that both Pip and the novel condemn

Orlick (he ends up in jail) seems to confirm Judith Butler's point about the way that condemnation works against the possibility of even partial self-knowledge. Although he writes a narrative of violence, Pip's disavowal of violence is by this reading a mask for his own violent impulses – which are articulated in his 'other', the pathologically and therefore irrationally violent Orlick.

But I want to suggest that, in accordance with Butler's analysis of the 'humility' involved in the acknowledgement of the other's 'opacity', the final purpose of Dickens's novel involves an acknowledgment of Pip as a moral being *despite* – or indeed *because of* – his opacity to himself. The novel suggests that we might acknowledge others just because in a fundamental sense these others don't know who they are, don't know themselves, so that we do not or cannot know them. Pip's failure to know others and himself (his failure to know himself *is* a failure to know others) is what this narrative is about ('The "I" is the moment of failure in every narrative effort to give an account of oneself', Butler declares (p. 37) – even while this very otherness to myself itself *constitutes* myself, my 'I', as well as 'the source of my ethical connection with others' (p. 37)). Ethically and in terms of the violence that is 'neither a just punishment we suffer nor a just revenge for what we suffer' we are, Butler puts it, 'in each other's hands' (p. 39).

Judgement, then, and ethics, and violence. The problem of the other in *Great Expectations* – the problem of the self and others, the self as other – is perhaps most economically expressed as Magwitch dies in prison, and in Pip's response:

> Mindful, then, of what we had read together, I thought of the two men who went up into the Temple to pray, and I knew there were no better words that I could say beside his bed, than 'O Lord be merciful to him, a sinner!' (p. 455)

Pip's misquotation from Luke 18: 13 transfers the mercy begged for from 'me' to 'him': be merciful to *me* says the tax collector, not him.[55] There is a surreptitious replacement of the other for the self here that may be said metonymically to stand for the procedure of the novel, for the whole 'autobiography', and it is one that links up importantly with self-knowledge, with knowing the self. The question the novel raises – the question that critics have never failed to discuss while always failing to resolve – is the question of the autobiographer's knowledge or ignorance of himself. Is it the case, as Hilary Schor suggests, not only that Pip is an 'insufferable' young man but that he 'remains insufferable to the end of the novel'?[56] Jeremy Tambling cites a comment by Dickens from his '*Copperfield* period': 'I know how all these things have worked together to make me what I am',[57] and argues that this is precisely what is *not* suggested of the protagonist in *Great Expectations* – a novel in which 'the expectation that the hero will learn through experience is belied'.[58] To the extent that Pip is Charles Dickens (and to a large extent of course he is nothing of the sort) this might be linked to A.O.J. Cockshut's sense that the novelist 'never came to understand himself or his own motives very well'. The assumption is that the hero of a narrative as well as that narrative itself should be able – and therefore that *we*, we readers, should be able – to 'understand' the hero's motives 'very well'. But perhaps, as Butler and others suggest, we can't – and perhaps this opacity of selfhood is intrinsic to one's ethical relation to the other, part of what Butler boldly and very properly calls 'life'. Such a hypothesis might then help us to think about the violence that is both endemic and extreme in Dickens's novel. Violence, which in this novel is almost exclusively an effect of *hands*, infects and affects almost every character and is evident in almost every turn of the novel's plotting. The novel opens, indeed, with the threat of violence from Magwitch, the escaped convict, and with Pip being violently grasped and turned upside down. But it doesn't stop there, and lines of violence can be traced from character to character and from plot-event to plot-event. On two occasions Magwitch is portrayed as locked in mortal combat with his nemesis Compeyson, the final fight ending in the (eventual) death of both men. Pip is also the subject of violence at the hands of his sister, whose bringing up by hand involves, above all, acts of 'battery'. And Pip in turn subjects Herbert Pocket to violence (comically, it should be said, and at Pocket's instigation) at their first meeting at Satis House. Although Joe is also subject to Mrs Joe's batterings, and although he is by nature gentle, passive, he is easily able to overcome, by violence, his employee, Orlick, when necessary. Orlick himself attacks Mrs Joe and leaves her for dead; he also breaks into Pumblechook's house and, together with his accomplices and in a Quentin Tarantino-style pantomime performance of violence that may itself be read as an encoding of extreme violence, slaps Pumblechook's face, pulls his nose, and stuffs flowers into his mouth; and he traps and tries to kill Pip in the sluice-house before himself being physically overwhelmed by Pip's allies. Molly fights with and kills her rival with her bare hands. And Bentley Drummle, Pip's other rival, severely beats Estella, beats her into a kind of proud submissiveness, once he has married her.

But perhaps the most curious act of violence is that which brings together the potential for both violence and tenderness contained in, and in *Great Expectations* explicitly articulated by, the hand. It occurs in a moment of nescience that is also manual, and that is centred on Pip's own actions. On his last visit to see Miss Havisham, Pip looks back as he is leaving, only to see his putative patron, and tormentor, in flames. He tries to put out the flames with two coats and a table cloth:

> that we were on the ground struggling like desperate enemies, and that the closer I covered her, the more wildly she shrieked and tried to free herself; that this occurred I knew through the result, but not through anything I felt, or thought, or knew I did. I knew nothing until I knew that we were on the floor by the great table, and that patches of tinder yet alight were floating in the smoky air, which, a moment ago, had been her faded bridal dress.
> ... I still held her forcibly down with all my strength, like a prisoner who might escape; and I doubt if I even knew who she was, or why we struggled, or that she had been in flames, or that the flames were out, until I saw the patches of tinder that had been her garments, no longer alight but falling in a black shower around us. (pp. 397–8)

By the end of the battle, the fire is out, Miss Havisham is mortally injured, and Pip's hands are seriously burnt: 'I was astonished to see that both my hands were burnt', he remarks, 'for, I had no knowledge of it through the sense of feeling' (p. 398). In (this) violence there is a certain nescience – an ignorance even as to the status of the violence itself, as to whether or not it is violence, or whether instead it is not finally an act of tenderness, of redress, of comfort, of love. In this most intimate manual relation with the other, this expression of the relation of violence that seems to move and motivate the novel, in this violent attachment, there is a final ignorance, a not knowing what one is doing, and a certain forgiveness that seems to be offered precisely in or as a result of that nescience.

What is Pip saying in the opening scene of the novel when he reads the family tombstones in the churchyard, other than: 'I am not me, therefore I am'; or 'I do not know who "I" am; I am only as an other, therefore "I" am'? He constitutes himself, his 'I', in this inaugural address, this inaugural act of reading and identification, only as opaque to himself and as therefore constituted by his (necessarily inadequate, failed, ignorant) understanding of others. He constitutes himself as a subject through his *ignorance – not* through any knowledge – of others, of other people.

Looking at others, or looking at least at their final, posthumous traces, at all that can be seen of them, at their gravestones, at what is (not) left of them, he says: that which I am not and don't know must be what I am. And, as Jacques Lacan would predict, the rest of Pip's life (which means the rest of his autobiographical narrative) is dedicated to obtaining and fixing on supplements for this misrecognition of the self – as blacksmith, beneficiary, lover, friend, brother, criminal, *petit bourgeois*, businessman, narrator ... although never, we might note, as novelist. He is saying 'I don't know who I am; I will therefore have to account for myself, name myself, by reference to others, whom I also don't know'.

And is this not finally the condition of each of us? That we know not who we are and therefore account for ourselves by appealing to unknown others? Is that not finally who we must be, who I am, what it must mean to be me, what it must mean for you to be you – some version of this profound sense of uncertainty, this interpersonal (mis-)identificatory nescience?

Notes

1 See Emmanuel Levinas's comment that 'knowledge as perception, concept, comprehension, refers back to an act of grasping ... The immanence of the known to the act of knowing is already the embodiment of seizure' ('Ethics as First Philosophy', trans. Seán Hand and Michael Temple, in *The Levinas Reader*, ed. Seán Hand (Oxford: Basil Blackwell, 1989), p. 76; see also *Totality and Infinity: An Essay on Exteriority*, trans. Alphonso Lingis (Pittsburg: Duquesne University Press, 1969), p. 80: 'a being is in relation with what it cannot absorb, with what it cannot, in the etymological sense of the term, comprehend' (quoted in Philip Weinstein, *Unknowing: The Work of Modernist Fiction* (Ithaca: Cornell University Press, 2005), p. 257). For a lucid overview of the history of the question of other minds in analytical philosophy see Anita Avramides, *Other Minds* (London: Routledge, 2001).
2 See Pam Morris on the use of free indirect discourse in *Middlemarch*: 'psychological realism is functioning here to confirm the availability of knowledge' of others (*Realism* (London: Routledge, 2003), p. 117). On the 'easy transitions from mind to mind' that characterize realist fiction see Lilian R. Furst, *All Is True: The Claims and Strategies of Realist Fiction* (Durham: Duke University Press, 1995), ch. 6 (p. 120). See also Brigid Lowe's argument that the aim of the Victorian novel is 'to transcend as far as possible the limits of individual experience' and to evoke sympathy for others (*Victorian Fiction and the Insights of Sympathy: An Alternative to the Hermeneutics of Suspicion* (London: Anthem Press, 2007), ch. 2 (p. 103). A more general case for reading fiction as a way of knowing others has recently been made by Lisa Zunshine

in the context of contemporary cognitive psychology in *Why We Read Fiction: Theory of Mind and the Novel* (Columbia: The Ohio State University Press, 2006).

3 See Philip Weinstein's comment on realist fiction as a genre that attempts to rectify the 'lopsided' Cartesian conception of knowledge (whereby 'the individual occupies a prior space of inner being; what is outside this space is speculative'), but ends up in 'its most revealing moments' looking as if it were 'a creature whose feet moved resolutely in the opposite direction of its arms' (*Unknowing*, p. 44). Nevertheless, for Weinstein, recognition – a version of Aristotelian *anagnorisis* – 'enacts realism's cardinal premise ... that human life takes on precious focus in time' (p. 66); the 'fundamental assumption' in realist fiction is 'the value of *knowing*' (p. 82). For a view that contrasts with (and is much more positive than) my own see Martha C. Nussbaum, 'The Window: Knowledge of Other Minds in Virginia Woolf's *To the Lighthouse*', *New Literary History* 26 (1995): 731–53: Nussbaum argues that the novel allows an ethical rather than epistemological take on the philosophical question of other minds.

4 Robert Pinsky, *Democracy, Culture and the Voice of Poetry* (Princeton: Princeton University Press, 2002), p. 39.

5 On the misnaming of narrators as 'omniscient' see Jonathan Culler, *The Literary in Theory* (Stanford: Stanford University Press, 2007), ch. 8, and Nicholas Royle, *The Uncanny* (London: Routledge, 2003), ch. 10: Royle suggests that the term and idea of 'telepathy' is a more accurate way of conceiving of the kinds of third-person narrators that have access to others' minds.

6 See Daniel C. Dennett's glancingly suggestive comment on the 'wonderful novels of the eighteenth and nineteenth centuries' as producing 'models' for 'theories of mind' – including especially, I would suggest, theories of others people's minds (*Breaking the Spell: Religion as a Natural Phenomenon* (London: Allen Lane, 2006), p. 396n. And see Dorrit Cohn, *Transparent Minds: Narrative Modes for Presenting Consciousness in Fiction* (Princeton: Princeton University Press, 1978), on this as an important structural feature of narrative fiction.

7 On free indirect discourse see Roy Pascal, *The Dual Voice: Free Indirect Speech and Its Functioning in the Nineteenth-Century Novel* (Manchester: Manchester University Press, 1977).

8 Stanley Cavell, *Philosophy the Day After Tomorrow* (Cambridge, Mass.: Harvard University Press, 2005), p. 150.

9 My equivocation in this sentence between substitution and supplementation is of course a crucial one: do we add to our knowledge of others through our sense of these external markers, or do these markers, these signs of inner life, in fact constitute a necessary substitution of such knowledge, standing in for what we can never know?

10 Quoted in Kerry McSweeney, *Middlemarch* (London: Allen and Unwin, 1984), p. 119.
11 Henry James, review of *Middlemarch*, in the *Galaxy* (March 1873), reprinted in Patrick Swinden, ed., *George Eliot, 'Middlemarch': A Casebook* (London: Macmillan, 1972), pp. 67–8.
12 The general or scientific knowledge embedded in the novel was in fact itself a cause of mild complaint in at least one review: 'We all grumble at *Middlemarch*', grumbles the anonymous reviewer (possibly R.H. Hutton), 'we all say that the action is slow, that there is too much parade of scientific and especially physiological knowledge in it' (review in the *Spectator* 1 June 1872, in Patrick Swinden, ed., *George Eliot, 'Middlemarch'*, p. 34).
13 Felicia Bonaparte, 'Introduction', in George Eliot, *Middlemarch*, ed. David Carroll (Oxford: Oxford University Press, 1998), pp. viii–ix: further references to this Introduction will be cited in the text; quotations from the novel are from this edition.
14 That the novel is about, in the first place, modes of knowing, about education, and therefore indeed about the social construction of (gendered) ignorance, is made very clear in a passage from the final page of the novel in the first edition (deleted in subsequent editions) on the 'modes of education which make a woman's knowledge another name for motley ignorance' (*Middlemarch*, p. 810). It is, after all, a novel that is concerned with the fact that, as the narrator comments, 'We are all of us born in moral stupidity, taking the world as an udder to feed our supreme selves' (p. 198), and with the distance from that postnatal condition that we can gain over a life time.
15 See Kay Young, '*Middlemarch* and the Problem of Other Minds Heard', *Literature Interpretation Theory* 14 (2003): 224, on Eliot's work as a project of epistemological questioning: 'George Eliot meditates on the nature of consciousness throughout her works of fiction with the insistence of a philosopher who cannot end the meditation. What does it mean to know? How does one know? These are the questions that structure Eliot's epistemological search.' Young argues that in *Middlemarch*, Eliot 'shifts' her investigation from the question 'what do *I* know' to 'what do I know of *you*?' (ibid.), and that access to others is achieved and that it is achieved most of all through the intimacy of sound. The problem of other minds is indeed announced early in the first chapter: 'So much subtler is a human mind', the narrator comments, 'than the outside tissues which makes a sort of blazonry or clock-face for it' (p. 9).
16 George Eliot, *Selected Essays, Poems and Other Writings*, ed. A.S. Byatt and Nicholas Warren (London: Penguin, 1990), p. 110.
17 George Eliot, *Middlemarch*, ed. Bert G. Hornback (New York: Norton, 1977), p. 648.
18 Swinden, ed., *George Eliot, 'Middlemarch'*, p. 55.
19 Ibid., p. 63; see also p. 64.

20 Ibid., pp. 100, 105, 166, 187.
21 Barbara Hardy, *The Appropriate Form: An Essay on the Novel* (London: Athlone, 1964), p. 121. For Hardy, it is when Will and Dorothea are together 'physically or in thoughts of each other, that the romantic glow seems false and the childlike innocence implausible and inappropriate' (p. 128). In an intriguing biographical study Richard Ellmann suggests that the 'flaw' in the novel might be explained by the fact that Ladislaw's original is a version of George Eliot's future husband, the young John Cross. According to Ellmann this would link Ladislaw directly with the question of ignorance since one of the attractions of Cross was his intellectual difference from Eliot's husband G.H. Lewes: Cross, Ellmann explains, was 'the opposite of her husband, and of most of her old friends, in knowing nothing ... of works in ancient languages, in metaphysics, or in science' ('Dorothea's Husbands', in Hornback, ed., *Middlemarch*, p. 763).
22 W.J. Harvey, Introduction to George Eliot's *Middlemarch* (Harmondsworth: Penguin, 1965), p. 21.
23 Kerry McSweeney agrees with Hardy, and implicitly with Harvey, when he comments that the chapter is 'not nearly as powerful and satisfying as many readers (including myself) would have liked it to be' because Eliot 'has scripted the scene to point up the childlike qualities of Dorothea and Will'; as he continues, 'the script fails to include any detailed notation of Dorothea's thoughts and feelings', and it indicates that Eliot is attempting to 'play down' the suggestion of Dorothea's 'active desire' in part at least in order to maintain a sense of her selflessness (*Middlemarch*, p. 117). For a partially dissenting view on the failure of the Lasdislaw character and on chapter 83 in particular see Laurence Lerner's 1967 essay 'Dorothea and the Theresa-Complex' (reprinted in Swinden, ed., *George Eliot, Middlemarch*, pp. 225–47): 'The scene in which they finally come together', Lerner argues, 'is moving and convincing, and to wish it away would be cynically to refuse one of George Eliot's genuine successes' – although even for Lerner it can be criticized for replacing 'a human relationship by an idealised ending' (p. 242).
24 Harvey, 'Introduction', p. 21.
25 Ibid., p. 21.
26 In one of her most extraordinary and idiosyncratic literary productions, *The Lifted Veil* (published in 1878), Eliot presents rather different objections to the possibility of our knowledge of others, in a text which, in so many ways (length, subject matter, narrative style and focus and so on) seem so markedly un-Eliot-like. The novella concerns Latimer's tortured clairvoyance, his 'unhappy gift' or 'curse' of 'insight', his 'wretched knowledge' of others, his 'diseased participation in other people's consciousness', and his recognition that his love for Birtha can be sustained only on condition of the 'real interest' in her provoked by his 'ignorance' (*The Lifted Veil* (London: Virago, 1985), pp. 21, 23, 26, 66): Birtha is therefore his 'oasis of mystery in the dreary desert

of knowledge' (p. 26); 'ready dullness, healthy selfishness, good-tempered conceit – these are the keys to happiness', he concludes (p. 37).

27 Karlin argues that 'psychological acuteness' is 'what the novel is famous for' and that this is in fact 'one of the defining elements of realist fiction'. He suggests that this acuteness is often signified by comments on characters' hands. As he comments, 'some of the novelist's most heightened or poignant passages are marked by the touch of hands'; and he notes that character is itself often designated by the look of individuals' hands (Daniel Karlin, 'Having the Whip Hand in *Middlemarch*', in Alice Jenkins and Juliet John, eds, *Rereading Victorian Fiction* (London: Palgrave, 2000), p. 31). Karlin does not, however, pay particular attention to chapter 83; nor does he link the attention paid to hands in the novel with psychological anepistemology, as I am trying to do here.

28 By contrast, the head and the heart, those other body-parts that are the focus for passion, are mentioned only four and two times respectively.

29 Karlin alludes briefly to this fact without elaborating on it when he comments that each of the stages of the 'culminating scene' in this chapter is 'marked by the holding or releasing of hands' ('Having the Whip Hand', p. 31).

30 This is made clear when it comes to Dorothea and Will's first trembling, impulsive kiss: 'Her lips trembled, and so did his. It was never known which lips were the first to move towards the other lips; but they kissed tremblingly, and then they moved apart' (p. 761). Again, the passive tense denotes a certain passivity and the whole action is reminiscent, in effect, of the neurophysiologist Benjamin Libet's recent work on the idea that the brain (or 'unconscious') begins to work prior to the subject's awareness that she will act, before any 'conscious' decision has been made (see *Mind Time: Temporal Factors in Consciousnesss* (Cambridge, Mass.: Harvard University Press, 2004)): you begin to act, in other words, before you know it, or before you know you are going to act. Interestingly, Libet links this with 'creativity', and with speech and writing, all of which, he suggests, are 'likely to be initiated unconsciously' (p. 108; see also pp. 96–7 and 107–9). It is perhaps not coincidental that contemporary with the writing of *Middlemarch* Shadworth Holloway Hodgson published *The Theory of Practice* (1870), which outlines a theory of epiphenomenalism (a theory made popular by Thomas Henry Huxley in his 1874 paper 'On the Hypothesis that Animals are Automata, and Its History'); or that George Henry Lewes was intimately involved in debates over the nature of the mind, the brain and consciousness (in *Physiology of Common Life* (1859/1860) and *Problems of Life and Mind* (1874–79)). In *Middlemarch* this nescient act also produces a moment of marked narratorial or authorial nescience, since the passive voice suggests that it is not, in the end, *for* Dorothea or Will to know this, but for the narrator or author – who herself remains unknowing.

31 Compare Dorothea Barrett's rather curious suggestion that although the pathetic fallacy has been used throughout the novel to 'illuminate Dorothea's

state of mind', it here 'echoes' the author's and the reader's 'discontent with the impending union' (*Vocation and Desire: George Eliot's Heroines* (London: Routledge, 1989), p. 140).

32 The pun is adapted from a phrase by Jean Laplanche that I discuss below (see Chapter 7).

33 Even in the final moment of decision, of the impulsive acceptance of each other's hand in marriage and rejection of the dead hand of Casaubon's will, hands are at work, although here silently at work, at work without words: Dorothea impulsively declares that she can live without her widow's inheritance: 'In an instant Will was close to her and had his arms round her, but she drew her head back and held his away gently that she might go on speaking' (p. 762). Hands are *not* mentioned here, but in the context of a chapter that compulsively observes their doings, they are still silently at work: if Will's arms are around Dorothea then his hands are presumably holding her too; and what does Dorothea hold Will's head back *with* if it is not with her hands? In this intimacy of touch there is finally no need even to say the word 'hand', since hands, lovers' hands are, so to speak, everywhere.

34 Judith Butler, 'Giving an Account of Oneself', *Diacritics* 31: 4 (2001): 22 (published in 2004): further references to this essay are cited in the text. Butler gives a useful summary of Lacanian notions of the ignorant subject – or the subject of ignorance – in an interview from 2000: Lacan's sense that 'the subject is produced on the condition of a foreclosure' means that 'there would always be a lack of self-understanding for any subject; that there would be no way to recover one's origins or to understand oneself fully . . . because the foreclosure of the past . . . is the condition of the subject itself. So, I come into being as the condition that I am radically unknowing about my origins, and that unknowingness is the condition of my coming into being – and it afflicts me. And if I seek to undo that [to undo that ignorance], I also lose myself as a subject; I become undone, and I become psychotic as a result' (Interview with Gary A. Olson and Lyn Worham, reprinted in Sara Salih, ed., *The Judith Butler Reader* (Oxford: Blackwell, 2004), p. 332). In 'Giving an Account of Oneself', Butler draws in particular on Cavarero's *Relating Narratives: Storytelling and Selfhood*, trans. Paul A. Kottman (London: Routledge, 2000); Cavarero in turn draws on Hannah Arendt's *The Human Condition* (Chicago: University of Chicago Press, 1958) and *The Life of the Mind* (New York: Harcourt and Brace, 1971).

35 See Weinstein, *Unknowing*, p. 4, on the idea that 'modernist narrative involves the discovery, not of who one is . . . but that one is other': it is my suggestion that this recognition cannot be restricted to 'modernist' narrative (Weinstein focuses on Proust, Kafka and Faulkner) but is part of an epistemological crisis implicit in Romantic and post-Romantic poetics more generally.

36 See George Eliot's objection to Dickens in 'The Natural History of German Life': while Dickens is 'gifted with the utmost power of rendering the external

traits of our town population', she says, he fails to properly represent their 'psychological character – their conceptions of life, and their emotions' (p. 111).

37 *Great Expectations* illustrates this contract in a remark that Pip makes about Biddy: 'Why it came natural to me' to tell Biddy 'everything' and why 'Biddy had a deep concern in everything I told her', Pip comments, 'I did not know then, though I think I know now' (Charles Dickens, *Great Expectations*, ed. Margaret Cardwell (Oxford: Oxford University Press, 1998), p. 94: quotations from the novel are from this edition). The remark itself denotes the structural assumptions of autobiography.

38 Butler, 'Giving an Account', pp. 33, 35. See also Michael Sprinker, 'Fictions of the Self: The End of Autobiography', in James Olney, ed., *Autobiography: Essays Theoretical and Critical* (Princeton: Princeton University Press, 1980), p. 334: 'If autobiography can be described as the self's enquiry into its own history – the self-conscious questioning by the subject of itself – then Nietzsche offers the most fearful warning for any autobiographical text: "The danger of the direct questioning of the subject *about* the subject and of all self-reflection of the subject lies in this, that it could be useful and important for one's activity to interpret oneself *falsely*".' As Sprinker goes on to remark, 'In the present century no one has taken this admonition more seriously than Freud'.

39 Charles R. Forker, 'The Language of Hands in *Great Expectations*', *Texas Studies in Literature and Language* 3 (1961): 280–93 (280).

40 Ibid., p. 281. As Forker comments, 'the obvious utility of hand symbolism in a novel where one of the major themes is manipulation – the treatment of people like things – can be abundantly illustrated in *Great Expectations*' (p. 285).

41 Ibid., p. 293. For an almost contemporaneous assessment of hands in the novel see also Jack B. Moore, 'Hearts and Hands in *Great Expectations*', *The Dickensian* 61 (1965): 52–6.

42 William A. Cohen, 'Manual Conduct in *Great Expectations*', *English Literary History* 60 (1993): 217–59 (p. 221).

43 Although I would also concede that there is a certain force in Valentine Cunningham's scathing satire on Cohen's reading in *Reading After Theory* (Oxford: Blackwell, 2002), pp. 99–105.

44 Such certainties are, in fact, more in evidence and less guarded or qualified in Cohen's work than in Sedgwick's. 'How can we make the silences [the Victorian silences about sex] speak?', Cohen asks, and answers his own question decisively: 'Precisely through attention to the rhetoric of unspeakability: such tropes as periphrasis, euphemism, and indirection give rise to signifying practices that fill in these enforced absences' (Cohen, 'Manual Conduct', p. 221): rather like the Freudian charge of 'disavowal', the logic of this would involve a (Foucauldian) double bind – the less you speak about sex the more you are (really) speaking about it.

45 Maurice Blanchot, *The Space of Literature*, trans. Ann Smock (Lincoln: University of Nebraska Press, 1982), p. 192.
46 A.O.J. Cockshut, *The Imagination of Charles Dickens* (New York: New York University Press, 1962), p. 11.
47 See Jeremy Tambling's comments that *Great Expectations* 'recognizes itself to be about the creation of identities, imposed from higher to lower, from oppressor to oppressed' ('Prison-Bound: Dickens and Foucault (*Great Expectations*)', in Stephen Connor, ed., *Charles Dickens* (Harlow: Longman, 1996), p. 124); Catherine Waters on *Great Expectations* as an 'autobiographical narrative apparently devoted to the faithful record of Pip's quest to establish his own identity' (*Dickens and the Politics of the Family* (Cambridge: Cambridge University Press, 1997), p. 173); and Hilary M. Schor on the novel as an autobiography with 'its requisite story of identity' (*Dickens and the Daughter of the House* (Cambridge: Cambridge University Press, 1999), p. 153.
48 See Cohen, 'Manual Conduct', p. 241. Forker maintains that Pocket's 'affectionate sobriquet' for his friend 'ironically summarised by a kind of pun the combined forces of manipulation – Mrs. Gargery, Wopsle, Miss Havisham, Estella, Magwitch – which have helped to make him what he is' ('The Language of Hands', p. 287), but fails to develop the renaming further.
49 The *OED* suggest that the colloquial phrase 'a handle to one's name' ('a title of rank, honour, or courtesy attached to a name') enters the language in the early nineteenth century (1833 is the first citation), and quotes the rather self-conscious use of the phrase from Thackeray's 1855 novel *The Newcomes* ('She ... entertained us with stories ... mentioning no persons but those who "had handles to their names", as the phrase is' ('handle', sb.4a). From this follows the slang sense of 'handle' as a personal name or nickname, which the *OED*, gives as its first citation from 1870. It seems likely, anyway, that the association of 'handle' (or Handel) and name is not entirely anachronistic in *Great Expectations*.
50 See Julian Moynahan's discussion of the 'peculiar parallel between the careers of the two characters' ('The Hero's Guilt: The Case of *Great Expectations*' (*Essays in Criticism* 10 (1960), p. 65), and of Orlick as Pip's '*alter ego*' or 'shadow' (p. 67), or as his 'double, *alter ego* and dark mirror-image' (p. 69), or his suggestion even of a 'complex unity' of crime and guilt that he calls 'Pip-Orlick' (70). In an interesting analysis of violence in the novel Schor suggests that Pip 'never sees himself as violent', instead displacing his violent impulses onto others: 'Orlick avenges Pip by beating Mrs Joe', while Bentley, who is himself uncannily *like* Orlick, 'accomplish[es] Pip's metaphorical ravishing of Estella, marrying the woman who doesn't truly love him, then literally beating her into submission' (*Dickens and the Daughter*, p. 172) (as Schor comments, by the end of the novel Bentley Drummle's violence towards Estella has succeeded in transforming her into 'a woman who can love Pip' (p. 173)). On Drummle as a 'reduplication' of Orlick and as

standing in 'the same analogical relationship to Pip as Orlick does' see Moynahan, 'The Hero's Guilt', p. 73: both, for Moynahan, are Pip's 'instruments of vengeance' (p. 74). Indeed, on at least one occasion, Drummle's appearance explicitly reminds Pip of Orlick (see *Great Expectations*, p. 354).

51 Another identification that Pip seeks to avoid – with Magwitch – is also mediated through assumed names: as an escaped convict, Magwitch assumes the name of Provis (see p. 326); but his sense of how he came originally, as a child, to know that his name was Abel Magwitch also has a source just as fanciful as Pip's assumption of 'Pip': he knew it 'Much as I know'd the birds' names in the hedges to be chaffinch, sparrer, thrush', he says (p. 342) – that is, by knowing it without knowing it.

52 See Moynahan's comment that the situation is 'absurd', as a dream can be, but that 'like a dream it may contain a hidden truth' ('The Hero's Guilt', p. 66) – and more directly, that the anomaly of Pip's belief in his own guilt and Orlick's 'relative lack of motive' can 'best be resolved on the assumption that Orlick acts merely as Pip's primitive instrument or weapon' (p. 72).

53 See ch. 17, especially pp. 126, 128.

54 See p. 467.

55 The point is made by Moynahan in 'The Hero's Guilt', p. 61.

56 Schor, *Dickens and the Daughter*, p. 154. See also p. 170 on the novel as a 'mystery' novel, with its 'necessary return', which is 'to revisit sites once of ignorance, now of knowledge'. As James A. Davies comments, Pip reveals a '*persisting* lack of self-knowledge' (*The Textual Life of Dickens's Characters* (Basingstoke: Macmillan, 1989), p. 95: italics added). Compare Moynahan's comment that the 'profoundest irony of the novel is not reached until the reader realises he must see Pip in a much harsher moral perspective than Pip ever saw himself' ('The Hero's Guilt', p. 71) – as this suggests, critics often *do* (attempt to) resolve this dilemma.

57 Tambling, 'Prison-Bound', p. 129, citing John Forster, *The Life of Charles Dickens* (London: Dent, 1969), 1: 32.

58 Ibid., p. 132.

6

Joseph Conrad's blindness

> The only indisputable truth of life is our ignorance. Besides this there is nothing evident, nothing absolute, nothing uncontradicted.[1]

Joseph Conrad 'never wrote a true short story', declares Ford Madox Ford in his memoir of his friend and collaborator.[2] Ford goes on to explain his sense of a 'true short story' as 'a matter of two or three pages of minutely considered words, ending with a smack ... with what the French call a *coup de canon*'. Conrad instead wrote '"long-short" stories', Ford argues, a form that is 'practically the same as that of the novel'. Ford gives as examples of short story-writers Maupassant, Chekhov and O. Henry, writers whose tales are 'practically stereotyped – the introduction of character in a word or two, a word or two for atmosphere, a few paragraphs for story, and then, click! a sharp sentence that flashes the illumination of the idea over the whole'. According to Ford, the reason for Conrad's inability to write such stories is summed up by the 'mystic word "justification"', the need to make the action seem inevitable because of a protagonist's 'character, because of his ancestry, because of past illness or on account of the gradual coming together of the thousand small circumstances by which Destiny ... will push us into one certain predicament'.[3]

As Ford's comments suggest, the problem of the short story for Conrad has to do simply with its shortness.[4] Length is, so to speak, a capital problem for Conrad: it would be in his interest to make *Lord Jim* as short as possible, he declares to David Meldrum in October 1899, 'but I would just as soon think of cutting off my head'.[5] Moreover, word-length in Conrad's writing has the practical financial dimension that, as a writer chronically short of cash, he relied on his writing, paid by the word, for an income. Conrad's letters of c.1898–1902 – his major period of short-story writing (or, more precisely, his period of major short-story writing) – display his intense concern with the rate of pay per thousand words from *Blackwood's* and other publishers of his fiction, but while, as Zdzisław Najder points out, short stories paid 'incomparably better than novels', the longer the (short) story the greater its financial worth.[6] In response to such tensions both within the demands of his art and between the artistic and the financial stringencies under which he was working, Conrad's early work articulates what we might term an optical pathology of composition. Discussing his 1902 long-short story 'The End of the Tether', Conrad links the shortness of the short story to the reader's ability properly to understand, properly to see the text, suggesting that the problem of length – the problem of word-length – in Conrad's fiction is also a problem of vision: 'I depend upon the reader *looking back* upon my story as a whole', he writes to David Meldrum. 'This is why I prefer the form which needs for its development 30000 words or so. When it runs into 120 thou: – like *Jim*', he goes on, 'it reaches failure' (*Letters* 2: 441).[7] In this sense, Conrad makes impossible demands on his own 'art' (as he calls it): to write at length is to 'fail' but to shorten his stories, to write short – truly short – stories is akin to authorial decapitation. Conrad's writing, that is to say, and his composition of short fiction, of short stories, requires a certain kind of readerly gaze, and the ability properly to look is explicitly related to the *brevity* of his fictions. But Conrad's writing also involves a certain blindness, a certain inability properly to see – a condition that Conrad refers to as 'optical delusions' (*Letters* 2: 230–1) – which makes his fiction work but which works at the same time against authorial and readerly vision. And the problem of optical delusions may indeed be said to characterize many of the key episodes in some of his most well-known short stories, including of course the '"long-short" stories' 'Heart of Darkness', 'The End of the Tether' and 'The Secret Sharer'.

In this chapter, therefore, I want to look at the problem of literary ignorance from the perspective of the nature of narrative form, in particular the narrative form of Conrad's short stories, and to suggest that a literary agnoiology would be able to account at least in part for the problem of Conrad's fiction and its relation to his life. Not to be able to see – nescience in that sense – is intrinsic not only to the thematics of Conrad's 'short' fiction and to his life, indeed, but also to the nature of short-story writing, to the process of composition, and to Conrad's poetics of the short (and long) story. It is through ignorance, by means of a certain compositional nescience, that Conrad's stories get written.

Conrad almost invariably underestimated the length of his stories.[8] While he obsessively estimates and re-estimates the word-length of his stories and novels, he never gets the word-count right. Between 1894 to 1902, for example, Conrad unerringly underestimates the length of his tales as he is writing them: in October 1894, Conrad estimates the 110,00-word *An Outcast of the Islands* at 36,000 words (*Letters* 1: 184; trans. 1: 185); in October 1896, he estimates the 55,000-word *The Nigger of the 'Narcissus'* at 30,000 words (*Letters* 1: 310); in September 1897, he estimates the 150,000-word *The Rescue* at 85–100,000 words (*Letters* 1: 380); in December 1898, he estimates the 35,000-word 'Heart of Darkness' at under 20,000 words (*Letters* 2: 140); between May 1898 and May 1900, he estimates the 130,000-word *Lord Jim* at between 13,000 and 100,000 words (*Letters* 2: 62, 166, 168, 184, 191, 271, 274); in May 1898, he estimates the 135,000-word *Chance* at 5,000 words (*Letters* 2: 62); in January and October 1900 respectively, he estimates the 25,000-word 'Typhoon' at 20,000 and 12,000 words (*Letters* 2: 237, 295); between May 1898 and June 1902, he estimates the 47,000-word 'The End of the Tether' at between 5,000 and 30,000 words (*Letters* 2: 62, 237, 376, 411, 413, 423, 429, 434); in October 1900, he estimates the 25,000-word 'Falk' at 5,000 words (*Letters* 2: 295); in January 1902, he estimates the 9,000-word 'Tomorrow' at 6,000 words (*Letters* 2: 367). In each case, the story gradually increases in length as Conrad proceeds with it, despite his own estimations and in spite of his own best efforts. As Owen Knowles comments, this process of gradual and tortuous accretion – the production of what Knowles calls the 'runaway' novel, and Conrad's inability properly to limit his gradually expanding texts, texts that expand always beyond the author's own repeatedly revised estimations – were clearly integral to his compositional practice. Such 'compositional stops and starts', Knowles suggests, are 'not so much an interruption of creative rhythms as conditions that came to be strangely essential to them'.[9] His inability clearly to discern the end of a story through the fog of writing is a problem to which Conrad himself confesses: writing to Ford in April 1901, for example, he declares that he is 'finishing' 'Falk' but that 'with me such a statement may mean anything' (*Letters* 2: 327). And writing in December to William Blackwood about *Lord Jim*, he decisively brings together this concern over the length of his narratives with the problem of eyesight. Reassuring his publisher seven months before he finally completes the novel that it is 'progressing' and stating rather vaguely that 'in five more days' time it will be still nearer the end which seems well in view now', Conrad admits that he 'suffer[s]' at times from optical delusions . . . where my work is concerned': 'Lord Jim', 'Heart of Darkness' and 'Youth', he suggests, will make a 'homogeneous book' because they are all 'inspired by a similar moral idea' – 'or is it only one of my optical delusions?', he asks (*Letters* 2: 230–1).

Since Conrad's most famous comment on his own work – the declaration in the Preface to *The Nigger of the 'Narcissus'* that 'My task . . . is, by the power of the written word to make you hear, to make you feel – it is, before all, to make you *see*'[10] – involves a figuration of writing as a mode of envisioning, critics have not been slow to link the poetics of Conrad's narratives to the question of vision.[11] Indeed, it is true that Conrad's literary judgements typically involve the question of eyesight, of seeing: to write, for Conrad, is to see and to make the reader see. Gabriela Cunninghame Graham's *Santa Teresa* (1894) 'makes one *see* and reflect', he tells the author's husband in a letter (*Letters* 2: 30). Similarly, writing to Cunninghame Graham's mother about her son's travel book *The Journey in Morocco*, he declares that the book is 'a contribution not towards mere knowledge but towards *truth* – to the *truth* hidden in men – in things – in life – in nature – to the truth only exceptional men can see, and not every exceptional man can present to the ordinary dim eyes of the crowd'. Cunninghame Graham is, he goes on, 'unapproachable in acuteness of vision' (*Letters* 2: 15). 'One can always *see* a lot in your work', he tells H.G. Wells, apparently without irony in reference to *The Invisible Man* (*Letters* 2: 126), and a year later he again flatters Wells in similar terms by saying how much he is impressed by his friend's 'capacity to give shape, colour, *aspect* to the invisible' and to 'bring out the *depth* of things common and visible' (*Letters* 2: 239).[12] Writing – indeed language itself – is for Conrad almost invariably figured in and through modes of vision, through envisioning. It is words, he declares to the writer Hugh Clifford in October 1899, that appeal to the 'mental vision of your readers': 'words should be handled with care lest the picture, the image of truth abiding in facts should become distorted or blurred' (*Letters* 2: 200). Conrad articulates a profound appreciation for the literary vision of others, particularly when it comes to their reading of his own work: having received praise for 'Heart of Darkness' and 'The End of the Tether' from Edward Garnett, he brings together his sense of the importance of the reader's vision with his sense of his own failing authorial eyesight: Garnett, Conrad declares, is the 'Seer of the Figures in the Carpet' who has 'grapple[d] with the foggishness of H of D, to explain what I myself have tried to shape blindfold, as it were'. Garnett, he suggests, has 'seen so perfectly' the 'Figure in the Carpet of the E of the T', since his friend has managed to describe the story 'in a line and a half with so much precision that even to me it has been a sort of revelation' (*Letters* 2: 467–8). Conrad's comments on his own work involve a similar rhetoric of vision and blindness. Writing defensively to William Blackwood in a major statement of his aesthetic 'creed' in 1902, for example, Conrad rests his literary reputation – and his reputation as a valued contributor to *Blackwood's Edinburgh Magazine* – on his ability to convey action 'observed, felt and interpreted with an absolute truth to my sensations' and to express the 'action of human beings . . . moving in a visible world' (*Letters* 2: 418).

More darkly, though, Conrad characteristically expresses the onerous, exhausting, repetitive and tortuous work of writing in terms that stress the invisibility of the visible, or in terms indeed of blindness. 'I am going on home now . . . and intend to stick on blindly to the work till it is done with', he tells Pinker of *Romance* in January 1902 (*Letters* 2: 366). Unable to write a certain story in March 1898 he tells Edward Garnett that it nevertheless 'weaves itself into all I see, into all I speak, into all I think' (*Letters* 2: 50), while in July he tells Arthur Quiller-Couch that the book he is 'struggling' with is 'a mass of verbiage with some dim idea so well lost in it that I, even I have a long time ago lost sight of it' (*Letters* 2: 78). Similarly, Conrad tells Ford that he 'dreamily dream[s]' how 'fine' *The Rescue* could be if only 'the thought did not escape, if the expression did not hide underground, if the idea had a substance and words a magic power, if the invisible could be snared into a shape' (*Letters* 2: 119). The 'hard, atrocious, agonizing' work of writing involves the impossibility of making the invisible visible, of 'snaring' the invisible 'into shape' (*Letters* 3: 327).[13] For Conrad, in a conception that he articulates in different ways on a number of occasions, there is the idea of a story before or behind the story, 'lurking in blank pages, in an intensity of existence, without voice, without form – but without blemish' (*Letters* 2: 119). And in a letter from April 1899, blindly flailing at the end of his tether, Conrad twists and interlinks his sense of melancholia and his chronic sense of his own inability to write into an extraordinary, knotted metaphor of monstrous vision, one in which and from which *The Rescue* cannot be rescued:

> The more I write the less substance do I see in my work. The scales are falling off my eyes. It is tolerably awful. And I face it, I face it but the fright is growing on me. My fortitude is shaken by the view of the monster. It does not move; its eyes are baleful; it is as still as death itself – and it will devour me. Its stare has eaten into my soul already deep, deep. I am alone with it in a chasm with perpendicular sides of black basalt. Never were

sides so perpendicular and smooth, and high. Above, your anxious head against a bit of sky peers down – in vain – in vain. There's not rope long enough for that rescue. (*Letters* 2: 177)

Here, as in Conrad's fiction, the disturbance of vision in writing, in composition, is linked to fundamental, existential and epistemological as well as literary doubt: what he sees, as the scales fall from his eyes, is a monster with baleful eyes, and his visual field is otherwise restricted to the basalt sides of a chasm and a patch of sky. Similarly, in a letter to Edward Garnett of September 1899, Conrad complains that writing is 'only piling crime upon crime' when, as now, 'everything under heaven is impalpable to the touch like shapes of mist': 'All is illusion', he comments, 'the words written, the mind at which they are aimed, the truth they are intended to express, the hands that will hold the paper, the eyes that will glance at the lines. Every image floats vaguely in a sea of doubt – and the doubt itself is lost in an unexpected universe of incertitudes.' In a self-parodic echo of Marlow's cry to his audience in 'Heart of Darkness', Conrad asks Garnett, with heavy Slavonic irony, 'Do you see how easy writing must be under such conditions? Do you see?' (*Letters* 2: 198).[14]

In a letter from 1898, Conrad plays over once again his trope of literary eyesight, expressing a certain ambivalence as to the ultimate literary merit of his writing. Gratified by some praise of a draft of *The Rescue* by Garnett he asks for confirmation that the tale is 'vivid – and seen': 'It is good news to me, because, unable to try for something better, higher, I did try for the visual effect. And I must trust to that', he goes on, 'for the effect of the whole story from which I cannot evolve any meaning – and have given up trying' (*Letters* 2: 85). Writing to Garnett about *Lord Jim* in November 1900, Conrad declares that the novel lacks 'power' – by which he means that it lacks what he calls '*illuminating* imagination': 'I wanted to obtain a sort of lurid light out [of] the very events', he says, lamenting the fact that he has, he thinks, failed to 'breathe the right sort of life into my clay – the *revealing* life' (*Letters* 2: 302). Two years later he writes to George Gissing about his waning literary self-confidence, again in terms of a disturbance of vision: 'There is a talking spectre, a ghostly voice whispering incessantly in one's ear of the narrow circle circumscribing all effort, of the shortness of one's vision and of the poverty of one's thought' (*Letters* 2: 464).[15]

For Conrad, it is not just a certain poetics or literary aesthetics that is tied up with blindness and eyesight, but the absurdity of the human condition itself, its intolerable existential comedy: life itself incurably involves blindness. In a letter of January 1898 to his left-wing friend Cunninghame Graham, for example, Conrad rages against what he sees as the misguided humanism of socialism in an entropic universe: the 'fate of a humanity condemned ultimately to perish from cold', he declares, 'is not worth troubling about . . . . In a dispassionate view the ardour for reform, improvement for virtue, for knowledge, and even for beauty is only a vain sticking up for appearances as though one were anxious about the cut of one's clothes in a community of blind men.' Neither thought ('we don't even know our own thoughts') nor language ('Half the words we use have no meaning whatever and the other half each man understands each word after the fashion of his own folly and conceit') nor religious beliefs (which 'shift like mists on the shore') escape Conrad's scorn and, true to his own despair, neither does the 'string of . . . platitudes' in his own letter.[16] As this suggests, Conrad characteristically expresses his own frequent bouts of depression – experiences, as we have seen, closely linked to his sense of his own blind inability to write – in terms of authorial blindness. Writing to Garnett in August 1898, for example, he declares that he is 'appalled at the absurdity of my situation – at the folly of my hopes, at the blindness that had kept me up in my gropings'. He is, he goes on, extending the metaphor, 'Most appalled to feel that all the doors behind me are shut and that I must remain where I have come blundering in the dark' (*Letters* 2: 85). Feeling like a 'damned paralyzed mud turtle' in September 1899, Conrad writes that he is 'unutterably weary of thinking, of writing, of seeing of feeling of living' (*Letters* 2: 197). At the same time, of course, it is precisely this inability to see, this groping, that enables Conrad, that forces him, to write. Not being able to see, or – what is the same, in fact, what is, at least, the condition of not being able to see – the *desire* to see, to be able to see, is for Conrad what marks the predicament of the writer.

But if seeing and not being able to see are what may be said to define Conrad's conception not only of his life but of his career as a writer, his mode of composition and his literary aesthetics, these conditions are also foundational within his other, earlier career as a seaman, the career that is so intimately tied up with and articulated in his writing, and which, at the same time, his writing is designed to escape. Indeed, blindness and eyesight may be said to operate as the hinge between Conrad's 'two lives', may be said to disrupt and disturb the neat opposition – chronological, psychological, national, professional, financial, geographical – between his two careers.[17] In a telling passage from his memoir *A Personal Record* (1908–9), for example, Conrad figures a certain way of looking as the cardinal moment of his career, as the origin of writing and the end of seamanship. In a momentous passage, he describes 'the day before my writing life began', drawing out in luxurious detail the look of the autumnal day, a day with 'an opaline atmosphere, a veiled, semi-opaque, lustrous day, with fiery points and flashes of red sunlight on the roofs and windows opposite, while the trees of the square with all their leaves gone were like tracings of indian ink on a sheet of tissue paper'.[18] Of this extraordinary act of visual memory Conrad comments that 'There is no reason why I should remember that effect more on that day than on any other day, except that I stood for a long time looking out of the window after the landlady's daughter was gone with her spoil of cups and saucers'. 'It is very clear', he goes on, that his younger self was in no hurry to 'take the plunge into my writing life' and that his 'whole being' was 'steeped deep in the indolence of a sailor away from the sea': 'For utter surrender to indolence you cannot beat a sailor ashore when that mood is on him', Conrad declares.[19] Writing, in other words, seems to come out of a kind of thoughtlessness, a thoughtless, vacant, indolent seeing of the kind characteristic of sailors on shore-leave.[20] The very definition of Conrad as a writer, his very first impulse to write, seems then to come from this dual identity as writer and (non-)seaman, as the mariner on vacation, vacantly, indolently looking. Indeed, the precondition on which Conrad will write appears to be the condition of his being a seaman who is *not* at sea. Nevertheless, there is what might seem a rather curious identification in Conrad's thinking of the desire to see in the writer with the desire to see in the seaman. The desire to see, indeed, characterizes Conrad's other life, the profession of the sailor – it puts the sailor apart at the same time that it aligns him with all of humanity: the desire to see for the seaman makes him both exemplary and unique. This point – the point of the seaman's sight and his blindness, his desire to see, as both general and singular – is directly expressed in a short paragraph from Conrad's 1906 memoir of the mariner's life *The Mirror of the Sea*:

> To see! To see! – this is the craving of the sailor, as of the rest of blind humanity. To have his path made clear for him is the aspiration of every human being in our beclouded and tempestuous existence. I have heard a reserved, silent man, with no nerves to speak of, after three days of hard running in thick south-westerly weather, burst out passionately: 'I wish to God we could get sight of something!'[21]

This is Conrad's maritime law just as it is the law of writing, his law of the sea/see, the law of his sea-stories as it is of his see-stories. It is this – the often appalling and appalled frenzy for the visible – that makes life at sea, for Conrad and for his readers, at once unique, individual, singular, exotic, other, and at the same time familiar, known, general, 'universal'. It is there in the critical moments of many of his sea-stories – in Jim's leap from the ship in *Lord Jim*, for example, or in the desperate search for a navigational marker in 'The Secret Sharer', or in Whalley's blindness at the end of 'The End of the Tether'. But this singular and general condition, the blind condition of vision itself, is the condition on which Conrad can write sea-stories, the condition on which he writes, indeed, just as it is the wager that he makes in embarking on board ship. And it is also the anxiety, the scandal, of Conrad's 'literary life',[22] a life that involves a continual uncertainty over the nature of his stories, their generic identity, their *length*. It is, in effect, the trap of Conrad's writing, a mark of the generic limits of his reception. The 'image' of Conrad as a 'writer of sea stories and the exotic', Zdzisław Nadjer remarks, 'was to give him a wide but short-lived, shallow, and misleading kind of popularity'.[23] And Conrad is, throughout his writing life, acutely aware that to be classified as a teller of sea-stories, as a sailor peddling his yarns, rather than as a serious writer producing non-maritime novels, is to be marginalized, ignored, forgotten: 'Behind the concert of flattery', he tells his French translator, 'I can hear something like a whisper: "Keep to the open sea! Don't land!" They want to banish me to the middle of the ocean.'[24]

The condition on which Conrad writes is that he has been at sea but is not now a seaman; and the condition on which he writes about life at sea is that he is not defined by or limited to being a writer who writes about the sea. These conditions of Conrad's writing, of his writing life, and of his poetics of the short story, engage with a vexing of the visible, of eyesight and blindness, which seems akin to that memorably analysed by Derrida in *Memoirs of the Blind*. Derrida argues that it is the condition, the very condition, of the sighted not to be able to see with regard not only to *invisibility* – which is self-evident, the invisible being that which is constitutively not to be seen by the sighted – but to the *visible*: 'the visibility of the visible cannot, by definition, be seen', declares Derrida citing both Plato and Merleau-Ponty, 'no more than what Aristotle speaks of as the diaphanousness of light can be'.[25] 'The visible *as such*', Derrida continues, 'would be invisible, not as visib*ility*, the *phenomenality or* *essence* of the visible, but as the singular body of the visible itself, *right on* the visible – so that, by emanation, and as if it were secreting its own *medium*, the visible would produce blindness'.[26] Derrida could be reading Conrad here, a writer whose stories are peculiarly concerned with such diaphanousness, with the invisibility of the visible, with certain forms of light. It would be impossible, for example, to overlook 'Heart of Darkness' in this context as a '"long-short" story' centrally concerned with a condition – darkness – wherein the visible cannot properly be said to be seen. The story opens with a three-page meditation on the nature of the visible, with speculations that end in a famously visual figuration of Marlow's peculiar narrative technique as a spinner of yarns wherein, by contrast with those of seamen, the 'kernel' of the story lies outside, 'enveloping the tale which brought it out as a glow brings out a haze, in the likeness of one of these misty halos that sometimes are made visible by the spectral illumination of moonshine' (p. 50). The second paragraph of the story is exemplary of Conrad's meditation on the invisibility of the visible, on the impossibility, at least, of properly seeing light:

> The sea-reach of the Thames stretched before us like the beginning of an interminable waterway. In the offing the sea and the sky were welded together without a joint, and in the luminous space the tanned sails of the barges drifting up with the tide seemed to stand still in red clusters of canvas sharply peaked, with gleams of varnished sprits. A haze rested on the low shores that ran out to sea in vanishing flatness. The air was dark above Gravesend, and farther back still seemed condensed into a mournful gloom, brooding motionless over the biggest, and the greatest, town on earth. (p. 47)

Everything in this scene looks towards the invisibility of the visible, to the blindness of our seeing. Nothing in the scene – a scene remarkable, indeed visible, in a sense, only for its visibility – can properly be said quite to be seen. The imperceptible welding of sea and sky is achieved 'without a joint'; the drifting sails '*seemed* to stand still'; the sprits 'gleam' in the uncertain light; the shore runs out to the sea in '*vanishing* flatness'; the dark air above Gravesend approaches, as such, the condition of invisibility; in the distance, above London, the 'mournful gloom, brooding motionless' can hardly be said to be seen, so wordy is the gloom, and since it is variably repeated no fewer than four times over the next two pages ('brooding gloom' (p. 47); 'Only the glow to the west, brooding over' (p. 48); 'that gloom brooding over' (p. 48); 'a brooding gloom in sunshine' (p. 49)) the phrase achieves a degree of permutational repetition that emphasizes the sheer textuality of this light, its linguisticity, its *language* of sight, its invisibility. The 'very mist on the Essex marches', Conrad goes on in diaphanous prose, 'was like a gauzy and radiant fabric, hung from the wooded rises inland, and draping the low shores in diaphanous folds' (p. 48).

It is, in the end, in the long-short story 'The End of the Tether' that Conrad most explicitly and most fully thematizes loss of sight. The circumstances surrounding the tale's composition have to do with a matrix of issues concerning seamanship, the self-portrait, the profession of authorship and blindness. It is not by chance that it is with regard to this story that Conrad makes one of his most important statements about the nature of the short story, linking it to the reader's ability to *see* properly, when he says, as we have noted, that the short story depends for its success on the reader being able to '*look back*' on the narrative as a whole (*Letters* 2: 441). In this respect, 'The End of the Tether' ties up questions of Conrad's double life – as writer and as mariner – and his concern over the proper length of a short story with the question of vision and blindness, of literary agnoiology, that characterizes his work more generally.

The plotting of 'The End of the Tether' is complicated – some might say over-complicated, for what is supposed to be a short story, however long – but some of its key lines can be quite briefly summarized. Whalley is the 65-year-old captain and part-owner of a small trading ship, the *Sofala*, working a monthly route amongst some of the more obscure coastal ports of South-East Asia. He is coming to the end of a three-year contract with Massy, the ship's grasping, misanthropic owner and engineer. Whalley has invested his remaining £500 in the ship for three years to keep the business going, having lost the rest of his not inconsiderable wealth in the crash of the bank in which he had invested the bulk of his life's savings. Whalley is rapidly going blind and increasingly relies on the ship's Malay Serang (the unnamed native boatswain) to take charge. He cannot let Massy know this for fear of being laid off from the captaincy and losing the ability to withdraw his money from the partnership for a further year. The money is intended for his daughter and Whalley's dream is to be able to move to live with her in Australia when the contract with Massy comes to an end in six weeks' time. He desires above everything to be able to give his daughter the remaining £500 and to see her just one more time. But he is unable to conceal his blindness – from the ship's mate, Sterne (who covets Whalley's position), from his friend Van Wyk, the hermit-like tobacco planter, or indeed from Massy himself. Massy is in dire financial straits, needing a new boiler for the ship and having no capital to pay for it or to cover the money that Whalley will imminently withdraw from the business. Realizing that Whalley is effectively blind, Massy hatches a plan to use this disability to sink the ship and collect on the insurance by misdirecting its compass so that Whalley will sail on to a sandbank: Massy will then be able to retire from what has become for him the hateful and financial unrewarding life of a seaman and ship's owner. The *Sofala* runs aground and all the crew escape except for Whalley, who, having understood that his blindness has been discovered (a fact that has the potential to invalidate the ship's insurance), is at the end of his tether[27] and goes down with the ship in an act of self-sacrifice designed to ensure that his daughter receives his part of the insurance payout. The story revolves around Whalley's blindness and its revelation, around his professional dedication to the sea, and around the ethical scandal of the risk he takes with other men's lives to secure a meagre financial future for his daughter.

'The End of the Tether' may be considered as an exemplary story in Conrad's oeuvre, and it is a story that has a peculiarly autobiographical tenor: Conrad himself confesses that the story will be 'essentially autobiographical' (*Letters* 2: 356), and 'very personal' (*Letters* 2: 376). John Batchelor, for one, has ingeniously suggested that the story is 'autobiographical' in a sense unintended by Conrad: he argues that the story not only records events from Conrad's earlier life at sea but also articulates an anxiety about the author's writing life and his need to deceive both his agent, Pinker, and his collaborator, Ford, about his literary output 'in order to provide for his family'.[28] But the self-portraiture of this story may be considered as even more direct than this since the ending of a seaman's career through optical delusions, through failing eyesight, is not, it seems, just a story for Conrad. In letters recommending Conrad for a grant from the Royal Literary Fund in July 1902, Sidney Pawling and Edmund Gosse both suggest that the end of Conrad's career at sea was a result of his failing eyesight.[29] The anxiety that the story articulates, in this respect, may be said to be a central concern of Conrad's professional lives. In as much as he is, as a writer, dependent on *losing* his sight he is, we might say, always on the point of losing this sense of sight (this blindness), of losing his 'literary' eyesight, his 'vision': he is always on the point of losing the sense – or indeed (and this is the point, the crux) always on the point of losing the loss of sense, losing the experience of losing his sense, of becoming blind – that enables him to write in the first place.

'*Idein, eidos, idea*: the whole history, the whole semantics of the European *idea*, in its Greek genealogy, as we know – as we see – related seeing to knowing', declares Derrida, in *Memoirs of the Blind*, in a passage that also punningly but unetymologically relates the will to know, *savoir*, and the will to see, *voir*.[30] The facts of Conrad's double profession, the work of the sailor and the work of the writer, and the shared concern in these careers with the problem of seeing and knowing, with seeing *as* knowing, and of both with blindness cannot help but lead us to a recognition of Conrad's attention to these knots in his writing. But in Conrad, at least, the relation of vision to knowledge is more difficult and more troubling than it might at first sight seem, and its trouble is nowhere more carefully explored than in 'The End of the Tether'. In this story, indeed, rather than a relation of mutual reinforcement, rather than a sense of their semantic homology, their synonymy, or their quasi-etymological – their verbal – identity, the sense of sight and the idea of knowledge are forced apart, untied or disentangled, disturbed, distrusted, dissipated. The problem is determined most clearly in a telling passage concerning the function of the pilot for the mariner: for the mariner the pilot is, by definition, the most clear-sighted, most 'clear-eyed' man, and for this reason he is someone whose very title, we are told, 'awakens' 'the idea of trust, of dependence'. The pilot can help the sailor who is 'groping for the land in the dark', 'groping blindly in fogs', the seaman whose 'range of sight on all sides' has been contracted to 'a shrunken horizon that seems within reach of the hand' (p. 222). But the pilot's superior eye sight is also his blindness, his *ability* not to see:

> A pilot sees better than a stranger, because his local knowledge, like a sharper vision, completes the shapes of things hurriedly glimpsed; penetrates the veils of mist spread over the land by the storms of the sea; defines with certitude the outlines of a coast lying under the pall fog, the forms of landmarks half buried in a starless night as in a shallow grave. He recognises because he already knows. It is not to his far-reaching eye but to his more extensive knowledge that the pilot looks for certitude. (p. 222)

The pilot's knowledge of the scene is '*like* a sharper vision' but originates in fact in the memory rather than in the eye: his knowledge originates in the invisible, in what he does not see. It is because he fails to look, because he can neglect to look, that the pilot can see and safely steer. The perhaps rather conventional figuration of the blind as seers – as poets, visionaries, prophets, revolutionaries – is here displaced: the man who sees most clearly does so by deliberately not looking, by blinding himself to what he can see.[31]

Thus 'The End of the Tether' suggests that there are some kinds of knowledge that have little bearing on what is seen, however directly, and Conrad explicitly figures this disturbance of knowledge and eyesight in terms of a certain colonial presumption. By contrast with Western eyes, with the vision of the mariners who own and direct the boat, the *Sofala*'s Serang has a direct visual apprehension of the world. He is aware, however, that such knowledge counts for little in the world of the colonizing Europeans:

> The record of the visual world fell through his eyes upon his unspeculating mind as on a sensitised plate through the lens of a camera. His knowledge was absolute and precise; nevertheless, had he been asked his opinion, and especially if questioned in the downright, alarming manner of white men, he would have displayed the hesitation of ignorance. He was certain of his facts – but such a certitude counted for little against the doubt what answer would be pleasing. (pp. 203–4)

While Massy, the engineer-owner of the *Sofala*, can't quite believe the evidence of his senses, can't trust his eyes, when the visually challenged Captain Whalley steers the ship too far north in crossing the Batu Beru bar and stirs up mud from the seabed, the Serang, by contrast, is 'not troubled by any intellectual mistrust of his senses' (p. 204): mental 'speculation' for him does not interfere with ocular perception. The Serang *knows* what has happened because he has seen it, but this is not the kind of knowledge that counts, being the kind of knowledge that is quite distinct from that of the white man and quite useless in his world.[32] He therefore feigns ignorance: to all colonial intents and purposes he *is* ignorant.

For Conrad's colonizers, then, eyesight works in some sense and to some degree *against* knowledge: it cannot be trusted. In 'The End of the Tether' this is most forcefully articulated in relation to the knowledge of blindness. Thus when Sterne sees – when he comes to know – for the first time that Whalley is blind, his knowledge affects his eyesight. This discovery, this 'enormity', reorganizes his 'outlook on what was possible in this world': it is as if 'the sun had turned blue, throwing a new and sinister light on men and nature . . . for a second the very colour of the sea seemed changed – appeared queer to his wandering eye' (p. 223). Similarly, Whalley's confession of blindness to Van Wyk has the disturbing effect of disturbing the eyesight of Van Wyk himself. As

Whalley leaves the house, Van Wyk possesses the aural percipience of the blind: 'Mr Van Wyk, arrested, seemed to count the footsteps right out of earshot' (p. 269):

> He walked between the tables, tapping smartly with his heels, took up a paper-knife, dropped it after a vague glance along the blade; then happening upon the piano, struck a few chords again and again, vigorously, standing up before the keyboard with an attentive poise of the head like a piano-tuner; closing it, he pivoted on his heels brusquely, avoided the little terrier sleeping trustfully on crossed forepaws, came upon the stairs next, and, as though he had lost his balance on the top step, ran down headlong out of the house. (p. 269)

While these actions are those of a sighted man, they also express those of the blind or partially sighted. You'd have to be blind not to see it, so emphatically is Van Wyk's blinded condition drawn out: the tapping of his heels recalls the tapping of a blind man's stick; his glance at the knife is 'vague', as if unseeing; he 'happens' upon the piano, as if he doesn't see it, and his poise is like that of a piano-tuner (a profession specifically coded by an association with the blind); the fact that Van Wyk avoids the terrier is itself remarkable for being remarked upon, as if the avoidance is not inevitable, as if he might not have seen the dog; and he seems to lose his balance on the steps, as if coming across them unawares, blindly. The revelation of Whalley's blindness, then, seems to produce a mimetic disturbance of vision in those that discover it.[33] But in the same way, Conrad's prose itself features a form of blindness, a disturbance of vision or an effect of optical delusion that affects our reading of the story: his prose performs blindness and forms it in the reader. As in 'Heart of Darkness', Conrad works, from the very opening sentence of 'The End of the Tether', to disturb our sense of the visibility (except in the most banal of senses) of language:[34] the 'low swampy coast', we are told in the first sentence, retains 'its appearance of a mere smudge of darkness beyond a belt of glitter'; the sun's rays seem to 'fall violently upon the calm sea' and to 'shatter themselves' into a 'dazzling vapour of light that blinded the eye and wearied the brain with its unsteady brightness' (p. 151). Every 'image' in the opening paragraph not only points towards a certain disturbance of vision, a certain blindness or blinding quality (a troubling indeed of the critical rhetoric of 'image' and the notion of the visual imagination) but enacts or produces a form of mimetic blindness, thwarting the reader's vision, blinding him or her, disengaging every sense of the relation of sight to knowledge, of reading to seeing, and of reading to knowing or apprehending.

* * * * *

'The End of the Tether' is too long (its end is not properly tethered to its beginning). That the story 'is stretched out far beyond the interest of its materials', Lawrence Graver declared in 1969, 'has been a critical commonplace for nearly sixty-five years', and, writing a quarter of a century later, John Lyon remarks that 'The weaknesses of the tale are its slow-moving nature and its related tendency towards descriptive excess'.[35] In this respect, too, the story is exemplary of Conrad's work, of his spinning out of a tale, even, it would seem, to the extent of untethering it from its readers' aesthetic satisfaction. Conrad is at the end of his tether; and writing is, for him, as we have seen, the condition of being at the end of one's tether.[36] His stretching of the story's tether is a result of his blind insistence on making his readers *see* what it is that he sees – which is to say on making his readers see a failure of sight, making them 'see' failing vision, making their own vision fail. In this respect, 'The End of the Tether', this brilliant, illuminating tale, may very properly be said to constitute a blind, a blinding short story. When Van Wyk wants to know what going blind is like, he struggles for the language of this loss: 'What is it like – like a mist – like ... [?]' Whalley's answer, though, is precise and 'undismayed': 'It is as if the light were ebbing out of the world' (p. 269).[37] Conrad's writing seeks to reveal the experience of losing sight, of this ebbing of light. As such, the relation of eyesight to knowledge in Conrad's '"long-short" stories' is catastrophically, apocalyptically or suicidally disturbed. As we have seen, this is particularly evident in the way in which Conrad's prose involves description, or when visual similes are employed and when the text evokes particular effects of light – evocations of phosphorescence, say, or of the diaphanous that it also repeatedly, prosaically produces.[38] These disturbances of vision, these textual-optical delusions, are finally tied up with the excesses of Conrad's 'short' stories, with the fact that they are almost invariably *long* short stories, too long even to *be* short stories. In Conrad's theory of the short story, the shortness of the story is associated with a visual effect, with the limitations involved in *seeing/seaing*, with the adventure story or the sailor's tethered yarn within the terms of which Conrad wished not to confine his work. By contrast, a certain form of knowledge (a knowledge that cannot be reduced to seeing, a knowledge associated with blindness or visual disturbance, with optical delusion, a kind of ignorance) is equated in Conrad's logic of the short story with the 'literary' tale, with what he calls the 'endless' 'question of *art*' (*Letters* 2: 194). In particular, as Ford Madox Ford suggests, Conrad's tales are lengthened, are extended beyond the uncertain bounds of the short story because of his need to motivate characters, to explore not just what they look like, not just how they appear, because of his need to allow a certain spectre of, a certain spectral illumination from, speculation: 'always there is just that shadow', Conrad remarks of 'The End of the Tether', 'that ghost of justification which should secure the sympathy of the reader' (*Letters* 2: 441).[39] In this respect, and for this reason, it might be said that Conrad wants us not to see but to see – to see ghosts, phantoms, spectres of character and motivation – wants us not to be blind but to be blind, not to know and yet to *know*, finally, that seeing is not knowing.

Notes

1 Frederick R. Karl and Laurence Davies, eds, *The Collected Letters of Joseph Conrad*, 9 vols. (Cambridge: Cambridge University Press, 1983–2007), 2: 348–9 (further references to this edition are cited in the text as *Letters*).
2 Ford, *Joseph Conrad: A Personal Remembrance* (London: Duckworth, 1924), p. 204.
3 Ibid., pp. 204–5. On the question of the length and genre of Conrad's works see also Gail Fraser, 'The Short Fiction', in J.H. Stape, ed., *The Cambridge Companion to Joseph Conrad* (Cambridge: Cambridge University Press, 1996), pp. 25–9. Fraser points out that Conrad rarely used the word 'novel' to refer to his own writings, using 'tale' or 'story' in the subtitles to seven of his longer works and referring to both novels and short stories in his letters as 'stories'.
4 As Norman Friedman hints, it may be no exaggeration to say that short-story theory has failed to move much beyond a recognition of the form's brevity – indicating that there may be nothing else to theorize: 'the oft-ridiculed formula "A short story is a story that is short"', Friedman declares, 'is not so circular as it at first appears' ('Recent Short Story Theories: Problems in Definition', in Susan Lohafer and Jo Ellyn Clary, eds, *Short Story Theory at a Crossroads* (Baton Rouge: Louisiana State University Press, 1989), p. 15). Compare Robert Coover's suggestion that not knowing what a short story is is 'as common a complaint as writer's block' ('Storying in Hyperspace: "Linkages"', in Barbara Lounsberry et al., eds, *The Tales we Tell: Perspectives on the Short Story* (Westport: Greenwood Press, 1998), p. 133). See also Joyce Carol Oates, 'Beginnings: "The Origins and Art of the Short Story"', in ibid., who suggests a limit of ten thousand words (p. 47).
5 *Letters* 2: 215. Conrad's anxiety about word-length in his stories may be noted in his habitual misspelling of 'length': in his letters he repeatedly reverses the word's ending, making of it 'lenght', as if unable to finish the word, or to finish with it: see, for example, *Letters* 1: 318, 319, 332 (where he first writes 'length' and then 'corrects' himself), 380, 383, 421; 2: 49, 106, 215, 227, 331; 3: 139. In fact, his letters suggest that Conrad is acutely conscious of the problem

Joseph Conrad's blindness 149

of the length of his short stories. Apologizing to William Blackwood for the fact that by January 1899 'Heart of Darkness' has become longer than originally conceived and is now clearly too long for a single number of *Blackwood's Edinburgh Magazine*, Conrad justifies his verbosity by declaring that the story has 'grown on me a bit' and that 'anyhow the value is in the detail' (*Letters* 2: 147); and writing about Henry James's 'The Spoils of Poynton' in February 1897 he comments that 'The only fault I find is its length. It's just a trifle too long. Personally I don't complain as you may imagine, but I imagine with pain the man in the street trying to read it!' (*Letters* 1: 339). Nevertheless, writing to his publisher T. Fisher Unwin in March 1898, and frustrated by his own prediction that his new collection of short stories, *Tales of Unrest*, might not sell well owing to a 'general *slump* in short stories', Conrad declares that this slump in sales is 'an illogical phenomenon' since 'the intrinsic value of a work can have nothing to do with its lenght [*sic*]' (*Letters* 2: 49). See also his defence of the length of *Romance* in February 1903: the novel is long, he admits, but this is 'not a crime' and it is 'swift enough in reading' – moreover, he says it is an 'incontrovertible fact that successful novels have been the long ones – always' (*Letters* 3: 20).

6 Zdzisław Najder, *Joseph Conrad: A Chronicle* (Cambridge: Cambridge University Press, 1983), p. 207; see also Fraser, 'The Short Fiction', p. 30. For examples of Conrad's expression of concern over payment for his short stories see *Letters* 2: 272, 376, 379, 380, 381.

7 Compare Conrad's comment in December 1902 that the story of thirty to forty thousand words is 'the form I like best but which I believe is in no favour with the public' (*Letters* 2: 461); and his later comment that 'it requires about 25000 [words] to give a good idea' (*Letters* 3: 33). For a brief discussion of the idea of memory and the short story in this context see Fraser 'The Short Fiction', p. 31.

8 On this point see, for example, Lawrence Graver, *Conrad's Short Fiction* (Berkeley: University of California Press, 1969), pp. 90–1.

9 Owen Knowles, 'Conrad's Life', in Stape, ed., *The Cambridge Companion to Joseph Conrad*, pp. 12–13; compare John Batchelor's comment that 'Conrad's achievements were arrived at partly by evasion, pretending to himself that he was engaged in one activity (taking time off to write a short story) whereas in reality he was engaged in another (embarking on a major novel)' (*The Life of Joseph Conrad: A Critical Biography* (Oxford: Blackwell, 1994), p. 45). The very term 'short story' seems in fact to have been problematic for Conrad: writing in July 1899, for example, he refers to a 'series of short stories (or rather short serials)' (*Letters* 2: 184–5). Compare his somewhat opaque comment on the 10,000-word 'Youth' that 'Some critics, at the time, called it a short story!' (*Letters* 2: 368). By contrast, however, early in his writing life Conrad comments in a letter to Marguerite Poradowska of February 1893 that 'It takes a small-scale narrative (short story) to show the master's hand' (*Letters* 1: 123; trans. 1: 124).

10 Conrad, Preface to *The Nigger of the 'Narcissus'*, ed. Robert Kimbrough (New York: Norton, 1979), p. 147.
11 See, for example, John G. Peters, *Conrad and Impressionism* (Cambridge: Cambridge University Press, 2001), p. 35; Frédéric Regard, 'Facing the Image: Joseph Conrad's "ineluctable modality of the visible"', *Paragraph* 20: 1 (1997): 134–53. See also Mark A. Wollaeger's comment, in his study of the 'skeptical "foundation" of Conrad's novels', that the statement about 'seeing' 'derives simultaneously from the primacy of perception in the empirical tradition and the visionary response to the epistemological limitations of that tradition' (*Joseph Conrad and the Fictions of Skepticism* (Stanford: Stanford University Press, 1990), p. xiv. Wollaeger notes that 'Ian Watt has established the importance of English empiricism to the rise of the novel' and comments that Conrad 'conjures the demon of radical scepticism latent in that tradition' (p. 193).
12 Compare *Letters* 1: 109 (trans. 1: 110–11) for similar comments on the author's ability to make visible what others do not see; see also *Letters* 2: 439.
13 Compare Conrad's comment that 'writing – *the only possible writing* – is just simply the conversion of nervous force into phrases' (*Letters* 3: 85).
14 Compare Marlow's question to his audience in 'Heart of Darkness': 'Do you see him? Do you see the story? Do you see anything?' (Joseph Conrad, *Youth/Heart of Darkness/The End of the Tether*, ed. John Lyon (London: Penguin, 1995), p. 79: further references to 'Heart of Darkness' and 'The End of the Tether' are cited from this edition in the text).
15 Compare Conrad's comments in a letter of October 1898: 'I am haunted by the idea I cannot write – I dare say a very correct idea it is too. The harm is in its haunting me' (*Letters* 2: 106).
16 *Letters* 2: 17; the platitudes, it would seem, are anyway in fact largely borrowed from Anatole France (see *Letters* 2: 17n.).
17 See Conrad's 'Author's Note' to the *Youth* volume for the phrase 'two lives' (p. 5).
18 Conrad, *A Personal Record: Some Reminiscences* in *The Works of Joseph Conrad: The Uniform Edition* (London: Dent, 1923), p. 73.
19 Ibid., pp. 73–4.
20 Conrad declares that as far as he knows, he was thinking of 'nothing whatever', and certainly not of writing a story, although he says that he may have been thinking of Almayer, the protagonist of the story (ibid., 74). See Conrad's declaration later in *A Personal Record* that 'the life at sea . . . is not, upon the whole, a good equipment for a writing life' (p. 108). On indolence see, for example, his comments to Galsworthy of April 1906: 'I have always that feeling of loafing at my work, as if powerless in an exhaustion of thought . . . I doubt not only my talent . . . but my character. Is it indolence . . .?' (*Letters* 3: 327–8).
21 Conrad, *The Mirror of the Sea: Memories and Impressions* in *The Works of Joseph Conrad: The Uniform Edition* (London: Dent, 1923), p. 87.

22 See *Letters* 3: 70.
23 Najder, *Joseph Conrad*, p. 325.
24 Quoted in ibid.; see also pp. 379–81. A letter to Garnett of August 1896 concerning *The Rescue* is instructive in this respect. Conrad explains that he must 'justify – give a motive' to his characters to avoid producing a 'Clark Russel[l] puppet show', to avoid being read, that is to say, as a writer of melodramatic maritime adventure tales – a fate, he says, that would be 'worse than starvation' (*Letters* 1: 296). But the justification, he goes on, 'is unfortunately of so subtle a nature that I despair of conveying it in say 20 pages well enough to make it comprehensible'. He tells Garnett that he needs to 'invent an illuminating episode that would set in a clear light the persons and feelings'. Concerned that he is 'breaking up mentally', Conrad explains that he feels that he has 'forgotten how to think – worse! How to write' and that he 'knock[s] about blindly in it till I am positively, physically sick' (ibid.). A year later he writes in similar terms of the same novel to William Blackwood: 'all the first part is given up to the presentation of [Lingard's] personality', he tells his prospective publisher. 'I aim at stimulating vision in the reader. If after reading the *part 1st* you don't *see* the man then I've absolutely failed and must begin again'. 'I know I can write – in a way', he goes on, 'I also know what I am aiming at – and it is not pure story-telling' (*Letters* 1: 381–2).
25 Jacques Derrida, *Memoirs of the Blind: The Self-Portrait and Other Ruins*, trans. Pascale-Anne Brault and Michael Nass (Chicago: University of Chicago Press, 1993), p. 45: Derrida quotes Merleau-Ponty from *The Visible and the Invisible*: 'When I say that every visible is invisible, that perception is imperception, that consciousness has a "*puntum caecum*", that to see is always to see more than one sees – this must not be understood in the sense of a *contradiction* – it must not be imagined that I add to the visible ... a nonvisible ... One has to understand that it is visibility itself that involves a nonvisibility' (quoted p. 52).
26 Derrida, *Memoirs of the Blind*, pp. 51–2.
27 The phrase is used of Whalley in this sense twice towards the end of the story (see pp. 293 and 298), although not, *pace* Lyon, in its 'more literal sense' (see p. 310).
28 Batchelor, *The Life of Joseph Conrad*, p. 296n.; see Conrad's comment to Garnett in June 1902 that 'all my art has become artfulness in exploiting agents and publishers' (*Letters* 2: 424). Of course, in a sense the story is precisely *not* autobiographical, since, unlike its protagonist Whalley, Conrad 'judged himself no longer to be physically fit' for the life of a seaman and 'concluded that in common honesty to his employers ... he must leave the sea', as Najder puts it (*Joseph Conrad*, p. x). According to Conrad himself in *A Personal Record*, however, the autobiographical speculation – 'is this or is this not "autobiographical"'? – is specious because the distinction is, at some level, itself specious: it can 'hardly be denied', he remarks that 'every novel

contains an element of autobiography' since, he says, 'the creator can only express himself in his creation' (pp. xvii–xviii). Compare a comment to T. Fisher Unwin in a letter of July 1896 on his work as 'fragments of my innermost being produced for the public gaze' (*Letters* 1: 293). Perhaps it would not be too much at this point to link Derrida's sense of the self-portrait as 'like a ruin that does not come *after* the work but remains produced, *already from the origin*, by the advent and structure of the work' and the ruin as 'that which happens to the image from the moment of the first gaze', ruin as 'the self-portrait, this face looked at in the face as the memory of itself, what *remains* or *returns* as a specter from the moment one first looks at oneself and a figuration is eclipsed' (*Memoirs of the Blind*, pp. 65. 68), with D.H. Lawrence's characteristically caustic and unforgiving assessment of the ruins, the ruin, as he sees it, of Conrad's work: 'why this giving up before you start, that pervades all Conrad and such folks – the Writers among the Ruins. I can't forgive Conrad for being so sad and for giving in' (quoted in Najder, *Joseph Conrad*, p. 373). As a ruin is precisely how Whalley sees himself: financially 'ruined' ('and of his ruin he was not ashamed': 'The End of the Tether', p. 154), and ruined by blindness – the ruin of a sailor and of a man.

29 See a letter to Gosse from Sidney Pawling dated June 1902 in the Yale Collection of American Literature, Beinecke Rare Book and Manuscript Library, where Pauling states that Conrad abandoned the sea on account of his 'impaired' eyesight. The editors of Conrad's letters report that 'although not as severely as Captain Whalley in "The End of the Tether", Conrad had trouble with his eyes' (*Letters* 2: 376n.); see also Najder, *Joseph Conrad*, pp. 283–4, who also mentions the fact that Conrad was 'greatly interested in and knowledgeable in optics'. Actual blindness, real physical, if temporary, blindness, also affected Conrad's wife in the year before he wrote 'The End of the Tether'.

30 Derrida, *Memoirs of the Blind*, p. 12. On the etymological error in linking *savoir* and *voir* see Martin Jay, *Downcast Eyes: The Denigration of Vision in Twentieth-Century French Thought* (Berkeley: University of California Press, 1993), p. 2.

31 The convention is also adhered to in 'The End of the Tether', however: in the 'illuminating moments of suffering' brought about by his encroaching blindness, Whalley 'sees' things, we are told, 'as he had never seen them before' (p. 286).

32 Compare John Peters's illuminating discussion of the relationship between 'primitive' and 'social' (visual) perception in Conrad's fiction in *Conrad and Impressionism*, ch. 2.

33 The point is indeed even more directly put at one point: Van Wyk looks 'upon his solitude, as if the fact of Captain Whalley's blindness had opened his eyes to his own' (p. 278).

34 A rather different sense of the invisibility of language is suggested in Conrad's praise of Constance Garnett's translation of Turgenev, in which the reader

'does not *see* the language' since the story is 'alive – as living as when it came from the master's hand' (*Letters* 1: 420).

35 Graver, *Conrad's Short Fiction*, p. 115; Lyon, 'Introduction' to *Youth/Heart of Darkness/The End of the Tether*, p. xiv; compare Najder, *Joseph Conrad*, p. 284. Lyon goes on to comment that 'The story's landscapes and seascapes are described, again and again, with prolix precision' but that 'even such weaknesses in the narrative can take on an expressive and ironic strength as the reader comes gradually to guess the secret of Whalley's blindness', and that 'the slow-moving narrative comes to parallel Whalley's own slow-moving caution, and the lavishly accurate descriptions mock Whalley's own unseeing eyes'. I would suggest that it is in fact the complications of plotting, caused by the desire to explore human character and motivation that slows down the story, rather than excessive description (there is, in fact, relatively little description as compared to the amount of character analysis). But my suggestion would be that rather than ironizing or 'mocking' Whalley's blindness, the tale's descriptions repeat it in, perform it for, the reader.

36 See Conrad's comment on the 'awful grind' of writing 'The End of the Tether' in *Letters* 3: 16; and (with reference to the accidental burning of part of the manuscript) his remark that that the story 'put an awful nervous strain on me' (*Letters* 3: 24).

37 The importance of this image is emphasized when it is twice repeated toward the end of the story (see pp. 292, 294).

38 Effects of phosphorescence frame – at its start and at its end – that other story of visibility and invisibility, 'The Secret Sharer': a 'faint flash of phosphorescent light' seems to issue from what looks like a corpse at the beginning of the tale just as a 'phosphorescent flash' distinguishes the captain's hat, the crucial navigational marker, at the end ('The Secret Sharer', in *Typhoon and Other Tales*, revised edn., ed. Cedric Watts (Oxford: Oxford University Press, 2002), pp. 183, 217). And phosphorescence plays its own minor part in 'The End of the Tether' – in the 'rigid phosphorescent wake' from the *Sofala*, for example, and in references to Venus, a.k.a. the morning star, a.k.a. Phosphorus, which lights Whalley's way as he inspects the *Sofala* in order to decide whether to take it on (pp. 152, 190–1).

39 Ironically, one might say, it is precisely Whalley's motivations (the question of whether he is weak or heroic) that are at the centre of critical controversy concerning this story, as Graver makes clear – this obscurity being, in his opinion, the other weakness of the story (see *Conrad's Short Fiction*, pp. 115–19); see also Graver's discussion of Conrad's inability to write a short story as being due to his 'concern for moral analysis' (pp. 39–40).

7

Children, death and the enigmatic signifier: Wordsworth and Bowen

Anyone who has spent much time with children cannot fail to know at least two things: first, that at a certain stage in their development, children believe that you, that the adult, knows, must know, the answer to their questions; second, that you don't; that you don't, can't know everything – that in fact you can hardly be said to begin to scratch the surface of knowing everything (some would say you can't know, really know, anything) and that if a child scratches the surface of your knowledge she will very quickly come upon its limits. And children do. That is what happens when they stop being children: they stop believing – knowing – that you know, that the adult knows. But this ineluctable curiosity of children is founded on a profound ignorance, the ignorance of adults' ignorance. The adult, like the psychoanalyst and like the narrator (and like the literary critic?) is the one who is supposed to know. But as Adam Phillips remarks, this knowledge, this supposed knowledge, involves knowing something 'of enormous consequence' – knowing that there is a 'sense in which nobody knows the answers'.[1]

In other words, children have a way of asking questions that has little respect for the limits of your knowledge. Indeed, we might say that one way of defining an adult, of knowing an adult when you see one, involves that individual's ability to know where the limits of another's knowledge might lie – and, one hopes, their tact in not exposing what is beyond those limits, except in certain distinctly limited, carefully regulated circumstances (in some aspects of the law courts, of political debates, of academic seminars and other colloquia, and so on). Being an adult involves, in part, knowing what it is, or what it might be, that other people don't know: being an adult *means*, in part, the ability to gauge your own as well as another's ignorance.

But it is the young, of course, that are ignorant – it is almost their defining trait. Why is it, you might ask, that they are so ignorant? And you might answer that from one perspective, at least, the question may be said to answer itself and may in fact simply seem to express ironical or sham or disingenuous ignorance: the answer – if the premise of the question is accepted, if we accept that children are, indeed, fundamentally ignorant – may seem self-evident. Being young just is the state of ignorance: infants, after all, are not called infants (*in-fans*, from *fari*, to speak) for nothing, but are precisely defined by their ignorance of speech – and their ignorance therefore, presumably, of almost everything that is ordinarily called, or that is worth, knowing, or that can be called 'knowing' in most senses of the term.[2] But it's not *just* a stupid question. From another perspective, the question may help us to get a purchase on the literary engagement with ignorance, that of both children and adults. In this chapter, I will look at a poem from the early nineteenth century and a novel from the early twentieth century. It may not be an entirely unconnected contextual fact that both texts were written by authors who were (at the time) childless. And it may also not be entirely coincidental that both are severely perplexed about the ignorance of children.

Before we look at these texts, however, I want to attend briefly to the presentation of childhood nescience in the discourse most intimately concerned with it, psychoanalysis. Psychoanalysis is, of course, fundamentally concerned with forms of ignorance, founded as it is in a theory of the unconscious, the unconscious as that which we do not or that which we cannot know. Along with scepticism, anepistemology and indeed literature itself, psychoanalysis may be said to constitute (part of and in part) a theory of ignorance, agnoiology. Do we – we humans, that is – want to know? Is that what we desire? Is that the human 'thirst', as St Augustine would have it, this 'epistemophilic impulse'?[3] From a psychoanalytic perspective, in fact, it would be possible to argue that knowing is just what we do not desire. We are driven, according to (one version of) Freud, more by an anepistemological impulse than by a desire to know – or, at least one might say that the desire not to know and what it is that we desire not to know, especially about ourselves, is what is interesting, troubling, traumatizing, about us (more so, at least, than what we may be said to know or want to know). As Adam Phillips puts it, psychoanalysis is 'a theory of the unbearable, of what one prefers not to know'.[4] While one might want to query the implied agency of such a 'preference' (do we, can we *choose* what we do not, cannot know? Do we have a choice in the matter of not knowing? What 'we', what bit of 'me', would be involved in such preferring?), Phillips's short introductory essay to his short, bracing book *Terrors and Experts* is itself an exemplary statement of the importance of ignorance for psychoanalysis. A neurosis, Phillips explains is, 'in Freud's language, a way of not knowing what one wants' (p. 4): for Freud, a neurosis 'would seem to be the result of a kind of ignorance – a not knowing about mental events that one ought to know of'.[5] The analyst, one might think, must therefore be 'an expert on the inevitability of ignorance' (p. 5). And yet Phillips's version of Freud – what he calls the post-Freudian Freud (as opposed to the Enlightenment Freud), a Freud that places new emphasis on the profound, irresolvable unknowability of the unconscious and on the opacity and centrality of language – is in fact 'an expert on the impossibility of self-knowledge' (p. 6). For the post-Freudian Freud, the injunction to 'know yourself' begins to 'beg all the questions': for this (version of) Freud, 'the issue becomes not only how can we bear our (forbidden) knowledge, but how can we bear our inevitable ignorance?' (p. 6). The subject is constituted by a 'radical and formative insufficiency', and one that 'cannot be solved by knowledge' – indeed, the project of self-knowledge is 'itself the problem' (p. 7). Psychoanalysis is therefore a 'primer of necessary ignorance' rather than the discourse or practice that allows us knowledge of and hence a cure for our selves (p. 8).

Psychoanalysis is, of course, fundamentally concerned with what children in particular know and do not know and with how they come to know – which (also) means how they come to be ignorant, unknowing, 'unconscious'. The two go together: the unconscious *is*, in a sense, childhood or a version of childhood, a kind of vault or entombment, a secret and inaccessible place that we carry with us from our earliest years.[6] It is clear, after all, that for Freud the unconscious is something that is created at a certain point in one's development – that it is not something that one is born with, so to speak, but is *made* as a result of certain life experiences. It is also clear that the unconscious is created and indeed populated at an early age. If our unconscious is us, what or who we are just inasmuch as we do not know what or who we are, it, the unconscious, is us as children, ourselves as ghosts of the past.

Melanie Klein and Jean Laplanche have written powerfully on the idea that ignorance is also the basis of human (mis)communication, in the sense that the origin of communication involves the necessary misfiring of adult speech. Communication, according to Laplanche, originates in and is learnt through miscommunication, through the constitutive inability of the child to understand the adult. Both Klein and Laplanche suggest in their different ways that we learn through ignorance, implying that learning *is*, in a sense, a function of ignorance. And for both theorists, it has to do with the child's constitutive inability to conceive of conception, of childbirth, of sex. 'The early feeling of *not knowing* has manifold connections', Klein declares: the feeling 'unites with the feeling of being incapable, impotent which soon results from the Oedipal situation. The child also feels this frustration the more acutely because it *knows nothing* definite about sexual processes.'[7]

'So we are sent back to the originary infantile situation', Laplanche declares, in a richly suggestive essay on the otherness that inhabits the transference in psychoanalysis: 'The sexual enigma is presented to the child by adults in an *address*, and this address is enigmatic in so far as the other (the one who sends it) does not entirely know what he is saying: he is other to himself'.[8] Building on Sándor Ferenczi's work, Laplanche argues that the adult world is 'characterized by the existence of messages', whether linguistic, prelinguistic or paralinguistic, 'which ask the child questions it cannot yet understand'.[9] For the child, Laplanche argues, the primal scene in particular is 'a seduction, a primary seduction', since it is an enigma that the child cannot process. 'The sight of its parents having intercourse', Laplanche goes on, 'allows, or forces, the child to see images and fragments of traumatic scenarios which it cannot assimilate because they are to a certain extent opaque to the actors themselves'.[10] Similarly, the 'two great enigmas' noted by Freud – gender difference and the origin of babies – produce traumatic effects through the fact that adults are unable to explain them.[11] It is not of course that adults are not, at some level and with varying amounts of precision, able to explain the biology of reproduction and childbirth to themselves or to each other (at least to their own satisfaction). The difficulty is in explaining these crucial factors of animal existence to those beings – those animals – that don't have the equipment (the language, the developed body) to comprehend. The adult's world, according to Laplanche, is 'a world of signification and communication' which 'swamp[s] the child's capacity for apprehension and mastery'. The adult's messages – whether verbal or, more commonly, gestural, vocal, embodied – constitute 'enigmatic signifiers' for the child. They are enigmatic, according to Laplanche, though – and this is the crucial point – not only because the child does not know the language but, more importantly, on account of the fact that 'the adult world is entirely infiltrated with unconscious and sexual significations to which *adults themselves* do not have the code'.[12] The human, in other words – who, or what, we are, those 'self-translating and self-theorizing being[s]' that we think of as us or me or like me –

begins in ignorance in a specific, technical sense: 'the first indication of perception, or the first inscription in the psychical apparatus is the enigmatic signifier [which is] inscribed before any attempt is made to translate it'.[13] Language, communication, according to Laplanche's version of Freud, is founded in the enigmatic signifier, founded in the child's – and therefore our, and therefore their (it is a circular or repetitive, and seemingly never-ending cycle) – ignorance. We are ignorant because of our parents, and our children are ignorant because we are, as their children will be. It 'deepens like a coastal shelf' as Philip Larkin says[14] – except that, from another perspective, it doesn't, that it remains at the same submerged level, except that it remains always, generation after generation, the same inherited, learned ignorance, an immense, never-ending, submerged plateau of ignorance. Ignorance is our inheritance, our education.

A specifically Kleinian analysis of miscommunication between adults and children, and the consequences for a thinking of literary texts, has recently been more fully developed by the critic Peter Brooks. In *Body Work: Objects of Desire in Modern Narrative* (1993), Brooks is concerned to explore the ways in which psychoanalytic conceptions of knowing and ignorance can begin to provide us with the kind of knowledge that we call 'insight' into literary texts. Although he draws on a Freudian sense of ignorance, the conclusions he comes to are very different and contrast usefully with those of Laplanche. *Body Work* is concerned with the body as 'an "epistemophilic" project' and with the sense that the desire to know is 'constructed from sexual desire and curiosity'. The topic of Brooks's book is, he explains,

> the nexus of desire, the body, the drive to know, and narrative: those stories we tell about the body in the effort to know and to have it, which result in making the body a site of signification – the place for the inscription of stories – and itself a signifier, a prime agent in narrative plot and meaning.[15]

While the body is often viewed as a pre-symbolic and pre-linguistic site, itself a 'fall from language' which returns us to 'a presymbolic space in which primal drives reassert their force' (p. 7), the very 'realm of unmeaning' indeed (p. 21), the focus of Brooks's investigation concerns the ways in which bodies come to mean and the ways in which our interest in or desire for narrative is both analogous to and itself an expression of the desire for the body. His book concerns what he calls a 'narrative aesthetics of embodiment, where meaning and truth are made carnal' (p. 21). Building on Melanie Klein's proposal for the child's 'epistemophilic impulse', whereby the pre-linguistic infant makes of body-parts, sex difference and sensations the 'first building blocks in the construction of a symbolic order' (p. 7), Brooks argues that even at this stage the body begins to mean and, indeed, that the body begins meaning, begins symbolization: it is through the body – the seemingly simply material, and therefore non-signifying, object – that meaning occurs. As Brooks points out, for Klein (as for Laplanche), the epistemophilic impulse originates in the question of sexuality, the question, specifically, of where babies come from: the desire to know arises out of specific questions concerning the body. According to Klein (and, like Laplanche, she is following Sándor Ferenczi here), the infant is ill-equipped (in terms of the formation of its own body) to answer such questions.

For Brooks, in perhaps the most telling sentence in his book, 'narrative desire, as the subtending dynamic of stories and their telling, becomes oriented toward knowledge and possession of the body' (p. 8). And yet, as Brooks also explains, there is a fundamental problem in the child's investigation of sexuality, a fact which makes it certain that the desire to know is necessarily stymied: the fact that 'sexual curiosity' is awakened before sexual maturity means that the child's 'primary investigation of knowledge' is 'frustrated at its very roots, setting up a model of the desire to know as an inherently unsatisfiable, Faustian project' (p. 9): in other words, 'the radical structuring of human nature by sexuality ensures that the body will always be a problem in meaning' (p. 14). There is, within this logic itself, a resistance to meaning, just as the body itself presents a resistance to conceptuality and meaning: what Brooks calls the 'ever-renewed struggle of language to make the body mean' (p. 22) is precisely that, nothing more than an 'ever-renewed struggle'. 'We still don't know the body', Brooks declares as he ends his book: 'Its otherness from ourselves, as well as its intimacy, make it the inevitable object of an ever-renewed writing project' (p. 286). The desire to know is 'from the beginning' frustrated, and indeed 'construct[s] itself on the model of frustration' since it is based around what Freud calls the 'diphasic onset' of human sexuality (the temporal deferral involved in the relationship between an intellectual interest in sex and the physical development of the body): the desire to know is, therefore, 'always in excess of the capacity of objects of knowledge to satisfy it' (p. 99), and 'since the epistemophilic project is always inherently frustrated, the body can never be wholly grasped as an understandable, representable object' (ibid.). The body remains, at some level, unreadable and unread, remains an absence, a blank, just a body. Brooks's 'aesthetics of narrative embodiment insists that the body is only apparently lacking in meaning' (p. 25), but we might attend to the surplus of non-meaning, the ineluctable resistance to meaning, that always remains with and in the body; if the body is 'a key sign in narrative and a central nexus of narrative meanings' as Brooks argues (p. 25), it might be countered that as 'sign' and 'nexus' the body remains, itself, non-meaningful.[16] And as Brooks argues, narrative is 'generated as both approach and avoidance, the story of desire that never can quite speak its name nor quite attain its object' (p. 103): narrators themselves, those that are 'supposed to know', know only a part or a series of parts, see only that which is 'partially obscured' (p. 105). The Oedipus myth, in which the knower, once he comes fully to know, is struck blind is, for Brooks, the 'ultimate mythic paradigm'. But it remains mythic since 'in reality, we do not reach that fullness of knowledge'. Instead, 'we are made to be content – and are not content – with parts, with revelatory moments, with undressings, with gaps in the veil' (p. 122). And this may be said to constitute the work of literature, how it works and how it works on us: it makes us both content and discontented with ignorance, with the limits of our knowledge and with knowing that we cannot know.

If Brooks is interested in the 'narrative aesthetics of embodiment' in which 'meaning and truth are made carnal' (p. 21), his book everywhere prompts us to consider the ways in which meaning and truth are *not* made carnal or ways in which the body – and therefore by Brooks's account, narrative itself – is not made meaningful: we might acknowledge, as Brooks has it, 'the meaningless mortality of the body' (p. 286), we might consider the anti- or an-epistemological urge or instinct. Such a project would not – or would not necessarily – be a matter of epistemophobia, although some of what Melanie Klein in particular has to say about the child's development seems to come close to such a fear. Instead, it has to do with a generalized and non-pathological resistance to knowledge, one that at the same time may be said to resist both the desire for mastery and the sadism that Klein and others see as subtending epistemophilia. In Laplanche, Klein and Brooks, psychoanalysis is founded on and sees the child's (and therefore the adult's) engagement with the world as founded, in the last resort, in ignorance.

According to certain strands in psychoanalysis, then, the ignorance of children is a function of their dysfunctional communication with us, with adults. While psychoanalysis emphasizes the child's ignorance of sexuality, and while a major, indeed canonical literary text such as Henry James's *What Maisie Knew* is precisely focused, despite the title, around a girl's sexual ignorance, there is another incomprehension that psychoanalysis is fundamentally concerned with and to which the literary tradition has paid due regard in a number of remarkable texts: the question of death. It is this question that I want to explore in this chapter, the question of the child's fundamental inability to comprehend, to know death, not least because it is a form of ignorance carried by the adult, ignorance that the adult indeed may be said to inherit from the child, from herself as a child. If for Laplanche and others the Lacanian 'enigmatic signifier' that grounds and instantiates communication itself is bound up with unacknowledged sexuality, it is also necessarily bound up in death, that aspect of their own lives that only adults properly know about but which even they cannot, by definition, finally know (the 'obstacle' of death, as Levinas puts it, is 'insurmountable, inexorable and fundamentally incomprehensible').[17]

What we know of children is that they are ignorant (and ignorant in part at least because we are, because what we teach them is, in part, our nescience). But what we don't know of children, what we cannot conceive or even at times believe, is also, from another perspective, the extent or richness or precise form of that ignorance. Wordsworth's poems of children are poems about their ignorance but also poems about *our* ignorance of them, ignorance produced or prompted by theirs. We are ignorant of children because of their ignorance, ignorant of their ignorance. We are not ignorant – to say it again – about the fact that they are ignorant (we *know* that they are ignorant, what else could they be?), but ignorant of what this ignorance entails. Somehow, despite having been children, having been (like) them, we cannot conceive of their ignorance. We cannot know them (and therefore cannot know ourselves). And this perhaps is why we read and write poems and novels about the ignorance of children.

'We Are Seven', the most famous of Wordsworth's poems of childhood, opens with a question (formulated, as it happens, by Coleridge) that, along with the question of procreation, goes, even in its quibbling modal verb, to the heart of our ignorance of the ignorance of the child: 'A simple child . . . What *should* it know of death?' (ll. 1, 4: italics added). Wordsworth later explained that the poem was designed to illustrate 'the perplexity and obscurity which in childhood attend our notion of death, or rather our utter inability to admit that notion'.[18] In other words, by Wordsworth's account, the poem was designed to demonstrate the child's, any child's, constitutive ignorance of death. But Wordsworth's prose account of his poem gives only the half of it, since the poem is also – or mostly – about the adult's ignorance of the child's ignorance of death, his refusal to admit or countenance it. If Wordsworth's poem of children is about what children do, or can, or 'should', know, or not know, it is also about our ignorance of children – of who they are, how they think, what they know, and what we know of them. But it is also just about ourselves, about our own, 'adult' ignorance – as, indeed, the frankly slippery syntax of Wordsworth's prose-comment on his poem suggests in 'attend' (rather than 'attended') and 'admit' (rather than 'admitted'). Because perplexity and obscurity attended our notion of death in childhood, this suggests, and because we were not able to admit the notion then, perplexity and obscurity attend our notion of death now, which still cannot in some sense be admitted.

The poem is, at first glance, straightforward.

> A simple child, dear brother Jim,
> That lightly draws its breath,
> And feels its life in every limb,
> What should it know of death?
>
> I met a little cottage girl,
> She was eight years old, she said;
> Her hair was thick with many a curl
> That cluster'd round her head.
>
> She had a rustic, woodland air,
> And she was wildly clad;
> Her eyes were fair; and very fair;
> – Her beauty made me glad.
>
> 'Sisters and brothers, little maid,
> 'How many may you be?'
> 'How many? seven in all', she said,
> And wondering looked at me.
>
> 'And where are they? I pray you tell'.
> She answered, 'Seven are we,
> 'And two of us at Conway dwell,
> 'And two are gone to sea.
>
> 'Two of us in the church-yard lie,
> 'My sister and my brother;
> 'And, in the church-yard cottage, I
> 'Dwell near them with my mother'.
>
> 'You say that two at Conway dwell,
> 'And two are gone to sea,
> 'Yet you are seven; I pray you tell
> 'Sweet Maid, how this may be?'

Then did the little Maid reply,
'Seven boys and girls are we;
'Two of us in the church-yard lie,
'Beneath the church-yard tree'.

'You run about, my little maid,
'Your limbs they are alive;
'If two are in the church-yard laid,
'Then ye are only five'.

'Their graves are green, they may be seen',
The little Maid replied,
'Twelve steps or more from my mother's door,
'And they are side by side.

'My stockings there I often knit,
'My 'kerchief there I hem;
'And there upon the ground I sit –
'And sing a song to them.

'And often after sunset, Sir,
'When it is light and fair,
'I take my little porringer,
'And eat my supper there.

'The first that died was sister Jane;
'In bed she moaning lay,
'Till God released her of her pain;
'And then she went away.

'So in the church-yard she was laid;
'And all the summer dry
'Together round her grave we played,
'My brother John and I.

'And when the ground was white with snow,
'And I could run and slide,
'My brother John was forced to go,
'And he lies by her side'.

'How many are you, then', said I,
'If they two are in Heaven?'
The little Maiden did reply,
'O Master! we are seven'.

'But they are dead; those two are dead!
'Their spirits are in heaven!'
'Twas throwing words away; for still
The little Maid would have her will,
And said, 'Nay, we are seven!'

In sixteen four-line and a final five-line stanza, the narrator recalls a dialogue between himself and a young girl. The eight-year-old girl insists on arguing that she has six brothers and sisters – 'We are seven' – even though two of them are dead. The narrator refuses to accept this and tries to make her understand that being dead means that the other two no longer count because they can no longer be counted, counted as brother and sister, counted as human. The two speakers cannot agree, and the poem ends in befuddled exasperation.[19] Like 'Anecdote for Fathers', its companion-poem, 'We Are Seven' has usually been read as examining and questioning the power-relations of children and adults with respect to the question of knowledge and ignorance. In both poems – despite Wordsworth's assertion that 'We Are Seven' is about the girl's ignorance – it is the arrogance of adult knowingness that seems to provide the central topic, and in both poems it is the adult's insistence on knowing that seems to amount to the expression of ignorance. According to this reading, in 'We are Seven' the narrator becomes a pedantic mathematician as he tries unsuccessfully and, we might think, untactfully to convince the girl either that her mathematics or that her conception of death, or family, or what it means to be human, is faulty. Stuck in his mode of thinking, one that cannot accept the confusion of the living with the dead, the narrator dogmatically (and repetitively) insists on his own version of 'knowledge', ignoring that of the young girl. This leads to an almost comic explosion in the last stanza as the infuriated speaker cries 'But they are dead; those two are dead! / Their spirits are in heaven!', with crass disregard for the defensive ignorance within the young girl's calculations.

The poem ends, then, as Susan Wolfson puts it, in a 'standoff' in which the speaker is able neither to 'persuade nor bully the little girl with his logic' and in which her 'simplicity' cannot prevail: what we are faced with at the end of the poem are 'two orders of knowledge that are self-enclosed and irreconcilable'.[20] And if the child is unenlightened by the end, so is the adult, the 'overbearing questioner' according to Maureen McLane, who in his 'mulishness' has been unable imaginatively to enter into the child's conception of life and death.[21] The child, for her part is, of course, unable to get it, to get, or get at, what the man is talking about. The dialogue amounts to a perversion of the Socratic *elenchus*, a distortion produced *precisely* through the man's assumption of (superior) knowledge (Socrates' *elenchus* is enlightening, *pace* what is commonly conceived of as 'Socratic irony', *only* because the Philosopher is, and knows he is, ignorant).[22] For the child, the strangely, insistently questioning stranger is enigmatic – and enigmatic, as Laplanche would have it, because he is, unbeknownst to himself, fundamentally perplexed, unknowing, nescient.

And the poem is not only of course *about* incompatible viewpoints with regard to death: in addition it *produces* or performs conceptual incompatibility, having been read in two different, indeed two fundamentally irreconcilable ways. In what is currently the dominant tradition of reading, the poem has been interpreted, as it is above, as a tale of charming childish insouciance imposed upon by the crass stupidity and tactlessness of the adult. The adult insists on imposing his sense of 'reality', of the reality of the meaning of death, on to the child: he attempts to 'force on the child a knowledge for which she is not prepared', as Frances Ferguson puts it.[23] This reading involves an ironic distance from the speaker's point of view, a sense that the poem is guarded about and even critical of the adult's motives and actions.[24] The banal literalization of the human condition that the speaker expresses, the reductive, uninformed, uneducated and unimaginative supposition that the dead cannot be *counted* – both literally and figuratively – is read as a wholly inadequate, indeed ignorant, response to the complex, imaginative, sophisticated grasp of the other reality of death, of the survival of what we term the dead, the uncanny sense that we are not only here and now but also elsewhere and not us, haunted, possessed by others, by our sisters and brothers, by the dead. According to this thinking, the error, the ignorance in this poem is the adult's as much as the child's: while we may know that we are all bound to die and that we will not be part of our family after our death, we cannot know what death is. The narrator simply replaces one myth of death (presence) with another (absence).

The second (minority) reading takes the poem – and the speaker – straight. In this reading, we sympathize with the speaker's frustration at the girl's 'wilfulness' – ''Twas throwing words away; for still / The little Maid would have her will'. While some might regard this reading as itself wilful, wilfully naive, indeed, or as overly literal, there are, there always have been, critics who read the poem in this way and there are cogent reasons for doing so.[25] It is, after all, undeniable that the girl does not understand something fundamental – from a 'rational' or 'adult' perspective – about life and death, about counting, and, perhaps more importantly, about conversational etiquette: when I ask how many of you there are, how many in your family, I don't expect you to count your dogs, or the mice that live in your wainscot, or your friends, or your dolls – or the dead. The alleged wilfulness of the girl is an expression of ignorance about this fact, a 'wilful' ignorance, a wilful refusal to understand the question. Although the interpretation has become far less prominent in contemporary criticism, it is evident in, for example, one of the most influential twentieth-century studies of the poet, Geoffrey Hartman's *Wordsworth's Poetry* (1964), where the interlocutors are characterized as 'the rational questioner and the obtuse little girl'.[26] And it is apparent in Alan Richardson's more recent suggestion that in a 'more subtle manner adult preconceptions and categories are affirmed' in the poem (the adult having, after all, the last word, even if the poem may be said to take its title and its actual last word, from the girl), at least in the sense that, while the poem might be seen in some sense to reverse the relation of adult to child, at the same time it 'maintain[s] the hierarchical structure of their relation';[27] and it is there in Francis Ferguson's recognition that the girl is ignoring or misunderstanding or simply ignorant of the fundamental principle of mathematics that counting 'always takes numbers to have references that are available to be pointed to'.[28]

So I want suggest that there are indeed, despite appearances, perhaps, and contrary to the assumption that the 'poem' necessarily 'knows more ... than the man',[29] two possible and indeed two valid but opposing readings of the poem. I want to insist, indeed, on a credible and coherent reading of the poem in which the man is *not* ironized, but is properly knowing, and in which the poem is about the strangeness, the uncanny insistence of the girl's fundamentally insouciant, *ignorant* claims about death. Indeed, such is the disturbing force of the poem, that I would go so far as to predict that at some point in the future, in the context of a concatenation of unpredictable theoretico-ideologico-cultural circumstances, the critical consensus will swing back to this position. The two readings essentially revolve around the issue of the answer to the rhetorical question that starts the poem: 'What should it know of death?' 'What ought the girl know about death?', the question might be asking, 'What does she need to be told?' – with one response (that sympathetic to the adult) being that she needs to know that her siblings are not going to come back, for a start, that she needs to know, that she should know, at least, what *we* know or think we know about death, that she needs to not be ignorant about it. And she needs to know that the adult has superior knowledge about this, as he does about other things. But taking a more child-focused perspective, we might also consider that the question might be asking whether it is appropriate or even possible for the child to know of death: 'What should it know?' is the question; 'Well, nothing, in essence', is the answer, 'since a child cannot comprehend death and is anyway better off not knowing about it, better off not knowing what adults think of as their understanding, their knowledge, of death'. And this is what you are up against when you try to explain death to a child: incomprehension, and ultimately frustration.

I want to suggest that a proper reading of the poem would acknowledge that it produces poetic or hermeneutic uncertainty or 'ignorance' since it is impossible to decide between the two readings. Who is to say in relation to this poem, we might ask, who is the teacher and who learns, who speaks the truth and who is ignorant, which is the adult and which the child? The child truly is the father of the man or the mother of the woman just in so much as the poem disturbs the categories of child and adult with regard to knowledge and ignorance. In this sense, at least, the poem indeed opens up the question of the undecidability of death, of our ignorance of it.[30] In other words, the poem is not only about the child's but about *our* ignorance; it involves an attempt to understand the *adult*'s 'utter inability to admit' the notion of death. The poem concerns not only what a young girl 'should . . . know of death', but what we do not, cannot know of it.

I want to say that the child is valuable for Wordsworth because of her potential for the deconstruction of knowledge, for her incisive questioning of what is known and of who knows. What children show us, help us understand, is that, or what, we do not know. Like the other myths of nostalgia so crucial to Wordsworth's writing – myths of nature, of simplicity, of the past as a golden age, even of an undivided and self-present self – the myth of childhood might, in fact, be understood as a complex interrogation of the possibilities of a different kind of knowledge, a different way of knowing. This is not to suggest, in an idealized or 'Romantic' sense, that the child is, as Wordsworth puts it in the Intimations Ode, a 'little philosopher', but to suggest rather that what we can learn from thinking about the ignorance of children is something about our own ignorance. Wordsworth's fascination with the ignorance of children, in other words, may have to do with his fascination with what *we* do not know. It is not as if adults, after all, know death, know what death is (only the dead would know that – if they are not beyond knowing anything, as we must surely assume is the case, even if we cannot know it). But what Wordsworth's poetic children teach, or recall to us, is what it is like not to know – they remind us of what it is like to be ourselves, in other words, since we, too, are ignorant (it is just that we, some of us, do not know, do not properly acknowledge it).

* * * * *

The question of death is raised in another, very different but equally compelling, scene that confronts us with the question of children confronting death. In the second chapter of Elizabeth Bowen's magisterial novel of children and childhood ignorance, *The House in Paris* (1935), there is an exquisitely difficult conversation about death between two children, Leopold and Henrietta. In this case, the incomprehension is not directly a result of adults speaking past, or enigmatically to, children (although that certainly happens at other points in the novel and is, indeed, one of its major concerns).[31] No adult is in fact present during the conversation – that is the point of the conversation. But at the same time, the conversation is steeped in the conflict, the irreducible perplexity, of the relationship between adult language and comprehension and the language and understanding of children.

The scene is set in a house in Paris where Leopold and Henrietta, two children who have never met before, are left alone together in the drawing room. By coincidence, both children are passing through the house, which is owned by the ailing, indeed dying, Mme Fisher, who lives with her adult, unmarried daughter. Miss Fisher (and by somewhat terrifying extension her ailing mother) is very temporarily – for the day only – *in loco parentis*, with all that that involves in terms of authority, power and the regulation of the children's knowledge and ignorance (there are some things that children just should not know . . .). Henrietta, an orphan aged 11, is on the way to meet her grandmother in Mentone in the south of France, while Leopold, who is 9, has travelled up from Italy where he lives with this adoptive parents, to see, for the first time since very soon after his birth, his biological mother. In the absence of grown-ups, the children's talk seems to enact something like a demented simulacrum of adults' conversations.[32] The conversation involves unconscious cruelty, the exposure of each other's and the children's own pain, their trauma of loss and abandonment, their insecurities and fears about their own identity and value, and their probing ignorance of death. 'Where does your mother live?', Leopold asks with 'animation':

> 'Oh, she's dead', said Henrietta, embarrassed.
>
> 'Oh, is she?' said Leopold, taken aback. His manner became a little touchy and wary, as though she had been laying a trap for him. Picking Henrietta's monkey up by the ears he examined it distantly: its limp limbs and stitched felt paws hung down.
>
> 'Don't!' exclaimed Henrietta. 'His ears may come off!'
>
> 'They seem quite firm', said Leopold, testing them. 'Why do you say "don't"? Do you think it feels?'

'Well, I like to think he notices. Otherwise there'd be no point in taking him everywhere . . . Have you been in Paris often, Leopold?'
'Does it squeak?' he went on, absorbed, digging at Charles's belly.
'No. Please put him down. Have you been in Paris often?'
'No. I live near Spezia. Italy's better than France'.
'Why?' she said, nettled.
'It's hotter', he said, raising his eyebrows, 'and not nearly so shabby. Besides, it has got a king still. Mentone used to be Italy till France took it away. Nobody goes to France when they can go to Italy'.
'Then why doesn't your mother go and see you in Italy?'
'Because it's too far', said Leopold loftily. Silhouetted against the unsunny muslin blind he began rocking backwards and forwards, from his toes to his heels. Creak – creak went his shoes on the parquet or jerked hastily back: his hands stayed in his pockets the whole time. He became his own rocking toy whose equilibrium flattered him; meanwhile showing Henrietta that he had no thoughts. She, however, refused to watch. Gazing up at the cornice picked out in grey and yellow, she thought: 'All he wants is somebody who will notice.'[33]

The pain in the thought of death, one's mother's death, at the beginning of this passage is first displaced into embarrassment and then, by Leopold, into a questioning of the animation of Henrietta's monkey, as if to ask what might be the difference between a dead mother and a toy monkey: both are objects of affection and both inanimate, unresponsive, and both are therefore curiously human at the same time as being curiously non-human. The pain of Leopold's probing questions, figured as the sadistic physical probing of the anthropomorphized toy monkey, is reciprocated by the marginally more sophisticated – and therefore more destructive – Henrietta, as she asks why his mother fails to visit Leopold in Italy. The question points unerringly to the fact that having an *absent* mother is, in practical terms, not very far from having a *dead* mother. 'What *is* the difference?' she seems to be asking, as if, like Leopold, she is an emerging epistemologist of pain. It is as if Henrietta is attempting to figure out a theory of death, and the question of whether it can be conceived of as something like absence and abandonment. Both Henrietta and Leopold are trying to understand what death means but also (as part of that enquiry, perhaps) trying to defend themselves against the hurt that they somewhere, however obscurely, somehow know because they know something that they wish they did not and because, at the same time, there is something they know that they do not know. Leopold's response is to become a rocking toy and to show Henrietta that he has no thoughts. The response is entirely reasonable since, just as the monkey is physically probed by Leopold's fingers, so Leopold in turn is being psychically probed by Henrietta's questions. Bowen in effect shows us the functioning of the unconscious in action: Leopold is repressing the thought and is constructing for himself his own unconscious, that place designed to encompass what cannot be encompassed by the subject, that which, in more than one sense, *cannot* be known

The conversation then turns to what should and should not be said (another, social, form of ignorance, or of the production of ignorance): Henrietta has been told by Miss Fisher that she should not talk about Leopold's relationship with his mother, while Leopold for his part has been instructed not to answer any of Henrietta's questions. But he does not know how to obey Miss Fisher, he explains, and anyway, as he remarks with something like the prodigious sophistry of the young and vulnerable, 'It's not my fault if you are here while I talk'. Leopold is troubled by Henrietta's questions and by the fact that she – and therefore others – might think that it is 'funny' that he lives away from his mother. So Leopold returns Henrietta's difficult enquiry into his coherent self by asking her a series of direct and pointed questions about her dead mother:

> 'Look – now your mother's dead so you can't possibly see her, do you still mean to love her, or is that no good now? When you want to love her, what do you do, remember her? But if you couldn't remember her, but heard you could see her, would you enjoy loving her more, or less?'
> 'I don't see what you mean', said Henrietta, distracted – in fact in quite a new kind of pain. She saw only too well that this inquisition had no bearing on Henrietta at all, that Leopold was not even interested in hurting, and was only tweaking her petals off or her wings off with the intention of exploring himself. His dispassionateness was more dire, to Henrietta, than cruelty. With no banal reassuring grown-ups present, with grown-up intervention taken away, there is no limit to the terror strange children feel of each other, a terror life obscures but never ceases to justify. There is no end to the violations committed by children on children, quietly talking alone. Henrietta dreaded what he might say next. Helpless tears began making her eyelids twitch.
> 'Why, are you still unhappy about your mother?' he said. (p. 31)

The authorial comments sum up the point of the whole passage: away from the so-called 'civilizing' influence of adults, 'there is no limit to the terror strange children feel of each other'. But the sentence goes on to turn this around to implicate adults too – 'a terror life obscures but never ceases to justify'. In another sense, however, the knowing (adult) generalizations of the narratorial commentary know too much, or claim too much – there is something jarring, overstated, in what are presented here as universal human truths about children. The commentary contrasts with the suggestiveness and subtlety of the exchange and of Leopold's questions, his ontological probing of the nature of loss. It is as if this 'adult' intrusion of narratorial commentary has forced itself, literal-mindedly, on the subtle inquiries and inquisitions of the children's helpless, desperate talk. What the conversation seems to illustrate is, in fact, the (here complex, messy, overlapping) conflict between the child's ignorance and that of the adult. Both Henrietta and Leopold are, in a sense, trying to become adults – Henrietta especially is on the verge of adolescence. And our fascination with the scene and Bowen's fascination more generally with adolescents and young adults (*The Hotel* (1927), *The Last September* (1929), *The Death of the Heart* (1938) all figure adolescents and young adults as protagonists) has to do, I think, with how they indicate things about ourselves that we do not know – not least our own ignorance.

The point is, as I say, not that we should (sentimentally and with, potentially, so much condescension) look at children as 'little philosophers'. They might, it is true, look, at times, like epistemologists, those strange beings that ask strangely naive, insouciant questions about the world, questions that most of us don't ask just because we see no need ('how do I know another person, or this table?' they (epistemologists) childishly ask – or indeed 'how do I know that this other person is not, in some essential way, more like a table or a stuffed toy monkey than like what I take myself to be?'). Indeed, children's questions may not seem so different, except in their formulation. In this respect, I suggest that our literary fascination with children has to do not so much with the sentimental or 'Romantic' (Wordsworthian, indeed) vision of children as somehow naturally wise – unencumbered as they are by the prison-house of language and learning, of an adult's socialized conception of herself and the world – but with the fact that their questions make us consider the limits of our own knowledge. We know, in essence, that the dead do not count and that a toy monkey cannot feel or that a mother being dead is not the same as a mother just being away from us but alive, not the same as having deserted us; we know that the fact that your mother is dead does not mean that you stop loving her. But in another sense, we do not know – we do not know what it means to count or not to count if a person is dead, and do not know what kind of absence is involved; we do not know, really know, psychologically grasp or accept, the difference between being abandoned and being orphaned; we do not know how or why or in what way being absent is different from being dead; do not know what love means when it comes to loving the dead. Children, in these texts at least, ask the kinds of questions we do not usually, or often cannot, ask, the kinds of questions that an epistemologist (that most childlike of philosopher) might ask, if she puts her mind to it (if an epistemologist may be said to have a mind, that is). And the function of such children may be said to involve the possibility of seeing, in the end, not their ignorance but the limits of our own knowledge, and of recognizing where knowing ends, of acknowledging what it is that we do not know. Children, children in literature, that is, function in this respect as an agnoiological force: rather than teaching us things they allow us to engage with our own ignorance.

Notes

1 Adam Phillips, *Terrors and Experts* (London: Faber and Faber, 1995), p. 2: Phillips suggests that in fact 'every child does somewhere' know this. See also Stanley Cavell *The Claim of Reason: Wittgenstein, Skepticism, Morality, and Tragedy* (1979), new edn. (New York: Oxford University Press, 1999), pp. 124–5.
2 There are, of course, various different kinds of knowledge. Berys Gaut usefully lists propositional knowledge, knowing how, phenomenal knowledge (i.e. 'knowledge of what it is like to experience something') conceptual knowledge, knowledge of values and significance, and so on ('Art and Cognition', in Matthew Kieran, ed., *Contemporary Debates in Aesthetics and the Philosophy of Art* (Oxford: Blackwell, 2006), p. 115): but most of these ways of knowing involve, at some level, language.
3 St Augustine, *Confessions*, trans. R.S. Pine-Coffin (London: Penguin, 1961), p. 35: for Augustine, this 'thirst' is a 'temptation', a 'futile curiosity'. 'Epistemophilic impulse' is from Melanie Klein, 'Early Stages of the Oedipus Conflict', in *Contributions to Psycho-analysis, 1921–1945* (London: Hogarth, 1948), pp. 204–9; see also p. 33 on 'the impulse for knowledge'.
4 Phillips, *Terrors and Experts*, p. 13: further references are cited in the text.
5 Ibid., p. 5: quoted from Freud's *Introductory Lectures on Psychoanalysis*.
6 See Nicolas Abraham and Maria Torok, *The Wolf Man's Magic Word: A Cryptonymy*, trans. Nicholas Rand (Minneapolis: University of Minnesota Press, 1986).
7 Klein, 'Early Stages', p. 188. As Phillips remarks, 'The so-called facts of life are hardly a convincing answer – for anybody – to why people have sex, or where babies come from' (*Terrors and Experts*, p. 1).

8 Jean Laplanche, 'Transference: Its Provocation by the Analyst', in *Essays on Otherness* (London: Routledge, 1999), p. 229.
9 Jean Laplanche, *New Foundations for Psychoanalysis*, trans. David Macey (Oxford: Basil Blackwell, 1989), p. 124. See Phillips on a child learning its first language: 'It impinges ineluctably on the child's development, making all the difference. The child may be inventive within it, but it is not the child's invention. It is, as it were, something the child has to catch; from the young child's point of view, language is what other people do; it is other people. And the learning of it will always be a paradoxical kind of trauma for the child (if not *the* paradigm of trauma itself), because the trauma can only be processed – the child will only be able to make sense of it retrospectively – in the currency of the trauma itself: in words' (*Terrors and Experts*, p. 4).
10 Laplanche, *New Foundations*, p. 127.
11 Ibid., pp. 127–8.
12 *Essays on Otherness*, pp. 126–7.
13 *New Foundations*, p. 131. This is a fact which, Laplanche argues, brings the possibility of Freud's notion of the 'experience of satisfaction' into question (ibid.). It is significant that Laplanche argues that the analyst, the 'one who is supposed to know' must resist knowing: 'if the analyst must be in the position of one supposed to know, he must obviously refuse knowledge, but he must also refuse to let himself know . . . This is the motor, the source of energy, and perhaps it is the source of a new energy, which propels the cure. The search for knowledge both enslaves and propels the analysand, just as it once propelled the small child' (*New Foundations*, p. 158).
14 Philip Larkin 'This Be the Verse', l. 10, in *Collected Poems* (London: Faber and Faber. 1988), p. 180.
15 Peter Brooks, *Body Work: Objects of Desire in Modern Narrative* (Cambridge, Mass.: Harvard University Press, 1993), pp. 5–6: further references are cited in the text.
16 As Brooks asserts, for the nineteenth-century novel in particular (this indeed is 'a central preoccupation of the nineteenth-century novel') the body 'cannot be left in nonsignifying somatic realm. It must mean. But it will do so only when made part of a web of signifying practices' (p. 53).
17 Emmanuel Levinas, 'Ethics as First Philosophy', in *The Levinas Reader*, ed. Seán Hand (Oxford: Basil Blackwell, 1989), p. 78.
18 *'Lyrical Ballads' and Other Poems, 1797–1800*, ed. James Butler and Karen Green (Ithaca: Cornell University Press, 1992), p. 745 (references to 'We Are Seven' are from this edition). It is significant that one manuscript version of this poem's title was 'We Are Seven; or death' (see p. 73). Susan Wolfson suggests that the opening question 'seems no question at all, but rather an invitation to share the speaker's bemused condescension', and points to the 'resonance of moral obligation' in its 'should' (*The Questioning Presence: Wordsworth, Keats, and the Interrogative Mode in Romantic Poetry* (Ithaca: Cornell University Press, 1986), pp. 44, 45–6).

19 But see Frances Ferguson's counter-intuitive comment that 'perhaps the most curious aspect of the poem is not how much the girl and the man disagree on but instead how much they agree on' (*Solitude and the Sublime: Romanticism and the Aesthetics of Individuation* (New York: Routledge, 1992), p. 164).
20 Wolfson, *Questioning Presence*, p. 46; as Wolfson comments, 'Even so, the denial of death by a child who "feels its life in every limb" is something the most forgiving of adult readers knows is doomed to revision as she matures' (ibid.); see also Wolfson's comment that such 'contrariety between adult and childhood orders of knowing is a fundamental Wordsworthian issue, and the absence of connection a perpetual Wordsworthian concern' (p. 48).
21 Maureen McLane, *Romanticism and the Human Sciences: Poetry, Population, and the Discourse of the Species* (Cambridge: Cambridge University Press, 2000), p. 54, 59: as McLane comments, from this perspective the narrator is 'stupid in a way he himself cannot have assumed' (p. 54). Compare Richard Gravil, *Wordsworth's Bardic Vocation, 1787–1842* (Basingstoke: Palgrave Macmillan, 2003), p. 98: '*We are Seven* ends with the persona as unenlightened as he began, and subject to a continuing dramatic irony'; and see Keith Hanley's assurance that the girl 'is definitely given the last word' (*Wordsworth: A Poet's History* (London: Palgrave, 2001), p. 96).
22 Compare McLane, *Romanticism and the Human Sciences*, p. 59, on the man's attempt to educate the girl through 'a kind of twisted Socratic method'. The method is also, of course, catechistic, and part of Wordsworth's purpose here seems to involve a critique of the overbearing religiosity and indeed mindlessness of certain (dominant) eighteenth-century forms of education.
23 Ferguson, *Solitude and the Sublime*, p. 165.
24 This is, as I say, the most common interpretation, at least in recent years: as Ferguson comments, 'critics have tended to defend the child and abuse the man' (ibid.). See, for example, Maureen McLane's sense that the 'increasingly pompous' speaker 'gets his comuppance' by the end of the poem and 'his sentimental indulgence quickly turns sour': the poem, she suggests, 'slyly allies us with the maid' (the very title seems to endorse the maid's viewpoint, McLane argues, since otherwise it might be called 'Ye are only five') ('Ballads and Bards: British Romantic Orality', *Modern Philology*, 98: 3 (2001): 438–9); see also Mary Jacobus, *Tradition and Experiment in Wordsworth's 'Lyrical Ballads' (1798)* (Oxford: Clarendon, 1976), pp. 102–3; Heather Glen, *Vision and Disenchantment: Blake's 'Songs' and Wordsworth's 'Lyrical Ballads'* (Cambridge: Cambridge University Press, 1983), p. 43; Paul Hamilton, *Wordsworth* (Brighton: Harvester, 1986), p. 54. The reading is now so dominant as hardly to need arguing: in a recent essay on Charles Dickens's *Old Curiosity Shop*, for example, Paul Schlicke briefly refers to Wordsworth's poem in terms of the 'wise insight' of the child contrasted with the 'obstinate literal-mindedness of an adult'; in her 'wisdom', the child 'steadfastly uphold[s] [her] innocent vision in the form of uncomprehending objections'

('Embracing the New Spirit of the Age: Dickens and the Evolution of *The Old Curiosity Shop*', *Dickens Studies Annual* 32 (2002): 11).

25 See Peter de Bolla's comment that 'It is almost as if in reading the poem one is forced to side with one or the other of the protagonists' and that the one that one sides with is 'usually the adult' (*Art Matters* (Cambridge, Mass.: Harvard University Press, 2001), p. 104) – de Bolla in fact sees any such response as 'odd', suggesting that the force of the poem lies in the 'even handedness' by which one is forced to consider both sides of the argument.

26 Geoffrey H. Hartman, *Wordsworth's Poetry, 1787–1814* (New Haven: Yale University Press, 1964), p. 144. Hartman does, however, suggest that 'The child's unconscious faith should have admonished the questioner to look once more, and consciously, through death' (p. 146).

27 Alan Richardson, 'The Politics of Childhood: Wordsworth, Blake, and Catechistic Method', *English Literary History* 56: 4 (1989): 860. In this spirit see Coleridge's objection to Wordsworth's sense of the child as a 'philosopher' in the 'Intimations' ode, an assertion that he links to 'We Are Seven' ('Surely, it cannot be that this wonder-rousing apostrophe is but a comment on the little poem "We are Seven"') (*Biographia Literaria*, 2 vols. eds James Engell and W. Jackson Bate (London: Routledge and Kegan Paul, 1983), 2: 138–41).

28 Ferguson, *Solitude and the Sublime*, p. 166.

29 McLane, *Romanticism*, p. 59.

30 The sense that the poem is undecidable has itself been acknowledged by some critics: see, for example, Wolfson, *The Questioning Presence*, p. 46; David Ferry *The Limits of Mortality: An Essay on Wordsworth's Major Poems* (Middletown, Conn.: Wesleyan University Press, 1959), pp. 84–5; Gravil, *Wordsworth's Bardic Vocation*, p. 98; and, as previously mentioned, De Bolla, *Arts Matters*, p. 104.

31 For a discussion of *The House in Paris* in relation to ways of knowing and ways of being ignorant see Andrew Bennett and Nicholas Royle, *Elizabeth Bowen and the Dissolution of the Novel: Still Lives* (London: Macmillan, 1995), ch. 3.

32 The conversation may seem to enact Martin Amis's confessional description of youth as 'that time of constant imposture, when you have to pretend to understand everything while understanding nothing at all' (*Experience* (London: Vintage, 2001), p. 54).

33 Elizabeth Bowen, *The House in Paris* (1935) (London: Penguin, 1976), pp. 29–30: further references are cited in the text.

8

Monsters and trees: epistemelancholia in David Hume and Henry James

Melancholy is the monster. It makes monsters of us, it monsters humanity: to be melancholy is to be human and to be melancholy is to be monstrous.[1] Melancholy is thought, philosophy, poetry and knowledge. Melancholy is the subject of speech and the subject who speaks; melancholy is beyond speech, beyond language. Melancholy is unique, singular and infinitely variable;[2] melancholy is universal, unchanging, is the condition of unchangingness.[3] Melancholy: human and non-human, in and out of nature, monstrous. Melancholy is a foreign body, an impostor, an impostume. Melancholy is a swelling or growth in the head – for Robert Burton 'a kind of Impostume in my head', for Byron's Tasso 'the mind's canker in its savage mood'.[4] Canker, then, 'an eating sore: a gangrene: a fungus disease in trees . . . anything that corrupts, consumes, irritates or decays'.[5] Melancholy is foreign to the subject, beyond reason or cause, outside consciousness, outside analysis; melancholy is thinking. Melancholy is truth and an aberration in perception, speech and the deformation and regression of language, the condition of inarticulacy.[6] There is nothing to say about melancholy; melancholy is the condition of having nothing to say.[7] A medical condition and the condition for poetry, literature, philosophy, the condition of writing: lack, absence, *différance*, deferral. Melancholy branches out towards all experience, perception, language, memory. Melancholy trees, the melancholy of trees: a monstrous, branching growth, an outgrowth, 'depression's dark wood' or a 'forest where the wolf howls and the obscene bird of night chatters'.[8] A place to hide after the Fall, a place where 'highest woods impenetrable / To star or sunlight, spread their umbrage broad'.[9] Melancholy is a jungle or a forest encountered in the middle of life, to be lost in, a loss: 'Nel mezzo del cammin di nostra vita / Mi ritrovai per una selva oscura, / Ché la diritta via era smarrita'.[10] The dark wood of life but also the endless, branching quality of melancholic thinking:

'I am almost sick and giddy with the quantity of things in my head', writes John Ruskin, 'trains of thought beginning and branching to infinity, crossing each other'.[11] This is the 'excess', in Julia Kristeva's formulation, of 'an unorderable cognitive chaos'.[12] Thinking is itself the sickness, the monster. Melancholy, then: the experience, as the melancholic novelist William Styron puts it, of being 'sapped'.[13]

In this chapter, I seek to investigate representations of melancholy – particularly those in the writings of Henry James and David Hume – in terms of a certain figuration of trees. I will suggest that trees, figures of monstrous outgrowths, are often represented as both analogues for and, more strikingly, causes of melancholia. But I also want to suggest that the pervasive literary discourse of melancholy – one that in some ways haunts literature from classical times to the present – is linked to ignorance and to the discourses of scepticism and agnoiology. The monstrous tree, in that sense, may be said to stand in for a kind of cognitive block or (un)natural outgrowth, a convoluted branching of thinking in which thinking, and knowing, cease. But first we need to establish the pervasiveness of the connection between melancholy and the (figure of the) tree.

Melancholy is dendritic. The arborescent diagrammatic contents pages of Burton's *Anatomy of Melancholy* instance the aleatory, endlessly branching nature of melancholic thinking, of a melancholic, thinking.

There is no reason for the tree. It is in the park, confronted by the 'black, knotty mass' of the root of a chestnut tree, that Jean-Paul Sartre's Roquentin experiences his monstrous existential 'revelation'.[14] In an experience more or less indistinguishable from the 'vastation' described by William James and his father or the 'breakdowns' related in a recent spate of confessional books by William Styron, Kay Redfield Jamison, Andrew Solomon and others, Roquentin suddenly sees the 'diversity of things', their 'individuality', as only 'an appearance, a veneer': 'This veneer had melted, leaving soft, monstrous masses, in disorder – naked, with a frightening, obscene nakedness' (p. 183). Trees become 'superfluous', without the 'slightest reason for being there', just like Roquentin, who is 'weak, languid, obscene, digesting, tossing about dismal thoughts' and who is also 'superfluous' (p. 184). And for Roquentin, the crisis brought about by his recognition of the 'absurdity' of the tree's root is finally an epistemological crisis: 'faced with that big rugged paw, neither ignorance nor knowledge had any importance; the world of explanations and reasons is not that of existence' (p. 185). The root exists 'in so far that I could not explain it' (p. 186). Fascinated, fixated on the thing of the root, its non-human non-intelligibility, its contingency, its superfluity, Roquentin *becomes* the root: 'I *was* the root of the chestnut tree. Or rather I was all consciousness of its existence' (p. 188). The tree's branches, too, are monstrous, endlessly multiplying and without origin: 'There were swarms of existences at the ends of the branches, existences which constantly renewed themselves and were never born'. Roquentin is 'stunned' by the 'profusion of beings without origins' (p. 190). This is a birth beyond reason, effect beyond cause: 'Every existent is born without reason . . . there was *no reason for it to exist . . . But it was not possible* for it not to exist' (pp. 191–2).

A tree is also the focus of an existential crisis for Virginia Woolf. As a child, the depressive and ultimately suicidal novelist hears that a friend of her parents, Mr Valpey, has killed himself. Woolf connects this death with an apple tree in the family's St Ives garden. Unable to walk past this tree of knowledge, she records standing looking at the 'grey-green creases of the bark' in 'a trance of horror': 'I seemed to be dragged down, hopelessly, into some pit of absolute despair from which I could not escape', she comments in a memoir completed only months before she took her own life.[15]

Kay Redfield Jamison, who uses the word 'dendritic' to describe melancholy thinking,[16] includes amongst other visual aids in *Touched with Fire: Manic-Depressive Illness and the Artistic Temperament* dendritic diagrams illustrating the prevalence of melancholy in the family trees of Tennyson, Schumann, Henry James, Woolf, Hemingway and Van Gogh.

'I don't know why, but I just don't trust trees. I appreciate that they are supposed to provide oxygen for us, but I'm not entirely sure that I believe that. They intimidate me – probably because I'll end up dressed in one before long.'[17]

The final entry in *Roland Barthes by Roland Barthes* is entitled 'The monster of totality'. And the final image is an illustration from Diderot's *Encyclopédie*, 'Anatomy: stems of the vena cava with their branches dissected in an adult body'.[18] The illustration shows the human body as a tree. 'To write the body', writes the melancholy semiologist Roland Barthes, 'Neither the skin, nor the muscles, nor the bones, nor the nerves, but the rest: an awkward, fibrous, shaggy, ravelled thing, a clown's coat'.[19] Barthes's book is a book of mourning – mourning for the author's mother and, as with all autobiographical writing, for his past selves – but also a book of melancholia, ending with the body figured as a tree.

The melancholy poet John Keats, a poet much possessed by trees, also figures the inside of the human body – in this case the inside of the head, the cerebellum – as *arbor vitae*. 'Ode to Psyche' is, amongst other things, an ode to and presentation of the poet's own psyche, which means for the medically trained poet a representation of his own brain's physiognomy. In the first stanza, the poet records coming across the mythical figures of Psyche and Eros as he 'wandered in a forest thoughtlessly'.[20] In the final stanza the inside of the head, the brain, is more fully described. Keats imagines building a temple to Psyche in 'some untrodden region of my mind', a region 'Where branchèd thoughts, new grown with pleasant pain, / Instead of pines shall murmur in the wind' (ll. 51–3). The pain of pines: tree-like thoughts as the painful substance of the mind, branching. Thoughts substitute for trees. Similarly, Byron's melancholic Manfred, who is 'Grey-hair'd with anguish', sees something like an objective correlative for his condition in trees: he is 'like these blasted pines, / Wrecks of a single winter, barkless, branchless, / A blighted trunk upon a cursed root, / Which but supplies a feeling to decay'.[21]

The tree of knowledge is also the tree of melancholy. As *homo sapiens* we have a taste for the tree, the 'tree of knowledge', a 'taste' in other words for knowledge, for the tree that also makes gods of us in our knowledge.[22] Having eaten of its fruit, Eve's sorrow is 'greatly multipl[ied]' and she is condemned to 'bring forth children' 'in sorrow', while Adam is condemned to eat of the ground 'in sorrow' for 'all the days of [his] life' (Genesis 3: 16–17). In Milton's adaptation of the story Satan begins his temptation of Eve with an apostrophe to the tree:

> O sacred, wise, and wisdom-giving plant,
> Mother of science, now I feel thy power
> Within me clear, not only to discern
> Things in their causes, but to trace the ways
> Of highest agents, deemed however wise.
>
> (*Paradise Lost* 9: 679–83)

Like Jacques Derrida, Milton's Eve has 'a taste for the secret':[23] she 'engorge[s]' the fruit of the tree 'without restraint' (9: 791), and then she too addresses the 'sovereign, virtuous, precious of all trees', remarking that the 'hitherto obscured, infamed' tree has been until now 'to no end / Created' (9: 795–9). Eve worships the tree's 'sciential sap' (9: 837). But as we know, unhappy consequences flow from Eve's tasting and from her and Adam's 'sapience': Satan is turned into a 'monstrous serpent on his belly prone' (10: 514) and with his 'accessories' becomes part of a 'thick-swarming' mass of 'complicated monsters' (10: 520–3).[24] For Adam and Eve the 'fleeting joys / Of Paradise' turn out to have been 'dear bought with lasting woes' (10: 741–2), and the threatened death on eating of the tree turns out to be 'not one stroke' as expected but instead 'endless misery / From this day onward' (10: 809–11). Milton's Eve may be said to have introduced epistemelancholia – monstrous word – into the world: she recognizes that she is 'to others cause of misery', that she is fated now to 'bring / Into this cursed world a woeful race' that will be, after a 'wretched life', 'Food for so foul a monster' as death (10: 982–6).

It comes as no surprise, therefore, that in the romantic-melancholic, totalizing-idealizing, binarizing nostalgia-hymn to the 'rhizome' which opens *A Thousand Plateaus*, Deleuze and Guattari reserve their scorn for the tree: 'We're tired of trees. We should stop believing in trees, roots, and radicles. They've made us suffer too much. All of arborescent culture is founded on them, from biology to linguistics.'[25] Deleuze and Guattari reject what they figure as the hierarchical nature of 'arborescent' thinking, as well as the discourses which exploit the tree as their structural model – 'from botany to biology and anatomy, but also gnosiology, theology, ontology, all of philosophy' they say, but they also include linguistics and genealogy, psychoanalysis and neuroscience, indeed all of 'Western reality' and 'all of Western thought' (p. 18). Our authors prefer the arboureal to the arboreal, they prefer grass: 'Many people have a tree growing in their heads', they declare, 'but the brain itself is much more a grass than a tree' (p. 15). It is the particular form of connectivity in trees that Deleuze and Guattari object to, since, by comparison with the utopian rhizome's ability to connect 'any point to any other point', the tree is, they argue, static, hierarchical, centred (p. 21). The tree is death, the death of desire: 'once a rhizome has been obstructed, arborified, it's all over, no desire stirs ... Whenever desire climbs a tree, internal repercussions trip it up and its falls to its death' (p. 14). We might take it that a dendritic reading would differ from a rhizomatic reading – the rhizomatic reading of the tree, in the first place – in the attention that it would pay to a certain undoing of certainty with respect to causality and connection. In this respect, it may be thought that Deleuze and Guattari have simply misinterpreted the tree, misinterpreted its melancholic monstrosity, its outgrowth, its canker. A monstrism of the tree would allow for an alternative reading of the aborescent. It is the happily totalizing and joyfully binarizing logic of the rhizome (articulated in particular in its opposition to the tree itself, of course) that dendritic logic might question, with its resistance to a totalizing connectivity, with its familial uncertainties, its monstrous organic and inorganic growths.[26]

* * * * *

Melancholy is the beast. Writing to Edmund Gosse in 1910, Henry James declares that 'black depression – the blackness of darkness and the cruellest melancholia are my chronic enemy and curse'.[27] A certain anachronism is invited by this statement, a certain retrospective reading of such a text as his 1902 story of 'melancholy and loneliness', his tale of 'desolation', his most 'modern' tale, the one invested with the most 'personal emotion',[28] 'The Beast in the Jungle'. The tale can be read in terms of the anachronism of melancholy,[29] and in terms of melancholy's monstrous epistemology. Julia Kristeva argues that 'Melancholy persons, with their despondent, secret insides, are . . . intellectuals capable of dazzling, albeit abstract constructions' and that 'Through their empty speech they assure themselves of an inaccessible . . . ascendancy over an archaic object that thus remains, for themselves and for all others, an enigma and a secret'.[30] James's tale concerns an unrevealed secret, an unopenable closet, an impenetrable crypt, but *at the same time* it can be read as a narrative of melancholy, a monstrous discourse of epistemological doubt and depression, of epistemelancholy. What we know of 'The Beast in the Jungle', what is to be known, to be revealed, is the beast, the monster. A dendritic as opposed to a linear or causal reading of the novel – but also as opposed to a rhizomatic reading – would explore the story through James's melancholy of 1910 and through both his own earlier depressive 'episodes', his constitutional melancholy and the 'vastations' of his immediate family. It would suggest that the truth of the beast, the monster of this narrative, waiting amongst the trees of the jungle, ready to spring, already sprung, is melancholia – and that the James family, and Henry James's writing life, were subjects to and the multiple subject of both transgenerational and intragenerational melancholy: for the James family, melancholy is infectious, dendritic.[31]

What Henry James adds to his plans for 'The Beast in the Jungle' when he comes to write it in the summer of 1902 is the beast and the jungle – figures and a certain logic of figuration, which are absent, in abeyance, in the earlier notebook sketches for the tale from February 1895 and August 1901.[32] This is not (only) to remark that in writing the story, writing it out, James develops the gothic, supernatural, uncanny, melodramatic or horror dimensions of the text but (also) that a certain logic – the logic of monstrism and of melancholy, of, in short, the dendritic – comes to determine or define James's writing. The significance of the beast, the monster, in James's tale is evinced by its *absence* in his germinal notes. While the composition of the tale was prefigured in two notebook entries, one from seven years and one from twelve months earlier, the figure of the beast – of monstrism and of melancholy – appears before 1902 only in this absence.

Something happens, then, in the summer of 1902 that develops the germ of a story about 'the idea of *Too late*', about a passion that '*might have been*' or about 'some affection language desired and waited for, that is formed too late' (from 1895), that develops a '*faintaisie*' about a man who fears that 'something will happen to him' and a woman who 'reads . . . his real case, and is, though unexpressedly, *lucid*' but who dies before the man realises that what was to happen was 'that nothing happens' (from 1901), into a tale centred the figure of a beast. What happens, we might surmise (but when? when will the story have been written? when is the desire of language formed? when will the germ be activated? what sprouting is James awaiting between 1895 and 1902?), concerns James's family tree, concerns an infection, a germ and germination – a tree-like, uncontainable growth, an other language, monstrous, beyond control – of an intertextual, dendritic monster. The 'Beast in the Jungle' is not just about the beast, the monster, but is itself a monstrous outgrowth, a melancholy canker, an imposthume. It just happens that James was reading his famous brother's just-published *The Varieties of Religious Experience* when he came to write the tale in 1902, to write it up from his notebooks. Indeed, Leon Edel comments that writing the tale provided a 'catharsis' for Henry James, a 'moment of vision and of insight such as his brother, William, described in his book'.[33] The 'moment of vision' that Edel refers to is described in William's lecture on 'The Sick Soul' where he produces the metaphor of the monster to figure his own devastating depression. William describes being in a state of 'philosophic pessimism and general depression of spirits' when he suddenly experiences 'a horrible fear of my own existence'. He imagines 'an epileptic patient' from an asylum, 'a black-haired youth with greenish skin, entirely idiotic'. The patient – but here, as the man becomes more bestial, the figures more extreme, it becomes unclear whether he is imagined or remembered – sits 'like a sort of sculptured Egyptian cat or Peruvian mummy, moving nothing but his black eyes and looking absolutely non-human': '*That shape am I*', William feels, and 'Nothing that I possess can defend me against that fate, if the hour for it should strike for me as it struck for him'. He becomes 'a mass of quivering fear': 'After this the universe was changed for me altogether', William concludes.[34] To the extent that this figuration of the beast – this identification of the subject with the beast, this horror that 'the hour might strike' at any time and that I will become the monstrous and monstrously suffering man – is what happens to Henry's story, we can say that the story is not Henry's. Nor is it however William's, since, in a footnote to his discussion of the monstrous 'experience of melancholia' (p. 161), William refers us back to a passage from his father's *Society the Redeemed Form of Man* (1879) in which a similar figuration occurs. The parallels between Willliam's experience and his father's are indeed remarkable, suggesting that William's experience of a monstered melancholy, his 'vastation', is impelled by a form of intertextual, a form of transgenerational, haunting. Henry James Sr records an experience from 1844 when he is suddenly subject to 'a perfectly insane and abject terror'. The terror is, as we must expect, 'without ostensible cause', but is figured in his 'perplexed imagination' as a 'damnèd shape squatting invisible to me within the precincts of the room, and raying out from his fetid personality influences fatal to life'.[35] What are we to make of these textual-familial relations? How do they relate? It is not simply that the accounts by his father and brother of a certain experience of melancholy, of monstrism, provided the novelist with an imaginative 'germ', a certain contagion, a certain psycho-pathological condition – a condition of writing – since the very nature of the relationship may be figured as a monstrous, uncontainable, dendritic series, a series which fundamentally undoes the certainties apparently contained by the organicism of seed, germ, germination, family tree, branches, undoes indeed (familial) relationship itself.

Both Henrys and William map their accounts of the beast on to a certain *thinking* of melancholia, a certain epistemelancholia. They relate, that is to say, the monstrous logic of melancholy to philosophical monstrism, to a certain questioning of the discourses of knowledge or truth. Henry James Sr's description is prefaced by an account of his sense that he had just made a small but significant breakthrough, an 'interesting discovery' which would 'extensively modify theology'. He notes that, rather than throwing 'a direct light upon our natural or race history' the book of Genesis 'was an altogether mystical or symbolic record of the laws of God's *spiritual* creation and providence'. By means of this idea he hopes to be able 'to be finally qualified to contribute a not insignificant mite to the sum of man's highest knowledge' (p. 160). It is this, it seems, this intellectual and conceptual breakthrough, this theologico-epistemological invention, that precipitates his 'breakdown', his 'catastrophe', his 'vastation' (pp. 162, 163). Henry James Sr, then, is brought to a point of crisis by philosophy, by a certain thinking, by indeed *knowing* something fundamental and fundamentally new. The breakdown, however, leads him to an alternative revelation – the revelation of non-revelation. The vastation itself is seen as a 'bottomless mystery' and he declares that 'The more . . . I worried myself with speculations about the cause of it, the more the mystery deepened' (p. 161). Beyond this mystery, however, is the recognition that 'The curse of mankind, that which keeps our manhood so little and so depraved, is its sense of selfhood, and the absurd, abominable opinionativeness it engenders' (p. 162). This opinion about opinionatedness prefaces Henry James Sr's account of 'the proper upshot of this incident', a loss of faith in truth and a loss of desire to know. He records losing all interest in his work, feeling certain, *knowing* that he has 'never caught a glimpse of truth'. He experiences what he calls 'an utter and plenary destitution of truth' and is 'sick to death in fact with a sense of my downright intellectual poverty and dishonesty': 'Truth, indeed!' he exclaims, revealing the truth:

> How should a beggar like me be expected to discover it? How should any man of woman born pretend to such ability? Truth must *reveal itself* if it would be known; and even then how imperfectly known at best! For truth is God, the omniscient and omnipotent God; and who shall pretend to comprehend that great and adorable perfection? And yet who that aspires to the name of man, would not cheerfully barter all he knows of life for a bare glimpse of the hem of its garment? (pp. 162–3)

This sickness, this monstrous melancholy,[36] is precipitated by and results in the theologian's epistemological sickness unto death, his sense of his own 'downright intellectual poverty and dishonesty'. And by the paradox that truth cannot but must be known. But the passage is also performative with regard to its *assertion* of doubt, its statement of the truth that truth lies beyond the human mind's imaginings, and its assertion of the full-emptiness, the present absence – the 'plenary destitution' – of truth.

William's confession of vastation is similarly epistemelanchological, embedded as it is in a book which analyses the truth-value of religious experience. But the philosopher is particularly concerned with the question of the accuracy of the melancholic's perception of the world. 'Let us see', begins William James, 'whether pity, pain, and fear, and the sentiment of human helplessness may not open a profounder view' of life (p. 136).[37] He begins his analysis with the founding sense of the insecurity, the ungroundedness, of human existence: 'Unsuspectedly from the bottom of every fountain of pleasure . . . something bitter rises up: a touch of nausea, a falling dead of the delight, a whiff of melancholy, things that sound a knell.' Human life, in other words, is determined by 'an irremediable sense of precariousness' (p. 136), by insecurity, nausea, melancholy. Even 'the happiest man', the man who is 'most envied by the world', is conditioned in his 'in most consciousness' by failure (p. 137). 'Suffering' and 'poisonous humiliation' are, James asserts, 'pivotal human experiences': something 'so ubiquitous and everlasting is evidently an integral part of life'. He quotes the cheerfully Beckettian comments of Robert Louis Stevenson that 'Whatever else we are intended to do, we are not intended to succeed' and that 'failure is [our] fate', and he remarks in a footnote that Stevenson 'adds with characteristic healthy-mindedness: "Our business is to continue to fail in good spirits"' (p. 138). The sentiment clarifies William's sense that optimism is defined by the possibility that failing will *continue*, will not end, that failing is endless – that optimism, that is to say, is pessimism.

William James's lecture ends, terrifyingly, with the reassertion that the monster of melancholia is the bound up with the 'every day', that there is no proper distinction to be made between 'melancholia' and the 'normal process of life', a normality which contains 'moments as bad as any of those which insane melancholy is filled with'. 'The lunatic's visions of horror', he insists, 'are all drawn from the material of daily fact': 'Our civilization is founded on the shambles, and every individual existence goes out in a lonely spasm of helpless agony' (p. 163). The logic of this recognition leads, indeed, to monsters – real monsters, loathsome, monstrous animals (but aren't all animals, all plants, somehow monstrous? – 'the vegetable kingdom abounds with monsters')[38] – that is to say, to *beasts*:

> Crocodiles and rattlesnakes and pythons are at this moment vessels of life as real as we are; their loathsome existence fills every minute of every day that drags its length along; whenever they or other wild beasts clutch their living prey, the deadly horror which an agitated melancholiac feels is the literally right reaction on the situation. (p. 164)

The revelation of melancholy involves a certain monstrism, a mixing up of things (human, animal, bestial, monstrous) which is itself the enactment of a monstrous logic, what we should call 'loathsome logic': and the loathsomeness inheres, not least, in the fact that the 'agitated melancholiac' is 'literally right'. It is his knowledge, what he *knows*, that makes him melancholic – just as (as we shall see) it is his ignorance, that which he cannot know, that (also) defines his melancholia.

Alice James also famously suffered from 'melancholia', and she may be said to have taken the epistemelancholia of her brothers and her father to its logical conclusion. Alice not only suffered from melancholia but constructed her existence around it. For her, thinking was itself the danger. Her biographer tells us that she experienced a 'breakdown' at the age of 19 from which she never fully recovered. For the rest of her life Alice was in or was defending her self from a state of what we would now call 'depression' (the terms are always, necessarily, in process, uncertain, conflicted, a site of conflict: this is the point, this is what we mean when we talk of epistemelancholia, this and the ideas that melancholia is an (an)epistemology, or even agnoiological, and that melancholics are both epistemophobic and epistemophiliac) and she defined the limits of her life according to the strictures of nervous disease.[39] Unlike her father, William and (arguably) Henry, Alice wrote little about her own condition. In the final years of her life, though, she wrote a journal in order to try to 'lose a little of the sense of loneliness and desolation which abides with me'.[40] In an entry for October 1890, she records her 'breakdown' of ' '67 or '68', when she 'broke down first, acutely, and had violent turns of hysteria',[41] and she explains her condition as a reaction to 'cerebration': 'conscious and continuous cerebration', she declares, 'is an impossible exercise and from just behind the eyes my head feels like a dense jungle into which no ray of light has ever penetrated'.[42]

The jungle, then. The various Jamesian accounts of melancholy congregate in or branch out from Alice James's minimal recounting, late in life, of the melancholy, dendritic nature of thinking itself as a site of thickly wooded, overgrown, impenetrable trees, as a monstrous outgrowth. And this, too, is the jungle of Henry James Jr's tale, a jungle literally, metaphorically inhabited by a beast. Conventional accounts of 'The Beast in the Jungle' suggest that it centres on the question of knowledge, of knowing, of secrets and of revelation. As one critic comments, the tale 'seems to hint at ultimate truths, at figures in the carpet, at clues and at riddles' and ultimately at 'Jamesian self-revelation and expiation'.[43] But the story is in fact constituted by a certain epistemological crisis. Its opening sentence, for example, is a veritable thesaurus of (un)knowing: 'What determined the speech that startled him in the course of their encounter scarcely matters, being probably but some words spoken by himself quite without intention – spoken as they lingered and slowly moved together after their renewal of acquaintance.'[44] The sentence opens with the question of 'determination', determination as a question ('What determined'); it makes the quasi-categorical assertion that the determination of the speech is insignificant ('scarcely matters'); it goes on to declare the narrator's uncertainty ('probably'); and it continues with the ignorance or disavowal of intentionality ('quite without intention').

The tale opens, then, by setting up a complex dialectic of ignorance and knowledge as a key problem both for its protagonist, John Marcher, and for the very subject who is supposed to know, for the narrator. And as the opening scene unravels we learn of Marcher's own strange, unaccountable disturbance concerning knowledge, his epistemophobia. He is, we are told, 'disconcerted' by the question of knowledge, of knowingness, and of ignorance in others: he is disconcerted 'almost equally by the presence of those who knew too much and by those who knew nothing' (pp. 64–5). Knowledge in others, the knowledge of others – always too much or too little – is itself unsettling, monstriferous.[45]

Eve Kosofsky Sedgwick's influential discussion of James's tale opens up new ways of knowing the narrative and suggests that it is concerned above all with a certain knowledge, with certain ways of knowing. But as Sedgwick herself almost acknowledges, almost knows, the contradiction within or fracturing of her own essay itself revolves around the question of knowing – of knowing sexuality, of knowing the truth of James's narrative – since the essay is both determined by the inescapable gesture of criticism – the unveiling, unravelling or revelation of meaning – and at the same time resistant to that critical demand. *Epistemology of the Closet* is, as Sedgwick herself asserts, concerned with the structuring and 'fracturing' of 'the major nodes of thought and knowledge in twentieth-century Western culture as a whole' by a crisis in 'homo/heterosexual definition'.[46] Sedgwick's analysis of James's tale is determined by the contradiction which drives her book, the paradoxical assertion and denial of homosexuality, the avowal of its historical truth and its disavowal, the specifying of a certain homosexual truth and the deconstruction of that identification, of that identity. Sedgwick asserts that 'to the extent that Marcher's secret has *a* content, that content is homosexual' and immediately insists that such a content is 'not only dubious' but 'actively denied' from within the tale (p. 201). Sedgwick knows, only too well – this, indeed, is the burden of her book, of her queer project as a whole – that her deliberations concerning James's sexuality and her mapping of his queerly bachelor life on to that of Marcher are precisely the kind of epistemology that 'animates and perpetuates the mechanism of homophobic male self-ignorance and violence and manipulability'. For Sedgwick, to point to '*a* possibility of "homosexual meaning" is to say worse than nothing' (p. 204), and yet this is what Sedgwick does point to even while she complicates matters by 'spelling out' what she sees as a 'series of "full" – that is, homosexually tinged – meanings for the Unspeakable' in James's tale. Or when, to put it differently, she 'hypothesizes' that Marcher's sexual identity 'importantly includes, though is not necessarily limited to, the possibility of something homosexual' (p. 205). Sedgwick's reading of the tale, then, is centred on the paradox of knowing the (homosexual) truth and resisting the grounds of such knowledge. If we were to read the tale through the figure of melancholy – through a certain monstrism, that is to say – we might draw out the epistemological question that cannot help but undo Sedgwick's reading. The problem of knowledge, of knowing, in 'The Beast in the Jungle', is intimately bound up with the question of the beast itself, which is to say that it has to do not only with a certain queer desire but also with a certain performance of melancholia.

'I am that queer monster the artist', James declares in an 1914 letter to Henry Adams.[47] While a post-Sedgwickian reading might be tempted to put the emphasis on 'queer' in this confession, we might also reflect upon 'monster'.[48] There is, indeed, something monstrous about the endless connectivity of an 'Art' which attempts to capture 'experience' when experience is famously described by James as 'a kind of huge spider-web of the finest silken threads suspended in the chamber of consciousness, and catching every air-borne particle in its tissue. It is the very atmosphere of the mind', James continues, 'and when the mind is imaginative ... it takes to itself the faintest hints of life, it converts the very pulses of the air into revelations'.[49] Not so much 'telepathy' or 'telepathy of disease',[50] then, as a working out and working through of a monstrous family tree and an unpredictable, uncontainable intertextuality,[51] monstrous in its organic and inorganic branchings, in its outgrowth: jungly. The 'vastations' described by Henry James Sr and by William are translated into a monstrous consciousness in James's tale, and figured in the 'visitation' of the beast (p. 106). The 'jungle' behind Alice's eyes becomes the beast-inhabited jungle thought up by Marcher, thought up by James, by the James family, in a tale deeply concerned with knowing and with not knowing, with truth but with a 'truth' that is, in its final apparition – as Marcher stands at the graveside, a monstrous, melancholy figure, a figured human become a lonely warning to us all – 'vivid and monstrous' (p. 106).

Melancholy is monstrous. The very words of melancholy suggest unnatural nature, suggest nature gone awry. Melancholy is an 'ogre' for William Styron, a 'gorgon'.[52] For James Clarence Mangan to be melancholic is to be 'shut up in a cavern with serpents and scorpions and all hideous and monstrous things, which writhed and hissed around me, and discharged their slime and venom over my person'.[53] Coleridge's melancholy thoughts are monstrous toads: 'My thoughts bustle along like a Surinam toad, with little toads sprouting out of back, side, and belly, vegetating while it crawls.'[54]

Our new word for melancholy, the comfortingly scientific, comfortingly sapient 'depression', slithers 'like a slug' through the twentieth century.[55]

Timothie Bright tells us that 'melancholick humour' causes the brain to 'forge monstrous fictions'; André du Laurens that the melancholic 'maketh himselfe a terrour unto himselfe, as the beast which looketh himselfe in a glasse ... hee is become a savadge creature, haunting the shadowed places, suspicious, solitarie, enemie to the Sunne'; Thomas Willis informs us that some melancholics 'undergo imaginary *Metamorphoses*' imagining themselves to be 'a Dog, or a Wolf, or some other Monster'.[56]

Burton's *Anatomy of Melancholy* – a work whose pagan god is Hercules, the slayer of monsters[57] – is full of monsters: in melancholics, imagination is 'most Powerfull and strong, and often hurts, producing many monstrous and prodigious things' (1: 152). There is, Burton declares, 'nothing so vaine, absurd, ridiculous, extravagant, impossible, incredible, so monstrous a Chymera, so prodigious and strange, such as Painters & Poets durst not attempt, which [melancholics] will not really feare, faine, suspect, and imagine unto themselves' (1: 395)

Scholars, Burton tells us, are peculiarly prone to melancholy, put upon as they are by 'irksome houres, laborious tasks, wearisome daies', and by their 'familiar attendants', 'Terrible monsters' (1: 307).

Our lack of 'charity', he insists, makes us at once melancholy and monstrous: the fact that we cannot 'compose our selves to [the] Christian Lawes of Love' is itself the 'cause of all our woes, miseries, discontent, melancholy'. Instead, we 'contemne, insult, vexe, torture, molest' each other, 'provoke, raile, scoffe, calumniate, challenge, hate, abuse ... to satisfie our lust or private spleene': 'Monsters of men as wee are, Dogges, Wolves, Tygers, Fiends, incarnate Divels ... our whole life is a perpetuall combate' (3: 33).

Melancholy is epistemology. Melancholics, and those who write about them (by and large melancholics *are* those who write about them),[58] agree that the origin of melancholy is a mystery – that melancholy is a closet, a crypt – that melancholy is that which cannot be known. And the more we know about it the less we know it, the very number of hypotheses concerning its origins and meanings being testimony to its 'all but impenetrable mystery'.[59] Melancholy, then, is a problem of knowledge, or ignorance. Sadly, however, knowledge is also a problem of melancholy. Julia Kristeva declares that she owes 'a supreme, metaphysical lucidity to my depression' and that there is 'meaning only in despair'; while others 'get their knowledge by Bookes', Robert Burton gets his by 'melancholizing'.[60]

Melancholy involves both knowing and not knowing, both knowledge and ignorance. But it is also fundamentally the enactment, the performance, of philosophical scepticism with regard to causality. While there are, indubitably, reasons to be melancholy, melancholy is in the end beyond reason: that is its point, its reason. If melancholy has its reasons then it is or it becomes not melancholy but something else – mourning, for example, or a reasoned (however irrational) response to unreasonable suffering, say politics or religion. Indeed, it should come as no surprise that, as we shall see, the philosopher David Hume identifies a certain monstering with melancholia and sees both as an effect of the deconstruction of causality, since such an ungrounding is nowhere more evident than in the melancholic condition. Burton refuses to pronounce on whether melancholy is 'a cause or an effect, a Disease, or Symptome', and quotes Du Laurens's definition of melancholy as 'a kinde of dotage without a feaver, having for his ordinary companions, feare, and sadnesse, without any apparent occasion' (Burton, *Anatomy*, 1: 162). Indeed, the unfixing of cause and effect may be considered as the very definition of melancholia – as Freud suggests in his brief but influential engagement with the condition in 'Mourning and Melancholia', in an argument that branches back to Aristotle's *Problems* 30, where melancholia is defined as 'groundless despondency'.[61]

Freud builds, then, on the ancient tradition that, as Stanley Jackson puts it, 'in melancholia the sadness or dejection was "without cause" or "without apparent cause"'.[62] He begins by asserting the comparability of mourning and melancholia, suggesting that an understanding of the former will lead to an understanding of the latter. Mourning, he suggests, is fundamentally to do with 'the reaction to the loss of a loved person'.[63] Melancholia, he continues, may initially 'be the reaction to the loss of a loved object' but may more fundamentally be due to a loss 'of a more ideal kind' (p. 253). But Freud goes on to suggest that melancholia may be to do with a loss that cannot so easily be defined, in which neither the analyst nor the subject himself can 'consciously perceive what he has lost' (p. 254). The latter hypothesis leads Freud to the suggestion that melancholia is 'in some way related to an object-loss which is withdrawn from consciousness' by contrast with mourning, in which 'there is nothing about the loss that is unconscious' (ibid.). The melancholic is characterised by an *inexplicable*, interminable, and finally untreatable mourning, in which 'we cannot see what it is' that absorbs the subject 'so entirely' (ibid.).[64] Melancholia is, according to Freud, a foreign body. Melancholia is a condition which relates to 'another person, the sexual object they have lost or which has become valueless to them' and one in which the object is subsequently 'set up in the ego itself . . . projected on to the ego'.[65] It is also 'foreign' to a strictly Freudian psychoanalysis, in the sense that Freud declares melancholics, together with paranoiacs and 'sufferers from dementia praecox', to be 'proof against psychoanalytic therapy'. Despite the fact that melancholics know themselves to be ill 'this does not make them more accessible' to treatment. This resistance to psychoanalysis is, Freud declares, in a remarkable confession, a challenge to the project of psychoanalysis as a whole: 'We are faced here by a fact which we do not understand and which therefore leads us to doubt whether we have really understood all the determinants of our possible success with the other neuroses.'[66]

It is not with the psychologist or psychoanalyst that melancholy ends, however, but with the philosopher: it is not so much in the undoing of psychoanalysis as in the undoing of philosophy. The philosopher, that theorist and lover of knowledge, of wisdom, the one who knows, who is supposed to know (even if what he knows is, as in Socrates' case, and Hume's indeed, his own ignorance), is a melancholic who performs, perversely, a certain monstrism. In his famous 'Conclusion' to Book One of the *Treatise of Human Nature*, the philosophical sceptic David Hume declares that his memory of 'past errors and perplexities, makes me diffident for the future' and that he is reduced 'almost to despair' by the 'wretched condition, weakness, and disorder' of his own 'faculties'.[67] He compares himself to a lone sailor who is solitary and suicidal: his situation makes him 'resolve to perish on the barren rock' on which he is stranded rather than 'venture . . . upon that boundless ocean, which runs out into immensity'. This sense of his predicament 'strikes' him with 'melancholy' and is indeed monstriferous: his 'philosophy' places him in a condition of 'forlorn solitude' and in relation to society he sees himself as a 'strange uncouth monster' (p. 172). Since he has declared his 'disapprobation' of the systems of 'metaphysicians, logicians, mathematicians, and even theologians', since he 'foresee[s] on every side dispute, contradiction, anger, calumny and detraction', and since when he 'turns [his] eye inward' he sees only 'doubt and ignorance', he is in the position of the abjected, monstrous and melancholy other:

> I . . . fancy myself some strange and uncouth monster, who not being able to mingle and unite in society, has been expell'd all human commerce, and left utterly abandon'd and disconsolate. Fain wou'd I run into the crowd for shelter and warmth; but cannot prevail with myself to mix with such deformity. I call upon others to join me, in order to make a company apart; but no one will hearken to me. Every one keeps at a distance, and dreads that storm, which beats upon me from every side. (Ibid.)

The philosopher as monster: dread warning. The philosopher as warning against philosophy. The philosophical melancholy of the sceptical, ignorant philosopher – what another philosopher terms Hume's 'melancholy turbulence'[68] – is not simply a side-effect of his conceptual and intellectual attacks on others, nor is it simply a social monstering. It is the very internal logic of the philosopher's thinking, his agoniology, that situates him as the melancholic subject, as the monster. The very experience of 'trac[ing] up the human understanding to its first principles' leads the philosopher into 'such sentiments, as seem to turn into ridicule all our past pains and industry, and to discourage us from future enquiries' (p. 173). It is thinking itself, philosophical or sceptical thinking, which produces melancholia. And yet this logic, the logic of connection, the logic of cause and effect – the philosopher is melancholic owing to his philosophical thoughts – is precisely what is disturbed by those very thoughts. It is indeed the very *undoing* of the logic of causality – and therefore the certainties of personal identity, inductive reasoning, perception, empirical investigation and knowledge itself – that is the *cause* of melancholy. But such a formulation simply repeats the errors of a certain causal reasoning. We must say, rather differently, simply that this suspension of the logic of causality and of personal identity – philosophy, in Hume's sense of it – *is* melancholy.

In the end, the philosophical undoing or suspension of the logic of cause and effect itself undoes philosophy.[69] Philosophical thinking radically undermines the thinking subject's desire for thinking, for philosophy, a thought which reveals the grounding double-bind of philosophy's desire:

> Such a discovery not only cuts off all hope of ever attaining satisfaction, but even prevents our very wishes; since it appears, that when we say we desire to know the ultimate and operating principle, as something, which resides in the external object, we either contradict ourselves, or talk without a meaning. (p. 173)

Hume's sceptical suspension of the logic of causal reasoning, in other words, amounts to an undoing of thinking itself, of philosophy, rigorously conceived. The desire of philosophy to discover the grounds of its own thinking is 'contradicted' by that very desire since what philosophy discovers is that the very notion of ground, of 'operating principle', is disturbed, put into abeyance, by the suspension of cause and effect (itself the 'presumed basis for all human knowledge').[70] This is what the philosopher doesn't want to think or wishes not to think, what philosophy resists. Since it is the 'determination of the mind which is acquir'd by custom' that produces the 'connection, tie, or energy' of cause and effect, seeking the truth of the 'original and ultimate principle' – that of cause and effect – is self-defeating: the principle has no origin other than thinking itself (p. 173). There is no principle of causality separate from thinking. Which means that there is no philosophical truth, only the desultory, alienating and monstrous work of philosophy, of thinking.[71] But this work of philosophy is at the same time the end of the work of philosophy, the end, indeed, of thinking (monstrous thought! 'unthinkable', thought). Scepticism is a 'malady which can never be radically cur'd, but must return upon us every moment' (p. 144). As Hume remarks, the 'understanding, when it acts alone, and according to its most general principles, entirely subverts itself, and leaves not the lowest degree of evidence in any proposition, either in philosophy or common life' (p. 174). In Hume's own case, his sense of the 'manifold contradictions and imperfections in human reason' has 'heated my brain' and results in a radical and melancholy state of uncertainty:

> Where am I, or what? From what causes do I derive my existence, and to what condition shall I return? Whose favour shall I court, and whose anger must I dread? What beings surround me? and on whom have I any influence, or who have any influence on me? (p. 175)

It is the condition of this questioning that its subject be in an abject state of melancholy:

> I am confounded with all these questions, and begin to fancy myself in the most deplorable condition imaginable, environ'd with the deepest darkness, and utterly depriv'd of the use of every member and faculty. (p. 175)

In the end it is, famously, not reason which saves the philosopher from this pit of despair, this 'philosophical melancholy and delirium', but its other, unthinking, 'everyday life', ignorance itself, the other ignorance of the ordinary: the philosopher leaves his closeted thoughts to dine, talk and play backgammon, and when he later returns to his anoiological speculations 'they appear so cold, and strain'd, and ridiculous, that I cannot find in my heart to enter into them any further' (ibid.). Rather than the consolations of philosophy, the monstriferous, dendritic disquisitions of philosophy require their own consolation of experience, their own antidote to melancholy in experience itself. The end of thinking is to stop thinking, the end of philosophy to stop philosophy, and the end of ignorance is ignorance. But this offers only momentary relief for a philosopher, even for one who finds himself 'absolutely and necessarily determined to live, and talk, and act like other people in the common affairs of life' (ibid., p. 175). For the philosopher, there is no ordinary life, only the enactment, the performance of a resistance to thinking, a performance of unthinking.[72] And the desire for the ordinary, for the non-philosophical, is itself governed by melancholy, for Hume's desire for the 'common affairs of life' (an impossible desire, a desire impossible to accede to, he admits) is produced by his 'splenetic' – his melancholy – 'humour'. To think is to be melancholy. But by a monstrous logic, not thinking, ending philosophy, the return to ordinary life, to the shambles, to ignorance (from ignorance) offers – we know, Hume knows – no salvation, no resolution or redemption, and no escape from the vicissitudes of epistemelancholia.

Notes

1 See Stanley W. Jackson, *Melancholia and Depression: From Hippocratic Times to Modern Times* (New Haven: Yale University Press, 1986), p. 404: 'With such distress, we are at the very heart of being human'; and see also Andrew Solomon, *The Noonday Demon: An Atlas of Depression* (London: Chatto & Windus, 2001), p. 401: 'To look at the evolutionary questions about depression is to look at what it means to be human.'
2 See Robert Burton, *The Anatomy of Melancholy*, 6 vols, ed. Thomas C. Faulkner et al. (Oxford: Clarendon, 1989–2000), 1: 395: 'The tower of *Babel* never yeelded such confusion of tongues, as this Chaos of melancholy doth variety of Symptoms'; see also 1: 407: 'The foure and twenty letters make no more variety of words in divers languages, than melancholy conceipts produce diversity of symptoms in severall persons'.
3 See, for example, Lewis Wolpert, *Malignant Sadness: The Anatomy of Depression* (London: Faber and Faber, 1999), p. 3, historical surveys such as Jackson's *Melancholia and Depression*, and, *pace* n.2, above, the universalizing impulse of much of Burton's *Anatomy*.
4 Burton, *The Anatomy of Melancholy*, 1: 7; Byron, 'The Lament of Tasso', l. 5.

5 *Chambers English Dictionary* (Edinburgh: Chambers, 1988), 'canker'.
6 The idea that the experience of melancholy cannot be expressed is often expressed, albeit often somewhat naively: Stanley Jackson, for example, declares 'I would be so bold as to suggest that there is no literal statement that would convey to a reader the distress of being in the throes of a severe depression . . . it would require the enhancement of a metaphorical expression to bridge the gap of understanding' (*Melancholia and Depression*, p. 396); similarly, Andrew Solomon asserts that depression is 'almost unimaginable to anyone who has not known it' and that metaphors – 'vines, trees, cliffs, etc' – constitute 'the only way to talk about the experience' (*Noonday Demon*, p. 29); see also William Styron, *Darkness Visible: A Memoir of Madness* (New York: Random House, 1990), pp. 7, 16–17, 83; and Wolpert, *Malignant Sadness*, pp. 1, 9; and see Julia Kristeva's very different discussion of the 'noncommunicable' nature of melancholia, its 'lack of meaning' and the 'spectacular collapse of meaning' experienced by the melancholic (*Black Sun: Depression and Melancholia*, trans. Leon S. Roudiez (New York: Columbia University Press, 1989), pp. 3, 53).
7 See Jean-Luc Nancy, *The Sense of the World*, trans. Jeffrey S. Librett (Minneapolis: University of Minnesota Press, 1997), p. 146: 'unhappiness is unhappiness, *and there is nothing else to say*'. Melancholy, 'unhappiness', Nancy continues, is 'as in-significant as joy': with joy, unhappiness is, is at, 'the nonsignifying origin of significance itself' (ibid.); see also Kristeva, *Black Sun*, p. 51: 'The depressed speak of nothing, they have nothing to speak of.'
8 Styron, *Darkness Visible*, p. 84; Henry James, Sr, on the 'natural inheritance of everyone who is capable of spiritual life' in *Substance and Shadow* (Boston: Ticknor & Fields, 1863), p. 75 (quoted in Jean Strouse, *Alice James: A Biography* (London: Jonathan Cape, 1980), p. 130).
9 John Milton, *Paradise Lost*, ed. Alastair Fowler (Harlow: Longman, 1971), 9: 1086–7; further references are cited in the text.
10 Dante's *Divina Commedia*, 1: 1–3; as quoted in Styron, *Darkness Visible*, p. 83.
11 Quoted in Kay Redfield Jamison, *Touched with Fire: Manic-Depressive Illness and the Artistic Temperament* (New York: The Free Press, 1993), p. 29.
12 Kristeva, *Black Sun*, p. 33. Kristeva comments that the depressed often have a 'singular and inventive' relationship with language – what she calls a 'hyperactivity with signifiers' – which 'recalls the puns of hypomanics' and which is 'coextensive with the cognitive hyperlucidity of depressed persons, but also with the manic-depressive's inability to decide or to choose (p. 59). The dendritic nature of melancholia in the sense of an overload of information is figured by Styron as like 'one of those outmoded small-town telephone exchanges, being gradually inundated by flood-waters' (*Darkness Visible*, p. 48). Styron comments on the way that the mind in depression is 'dominated by anarchic *disconnections*' (ibid., p. 14; italics added): an excess

of connectivity and an absence of connection become, at some point, indistinguishable.
13 Styron, *Darkness Visible*, p. 47. Part of my purpose in this chapter is to explore the connection between melancholia and trees. But I am also interested in the connection between literature and trees. As J. Douglas Kneale comments, 'The connection between trees and poetry is as old as trees themselves' ('Gentle Hearts and Hands: Reading Wordsworth After Geoffrey Hartman', in Helen Regueiro Elam and Frances Ferguson, eds, *The Wordsworthian Enlightenment: Romantic Poetry and the Ecology of Reading* (Baltimore: The Johns Hopkins University Press, 2005), p. 239). As old as poetry, Kneale means, presumably (unless he can conceive of poems before people . . .).
14 Jean-Paul Sartre, *Nausea*, trans. Robert Baldick (Harmondsworth: Penguin, 1965), p. 182; further references are cited in the text.
15 Virginia Woolf, 'A Sketch of the Past', in *Moments of Being: A Collection of Autobiographical Writing*, 2nd edn., ed. Jeane Schulkind (San Diego: Harcourt, 1985), p. 71.
16 See Jamison, *Touched with Fire*, p. 29; Jamison uses the word to describe the characteristic thought-processes of Samuel Taylor Coleridge in particular (see pp. 109, 220). For Jamison's account of her own depression see *An Unquiet Mind: A Memoir of Moods and Madness* (London: Picador, 1996).
17 Jarvis Cocker, the melancholic lead-singer with the rock band Pulp, speaking at a concert at the Hay-on-Wye Literary Festival, 24 May 2001, as reported in *The Observer*, 27 May 2001 (*The Observer Review*, p. 10).
18 *Roland Barthes by Roland Barthes*, trans. Richard Howard (New York: Hill and Wang, 1977), p. 186; the illustration is on p. 181. Coincidentally, perhaps, the cover to the English translation of Nancy's *The Sense of the World* incorporates a similarly dendritic human body.
19 Ibid., p. 180.
20 Keats, 'Ode to Psyche', l. 7, in *John Keats: The Complete Poems*, ed John Barnard, 3rd edn. (London: Penguin, 2003), pp. 340.
21 Byron, *Manfred* 1.2.66–9, in Jerome J. McGann, ed., *Byron: The Oxford Authors* (Oxford: Oxford University Press, 1986), p. 284.
22 'For God doth know that in the day ye eat thereof, then your eyes shall be opened, and ye shall be as gods, knowing good and evil' (Genesis 3: 5).
23 See Jacques Derrida and Maurizio Ferraris, *A Taste for the Secret*, trans. Giacomo Donis (Cambridge: Polity, 2001), p. 59: the cover-art of the English translation includes a detail of Eve from a diptych by Lucas Cranach from c.1528, emphasizing the shared transgressive urge to sapience in the lover of wisdom and the mother of all humanity. Milton, of course, famously plays on the 'taste' of 'wisdom' in his use of 'sapience' at *Paradise Lost* 9: 797 and 1018.
24 Even Milton's language is monstrous here, syntactically, lexically, referentially, phonetically: 'Scorpion, and asp, and amphisbaena dire, / Cerastes horned,

hydrus, and ellops drear, / And dipsas (not so thick swarmed once the soil / Bedropped with blood of Gorgon, or the isle / Ophiusa)' (10: 524–8).
25 Gilles Deleuze and Félix Guattari, *A Thousand Plateaus: Capitalism and Schizophrenia*, trans. Brian Massumi (London: Athlone, 1988), p. 15; further references are cited in the text. I wish to thank David Punter for reminding me of the significance of trees in Deleuze and Guattari's work.
26 A disquisition on the connectivity of the tree might start, for example, with John Ashbery's poem 'Some Trees' from *Some Trees* (New York: Corinth Books, 1970), p. 51, with a reading of the characteristic Ashberyan syntactical reproduction of a certain melancholy tree-like deformation, of the forming and un-forming of logical, consequential and linear connectivity in language. On some of the many, monstrously many connections that might be made between literature and trees (specifically in response to the complex 'intertextual filaments' of Wordsworth's 'Nutting', an exemplary poem of melancholic violence and trees) see J. Douglas Kneale's learned thoughts in 'Gentle Hearts and Hands', pp. 239–46.
27 Leon Edel, ed., *Henry James Letters*, 4 vols (Cambridge, Mass.· Harvard University Press, 1984), 4: 556. See Sheldon M. Novick's comment on Henry James's depression in 1867 that 'depression was a state that would recur with varying severity throughout his life' (*Henry James: The Young Master* (New York: Random House, 1996), p. 165).
28 Leon Edel, *Henry James*, 5 vols (London: Rupert Hart-Davis, 1953–72), 5: 137, 142.
29 The anachronism of melancholy is suggested by a number of commentators: see, for example, Solomon, *Noonday Demon*, pp. 16, 29. According to one reading of 'The Beast in the Jungle', the tale concerns a certain anachronism whereby Marcher comes to the realization that the beast has always already leapt.
30 Kristeva, *Black Sun*, p. 64.
31 See Strouse, on the 'Jamesian notion about a constant level of family health and pleasure' which involved one member of the family sacrificing their health at any one time for that of the other members: he or she 'was making a sacrifice so that the others could remain healthy'. Strouse quotes a letter home from Henry in 1869, for example: 'I have invented for my comfort a theory that this degenerescence of mine is the result of Alice and Willy getting better and locating some of their diseases on me.' Rather differently, Strouse also points out that 'everyone in the James family claimed to suffer so intensely with and for the others that ill health seemed almost contagious (though happiness was not). William and Alice in particular were said when sick to have such "morbid sympathy" with suffering that they were not told about the ailments of others, as the news would have been too much to bear' (*Alice James*, pp. 111–12). For the James melancholic family tree see Jamison, *Touched by Fire*, p. 215.

32 Leon Edel and L.H. Powers, eds, *The Complete Notebooks of Henry James* (New York: Oxford University Press, 1987), pp. 112, 199.
33 Edel, *The Master*, p. 143.
34 William James, *The Varieties of Religious Experience: A Study in Human Nature* (London: Longmans, Green and Co, 1909), p. 160; further references are cited in the text.
35 F.O. Matthiessen, ed., *The James Family* (New York, 1947), p. 161; further references are cited in the text.
36 'Monstrous melancholy' is Philip Melancthon's term for the 'grand sinne of Atheisme, or impiety', as quoted by Burton in *Anatomy*, 3.395; Henry James, Sr's account of his collapse seems to involve both faith and absolute doubt, ignorance, at the same time.
37 Much of Burton's vast, burgeoning, monstrous, endless book is taken up with his attempt to convince the reader that melancholy is a rational response to human existence – of, in other words, the truth-value of the melancholic's intellectual position. The sentiment is not uncommon amongst theorists of melancholia: Freud comments in 'Mourning and Melancholia' that the melancholic has a 'keener eye for the truth than other people who are not melancholic' (*The Pelican Freud Library, Volume 11*, ed. James Strachey et al. (Harmondsworth: Penguin, 1984), p. 255), and Andrew Solomon suggests that depressed people may have 'a more accurate view of the world around them than do nondepressed people. Those who perceive themselves to be not much liked', he goes on, plaintively, 'are probably closer to the mark than those who believe that they enjoy universal love' (*Noonday Demon*, p. 433); compare Wolpert, *Malignant Sadness*, p. 96. Søren Kierkegaard hints at something similar when he declares that the condition of 'despair' is not uncommon but that what is strange is that 'one should truly not be in despair' (quoted in Solomon, *Noonday Demon*, p. 316). Truth is, of course, itself the question of melancholy – not only because of the possibility that melancholics are undeceived with regard to the 'truth' of the human condition, its fundamentally melancholic nature, but also because part of the condition of melancholia is the melancholic's certainty, his *knowledge* that he is undeceived (see, for example, Solomon, *Noonday Demon*, p. 129).
38 Quoted from a 1793 entry in the *OED* ('monster' sb and a; 2a).
39 While melancholy or depression may be said to have characterized her condition, her biographer records that she was variously diagnosed as suffering from 'neurasthenia, hysteria, rheumatic gout, suppressed gout, cardiac complication, spinal neurosis, nervous hyperesthesia, and spiritual crisis' (Strouse, *Alice James*, pp. ix–x); see also Leon Edel, ed., *The Diary of Alice James* (London: Rupert Hart-Davis, 1965), p. 8.
40 *The Diary of Alice James*, p. 25.
41 Ibid., p. 149.
42 Ibid., pp. 149–50; see Strouse, *Alice James*, pp. 117–31, on Alice's breakdown; and see also pp. 107–8, on the nineteenth-century identification of thinking with nervous exhaustion, particularly for and amongst women.

43 Michiel W. Heyns, 'The Double Narrative of "The Beast in the Jungle": Ethical Plot, Ironical Plot, and the Play of Power', in Gert Buelens, ed., *Enacting History in Henry James: Narrative, Power, and Ethics* (Cambridge: Cambridge University Press, 1997), p. 120.
44 Henry James, 'The Beast in the Jungle', in *The Jolly Corner and Other Tales*, ed. Robert Gard (London: Penguin, 1990), p. 64; further references are cited in the text.
45 See Stephen Spender's general remark on James's novels that 'The amount his characters have to suffer ... is prodigious. Intelligence is all, and intelligence is the costliest of all' (quoted in Strouse, *Alice James*, p. 129).
46 Sedgwick, *Epistemology of the Closet* (London: Penguin, 1994), p. 1; further references are cited in the text.
47 Edel, ed., *Henry James Letters, Vol. IV*, p. 706. James is replying sympathetically to a letter from Adams on what James describes as a 'melancholy outpouring' of 'unmitigated blackness' (ibid.).
48 In fact both homosexuality and depression may be said to be closeted conditions – with regard to depression, see Solomon's comment on 'coming out about depression' (*Noonday Demon*, p. 365) and Styron's remarks on the 'taboo' and the 'secrecy and shame' of the condition and his sense that in talking about it he had 'helped unlock a closet' (*Darkness Visible*, p. 34); see also Jamison, *An Unquiet Mind*, pp. 199–209. For a suggestive reading of the closet in Sedgwick, James, epistemology and cinema, see Stanley Cavell, 'Postscript (1989): To Whom It May Concern', *Critical Inquiry* 16 (1990): 248–89.
49 Henry James, 'The Art of Fiction', in *Selected Literary Criticism*, ed. Morris Shapira (Cambridge: Cambridge University Press, 1981), p. 56.
50 See Jacqueline Rose, 'Jeffrey Masson and Alice James', *Oxford Literary Review* 8 (1986): 191.
51 Intertextuality is itself a form of melancholia according to Harold Bloom: 'A poem', he says, 'is a poet's melancholy at his lack of priority' (*The Anxiety of Influence: A Theory of Poetry* (New York: Oxford University Press, 1973), p. 96); see also his comment that 'To *know* is to have become belated; not to know, not to understand, is to become early again, however self-deceivingly' (*Poetry and Repression: Revisionism from Blake to Stevens* (New Haven: Yale University Press, 1976), pp. 159–60).
52 Styron, *Darkness Visible*, pp. 76, 79.
53 Quoted in Jamison, *Touched with Fire*, p. 24.
54 Quoted in ibid., p. 109.
55 Styron, *Darkness Visible*, p. 37.
56 Quoted in Jackson, *Melancholia and Depression*, pp. 85, 87, 348.
57 See, for example, Burton, *Anatomy*, 1: 47, 84, 106–7, 115, 356; 3: 42, 392.
58 See Kristeva's opening remark in *Black Sun* that 'For those who are racked by melancholia, writing about it would have meaning only if writing sprang out of that very melancholia' (p. 3); compare Wolpert, *Malignant Sadness*, p. ix.

59 Styron, *Darkness Visible*, p. 77.
60 Kristeva, *Black Sun*, pp. 4, 6; Burton, *Anatomy*, 1: 8. See Michael O'Connell's comment that Burton's *Anatomy* is both a medical treatise on melancholy and, at the same time, a book 'on human knowing' (*Robert Burton* (Boston: Twayne, 1986), p. 49).
61 See Jackson, *Melancholia and Depression*, p. 315; compare Kristeva's remark that melancholia is 'a breakdown of biological and logical sequentiality' (*Black Sun*, p. 20); and compare Solomon, *Noonday Demon*, pp. 29, 38–40, 56, 63. In this sense, rather than being more accurate in their perceptions than others (see n. 37, above), melancholics are diagnosed as deluded according to the classical logics of sequence and consequentiality – as having, for example, 'erroneous beliefs' (Wolpert, *Malignant Sadness*, p. 99).
62 Jackson, *Melancholia and Depression*, p. 224.
63 Freud, 'Mourning and Melancholia', p. 252; further references are cited in the text.
64 This kind of thinking is pervasive in recent accounts of depression: see Solomon's comment that 'Grief is depression in proportion to circumstance; depression is grief out of proportion to circumstance' (*Noonday Demon*, p. 16); and see Wolpert, *Malignant Sadness*, p. 79: 'depression is sadness out of control'.
65 Freud, 'Introductory Lectures on Psychoanalysis', in *The Pelican Freud Library, Volume 1*, ed. James Strachey et al. (Harmondsworth: Penguin, 1973), p. 477.
66 Ibid., p. 490. It is no doubt for this reason that Freud dwells so little upon melancholia in his work, aside from in 'Mourning and Melancholia' and in a few isolated comments in the Introductory lectures.
67 David Hume, *A Treatise of Human Nature*, ed. David Fate Norton and Mary J. Norton (Oxford: Oxford University Press, 2000), p. 172 (further references are cited in the text).
68 John J. Richetti, *Philosophical Writing: Locke, Berkeley, Hume* (Cambridge, Mass.: Harvard University Press, 1983), p. 227.
69 See Annette C. Baier, *A Progress of Sentiments: Reflections on Hume's 'Treatise'* (Cambridge, Mass.: Harvard University Press, 1991), p. 19: 'by now, when reason is subverted, there no longer are "reasons" for the present position, or non-position'.
70 Richard Tarnas, *The Passions of the Western Mind* (London: Pimlico, 1996), p. 337.
71 Compare Richetti's comments that 'The Hume of this conclusion enacts those confusions bound to beset the understanding which the *Treatise* has already explored' (*Philosophical Writing*, p. 228); see also Baier, *A Progress of Sentiments*, p. 1; and see her comment that the *Treatise* is 'a dramatic work which presents and does not merely describe a new turn in philosophy' (ibid., p. 27).

72 The escape from philosophy as presented in the *Treatise* in fact repeats Hume's 'real life' attempt, in 1734, to leave philosophy and its attendant symptoms of melancholia behind and to take up a position with a 'considerable trader in Bristol'. He resolved to 'forget myself, & everything that is past, to engage myself, as far as is possible, in that Course of Life, & to toss about the World, from the one Pole to the other, till I leave this Distemper behind me' (David Hume, 'A Kind of History of My Life', in David Fate Norton, ed., *The Cambridge Companion to Hume* (Cambridge: Cambridge University Press, 1993), 350). After just a few months of such a life, ordinary life, Hume escaped to France where he wrote *A Treatise of Human Nature*.

9

American ignorance: Philip Roth's American trilogy

When questioned, Philip Roth can be peculiarly insistent on the subject of his own, authorial, ignorance:

> Robert McCrum: Do you think sex is the Western novel's deepest theme?
> Philip Roth: I don't know.
> Robert McCrum: So what is the purpose of fiction?
> Philip Roth: God only knows.[1]

'I don't know anything about anything', Roth complains in another interview, from 1984, half-jokingly contrasting himself with John Updike, who 'knows so much', who knows 'about golf, about porn, about kids, about America' (*CPR* 151). For Roth, ignorance includes, especially, the question of knowing about oneself: 'blank space is part of who one is to oneself', he suggests in a 1988 interview. And there are important if sometimes subtle discriminations to be made with respect to ignorance: 'there's a difference, on the one hand, between not knowing and not knowing that you don't know and, on the other, not knowing and knowing *why* you don't know – and even, paradoxically, knowing what it is you don't know' (*CPR* 234).

Roth has also declared his interest in what is not or cannot be known, in the human capacity for ignorance more generally. Speaking recently about *The Plot Against America* (2004), for example, he comments on the human ignorance of ageing:

> There may be a biological blinder about age that's built in. You are not supposed to understand until you get there. Just as an animal doesn't know about death, the human animal doesn't know about age. When I wrote that book about my father in old age, *Patrimony*, I thought I knew what I was talking about, but I didn't really.[2]

The move here from a general statement about human ignorance to a comment on his personal or authorial ignorance is something of a Roth idiom or reflex. Authorship, the predicament of the writer – the subject, the topos which, along with the vicissitudes of (male) human sexuality and being Jewish, may be said to characterize or even to define his writing – is bound up for Roth in ignorance. In the essays and interviews collected in *Reading Myself and Others* (1985) and in *Conversations with Philip Roth* (1992) authorial ignorance is a recurring topic. In an essay from 1974, Roth describes his working method as 'playing in the mud' ('I did not have any idea where I was going', he explains: *RMO* 31), and he comments in an interview from 1972 that he doesn't know what he's saying until he's said it:

> I often feel that I don't really know what I'm talking about until I've stopped *talking* about it and sent everything down through the blades of the fiction-making machine, to be ground into something else, something that is decidedly *not* a position but that allows me to say, when I'm done, 'Well, that isn't what I mean either – but it's more like it'. (*RMO* 62)[3]

Suspicion about having fixed intellectual, ethical or political 'positions' is expressed elsewhere in Roth's essays and interviews, and is even presented as the driving force, the essence, indeed, of writing: 'one of the strongest motives for continuing to write fiction', Roth comments in an interview, 'is an increasing distrust of "positions", my own included' (*CPR* 60).

In this chapter, therefore, I will examine the work of one of America's pre-eminent contemporary novelists in order to focus in more depth on the question of authorial ignorance. Throughout this book, I have been attempting to suggest that a key dimension of the constitution of the literary since especially the Romantic period has been in terms of the idea that at some level, in some ways, the author may be said to be ignorant of what she is doing. In this chapter and the next I want to focus on this question in relation to contemporary writers – a novelist and some poets – in order to think in particular about the political and indeed ethical valency of such authorial ignorance. In the end, I want to suggest, it is fundamentally part of the force of literature that contemporary writers engage with when they describe themselves as not knowing. Authorial ignorance, I would propose, is a crucial if often overlooked concern in contemporary literary practice particularly in its relation to larger question of politics and the ethical. And there is perhaps no one – no major contemporary writer in English – who is more consistently concerned with the question of the nature of authorship and its ethical relation with ignorance than Philip Roth.[4]

The problem of ignorance for Roth – a kind of contemporary Socrates – is also that of knowingness. His oeuvre as a whole may, after all, be read in terms of a resistance to all those people who know about other people and especially know what is wrong with other people, either through the powers invested in them through their place in society – the mother, the Rabbi, and even God in *Portnoy's Complaint*, the father in *Zuckerman Unbound*, the legal establishment and the psychoanalyst in *My Life as a Man*, the judge in *The Ghost Writer*, the academic in *The Human Stain*, the literary critic in *The Anatomy Lesson*, the politician in *The Plot Against America*, the policeman in *Sabbath's Theater*, the secret police in *The Prague Orgy* and Mossad in *Operation Shylock*, public opinion in *Sabbath's Theater* and *The Human Stain*, the literary biographer in *Exit Ghost* and the goy passim – or just through their own blind ignorance. The author's job, by contrast, is to *not* know what's wrong. *The Anatomy Lesson*, Roth comments in a 1984 interview, 'is about not knowing':

> Look, diagnoses abound in this book. Everybody *else* knows. They've all got [Nathan Zuckerman] pegged, just like Appel. All his women know what's wrong with him. Even the trichologist who treats his baldness knows why he's losing his hair: 'undue pressure'. This book is *crammed* with people who know what's wrong with Zuckerman. I leave the diagnosing to his comforters. I try to stay out of it. (*RMO* 114)

Fiction, according to Roth in another interview, 'derives from that unique mode of scrutiny called imagination': it is a 'way of knowing the world as it's not otherwise known' (*RMO* 155, 154). But the knowing involved is a kind of end-stopped knowing, since what you know is just that book, that novel:

> What you know from Flaubert or Beckett or Dostoyevsky is never a great deal more than you knew before about adultery or loneliness or murder – what you know is *Madame Bovary*, *Molloy*, and *Crime and Punishment*. (*RMO* 155)

So Kafka's novels, to take a favourite Roth example, cannot be called 'ways of knowing the world', or, to put it more precisely, they are ways of knowing the world that 'look to most people like no way of knowing anything' (*RMO* 155).

Roth suggests that the author writes through his obsessions and that those obsessions are, by definition, that which the writer does not know, cannot know. The novelist 'suffers from serious ignorance of his obsessional theme', Roth comments in an interview from 1985; and he 'lays siege' to the theme again and again because it is 'the one he least understands – he knows it so well that he knows how little he knows' (*RMO* 160).[5] This theme of authorial ignorance and obsession might itself be seen as something like an obsession for Roth. He comments elsewhere, for example, on the artist's 'ingenuity, anxiety, isolation, dissatisfaction, relentlessness, obsessiveness, secretiveness, paranoia, and self-addiction' (*RMO* 290); and in *The Prague Orgy* Roth's so-called 'alter-ego', his narratorial obsession, indeed, over ten novels[6] and the major figure for his exploration of authorship, the obsessive Nathan Zuckerman, remarks on 'the ever-recurring story that's at once your invention and the invention of you' (*PO* 84). The question of authorial ignorance occurs and recurs in Roth's fiction, often with comic results. In *Operation Shylock* (1993), Smilesburger, the unnervingly knowing Mossad agent who advises the character 'Philip Roth' about the inadvisability of publishing his book, is clear about the author's ignorance: 'This is not a report of what happened', he tells Philip Roth, 'because, very simply, you haven't the slightest idea of what happened. You grasp almost nothing of the objective reality. Its meaning evades you completely' (*OS* 390).

Like knowledge for Rabelais's Gargantua, ignorance, for Roth is or should be endless, bottomless:[7] 'For all that the world is full of people who go around believing they've got you or your neighbour figured out', Zuckerman comments towards the end of *The Human Stain*, 'there really is no bottom to what is not known' (*HS* 315).

It is in Roth's second Zuckerman trilogy, the so-called 'American' trilogy of *American Pastoral*, *I Married a Communist* and *The Human Stain* (1997–2000), that the question of ignorance and, in particular, of authorial ignorance has been most fully investigated. Divided as it is into three Miltonic parts ('Paradise Remembered', 'The Fall', and 'Paradise Lost') *American Pastoral* in particular is, from the start, in its formal structure, fundamentally implicated in the discourse of ignorance. The Biblical narrative of the Fall might be read in terms of both epistemophilia (in Eve and, more reluctantly, in Adam) and epistemophobia (in Adam and, rather differently, in God), and, like John Milton's epic poem of originary and tragic epistemophilia and epistemophobia, Roth's novel revolves around knowing and not knowing. Like John Milton, and like the Bible, Philip Milton Roth[8] is interested in, and his writing may be said to be centred on, the consequences of (transgressive) (sexual) knowledge.[9] And, to a significant extent, at least, around the mouth – the organ (if that is what it is) of the body that has been, at least since the writing of Genesis, bound up with such terrible knowing (through transgressive tasting, and through fork-tongued speech), and with such saving ignorance.

American Pastoral tells the story of Seymour Levov, an American Jew known familiarly as 'Swede' for his Scandinavian-seeming stature and good looks. Levov is famous throughout Newark for his sporting prowess, and he grows up to marry an Irish-American Catholic girl, Mary Dawn Dwyer (Miss New Jersey for 1949), to take over his father's glove factory and to successfully carry on the family business. Levov's desire to belong to the assimilationist bourgeois ideal of Wasp America as a successful businessman, owner of a substantial colonial-era farmhouse in rural Old Rimrock, NJ, and devoted husband and father, is shattered as his life collapses around him when, his troubled, stuttering daughter Merry, at the age of 16 in 1968, in seemingly 'inexplicable' revolt against the comforts of her wealthy, liberal American upbringing and in violent protest against the Vietnam War, sets off a home-made bomb at Rimrock post office.[10] The bomb kills the local doctor but fails to stop the Vietnam War. Merry goes into hiding and is not heard of for five years until a messenger, a girl similar in age who calls herself Rita Cohen and who had turned up at Levov's factory four months after his daughter's disappearance to sexually tease and psychically torment him with details about his daughter's life, finally reveals Merry's whereabouts. Merry, it turns out, has committed further bomb outrages, killing a total of four people, and has twice been raped in her lost years on the run. But her experiences have led her to make a second dramatic change in her identity and affiliation and she has become a non-violent, radically self-denying Jain. Fearful of harming any living thing, animal or plant, afraid of the harm done in using water to wash herself, she even wears a veil to avoid destroying microbes by breathing them. Although she has lost her stutter, Merry is stinking and half-starved, living in dire, squalid conditions in a slum in Newark not far from Levov's factory: she wears 'a scarecrow's clothes' and is 'stick-skinny as a scarecrow . . . the scantiest farmyard emblem of life, a travestied mock-up of a human being, so meager a likeness to a Levov it could have fooled only a bird' (*AP* 239). For Seymour Levov, this transformation is beyond comprehension and the novel revolves around the sheer nauseating inexplicability of what the daughter of this successful and successfully assimilated Jewish man has become: 'the inexplicable had forever displaced whatever [Levov] once thought he knew . . . she was unknowable', Zuckerman, the narrator, comments (*AP* 266). The novel revolves around the profound, unanswered and unanswerable question of causality, with which it ends – a far from straightforward and indeed highly ambiguous, highly ironized, even duplicitous 'rhetorical' question: 'And what is wrong with their life?', Zuckerman asks in bafflement as the novel closes, 'What on earth is less reprehensible than the life of the Levovs?' (*AP* 423).[11]

One explanation – one that torments Levov – involves his daughter's mouth and in particular her stammer, and the misuse of her mouth in an erotic kiss. At the sultry end of one long, hot summer holiday, when she is 11 and he is 36, Merry asks Levov in her stuttering way and 'half innocently, half audaciously', to kiss her 'the way you k-k-kiss umumu-mother' (*AP* 89). Disturbed by the intense but unfamiliar and forbidden eroticism of his daughter's pubescent body he refuses, but with an uncharacteristically mocking negative that mimics her speech, 'N-n-no' (*AP* 90). And then, trying to row back from this unprecedented paternal rebuke, he loses 'his vaunted sense of proportion' and does the unthinkable: he 'drew her to him with one arm, and kissed her stammering mouth with the passion that she had been asking him for all month long while knowing only obscurely what she was asking for' (*AP* 91).[12] Five years later, Merry bombs the local post office and disappears, and in her absence Levov cannot stop questioning himself about this kiss, about whether it is the kiss, or his subsequent defensive withdrawal from her, that has led to her act of terrorism: 'once the inexplicable had begun', Zuckerman comments, 'the torment of self-examination never ended' (*AP* 92). In this disordered, uncomprehending state of mind, Levov generalizes from his daughter's mouth: 'there was no fluency anywhere', he thinks, 'It was *all* stuttering'. And ultimately he – his life, his sense of life – is centred in and indeed *becomes* the mouth: in Zuckerman's conception, Levov pictures his life as a 'stuttering mouth and a grimacing face – the whole of his life without cause or sense and completely bungled' (*AP* 93).

The question of the mouth – the intimate eroticism of the mouth as well as its connection with ignorance – might be traced more widely in Roth's fiction. For Roth, indeed, one of the human sites of ignorance – in a sense, the source of all ignorance, the place where ignorance may be said to begin or at least to be articulated since it is the place of speech itself – is the mouth. For 'loudmouth' Roth (*CPR* 200), the most mouthy of writers and the writer for whom the rhythms of speech themselves constitute a very particular technique and style, the very force of his writing indeed, the mouth is where you are, what you are. One way to open up Roth's oeuvre (if not his mouth) is to consider the mouth.

Roth's novels are full of mouths – mouths open, broken, violated, eroticized, investigated, repaired, ontologized. In *The Anatomy Lesson* (1983), Nathan Zuckerman slips, under the influence of drugs and alcohol, and breaks his jaw against a gravestone. When he comes round he is in hospital and 'The whole of his mouth, from ear to ear, was just pain' (*AL* 263). While the rest of his body functions and is uninjured, the pain in his mouth, the pain that is his mouth, means that 'he himself had become his mouth' and that he has 'turned from a neck and shoulders and arms into a mouth. In that hole was his being' (*AL* 266). The hole is Zuckerman's whole, the whole of him. As he recovers over the next few days, the speechless writer thinks of himself as 'nothing but a broken mouth' (*AL* 277):

> Nothing existed but the inside of his mouth. He made all sorts of discoveries in there. Your mouth is who you are. You can't get very much closer to what you think of as yourself. The next stop is the brain. No wonder fellatio has achieved such renown. Your tongue lives in your mouth and your tongue is you. (*AL* 278)

And Zuckerman begins to fantasize about being a doctor, even being a 'maxillo-facial surgeon'. And then, grasping some of the soiled bedsheets that are awaiting collection in a hospital corridor he imagines that by embracing sickness he will escape the unbearable obsession of writing, escape from literary self-consciousness into life, into the mouth that is life: '*This is life*', he thinks, '*With real teeth in it*' (*AL* 290).

The Counterlife (1986) has 'a lot to say about the erotics of speech', as Hermione Lee puts it (*CPR* 260), since the now impotent Nathan Zuckerman talks endlessly to Maria, and, for him, her voice, 'her talking tongue', is 'the sole erotic implement' (*C* 184). But mouths, of course, are erotic in other ways than talk. 'The mouth', says Wendy, the appealing young dental assistant in a reflective moment, 'is really the most personal thing that a doctor can deal with' (*C* 31). Wendy is being interviewed for the job by the dentist, Henry Zuckerman, brother of the novelist Nathan.[13] Henry is becoming excited by this erotically charged exchange with the 'slight, young blonde' who is 'petitioning for a job'. He speaks of her mouth and asks her about her awareness of her mouth, all the time looking at it, and always on the verge of revealing his own inappropriately sexual energies, thoughts, desires. He tries to avoid talking about sex but can't, because he's talking about mouths:

> 'Most people, as you must know by now, don't even think that their mouth is part of the body. Or teeth are part of the body. Not consciously they

don't. The mouth is a hollow, the mouth is nothing. Most people, unlike you, will never tell you what their mouth means. If they're frightened of dental work it's sometimes because of some frightening experience early on, but primarily it's because of what the mouth means. Anyone touching it is either an invader or a helper. To get them from thinking that someone working on them is invading them, to the idea that you are helping them on to something good, is almost like having a sexual experience. For most people, the mouth is secret, it's their hiding place. Just *like* the genitals. You have to remember that embryologically the mouth is related to the genitals[. . .] The mouth, you mustn't forget, is the primary organ of experience . . .'. On he went, looking unblinkingly and boldly at hers. (*C* 33–4)

Predictably, perhaps, Henry Zuckerman hires Wendy, and they end up having sex (including, of course, oral sex)[14] after-hours in the dentist's surgery.

Roth's next novel, *Deception* (1990), is like something out of Samuel Beckett in its narrative is dislocations and emotional attenuations. And like a Beckett fiction but erotically charged, the novel is almost all mouth, structured as it is around a series of dialogues with narratorial or authorial direction almost completely absent: the reader is left to piece together the details of scenes by seeming to overhear the disembodied voices.[15] There's a sense in which the novel is all mouth and, since the voices are *dis*embodied, anything but mouth. But *Deception* also revolves thematically around the ways of mouths, around what they do, what they're for and around the way they can seem to work as quasi-autonomous organs. Philip's deracinated lover has become a mouth, only a mouth, all mouth. She sees herself in her family life as just a mouth and as a provider for other mouths. Her function in her failing marriage is both to provide a mouth and to provide for mouths both sexually and for nourishment. 'I have to do everything', she tells Philip: 'Fucking, sucking. Everything. Cooking. There are all these substances in and out of people's mouths. It does sometimes feel that way. I have to make everything right and happy. A barrel of fun' (*D* 62). And in *Deception* mouths are explicitly linked with sexual seduction by means, not least, of talking. Philip's cynical Czech friend Ivan accuses him of having seduced his wife and having done so by talking. Other men, according to Ivan, talk to women 'as part of the seduction leading up to the fuck': they let the women start their story, 'then when they believe they have been sufficiently attentive, they gently press the moving mouth down on the erection'. Conversely, and for Ivan perversely, Philip gets women into bed 'to talk to them' (rather than talking to them to get them into bed) (*D* 86–7). Philip's wife seems to agree about her husband's perversity: finding his notes for a novel – this novel – about a man named Philip, she accuses him of having a lover, and of lovingly writing down every word she says: 'you're an "écouteur – an audiophiliac"', she protests, echoing Ivan's sense of the perversity of Philip's oral obsession. (*D* 175).[16]

The mouth can of course function as the site of violation, of violence even, as is made clear in what must be – after pretty much the whole of the Brucknerian hymn to obscenity and sexual transgression that is *Sabbath's Theatre* (1995) – one of the most challenging scenes in Roth's sexually confrontational oeuvre. The scene occurs in *The Dying Animal* (2001), when David Kapesh has violent and not entirely willing oral sex with his young Cuban lover Consuela Castillo. Kapesh props her up on the bed, kneels over her and 'rhythmically, without letup . . . fucked her mouth' while holding on to her hair, twisted round his hand, 'like a thong, like a strap, like the reins that fasten to the bit of a bridle' (*DA* 30). He comes, and then there is the 'bite back': she snaps her teeth at him, indicating what she could have done, what she wanted to do but didn't (*DA* 31). And in biting, biting back at him, she attains her own mastery, mastery over her lover.[17]

But the question of the mouth – with respect in particular to the oral obstruction of the stutter and to the scandal of an incestuous kiss and its irretrievable causality (what it causes to happen as well as, in a different sense, the opacity of what it is caused by) – haunts Seymour Levov and haunts *American Pastoral* with a peculiar intensity.[18] The tragedy of Swede Levov is determined in many ways, at least in his own conception (or, therefore, in Nathan Zuckerman's), by the mouth, by the forbidden kiss. There are, of course, other explanations – political, religious, moral explanations – for the fall of Swede Levov. Indeed, the causal logic of Swede's fall has been a major question in the novel's reception. Timothy Parrish, for example, suggests that the reason for Levov's downfall is to be located in the 'loss of his Jewish identity',[19] and Debra Shostak hints at a similar conclusion when she comments that Levov 'fatally' represses the ethnic and cultural differences between his own Jewish and his wife's Irish-Catholic background.[20] Marshall Gentry has helpfully listed a number of other ways in which reviewers of the novel have construed the cause of Levov's fall –including its being an effect of the evil eye, of sheer irrationality, of the randomness of events, of Levov's 'inexplicable' daughter, of the '1960s revolution', of liberal permissiveness, of the 'flaws of 1960s leftist politics', of Jewish assimilation and of the obsolescence of ladies' gloves (on which Levov's wealth is based).[21] And Gentry presents his own solution to the conundrum of Swede's fall by arguing (somewhat unconvincingly) that 'these conclusions are understandable but wrong-headed' since in fact Roth is 'more aware than Zuckerman is of the limits of Swede's world', and that the novel is in fact a 'feminist' critique of American masculinity, as articulated by the novel's female characters.[22] But as this suggests, critics have tended to play down the significance of the mouth and the unacceptable kiss – to play down what might nevertheless be seen as the transgressive, incestuous sexual drive of *American Pastoral*. I want to suggest that the conundrum of causality in this novel is linked to the mouth, and to the kiss, but that this very causality, this rationality, is at the same time undermined by the mouth. The mouth constitutes both the causality of violence and its other, the deconstruction of causality, of reason.

It is, indeed, in another function of the mouth, the mouth as exit rather than entry into the body, the site of regurgitation rather than accommodation, and of disgust rather than desire, that the mouth and ignorance – the inexplicable, non-understanding – come powerfully together, come together in vomit.[23] In a pivotal scene in *American Pastoral*, the mouth is again associated with (male) violence and violation, but this time in a way that is anything but sexual. This central scene of ignorance links a number of the mouth's functions – kissing, stuttering (a kind of oral infarction of speech) and vomiting – with the inexplicable. Vomiting and stuttering in particular involve contrasting involuntary reflexes that overpower rational or cognitive control of the body, a revolt of the body against the body and, more to the point, a revolt of the body against one's mind, against consciousness, against reason. The body's violent abjection may itself be said to constitute the embodiment of ignorance. In what is arguably the most decisive and certainly the most challenging scene in *American Pastoral*, Levov meets the stinking, emaciated, religiously fanatical Merry in her 1973 incarnation as a Jain. He interrogates her insistently about her life, about becoming a terrorist, and about her subsequent decision to become a Jain, as he desperately tries to understand, to get a grip on, what he sees as the insanity of her actions, on how they came about, on their logic or causality. But Merry's complacent, self-abnegating answers ('The truth is simple. Here is the truth. You must be done with craving and selfhood', etc. (*AP* 264)) make no sense to Levov and, ripping the veil from her face, he violently commands her to speak, to say who she is, what she is, to say something that will make sense of her condition. But as he pulls open her mouth he smells her body, a 'human mess stinking of human waste'; her smell is 'the smell of everything organic breaking down. It is the smell of no coherence' (*AP* 265). He responds by vomiting:

> A spasm of gastric secretions and undigested food started up the intestinal piping and, in a bitter, acidic stream, surged sickeningly onto his tongue, and when he cried out, '*Who are you!*' it was spewed with his words onto her face. (*AP* 265–6)

Levov's violently questioning speech, his ignorance, his uncertainty, becomes one with vomit, becomes vomit, in this moment of violent bodily and cognitive abjection, this moment when 'the inexplicable had forever displaced whatever he once thought he knew', this moment when Levov finally understands that his daughter is 'unknowable' (*AP* 266).[24]

It is, thematically, around Levov's ignorance, his sense that there are things that cannot finally be known, that *American Pastoral* revolves. But it is also around the question of ignorance generally and around authorial ignorance in particular. The question of authorship and autobiography – authorship and autobiography *as* a question – is, as I have suggested, the Rothian theme above all others, from early versions of a Newark Jewish boyhood in *Goodbye Columbus* (1959) and, notoriously, *Portnoy's Complaint* (1969) to a number of more or less ambiguously autobiographical books including *The Counterlife* (1986), *The Facts* (1988), *Deception* (1991), *Patrimony* (1991) and *Operation Shylock* (1993),[25] to the development of an authorial alter-ego in Nathan Zuckerman (in particular) as, in part, a defence against attacks on Roth's work for its indiscreet autobiographicity, in novels from *My Life as a Man* (1974) and *The Ghost Writer* (1979) to *The Human Stain* (2000). Roth's work, particularly his recent work, presents an exemplary instance of an author thinking hard about what it means to be an author, and (amongst other things) coming up against and indeed celebrating the conundrum or enigma of authorial ignorance.[26] 'I wish . . . I knew that much about anything', E.I. Lonoff, the Rothian figure of the established author complains in *The Ghost Writer*, but 'I've written fantasy for thirty years' (*GW* 16) – suggesting that writing 'fantasy' and knowing much about anything at all are mutually exclusive.[27] Each of the novels in Roth's second Zuckerman trilogy, his 'American' trilogy, concerns authorial ignorance, the *constitutive* or necessary ignorance of the author: in these novels, ignorance is both a major theme and the mechanism through which stories get told.[28] And in addition to the sense of anguished bewilderment that dominates the novels, all three are also concerned with a positive sense of ignorance, with a positive valuation of ignorance, with, at least, recommending the Socratic virtue of knowing that one doesn't know.

This is not of course to say that ignorance is not a great evil in Roth's imaginative universe. In many ways, all of Roth's novels may be read thematically as, in part, impassioned indictments of various forms of cultural and moral ignorance – beginning with the Nazi Holocaust and the development of Jewish cultural identity within the context or in the long shadow of that vast, ignorance-fuelled crime. But the American trilogy in particular presents the history of America in the second half of the twentieth century in terms of the ignorance that presents itself as knowledge. In this respect, each novel may be said to be written against 'knowing', against knowing that you know – against the knowingness of a radical left-wing critique that leads to terrorism in *American Pastoral*; against the coercive insistence on knowing a person's political allegiances of the MacCarthy era in *I Married a Communist*; and against the politically correct assumption that we can know an individual's motivations, and the 'ecstacy of sanctimony' (*HS* 2) that such knowing entails in *The Human Stain*.[29] This, for Roth, is the ultimate ignorance, the ignorance that is involved in the certainty of knowledge. In *American Pastoral*, it is precisely the knowing ignorance embodied in the anger and violence of the American political terrorists with whom Merry has become embroiled – the phenomenon that Zuckerman sums up as 'the indigenous American berserk' (*AP* 86) – that allows or persuades them to bomb and to kill. Rita Cohen, the spokeswoman for the group, is a 'child', physically and mentally – she is defined indeed, according to Zuckerman, by her ignorance:

> She was twenty-two years old, no more than five feet tall, and off on a reckless adventure with a very potent thing way beyond her comprehension called power. Not the least need of thought. Thought just paled away beside their ignorance. They were omniscient without thinking. (*AP* 134)

'You know nothing about anything', Levov tells her when he finds Merry, 'You don't know what you are talking about', 'You don't know what you're saying', 'Nothing', he insists, 'is further from your understanding than the nature of reality' (*AP* 135, 136, 139).[30]

Thematically, then, ignorance has a central place in the novel as one of the great evils in Roth's moral universe. But as Levov's indictment of

Merry might suggest, the greater, the even greater evil for Roth, for his book, is Plato's second or 'double' ignorance, ignorance, that is to say, that is constituted by the conceit of wisdom.[31] This is the ignorance that is encapsulated in a form of *knowing*, in knowing that you know, even though (or because) you don't. The greatest ignorance is this: that you don't know that you don't know. What is maddening for Levov about such ignorance is that it is represented as knowledge, as, for example, the 'know-it-all-ism of [Merry's] absurdly innocent, profoundly insane ... solemnity', as he fulminates (*AP* 254). If all three of the American trilogy novels are bound up with a Socratic ethics of ignorance, with a severe indictment of ignorance, they also involve the idea – also in its way Socratic – that 'What we know is that, in an unclichéd way, nobody knows anything', that 'You *can't* know anything', that 'The things you *know* you don't know' as Zuckerman puts it in *The Human Stain* (*HS* 209). All three novels are designed, in the end, to teach that 'the worst lesson that life can teach' – the worst that we can learn, but a lesson that seems nevertheless to be unavoidable – is that life, as Roth (or Zuckerman) comments in *American Pastoral*, 'makes no sense' (*AP* 81).[32]

American Pastoral in particular is, then, thematically centred on ignorance, indeed on not only Levov's ignorance of his own daughter's motivations but on authorial ignorance – on the inability of the author-figure to provide a satisfactory answer to the question of how and why chaos intrudes on the orderly Levov family life. But what I also want to emphasize about the analysis of ignorance in this novel is what we might call the literary technics of ignorance, the technical, narratological and authorial dimensions of not knowing around which the novel is plotted. 'How to tell the story', is what is in question: as Roth puts it in a 1983 interview, 'This is my greatest source of confusion and my greatest source of pleasure' (*CPR* 141).

Nathan Zuckerman is not just the narrator of the second 'Zuckerman' trilogy but is explicitly presented as an author, and implicitly as a stand-in or alter-ego or 'mouthpiece' for Roth himself.[33] In each of these novels, the central subject around which the mystery of identity and the narratives of transgression, purity and punishment revolve – Seymour Levov in *American Pastoral*, Ira Ringold in *I Married a Communist*, Coleman Silk in *The Human Stain* – is dead. There is, there can be, no solution either to the truth of narrative or to the mystery of identity: there is only ignorance and therefore speculation, imagination, writing: only authorship. And *American Pastoral* is exemplary in this respect. The tale of Swede Levov is framed by a brief meeting between the middle-aged narrator, Roth's long-standing alter-ego the now-famous but reclusive author Nathan Zuckerman, and his schoolboy hero Levov. Levov asks Zuckerman to write a memoir of his father but fails to tell him two salient facts about his own life – that his daughter is an erstwhile terrorist and that he himself is dying from cancer. It is only a few months later, when Zuckerman happens to meet Levov's brother Jerry at a high-school reunion, that he learns that Levov has died and that his daughter was the 'Rimrock Bomber'. From this and a few other fragmentary details, Zuckerman begins to piece together – but also to imagine – the Swede's story. Although Zuckerman may seem to disappear into his narrative, he – the substitute author – is everywhere present, in every word and every imagined action.[34] Since almost everything that we learn about Levov's adult life is imagined by Zuckerman, we could say that there is almost nothing of Levov here, that it is all Zuckerman. And it is, I think, in this question of piecing together – the question of how stories get told, how anyone, but especially how authors can know anyone and anything – that Roth's interest lies, as much as it lies in the passionate and passionately moral questions of good and evil, of causality and the randomness of events, of political ignorance masquerading as informed radical critique, and ultimately of the intolerable senselessness of things around which the plot overtly revolves.

Roth's novels also – or therefore – consistently propose that it is the work of the author, in fact the very definition of an author, not to know – and therefore to imagine. So while Zuckerman knows a little of his subject, 'Swede' Levov, he decides that 'anything more I wanted to know, I'd have to make up' (*AP* 74). Zuckerman's task is to 'dream', as he puts it, 'a realistic chronicle' (*AP* 89).[35] In *The Human Stain*, Roth presents an almost identical authorial-narrative predicament: for Zuckerman in this novel, both Coleman Silk and his lover Faunia Farley are at some level 'enigmatic', are indeed 'blank'. Zuckerman does not know whether Silk told his lover his life-long secret – the secret that, although he is a fair-skinned Negro, he has spent his adult life passing for a 'white' Jew. Zuckerman doesn't know whether Silk told her before they both died in a car crash, and yet he *knows* Silk did:

> How do I know she knew? [Zuckerman asks] I don't . . . I can't know. Now that they're dead, nobody can know. For better or worse, I can only do what everyone does who thinks that they know. I imagine. I am forced to imagine. It happens to be what I do for a living. It is my job. It's now all I do. (*HS* 213)[36]

Debra Shostak has written well on, amongst other things, knowledge and epistemophilia in Roth – on the 'relentless' 'epistemophilic urge' that is at the 'source of the fall – and at the source of writing'. Glossing this passage from *The Human Stain*, Shostak links transgressive knowledge – the type of knowing that returns us ultimately to the Bible – with secrets, and comments that 'The secret is the sin; the secret is the motive for and kernel of narrative; the secret is what makes the subject more than an object in someone else's narrative; and the secret is what imparts meaning to history'.[37] Shostak is right about the significance of secrets in Roth's fiction as well as about their importance for narrative more generally, but I would suggest that what is finally at work in these novels is not so much the secret – which seems to imply agency, knowledge and a veiled or disguised or hidden truth – as ignorance – which needs to imply none of the above. Roth is concerned as much with what we might call the 'anepistemologic' drive[38] and with agnoiology, as with knowledge, information and the impulses of curiosity. In *American Pastoral* and *The Human Stain* in particular, Roth presents making up, imagining, dreaming, as a way of 'knowing', of knowing when you do not know. And this is the paradox, the Rothian paradox of authorship, of the author's 'job': anything more Zuckerman wants to *know* about Levov or about Coleman Silk he has to make up.[39] For Roth, imagination – and therefore authorship – begins where knowledge ends. Imagination, writing, just is, from a certain perspective and in a certain sense, ignorance. Or to put it more accurately, Roth suggests that imagining is 'knowing', but knowing also that you do not know. Reprising a lifetime's fascination with the complex and ambiguous relationship between fact and fiction,[40] Roth has Zuckerman admit in *American Pastoral* that he is 'working with traces' of Levov, and that 'what he was to Jerry', 'things I was ignorant of or I didn't want' are simply 'expunged'. The question of whether 'the Swede and his family came to life in me any less truthfully than in his brother' is met with a rhetorical shrug: 'well, who knows? Who *can* know?' (*AP* 76–7). The point is made again and again in Roth's work, and is structural to the technique of all three of the 'American' novels: *American Pastoral* in particular is based around Zuckerman's inability to understand, to know, what it is that he is supposed, as a novelist, as indeed an author, to know – his 'subject', 'Swede' Levov. The novel is based around Zuckerman's inability to get a sense of and even to imagine the Swede's subjectivity, what Zuckerman calls his 'substratum' (*AP* 20). Instead, the author, Nathan Zuckerman, has to imagine or 'dream' him.[41] And the importance of dreaming – the importance of the mechanism of narrating that Roth so carefully builds up, each time differently, in these three novels – is emphasized by one of the epigraphs to *American Pastoral*, lines from Johnny Mercer's 'Dream', a song that urges us to dream so that things 'might come true', to 'dream, dream, dream'.

But the question is in fact wider than this for Roth – or for his stand-in, Zuckerman: we get people wrong, we misunderstand them, Zuckerman declares, we cannot but misunderstand them, we 'mangle [them] with our ignorance every day'. That, he says, is what 'living' is about: 'It's getting [people] wrong that is living, getting them wrong and wrong and wrong and then, on careful consideration, getting them wrong again. That's how we know we're alive', he asserts, because 'we're wrong' (*AP* 35). It's all error', as Zuckerman sums it up towards the end of *I Married a Communist*, when Murray Ringold explains that his brother, Ira, never 'discovered his life': 'There's only error. *There's* the heart of the world. Nobody finds his life. That *is* life' (*IMC* 319), Murray explains. There's a kind of impassioned ethics about such a vision of what life is about, and it privileges precisely literature or fiction or authorship, since an author – an author like Zuckerman or like Roth – is professionally bound, since that's his job, to get people wrong, to get them wrong by imagining them.[42] Swede's brother Jerry finds being wrong 'unendurable', so he has become a surgeon: 'the operating room turns you into somebody who's never wrong, he says, 'Much like writing'. But Zuckerman disagrees: 'Writing turns you into somebody who's *always* wrong. The illusion that you may get it right someday is the perversity that draws you on' (*AP* 63: italics added). But it *is* an illusion. The author is never right. The author, in Roth's version, is a specialist in getting it wrong.[43]

What Roth's American trilogy produces, then, is a particular spin on authorial ignorance: the novels suggest that the work of the author *begins* at the point where his knowledge ends. That is what he is paid for (if he is paid), it is why he writes, it is *how* he writes. The author writes *because* of his ignorance and he writes not in order to resolve it but instead to counter the deadly, indeed potentially totalitarian other fiction of omniscience, of knowing. For Roth, I suggest, the point of literature, the ethical and political force of the literary – of storytelling – is to make us know not *what* but *that* we don't know.[44] It is the nature of the human, what it means to be human, each of these novels asserts, to live in error and ignorance – error and ignorance as a kind of knowing. Nathan Zuckerman's self-denying seclusion in his isolated house on an American mountain is in part a place that, by saving him from contact with others, allows him a sense of the non-human and seems to save him from error, as is made plain at the end of *I Married a Communist*: 'What you see from this silent rostrum up on my mountain on a night as splendidly clear as that night Murray left me for good . . . is that universe into which error does not obtrude. You see the inconceivable: the colossal spectacle of no antagonism' (*IMC* 323). And yet it is the task of the author – it constitutes indeed the author's, the novelist's very identity, his *human condition* – to be able to express or enact or produce the error of ignorance. Like the narrator, who begins, etymologically as well as tropologically, in knowledge, in knowing, the author is, seemingly, the one who knows or, more properly (like Lacan's version of the psychoanalyst) the one who is supposed to know. But what Roth suggests, or confirms, what comes out of his mouth, sometimes like vomit, what comes out of his pen, is that what the author in fact knows and what he lets us know is, in the end, his own ignorance. What he knows, finally, is that he does not know.

Notes

1 Philip Roth, interview with Robert McCrum in *The Observer*, 1 July 2001. In this chapter, I will use the following abbreviations for Roth's books: *AL: The Anatomy Lesson* (1983) (New York: Vintage International, 1996); *AP: American Pastoral* (1997) (London: Vintage, 1998); *C: The Counterlife* (1986) (New York: Vintage, 1996); *CPR: Conversations with Philip Roth*, ed. George J. Searles (Jackson: University Press of Mississippi, 1992); *D: Deception* (1990) (New York: Vintage International, 1997); *DA: The Dying Animal* (2001) (London: Vintage, 2002); *F: The Facts: Novelist's Autobiography* (1988) (New York: Vintage, 1997); *GW: The Ghost Writer* (1979) (New York: Vintage, 1995); *HS: The Human Stain* (2000) (London: Vintage, 2001); *IMC: I Married a Communist* (1998) (London: Vintage, 1999); *MLM: My Life as a Man* (1974) (London: Jonathan Cape, 1974); *OS: Operation Shylock* (1993) (New York: Vintage, 1994); *PO: The Prague Orgy* (1985) (New York: Vintage, 1996); *RMO: Reading Myself and Others* (2001) (New York: Vintage 2001); *ST: Sabbath's Theater* (1995) (London: Vintage, 1996).
2 Quoted in Al Avarez, 'The Long Road Home', *The Guardian*, 11 September 2004.
3 Compare Roth's comment on the story 'On Air' in another interview: 'And I said, "I didn't know what I was thinking about when I wrote it". And that is true to some degree – I didn't want to know; the idea was *not* to know. But I also did know . . . I was trying to blow up more of myself' (*RMO* 134).
4 In fact, Samuel Beckett might be said to rival Roth in his fascination with ignorance, literary and other: there should be a section, indeed there should

be a chapter on Beckett in this book. In fact, I should have written a book on Beckett and ignorance. Such a book might begin with a comment made by Beckett to James Knowlson in October 1989 that he 'realised that Joyce had gone as far as one could in the direction of knowing more' but that Beckett 'realised that my own way was in impoverishment, in lack of knowledge and in taking away, in subtracting rather than in adding' (quoted in Knowlson, *Damned to Fame: The Life of Samuel Beckett* (London: Bloomsbury, 1996), p. 352); or with his comment to Israel Shenker in May 1956 that while Joyce is 'tending towards omniscience and omnipotence as an artist', Beckett is 'working with impotence, ignorance' (quoted in ibid., p. 772). A novel like *Molloy*, for example, could be conceived just as a book about not knowing, about what it is like not to know. Molloy himself is a kind of sage of ignorance, almost spiritual in what he fails to know and in his dwelling on not knowing: 'For to know nothing is nothing, not to want to know anything likewise, but to be beyond knowing anything, to know you are beyond knowing anything, that is when peace enters in, to the soul of the incurious seeker' (Beckett, *Molloy, Malone Dies, The Unnamable* (London: Calder, 1994), p. 64).

5 See also a 1983 interview on the Rothian writer as a 'monomaniac', or 'graphomaniac' (*CPR* 147).

6 I.e. part one of *My Life as a Man*, the first Zuckerman Trilogy (*The Ghost Writer, Zuckerman Unbound, The Anatomy Lesson*) and epilogue (*The Prague Orgy*), *The Counterlife*, and the second Zuckerman Trilogy (*American Pastoral, I Married a Communist, The Human Stain*) and *Exit Ghost* (2007).

7 See François Rabelais, *The Histories of Gargantua and Pantagruel* (1532–34), trans. J.M. Cohen (London: Penguin, 1995), p. 195: 'In short, let me find you a veritable abyss of knowledge', Gargantua implores Pantagruel; and see Andrew Martin *The Knowledge of Ignorance: From Genesis to Jules Verne* (Cambridge: Cambridge University Press, 1985), p. 28. There may perhaps be an echo here of Plato's image of the philosopher as falling into a well because he's looking at the stars (*Theaetetus* 174a–b).

8 It would be no exaggeration (not least since it happens to be true) to say that Roth's middle name is Milton. Roth makes play of his second name in at least two other novels: in *The Anatomy Lesson*, Nathan Zuckerman is obsessed by a review of his novel *Carnovsky* by the critic 'Milton Appel'; eventually, Zuckerman adopts Milton Appel's name – perhaps playing on the bilingual possibilities of the name as '(Je) m'appelle (Milton)' – telling people that he is a pornographer and publisher of the fictional magazine *Likety Split*. And in the first draft of part of *American Pastoral* (from 1972) Levov's first name was Milton (see Debra Shostak, *Philip Roth – Countertexts, Counterlives* (Columbia: University of South Carolina Press, 2004), pp. 123, 241).

9 See Timothy L. Parrish, 'The End of Identity: Philip Roth's Jewish *American Pastoral*', in Jay L. Halio and Ben Siegel, eds, *Turning Up the Flame: Philip Roth's Later Novels* (Newark: University of Delaware Press, 2005), p. 142, on

the 'familiar Rothian theme' concerning the recognition that (as Marcia Umahoff puts it in *American Pastoral*) 'without transgression there isn't very much knowledge' (*AP* 360).
10 See *AP* 92. On inexplicability see also Coleman Silk's sense of understanding nothing in *The Human Stain* (125–6), and Zuckerman's sense of Faunia Farley's 'inexplicable life' (*IIS* 163–4).
11 See also *AP* 138: 'What *is* the grudge? What *is* the grievance? That was the central mystery.'
12 The sexualization of his daughter is grotesquely reinforced for Levov in the last of a series of meetings with Rita Cohen – herself a kind of temporary nightmarish substitute or wish fulfilment for his missing daughter – in the months after Merry's disappearance. They meet in a hotel room, and Rita taunts Levov sexually, exposing her vagina, making him look at her and promising that if he has sex with her she will lead him to his daughter: '"Let's f-f-f-fuck, D-d-d-dad"', she taunts (*AP* 143); and holding her hand towards him, a hand covered in her own vaginal fluid, she says '"You know what it tastes like? Want me to tell you? It tastes like your d-d-d-daughter"' (*AP* 147).
13 Nathan Zuckerman's brother has been a dentist since his first appearance, in *My Life as a Man* (see *MLM* 14).
14 While oral sex figures in most Roth novels, it plays perhaps the most significant part, plot-wise, in *The Human Stain*, where it is (allegedly) while she is 'blowing' her lover in a pickup truck outside her apartment that Faunia Farley's two children die in a fire (*HS* 67).
15 See, Shostak, *Philip Roth*, p. 69. As Shostak comments, Roth's *I Married a Communist* (1998) is also 'virtually all talk' (p. 251), although in this case it is rather more conventionally the talk of the Conradian or Marlovian narrator, Murray Ringold, who talks about his brother's life to Nathan Zuckerman for six days.
16 See Roth's somewhat understated comment on the novel that 'talking and listening are almost erotic activities' (*CPR* 255).
17 Bite-back, or 'payback', might be seen as a kind of motto or indeed *modus operandi* for the whole of Roth's oeuvre in at least three ways. In the first place, there is the dialectical movement from one novel to another – from the transgressive energies of Mickey Sabbath in *Sabbath's Theatre*, for example, to the conformist quiescence of Seymour Levov in *American Pastoral* (see Shostak's comment on Roth's '*Stance* of having no fixed position', which she links with the dialogical or dialectical or contradictory movement from one novel to the next (*Philip Roth*, pp. 6–7); see also *CPR* 211 and 235, where Roth himself comments on this movement of succession of the 'swing' from one novel to the next; and see *CPR* 258, where he comments that what kicks a new book off is 'often an argument with your previous book – you try to undo it'). Secondly, there is a thematic concern

with 'payback': there are, for example, the comments on retribution in *The Human Stain* (e.g. p. 63) and Les Farley's sense that 'It *was* payback, *all* payback, the death of the kids was payback and the carpenter she was fucking was payback' for his actions in the Vietnam War (*HS* 67). And thirdly, there is payback as constituting the internal workings of the narratives – just one example, again from *The Human Stain*: in his (imagined) stream-of-consciousness rant against his ex-wife, Farley fulminates that rather than just 'fingering' her, Faunia's stepfather 'Should have fucked her, that would have straightened her out a little' (*HS* 70), a violent sexual logic that is echoed at the start of chapter 3, when Coleman Silk overhears three college professors musing on the idea that had Bill Clinton 'fucked [Monica Lewinsky] in the ass' she would have been too ashamed to have spoken about the affair to her friend (*HS* 146–51): we might understand there to be a characteristically Rothian kind of narrative 'payback' at work here in the sense that Farley's raging, unhinged comments on Faunia return in the later scene, ironizing or undermining or recontextualizing the professors' comments and distancing the implied author from any kind of immediate identification with their thoroughly disreputable – if not entirely un-Rothian – opinions.

18 See, for example, *AP* 173, 240.
19 Parrish, 'The End of Identity', p. 133.
20 Shostak, *Philip Roth*, p. 104.
21 Marshall Bruce Gentry, 'Newark Maid Feminism in Philip Roth's *American Pastoral*', in Halio and Siegel, eds, *Turning Up the Flame*, pp. 162–3; Gentry's list oddly misses what is perhaps the most immediate factor (since this is Merry's own justification for resorting to terrorism), the social and political trauma of the Vietnam war – a factor which also features significantly (in the murderous, retributive figure of Les Farley) in *The Human Stain*.
22 Ibid., p. 163.
23 For a provocative theorization of the human contamination or concatenation of desire with disgust see Jonathan Dollimore, 'Sexual Disgust', *OLR* 20 (1998): 47–78.
24 Compare Shostak's comment (in the rather different context of a discussion of *The Dying Animal* (2001)), that in Roth's work 'abjection typifies human subjectivity because it is inevitably constituted by the body' (*Philip Roth*, p. 60).
25 Each of the books is, of course, differently autobiographical and each explores a slightly different relationship of 'fact' to 'fiction'. Perhaps most surprising in this list are *Patrimony*, which is presented as 'straight' autobiography but which also necessarily involves a certain ordering and selection, and *Deception*, which most readers and critics have taken to be a novel – a work of fiction – but which has a protagonist named Philip and which Roth himself refers to in an interview as an 'autobiography' (see Margaret Smith, 'Autobiography: False Confession?', in Halio and Siegel, eds, *Turning Up the Flame*, p. 104).

26 As Charles Berryman comments, Roth 'confirms in modern literature a tragic-comic vision of the writer's fate' ('Philip Roth and Nathan Zuckerman: A Portrait of the Artist as a Young Prometheus', *Contemporary Literature* 31: 2 (1990): 189). The complexity of the relationship between author and character is suggested by Roth's comment in *The Counterlife* that 'it is the *distance* between the writer's life and his novel that is the most intriguing aspect of his imagination' (*C* 210); as it is by Nathan Zuckerman's comment on Philip Roth as a 'self-conscious author' in *The Facts* (*F* 195). This 'theme' is of course one that Roth himself has repeatedly engaged with in his novels, from *My Life as a Man* on (see *MLM* 240, on the importance of the artist's 'powers of detachment' and on 'denarcissizing himself'); and it is commented on in almost every interview collected in *Conversations with Philip Roth*. Critics have, of course, also repeatedly referred to and discussed it: see, for example, Alexander Nurnberg, '"I, Philip": Late Roth', *Arete* 16 (2004): 129–42; Elaine M. Kauvar, 'This Doubly Reflected Communication: Philip Roth's "Autobiographies"', *Contemporary Literature* 36: 3 (1995): 412–46; Patrick O'Donnell, 'The Disappearing Text: Philip Roth's *The Ghost Writer*', *Contemporary Literature* 24: 3 (1983): 365; Siegel, 'Introduction', in Segal and Halio, ed., *Turning Up the Flame*, pp. 17–30; Shostak, 'Philip Roth's Fictions of Self-Exposure', in ibid., pp. 31–57, and *Philip Roth*, pp. 8–12 and passim; Derek Parker Royal, 'Texts, Lives, and Bellybuttons: Philip Roth's *Operation Shylock* and the Renegotiations of Subjectivity', in Halio and Segal, eds, *Turning Up the Flame*, pp. 68–91; Smith, 'Autobiography', pp. 99–114. In a recent interview Roth rejects the premises of the question about the relationship between the author and his characters/narrators: '"I just don't understand the question", he says: '"I don't read or perceive books in that way . . . Am I Roth or Zuckerman? It's all me. You know? That's what I normally say It's all me. Nothing is me"' (interview with Martin Krasnik, *The Guardian*, 14 December 2005).

27 *The Ghost Writer* revolves, conceptually, around a telling sentence of authorial ignorance from Henry James's story 'The Middle Years', which Lonoff uses as a kind of motto and on which the aspiring writer Nathan Zuckerman dwells: 'We work in the dark – we do what we can – we give what we have. Our doubt is our passion and our passion is our task. The rest is the madness of art' (*GW* 77).

28 Ignorance as a theme is perhaps somewhat less evident in *I Married a Communist*, which is (as Roth comments in an interview) 'a book about people being educated at a very fundamental level': 'Everybody is educating everybody else', he comments (www.houghtonmifflinbooks.com/authors/roth/conversation.shtml). But education, as we have, I hope, begun to establish in this book, is itself a function or expression of, is bound up with, ignorance.

29 *The Human Stain* is perhaps most clear about the evil of knowing, revolving as it does around a note sent to Coleman Silk declaring that 'Everyone knows'

that he is 'exploiting' Faunia Farley (see *HS* 38ff), as well as around a linguistic quibble regarding the meaning of the question 'Does anyone know these people? Do they exist or are they spooks' (*HS* 6; see also pp. 84–5). The title, itself, indeed, is wrapped up in the question of ignorance, at least in the sense of error: the 'human stain', which is in part the Presidential semen 'stain' on Monica Lewinsky's dress that everyone (in 'real life') knows about, is more generally the stain that is in or on 'everyone' as, according to Faunia, the human condition of 'Impurity, cruelty, abuse, error, excrement, semen' (*HS* 242).

30 Similarly, before the bombing, Levov sees his daughter as irrationally driven by what he calls her 'ignorant hatred' of America (*AP* 213) and he hears her revolutionary critiques of the society that he loves as 'ignorant raving' (*AP* 240) (Levov, by contrast, is characterized by his love for America: 'That violent hatred of America was a disease unto itself. And he loved America. Loved being an *American*' (*AP* 206)).

31 See Plato, *Laws* 9: 863c.

32 Dawn's defensive reaction against the community's belief that her daughter is the Rimrock Bomber proleptically ironizes such assertions: 'Dynamite? What does Merry have to do with dynamite? No! It isn't true! Nobody knows a *thing*!' (*AP* 140).

33 See Shostak, 'Philip Roth's Fictions', p. 48, on Zuckerman as a 'mouthpiece' for Roth in *American Pastoral*. And see S. Lillian Kremer, 'Philip Roth's Self-Reflexive Fiction', *Modern Language Studies* 3/4 (1998): 57, on Zuckerman as the 'primary vehicle for Roth's portrait of an artist'; 'Like other postmodernists', Kremer claims, Roth 'privileges the artist as a new type of hero and often projects the inner life of the self as the field of action' (71).

34 Shostak takes a different view to mine of the significance of introducing Zuckerman only to have him disappear from the narrative a quarter of the way through the novel, suggesting that this strategy involves 'a structural metaphor for Roth's theme: the unreadable "reality" of the visible world renders the perceiving subject as fleeting as his subject of perception' ('Philip Roth's Fictions of Self-Exposure', p. 50; see also *Philip Roth*, p. 237, on the idea that Zuckerman 'simply disappears forever into a narrative voice that, were it not for that opening, would be taken for a conventional third-person narrator indistinguishable from the implied author'). But I take such a view to be fundamentally misconceived with regard to the epistemological conundrum that Roth presents in the novel: Shostak overlooks the fact that Zuckerman does not in fact disappear, that everything from the moment that Zuckerman begins to 'pull away from myself' and to pull away from the reunion and start to imagine, to 'dream' the 'realistic chronicle' of Swede Levov, is in fact Nathan Zuckerman, and that (for example) the alternative narratives towards the end of the novel – of Merry finding her way back to the Levovs' house and Levov's father dying, on the one hand, and the drunk Jessie Orcutt stabbing Lou Levov in the face with a fork, on the other – are part of that imagining and are indeed moments where there is a kind of

imaginative-narratorial slippage that exposes Zuckerman's presence, just as the novel's final questions, for another example, return us explicitly and unmistakably to Zuckerman's narrative voice.

35 There are, indeed, specific moments where ignorance fades into imagining and thereby 'knowing': one such moment occurs towards the end of *The Human Stain*, when Zuckerman describes the origin of the novel as occurring as he stands by Coleman's grave and hallucinates or imagines ('hears') Coleman and Faunia's voices: 'And that is how all this began: by my standing alone in a darkening graveyard and entering into professional competition with death. "After the kids, after the fire", I heard her telling him, "I was taking any job I could ..." (*HS* 338).

36 This final comment – 'It's now all I do' – alludes to the implicit link, in Roth and in the Western literary as well as theological tradition more generally, between sexual potency and knowledge: what Zuckerman means here is that what he doesn't do now is sex, since he's now impotent (as a result of prostate cancer). In other words sexual knowledge in the so-called 'Biblical' sense, the theme that has been at the forefront of Roth's oeuvre since the 1950s, has now finally be de-linked from narrative knowledge. Since, as Parrish suggests, Zuckerman's identity 'has been at times almost indistinguishable from the actions of his penis', his life now seems at an end and he has 'no more stories to tell about himself except through others' ('The End of Identity', p. 134).

37 Shostak, *Philip Roth*, pp. 265, 240.

38 Perhaps one could conceive of the relationship between the 'epistemologic drive' and the 'anepistemologic drive' as something like the relationship between the Freudian conception of the relationship between eros and thanatos, the 'pleasure principle' and the death drive, as articulated in *Beyond the Pleasure Principle*.

39 Imagining as knowing is not of course limited to authors, it is just part of their job description: Levov, for example, is also imagined as knowing through imagining, in his fear of knowing what happened to Merry as she was raped: he fears 'seeing everything he does not want to see, knowing everything he cannot stand to know. He cannot sit there imagining the rest of that story' (*AP* 274–5).

40 See Royal's comment that 'It is not an exaggeration to state that Philip Roth is obsessed with the play between the world that is inscribed on the page and the world that is not' ('Texts, Lives, and Bellybuttons', p. 68).

41 On Levov's unknowability see also *AP* 275–6; Zuckerman speculates that it is in part Levov's own 'dumbness' (*AP* 356), the fact that he is lacking in insight of others, that makes him unknowable (*AP* 409–10). A different mode of unknowability or a different motive for it, is represented by Levov's neighbour, the predatory and irretrievably Waspish architect William Orcutt, who has had an affair with Levov's wife and who develops unknowability in order to deceive others: he can then 'fuck his neighbor's wife' while presenting himself as 'the ever-reasonable unknowable man' (*AP* 382); for him, being

'unknowable is the *goal*. Then you moved instrumentally through life, appropriating the beautiful wives' (*AP* 383). Shostak is right, I think, to point to the way in which Zuckerman's inability to know Levov mirrors Levov's own inability to understand his daughter; as she comments, in this respect, at least, Zuckerman 'disappears into the Swede's story' as much as Levov 'disappears into Nathan's' (*Philip Roth*, p. 247).

42 Nathan Zuckerman's concern with human error goes back as far as *My Life as a Man*, where his concerns as a writer are summed up as 'human character, human possibility, human error, human anguish, human tragedy' (*MLM* 17). The notion of authorial ignorance is, of course, rather different from the claim made by at least one critic that *American Pastoral* expresses Roth's 'blind spot' in that the novel both deconstructs the pastoral and expresses its own pastoral nostalgia for a pre-1960s America (see Andrew Gordon, 'The Critique of Utopia in Philip Roth's *The Counterlife* and *American Pastoral*', in Halio and Siegel, *Turning Up the Flame*, pp. 151–9, especially pp. 157–8). Getting Levov 'wrong' runs as a motto especially through the first two frame-narrative chapters ('I was wrong', Zuckerman declares on p. 21; 'I was wrong. Never more mistaken about anyone in my life', he repeats on p. 39 (see also *AP* 80 and 82)). But this of course presents us with the (sceptic's) paradox that, in order to know that he was wrong, Zuckerman must know, correctly know, Levov, which is precisely what he declares he is unable to do. This paradox of authorial nescience may itself be construed as part of the serious ignorance, the profound, bottomless ignorance, the consummate error, of the Rothian author.

43 In *The Anatomy Lesson* a somewhat unhinged Zuckerman also fantasizes about being a doctor. And he also entertains hyper-Cartesian thoughts about doubt: 'doubt is half a writer's life. Two-thirds. Nine-tenths. Another day, another doubt. The only thing I never doubted was the doubt' (*AL* 268). The author, Roth himself, has expressed similar thoughts in interviews: while as a doctor (as a gynaecologist, for example) he would 'know that I could do it', as a writer 'I'm not at all sure that I can do it when I'm writing' since for a writer there's a 'sustained level of doubt that sustains you in some way' (*CPR* 218). For a related but rather different assessment of Zuckerman in the American trilogy as representing 'the vexing epistemological project of the historian' see Shostak, *Philip Roth*, p. 232.

44 Compare Ross Posnock's somewhat prickly remark that 'Roth is the hedgehog who knows one big thing – unknowability. This is the epistemological human stain we are morally required to embrace' ('Purity and Danger: On Philip Roth', *Raritan* 21: 2 (2001): 101). But perhaps one could say that Roth is concerned not so much with 'unknowability' as with the more interesting, more fertile state of not knowing. And Roth is also concerned in many of his novels with what, in *The Prague Orgy*, he calls the 'unforeseen consequences of art' (*PO* 61; see also 5) – indeed after the publication of *Portnoy's Complaint* this becomes a central part of Roth's concern with authorship.

10

The politics of authorial ignorance: contemporary poetry

It's a curious fact, one that might help us to distinguish literary texts from other forms of writing – history books, say, or political memoirs, or scientific textbooks, or certain kinds of philosophical writing – it's a curious fact that, as I have tried to suggest throughout this book, ignorance, authorial nescience, is well founded as a principle of literary composition, particularly in Romantic and post-Romantic writing. But it is even more striking that declarations of authorial ignorance became, in the twentieth century, something like a rite of passage, and indeed just what poets in particular were – as they still are, I think – expected to declare (stopped at customs, a writer today is not likely, as Oscar Wilde is alleged to have done, to say 'I have nothing to declare except my genius'; rather, she might be inclined to make an equivalent declaration: 'I have nothing to declare but my ignorance'). Authors seem to fall over themselves to confess that, at some level, they do not know what it is that they are doing, or how, or why they are doing it. During the last century in particular, ignorance has become something of a mark of pride, even a clannish badge of membership of the profession of (literary) authorship. What authors typically decry or exclude or disavow is the possibility that they possess precisely that to which their professional title seems to entitle them – their own authority over their work: contemporary authors' versions of the author are indeed peculiarly concerned to resist that figure's authority, his or her historic *auctoritas*. The author as unknowing, as not, or as not quite, conscious of what he or she does, as well as impersonal or as multiple, are the most common forms of twentieth- and twenty-first-century versions of authorship.[1]

In a letter to I.A. Richards of November 1931 concerning *Ash Wednesday*, to take an initial and notable example, T.S. Eliot writes in carefully discriminatory ways about the question of the visibility, the knowability of allusions in his poem. The question of allusion is always of course bound up, necessarily bound up, in *questions* of ignorance – in, indeed, the indeterminacy of both authorial and readerly knowledge of verbal or textual 'sources' and resources. According to Harold Bloom, indeed, criticism is itself (therefore) determined by allusive knowledge: criticism, Bloom suggests, is 'the art of knowing the hidden roads that go from poem to poem'.[2] But in his letter Eliot complicates such knowingness, in the poet as in the reader or critic:

> As for the allusions you mention, that is perfectly deliberate, and it was my intention that the reader should recognize them. As for the question why I made the allusions at all, that seems to me definitely a matter which should not concern the reader [*amended from* author]. That, as you know, is a theory of mine, that very often it is possible to increase the effect for a reader by letting him know [half *deleted*] a reference or a meaning; but if the reader knew more, the poetic effect would actually be diminished; that if the reader knows too much about the crude material in the author's mind, his own reaction may tend to become at best merely a kind of feeble image of the author's feelings, whereas a good poem should have a potentiality of evoking feelings and associations in the reader of which the author is wholly ignorant. I am rather inclined to believe, for myself, that my best poems are possibly those which evoke the greatest number and variety of interpretations surprising to myself.[3]

The letter makes it clear that, for Eliot, poetry involves a complex interplay between knowledge and ignorance (both the reader's and the author's), and that the work of composition involves interaction between the two.[4] But this movement is apparent in the larger shape of Eliot's statement: he begins with the question of how much *readers* know about the sources of a poem and ends with the assertion that the *author* might be 'wholly ignorant' of certain 'feelings and associations' in a text. This idea of the poet as 'wholly ignorant' of what a reader might properly make of the poem discriminates the poetry or poetics of ignorance from any idea of the text as constituted by a joint endeavour of poet and reader in, say, the reader-response theories of Wolfgang Iser or Hans-Robert Jauss, where reading is presented as a kind of synthetic understanding, just as much as it obviously disturbs any straightforward idea of authorial intentionality.

In a 1959 interview in *The Paris Review*, Eliot was even more direct about his own authorial ignorance: asked if his intention in *The Waste Land* was to promulgate a Christian message, he denied that it was but then went on to question the question. 'I wonder what an "intention" means!', he commented, 'One wants to get something off the chest. One doesn't know quite what it is that one wants to get off one's chest until one's got it off. But I couldn't apply the word "intention" positively to any of my poems. Or to any poem'. In *The Waste Land*, he says later in the same interview of one of the most highly regarded, most canonical and most exegetically worked-over poems in the English language, 'I wasn't even bothering whether I understood what I was saying'.[5]

Such confessions of poetic ignorance are pervasive in the twentieth-century Anglo-American literary tradition, although lyric poets seem particularly prone to them.[6] In his mid-century essay 'The Noble Rider and the Sound of Words', for example, Wallace Stevens argued that poetry should be understood in terms of 'thoughts and not only our own thoughts but the thoughts of men and women ignorant of what it is that they are thinking'.[7] 'In the writing of a poem', Robert Lowell declared in 1982, 'all our compulsions and biases should get in, so that finally we don't know what we mean'.[8] More recently, Seamus Heaney echoes Eliot's 'Tradition and the Individual Talent' in a 1999 interview in which he says that 'The constant problem, the constant question' for the poet, is 'the relationship between the conscious and the unconscious aspects': 'If you see too much intention in another person's work', he remarks, 'you resist it. [But] If you see too little, if it's not been brought far enough, you regret it.'[9] More matter-of-factly, the Australian poet Les Murray remarked in 1991 that 'If I know the end of a poem before I start, it's probably going to be a dead poem'.[10] And Paul Muldoon (one of the most densely allusive of contemporary poets) has argued, more guardedly, in a preliminary 'Ars Poetica' published in 1998, for the 'primacy' of a poet's 'unknowing' *as well as* his 'almost total knowingness'.[11]

There is ample evidence of this in the contemporary discourse of poetics – by which I mean the kinds of things that poets (in particular) themselves say about their poetry. It is something of an open secret – outside of the academic study of literature, at least – that *not* knowing is, for a poet, as important as knowing. For convenience, I will attempt to illustrate this by briefly looking at a recent book edited by Clare Brown and Don Paterson which comprises a series of short accounts by poets of their own poetry. The essays selected by Brown and Paterson were written over the last fifty years for the UK-based Poetry Book Society: on selecting a book for recommendation, the Society has a practice of asking the chosen poet to publish some comments on his or her work in its *Bulletin*. Brown and Paterson decided to give their book a title borrowed from a comment by one of the writers, the Scottish poet Kathleen Jamie, *Don't Ask Me What*

I Mean, and they comment that the gist of the statement 'uttered in arrogance, in anger, in forlorn desperation, and all points between' had been 'the most common response to the request for an article'.¹² In other words, the title was designed to indicate a common problem that the poets themselves had in talking about, in conceiving of and indeed in writing poetry. Again and again, as Brown and Paterson point out, poets unprompted (or prompted only by the request for a comment on their poems) would declare their ignorance.

In fact, although Brown and Paterson do not remark on it in their brief Introduction, these expressions of poetic ignorance have a number of different aspects. And it is, I think, worth trying to tease out the different ways in which the question of poetic ignorance appears in the poets' conceptions of their work and their working methods. Ignorance is a pervasive trope of authorship in contemporary poetry, I want to suggest, as well as being important thematically and technically, but it has multiple expressions. In what follows I have attempted to summarize the various kinds of statement that the poets make.¹³ We can call it 'Thirteen ways of looking at a poet'.

1. *I don't know where my poems come from*. 'And how does it happen, if it happens?' Michael Hofmann asks, 'What makes some things exhaustible and others practically not? If I really knew the answer, I'd bottle it' (p. 121; 1999). Oliver Reynolds agrees, extending such ignorance to a poem's audience as well: 'The book's destination is obscure (nor is much known of whence it came)', he remarks (pp. 240–1; 1985). When one talks about poetic composition, George Barker speculates, 'one is hinting at a matter about which no one knows anything' (p. 11; 1962). And commenting on *Door into the Dark*, Heaney explains that the title came from the opening line of his poem 'The Forge', which 'uses the dark, active centre of the blacksmith's shed as an emblem for the instinctive, blurred stirring and shaping of some kinds of art': but 'I cannot say why I should be possessed by past language and landscape', he comments (pp. 101, 102; 1969, 1975).

2. *It's not my job to explain my poems*. 'What [a poet] would probably like to say, if he is honest', Kingsley Amis says, in a moment of disarming honesty, 'is that he will see his readers or anyone else damned before he will reveal his almost total ignorance of what on earth he is up to as a poet. . . . Who am I to say what [my poems] are like or what they mean? That is the reader's job' (pp. 1–2; 1956).

3. *Poetic composition is not, can never be, fully rational or conscious.* Sarah Maguire is very clear on this point: 'all writers have their own

unconscious triggers and obsessions to work out', she comments, 'things which affect us and move us into writing; so, to a large extent (the unconscious part), I'm not in full control of these tropes: they turn me' (p. 170; 1991). 'To become conscious of a book's themes is to come out of the place where the poetry happens', comments Kathleen Jamie (p. 126; 1999). Writing forty years earlier, Elizabeth Jennings concurs: 'I find that the more poems one writes, the more mysterious the whole creative process becomes' she explains: 'I write poems in order to know, to discover, to get things clear ... I cannot say what my next poems will be like; writing a poem is, like mystical experience, a gratuitous gift' (pp. 133–5; 1961). Peter Levi suggests that 'Once the decision has been made, nothing can exist but the poem' but that such decisions 'are incommunicable and often subconscious' (p. 148; 1960). This is one of the most common responses, and it is often expressed in terms of mystery. W.S. Mermin, for example, comments that poetry for him is a 'mystery', one that 'gives us a feeling of illumination'; and he means this in a 'religious' sense, he says, thinking of poetry as 'a way of using what we know, to glimpse what we do not know' (p. 178; 1956). Andrew Motion, in a characteristically mystical moment, but one which leaves open the question of whether poetry allows an access of knowledge, comments that 'I think my poems (like many other people's, I dare say) are only partly the product of conscious workings; they also rely deeply on primal, swampy, dimly perceived things' (p. 188; 1997). Most recently, Alice Oswald has likened her poems to those of John Clare, which seem at times as if 'the mind has disappeared altogether and the world's going on as no human has ever thought it'. Something similar can be said about her own poems: in her collection *Dart*, she comments: 'The idea of a map poem or song line (which is how I see *Dart*) is just that – the structure comes off the river, the transitions are geographical not rational' (p. 208; 2002).

4. *I don't know what to say about my poems.* According to Douglas Dunn, 'almost everyone' says 'the same thing' about their poetry: 'I don't like writing about my work; or, I never know what to say about my poetry' (p. 70; 2000).

5. *I don't understand my poems; or I don't know what my poems are saying (if they're saying anything).* This is clearly related to 4, since if I don't know what my poems mean I can have little to say about them, and to 3 in the sense that my ignorance may be explained by recourse to the unconscious or to mystery. George Barker, for one, is stuck for words: 'Since I really do not know what these poems are supposed to say, apart

from the things that they do in fact say, it's a little difficult to speak' (p. 9; 1954). Jamie McKendrick understands the awkwardness, the embarrassment of the predicament: 'Many poets must experience a similar embarrassment when asked, politely or sceptically, what their work is about – that of not knowing the simple answer they of all people should know' (p. 162; 1997). Robin Skelton is equally forthright, suggesting that he may think he knows, but he doesn't: 'Of course I do have views about my own poetry. I sometimes even imagine that I know what I am trying to do, though mostly such opinions are mere deductions from past work, and a new poem very often shows them to be false' (p. 268; 1955).

6. *It is the poem or language that invents or writes itself, not the poet.* One reason for suggesting that I do not know what my poem is saying, says the poet, is that it is not in any important sense *I* that wrote it. 'A man does not invent poems; they discover him', George Barker remarks (p. 11; 1962); while John Burnside muses that 'I have come to feel that the poems I write are not so much made, or composed (by me), as heard' (p. 23; 2000). Michael Longley says that he 'lives' for 'those moments when language itself takes over the enterprise, and insight races ahead of knowledge' (p. 153; 1995). And Anne Rouse suggests that in what she calls a 'real poem' words 'start up their own life and force both reader and writer to think freshly' (p. 250; 1993). For Geoffrey Hill this is something of the magic of language: 'At one point in *The Orchards of Syon* (XXIII) I say "I write/to astonish myself"', he remarks: 'This self-astonishment is achieved when, by some process I can't fathom, common words are moved, or move themselves, into clusters of meaning so intense that they seem to stand up from the page, three-dimensional almost' (p. 117; 2002). There is nothing new or original in this, of course, linked as it is to the ancient tradition of inspiration. But what such remarks suggest is the continuing vitality of the tradition of poetic ignorance down to the twenty-first century.

7. *As I begin a poem I don't know where it will go, or how it will work out.* Rhyme, according to Ciaran Carson, is 'a powerful springboard from which to launch oneself into the unknown: in *Opera Et Cetera*, each poem is given a title from the alphabet and 'each time that I sat down to try another letter, I had no idea what I would write; nor would I have any clue about the outcome' (p. 25; 1996). 'While trying to write poetry', X.J. Kennedy comments, 'sometimes I neither know nor care what I mean by the words that start coming in stealthily': 'If the poem is lucky', he goes on, 'it arrives at some facts that its writer had not known he knew' (p. 141; 1971). While, as Sean O'Brien comments, 'It's hard to write about

your own books without sounding omniscient' the facts of writing are rather different: 'the writing of *HMS Glasshouse*', he confesses, 'began in ignorance with a poem whose title stuck, and the book's shape only began to emerge fairly late' (p. 202; 1991). James Reeves suggests that poets tend to write poems 'as best [they] can' but that the poems 'usually turn out quite different from what one imagines they will be like when one starts': it is as if they have 'a life of their own which they are determined to live in their own way' (p. 237; 1960).

8. *The poem tells me something about myself that I did not know before.* According to Donald Davie, 'the image of himself and his own world' produced by a poet's poems is 'as disconcerting to him as to anyone else; the poems in print give back to him the image of a stranger' (p. 49; 1959). Douglas Dunn records a similar sense of discomfort on reading his own poems: 'there's the most hellish event of all, when you find out for yourself just who and what you are in your work' (p. 71; 2000).

9. *What a poem says is not necessarily what I wanted to say.* 'Poems are what they say,' comments Patric Dickinson, 'which is not always what the poet intended' (p. 324; 1964).

10. *I cannot say or predict what my poem will mean to another person.* This is a variant on (9), coming at it from the other end, as it were. 'I can't imagine what they mean to anyone else', comments P.J. Kavanagh: 'But it is fine they mean something, because that, mysteriously, is what one intends' (p. 136; 1959). One intends, *that* they should mean, that is to say, but not *what* they are to mean.

11. *If I could tell you about my poems I would not need to write them.* 'If I could concisely explain myself or poems or my poems or writing', Geoffrey Grigson remarks, 'I should try not to write them' (p. 93; 1969).

12. *I can only write because I do not know.* A variant of (11), this is an idea expressed by a number of poets in Brown and Paterson's volume. Harry Guest, for example, comments that 'I don't know why or how I write poetry and suspect that if I knew I wouldn't be able to any more' (p. 327; 1976); while Dom Moraes concurs, saying that 'if a poet knew why he wrote poetry he would cease to write it' (p. 185; 1960). Pauline Stainer seems to be suggesting something similar when she comments darkly that she is 'wary of explaining poetry. Metaphor is a dark and arterial currency. We sleepwalk into the well' (p. 277; 1989).

13. *It is not I that makes a poem happen.* For Derek Mahon, 'there's a helplessness involved: one does what presents itself to be done' (p. 173; 1982). Paul Muldoon actually wills this lack of will: 'I try to leave the will out of writing poems, preferring to let them have their way', he says: 'But

I did have one or two demi-semi-conscious aims' in writing the poems collected in *Hay* (p. 193; 1999). But for C.K. Williams the question is undecidable: 'one can never quite be sure what one has earned, and what's been given, probably despite yourself; either will do' (p. 307; 1999).

While such abnegations of authority might look like abrogations of intellectual or ethical or political responsibility – while they might seem to be saying that poetry is for poetry's sake and that I, as poet, am not to be, cannot be, held responsible, intellectually or ethically or politically responsible, for my work since I am, at some crucial, some ultimate level, ignorant of what I am saying – in fact, I want to suggest, these forms of 'ignorance' may be seen to comprise or produce a crucial political valency. I want to suggest that poetic ignorance, as it is commonly presented by contemporary poets, has an incisive political charge. And that this response of irresponsibility, of nescience, may be linked to the wider issue of the politics of ignorance.

In *Ignorance and Liberty* (2003), the Italian political philosopher Lorenzo Infantino has argued for a recognition of ignorance as something like a founding principle of the democratic state.[14] Building on Karl Popper's classic wartime critique of the totalitarianism implicit in Plato's conception of an ideal Republic presided over by 'philosopher-kings' in *The Open Society and Its Enemies* (1945), Infantino argues that the principle of 'gnoseological fallibilism' – the possibility that anyone, including a state's political leaders, can be mistaken, can be held not to know – is intrinsic to democracy itself. Authoritarian and totalitarian states are founded, by contrast, he suggests, on the position that the leader or leaders *cannot* be mistaken, that they must, by definition, have knowledge of every aspect of the state's workings; it is a principle of totalitarianism that the leader(s) have knowledge that cannot – typically on pain of imprisonment, exile, torture or death – be questioned. 'The ignorant man should follow the leadership of the wise and obey his orders', the Athenian declares in Plato's *Laws* 3 (690b), explaining that this distinction – between the wise and the ignorant – is the most important principle in deciding who a leader should be.[15]

The principle of fallibilism – the proposition that we share what José Ortega y Gasset calls 'original ignorance'[16] – entails that, like all other people, political leaders are 'ignorant and fallible'. While it may seem self-evident – to any but political leaders, at least – the point is, in Infantino's view, both fundamental and often contested, since ('since' in both cases) it entails the principle that there must be limits on the power of a state's rulers (p. 5). In a system of political fallibilism, or 'democracy' (to use a politically vital if, especially since 9/11, a much misused word), there can be no 'privileged point of view': instead there is intellectual equality based on the recognition of 'our common ignorance' (pp. 32–3). The point is not that we are all always ignorant (and that is not Socrates' point, nor for that matter, for example, Philip Roth's) but that we all can be, that we all are potentially fallible – and that that fallibility should be accepted, acknowledged, and indeed that our knowledge of our potential ignorance should be used to nourish and sustain democracy. As a consequence, a truly democratic state will be organized around political institutions that are designed to prevent 'bad or incompetent rulers . . . from doing too much damage' (that – preventing too much damage – being about the best that anyone can hope for in an anthropo-political context).[17] Following the standard distinction between the authentic, perplexed Socrates of the early dialogues and the distorted image of Socrates as knowing that Plato presents in the later dialogues (in the *Republic*, in particular), Infantino suggests that what Socrates teaches us is that the principle of human ignorance, *not* knowing as 'a common feature of all of us', works against any individual (or group of individuals) taking power 'on the basis of a presumed superior knowledge' (p. 35). The 'open society' is, for Infantino, 'based on the recognition of everyone's ignorance'. This, he suggests, directly contrasts with Plato, who, as 'Socrates' Judas',[18] in fact 'reversed' his master's position (p. 48). Plato's idea of knowledge, Infantino argues, is based on an 'arbitrary psychologism' in which the philosopher, the 'philosopher king', is the only one who truly 'knows' reality and is therefore the one who must have a 'monopoly of knowledge'. It is simply by virtue of that superior knowledge, Plato argues, that the philosopher should have absolute and unquestioned power (pp. 38, 39).

Indeed, Infantino perceives a fundamental structural problem in the Platonic philosopher's access to knowledge, in that it is gained by internalized reflection, by 'looking exclusively within our soul and searching'. This does not allow for an increase in rationality resulting from the attempt, intrinsic to philosophical notions of democracy, to 'disprove', in every way possible, our 'cognitive hypotheses' (p. 38). 'Critical discussion', which is itself an intrinsic dimension of the democratic process and which 'corresponds to Socratic method', is replaced, in Plato, by 'conversion': 'Truth is no longer the impermanent product of a free exchange of ideas', Infantino explains, but rather 'an attribute of a special group, the Platonic philosophers, who possess knowledge that combines truth and virtue, to which everyone else must be *converted*' (p. 64). For Plato, knowledge is 'a pure conversion' rather than debate, rationalization, argument (p. 135). In order to 'convert' everyone else, the 'habitat of critical discussion' – a 'habitat' that includes private property, the market and 'the entire system of laws and values associated with them' – must be 'eradicated' (p. 73). And it is Infantino's point – as it was Popper's point before him (Plato's 'political demands', Popper says, are 'purely totalitarian')[19] – that we would be able to replace Plato's name here with the names of some of the tyrants who might be said to have dominated, if not characterized, the political history of, not least, twentieth-century world politics – Stalin and Hitler, certainly, but since them Mao Zedong, Pol Pot, Idi Amin, Augusto Pinochet, Nicolae Ceausescu, Slobodan Milosevic, General Suharto, Charles Taylor, Papa Doc Duvalier, Sadam Hussein, Robert Mugabe, Kim Il Sung . . . And even in allegedly 'democratic' societies there has always been and there continues to be, as the twenty-first century commences, a worrying tendency for political leaders to link their decisions to the commitment and conversion of political and religious faith, thus removing political decisions from the strictures and balances of rationality, debate and argument.

For Infantino, then, ignorance and fallibility are 'our major problem'. Individuals and societies make mistakes because they are fallible. But accepting our fallibility, our ignorance, is also the 'solution' to the problem. If we can 'stop claiming that there can be any privileged source of knowledge' we can 'start a process that is continually open and can mobilize the largest possible quantity of knowledge' (p. 89). 'Recognition of our ignorance and fallibility', Infantino declares decisively, 'leads to an open society. The presumption of holding a "monopoly of the truth" destroys all systems of liberty and is conducive to the revival of tribalism' (p. 133); the idea that there is, or can be, a 'privileged' source of knowledge 'always violates the egalitarian theory of rationality, and this always produces illiberal social systems' (p. 144). Infantino sums up the political consequences of ignorance as follows:

> The difficult struggle man has been involved in since the time of ancient Athens is among those who consider themselves ignorant and fallible, and thus believe there must be free social cooperation, and those who fear liberty and fight it in the name of superior knowledge, of which they declare themselves to be the bearers. Recognition of our ignorance and fallibility has taught us tolerance and made it possible for people with different philosophical and religious world-views to live together. It has brought us to the egalitarian theory of reason and juridical-formal equality, where

> general abstract norms define the limits of our actions but we are left to choose the content of our life. It is a *habitat* that recognizes fallibility, so it permits us to explore the unknown and correct our errors. Private ownership and the market bring economic development; democracy produces political development; and critical discussion leads to an increase in our rationality. In other words, we need comparison and competition. At the same time, this *habitat* allows us to avoid intellectualistic *hubris* and find new solutions by mobilizing our knowledge. Therefore, our problem is an '*ecological*' one; we must create an institutional-normative context that permits us to live by competition. (p. 148)

Infantino's political ignorance theory is not a plea for more ignorance – the tyrants, despots and their oppressive state machineries have enough of that, and indeed thrive on the dissemination of ignorance, on disinformation and on the destruction of the technological, social, intellectual and institutional modes and means of knowledge production and exchange. It is, rather, a plea for more knowledge. But his argument *is* also, from another perspective, a plea for a recognition of the fact that ignorance and the acceptance of the knowledge that we are all ignorant (the *only* truth that you might think that humans could agree on . . . or perhaps, on second thoughts, precisely the truth that humans will *never* agree on) is necessary for that earnest dream of Western liberalism, an open, properly democratic and non-totalitarian society.

What I want to suggest – and this is the reason that I have summarized Infantino's argument in some detail – is that the ignorance or 'perplexity' that the 'early' or 'authentic' Socrates appeals to, ignorance that is for Infantino fundamental to democracy itself, constitutes, in effect, something of the political force of the institution of literature as it is conceived in the Romantic period and beyond. To put it crudely, there is a development in generally accepted conceptions of authorship from Chaucer to the eighteenth century that goes along with changes in cultural, economic, political conceptions of authority more widely. The move is from an understanding of authorship within the medieval conception of *auctoritas*, whereby authority is invested in tradition, in what has gone before, to a conception of authority as self-sufficient and self-originating in the Romantic period.[20] The danger, of course is that the newly subjectivized authority of the literary author leads to a new kind of unquestioned authorialism, to the unquestioned authority of the genius-figure, whether author or artist, to the 'egotistical sublime' that Keats thought he perceived in Wordsworth, or indeed to the figuration of the political leader *as* a kind of artist (tyrants, of course, only too often fashion themselves as poets (Chairman Mao, Radovan Karadzic), or artists (Hitler), or men of culture, of critical taste and discrimination (Stalin) . . .). And the Romantics' fascination and even identification with the French Enlightenment dictator Napoleon Bonaparte, or the Shelleyan claim that poets are the unacknowledged legislators – the 'secret police' of the world, as Auden puts it[21] – might in some ways bear out such a link between the Romantic artist and the totalitarian leader. But this is only half of the story of Romanticism and of the 'consecration' of the artistic genius,[22] since there is, at the same time, something like an in-built defence against this threat. Poets – and more generally Romantic and post-Romantic authors – *disclaim* responsibility for their work, for the valency in the end even of their own subjectivity, arguing that they are in fact, professionally ignorant. This constitutes the danger of Romantic authorialism, of course, since it can so easily lead to the vatic conception of the author or poet as endowed with mysterious authority invested in them through inspiration – the poet is a 'legislator', even if not properly acknowledged as such. But this condition of authorship is also the poet's vulnerability, his fallibility, the fragility and uncertainty of his vision.

We might come to this point, or get a better fix on this point, by considering Derrida's rich conception(s) of the 'strange institution of literature', since my concern in this book has been to trace some of the ways in which ignorance is linked to the very idea, to the very institution, of literature as it has been conceived, developed and debated over the last two centuries in particular. Part of the force of Derrida's career-long attention to the question of literature has to do with the multiplicity, the sheer exuberant plurality, indeed, of his definitions and redefinitions of what he takes to be beyond or without definition. And within this definitional multiplicity there often lurks a sense of the ignorance of literature, its engagement with undecidability or aporia, with agnoiology. Literature – or writing more generally – is constituted for Derrida by a certain relationship with the signature or with the name or the date and is also (therefore) a mode of performativity;[23] the literary text is both singular – singularly singular, 'absolutely singular', indeed[24] – and necessarily an instance of something more general, necessarily involving a certain exemplarity;[25] literature is both unique and also 'only exemplary of what happens everywhere, each time that there is some trace'.[26] In literature, for Derrida, there is a suspension of the 'thetic relation to meaning or referent', of the ' "thetic" naivety of the transcendent reading'

(*AL* 45); and literature is constituted in the distinction between an author and a narrator;[27] literature, he suggests, is involved in the readerly production of a certain identification, of certain kinds of identifications (with characters, narrators, authors, let us say (*AL* 39)). There is 'no – or hardly any, ever so little – literature', or at least no 'essence' or 'truth' of literature;[28] literature has 'no essence or substance', it 'is not. It does not exist.'[29] Literature, again, 'is' itself the 'place' or the 'experience' of the 'trouble' we have in defining literature, and the experience of the '"trouble" we also have with the essence of language, with truth and with essence, the language of essence in general' (*AL* 48); literature is 'in place of the secret' and a passion of or a passion for the secret;[30] literature is 'on the edge of everything, almost beyond everything', it is 'the most interesting thing in the world' and in fact something that may indeed be 'more interesting than the world' (*AL* 47).

But perhaps Derrida's most potent definition of literature links it with democracy, with a democracy to come: literature, he suggests, in an interview published in 1992 (from which some of these other definitions come) is a 'strange', a fictive or 'institutionless institution', one that 'allows one to *say everything*, in *every way*' (*AL* 42). And this 'authorization to say everything' is linked, in the West and in its 'relatively modern form', Derrida argues, with 'the coming about of the modern idea of democracy' (*AL* 36–7). The possibility of saying 'everything' is, in principle and with a few exceptions, that on which democracy is supposedly founded: it is that which supports democracy, makes it possible and it is at the same time that which democracy makes possible. This possibility of 'saying everything in every way' *is* in a sense, and in principle, precisely what is meant by 'democracy': this is what democracy just is. Referring to a letter protesting against the Ayatollah Khomeini's fatwa issued against Salman Rushdie after the publication of *The Satanic Verses*, Derrida argues that, if literature has a 'critical function', such a conception would be intelligible only within the 'Western' concatenation of 'politics, censorship, and the lifting of censorship to the origin and institution of literature'. But Derrida suggests that any such 'critical function' is, in fact, 'very ambiguous', in the sense that literature also lays claim to a certain irresponsibility, a refusal 'to reply for one's thoughts or writing to constituted powers' – which is, in turn, Derrida goes on, 'perhaps the highest form of responsibility' (*AL* 38). Democracy, or democracy-to-come, allows not only for 'free speech' but also for the possibility of *not* speaking.[31] And not speaking, or speaking (or writing) in ways that amount to a resistance to speech – a resistance to meaning, to the thetic (literature as a 'suspension of the thetic relation to meaning or referent'), to making sense – is just what may be said to be instituted in and by the literary event, by the literary speech act. I want to suggest that this irresponsible or non-responsive responsibility is captured in the capacity of literature to engage with, to perform, to encompass not knowing – literature as the site or institution of 'a certain irresponsibility' (itself a high responsibility, itself involving a demand as well as a resistance) that I am calling 'ignorance', ignorance that is at the heart of the open society, of tolerance, of democracy.

Few contemporary poets have been as troubled by the question of political responsibility, of being called to speak, to speak up or speak out, and of the responsibility that poets (also) have to resist such pressures, as Seamus Heaney. For almost the whole of his career, there has been, as Heaney puts it, 'A public expectation . . . not of poetry as such but of political positions variously approvable by mutually disapproving groups'.[32] It is a question that is heard throughout his Nobel Lecture, 'Crediting Poetry' (1995), for example, as it is in many of Heaney's published essays and interviews. And it is there in a number of poems, most famously in 'Whatever You Say Say Nothing', and 'Exposure' from *North* (1975), and in 'Flight Path' from *The Spirit Level* (1996).

Alasdair Macrae has commented that, since the publication of his first book, Heaney has had 'constant and contradictory advice and admonishments from critics eager that he should write of Ireland in accordance with their views of the situation'.[33] Critics and commentators have argued that Heaney is too political, that he is not political enough, or that his politics are somehow incorrect (including but not limited to the suggestion that he is 'politically incorrect'). Edna Longley, for example, argues that Heaney is too political and that his poetry 'suffers' when it 'comes to or from political conclusions'.[34] For some, including Connor Cruise O'Brien, Blake Morrison and James Simmons, Heaney's poetry is imbued with the language of his 'tribe' (Catholic, nationalist, republican), to its own detriment.[35] To others – notably Desmond Fennell – Heaney's famed 'reticence' with regard to politics amounts to a culpable refusal of the responsibility of the poet to engage with contemporary Northern Irish politics; while David Lloyd and Ciaran Carson argue that Heaney's mythologizing of contemporary politics amounts to a mystification and obfuscation of political violence which can even amount to its celebration (Heaney is the 'laureate of violence', in Carson's telling phrase).[36] What Richard Kirkland sees as Heaney's consistent retreat from the political is said to result in recourse to the evasions of the 'notional closure' involved in the 'well-made poem', which compensates for his inability to reconcile the 'contradiction' of his 'liberal' political position.[37] Lloyd and James Simmons suggest that Heaney's political positions are based on racial and national essentialisms, as a 'retreat into the tribe'[38] rather than (as they ought to be) on class identity; similarly, Thomas Docherty suggests that Heaney has a 'blindspot' in his 'relation of politics to aesthetics'.[39] For some, Heaney's politics are plain enough, but suspect or politically incorrect: Patricia Coughlan asserts that he expresses an 'unconscious equivocation' with regard to sexual politics;[40] while Kirkland argues that Heaney expresses a 'fundamentally bourgeois poetic'.[41] Heaney is said to express a 'culpable ambiguity' with respect to Northern Irish terrorism,[42] and ultimately to lack a 'moral centre'.[43]

In fact, as this suggests, the heaviest critical charge against Heaney remains that of political obscurantism or evasion (and thereby the mythification and even celebration of political violence) and his writing registers, in various ways, the force of that charge. Perhaps his clearest response is the assertion in his 1984 essay on contemporary Northern Irish poetry, 'Place and Displacement', that 'It is a superficial response to the work of Northern Irish poets to conceive of their lyric stances as evasions of the actual conditions': the 'purely *poetic* force' of those poets' words, Heaney argues, in what is only apparently a paradox, is itself 'the guarantee' of the poet's *political* commitment (*FK* 118; italics added). This sense of the responsibility that a poet has towards the personal, and of the personal, individual, singular *as itself political*, is evident in other comments, as is Heaney's other defence, that of uncertainty ('Incertus' was, after all, his early pen-name),[44] of ambiguity, or of ambivalence.[45] Heaney has argued, for example, that the Northern Irish poet can learn from Osip Mandelstam and other Eastern-bloc poets, in their attempts to 'survive amphibiously' – to survive within both 'the realm of "the times"' and the 'realm' of a poet's 'moral and artistic self-respect' (*GT* xx).[46] The poet's condition is the condition of doubleness, of 'the challenge to be in two minds' (*RP* 202), or of 'The drama . . . that is played out in every poet between the social self and a deeper self' (FK 359), Heaney suggests, as well as of 'reticence'. In poetry and in his prose apologetics, Heaney has repeatedly resisted articulating *either* an affirmation *or* a repudiation of the call for direct expressions of 'political positions'. Instead, he affirms the necessity of being both 'socially responsible and creatively free' (*RP* 193), in a response to calls to take (political) responsibility that can look like no response at all since it looks like the political obfuscation of an appeal to the aesthetic – to the claim that art is for art's sake, that it is 'autonomous' and necessarily non-political and ahistorical. But Heaney's response should in fact be seen as a version of what Derrida conceives of as the political responsibility of literature to articulate what may be read as a certain 'irresponsibility', the 'refusal to reply for one's thoughts or writing to constituted powers' (including, we might say, the 'constituted powers' of critics, journalists and reviewers).[47] Thus, in the prefatory essay to *The Government of the Tongue*, Heaney suggests that lyric poetry, 'however responsible', always has 'an element of the untrammelled about it'; it involves 'a certain jubilation and truancy', he suggests, 'a sensation of liberation and abundance' (*GT* xviii).[48] As he comments in the title essay to the same collection, the

> vitality and insouciance of lyric poetry, its relish of its own inventiveness, its pleasuring strain, always comes under threat when poetry remembers that its self-gratification must be perceived as a kind of affront to a world preoccupied with its own imperfections, pains and catastrophes.

'What right', Heaney asks, 'has poetry to its quarantine?' (*GT* 99). Such statements of aesthetic or poetic freedom, insouciance, and indeed *jouissance*, always come with qualifications ('however political'; 'What right has poetry...?'). For Heaney, in other words, the politics of poetry involves precisely its capacity both to engage with and to evade or resist the 'repetitive intolerance of public life' (*GT* xxi) – that, that evasion as well as that engagement, is what makes poetry political. Poetry is political in this sense precisely by way of its refusal of the political as it is conceived or defined in other, more mundane, more coercive, less 'tolerant', less 'subtle' ways. That irresponsibility *is* its way of being answerable, being responsible.

A crucial *political* question for Heaney is the question of exemplarity and in particular the question of the imbrications of the personal or individual with larger social configurations of the political. The question is posed in the foreword to Heaney's first collection of essays, *Preoccupations* (1980), for example: 'how should a poet properly live and write?', he asks, 'What is his relationship to be to his own voice, his own place, his literary heritage and his contemporary world?' (*P* 13). And it is a question that is raised in two of Heaney's most famous and most famously direct poems of poetico-political engagement or expression. In 'The Flight Path', Heaney tells of an encounter between himself and an IRA man in a train to Belfast. The IRA man asks the poet why he doesn't 'write /

Something for us': 'If I do write something', Heaney replies in an inscrutably ambiguous answer, a response that is hardly a response at all, 'Whatever it is, I'll be writing for myself'.[49] Critics have tended to see the answer simply as a retreat from political engagement, into the personal or private. In fact, though, there is a linguistic trickiness or slipperiness at work here that allows for both political engagement and political evasion. The point is that Heaney does not deny that he will write 'Something for us'. He insists instead that if he does so it will (also) be 'for myself': he says, in effect, *both* – in an example of the kind of speech act that can be truly effected, and effective, perhaps, *only* in poetry.[50] The lines have been (mis)read as a refusal of political accountability – as declaring, in effect: 'if I write I will *only* write for myself'.[51] But it should rather be read in terms of the exemplarity of poetry, of literature, that Heaney repeatedly urges, the sense that 'the self is interesting *only* as an example' (*P* 14; italics added); 'if I write something for you (or for us)', he might saying, 'I will also be writing for myself'.

The turns of the phrase, the line's poeticity – its refusal, embedded in the delicate equivocation of the phrase – is akin to another verbal slippage, in 'Whatever You Say Say Nothing'. In this poem, the title is repeated within the poem but with a subtly different grammar:

> The famous
> Northern reticence, the tight gag of place
> And times: yes, yes. Of the 'wee six' I sing
> Where to be saved you only must save face
> And whatever you say, you say nothing.[52]

The grammatical difference between the poem's title ('Whatever You Say Say Nothing') on the one hand, and the internal line itself ('Whatever you say, you say nothing') on the other hand, is subtle but crucial, moving as it does, with that extra 'you' and the comma, from the imperative mood of the title to the indicative mood of the poem, from proscription to description. The point is that it is precisely the question of what Heaney calls the 'tolerances and subtleties' of poetic language that produces an evasion that is also an *assertion* of the political.[53]

Part of what is at work here is, no doubt, Heaney's career-long resistance to being co-opted for propaganda purposes, and in particular for the legitimation of political violence on either or any 'side' of the Northern Irish conflict. 'We live here in critical times', Heaney comments in a 1974 essay, 'when the idea of poetry as an art is in danger of being overshadowed by a quest for poetry as a diagram of political attitudes.

Some commentators', he continues, 'have all the fussy literalism of an official from the ministry of truth' (*P* 219–20).⁵⁴ But it is also a problem of knowledge, or ignorance. In a 1977 interview with Seamus Deane, Heaney quotes John Montague's assessment of Patrick Kavanagh that he has 'liberated us into ignorance', suggesting that such liberation has to do with 'an insouciance and trust in the alacrities and cunnings of our perception'.⁵⁵ For Deane, this makes Kavanagh a potentially 'dangerous exemplar' since he is a poet who 'espouses ignorance of the day to day'. Heaney demurs, and attempts to suggest that he is looking for a kind of writing that articulates (as *North* does) 'two different kinds of utterance ... one symbolic and one explicit'.⁵⁶ And again it comes down to the question of exemplarity: Deane asks Heaney whether he is 'seeking ... a kind of singular universal'. 'Yes', Heaney replies, 'but it is a damnable problem':

> The more one consciously tries to convey this imprint the more it seems to elude you. You see, the lift-off and push of the innocent creative moment can never be fully schematic. Indeed, a too conscious awareness of the experience which gave rise to a poem can very often impede its creation. The all-important thing here is the emerging authority which one senses in the poem being written, when you recognise that there are elements in the poem which are capillaries into the large brutal scheme of things, capillaries sucking the whole of the earth.⁵⁷

And here's the problem, the problem of self-consciousness, of knowledge, when poetry (also) needs a certain ignorance or insouciance. This, for Heaney, is the problem of poetry, and the involvement, in the end, of poetry in politics – which is also the involvement of poetry in ignorance. While poetry 'below a certain level of awareness does not interest me', Heaney comments in another interview, quoting Czesław Miłosz, the 'problem' with specifically *political* poetry is that it is 'howling that it's aware'.⁵⁸

For Heaney, the 'ultimate fidelity' of poetry is not to the 'corrective pressures of social, moral, political and historical reality' but to the 'demands and promise of the artistic event' (*GT* 101).⁵⁹ In the title essay from *The Government of the Tongue*, Heaney attempts to illustrate this point – the point that the 'government of the tongue' involves *both* a restraint on the tongue, on poetry, a 'denial of the tongue's autonomy and permission' (*GT* 96), *and* at the same time an affirmation of poetry's 'right to govern' itself (*GT* 92). He appeals to that 'most reticent and mannerly of poets', Elizabeth Bishop, and in particular to 'At the Fishhouses' for confirmation of this point. Heaney focuses especially on the last thirteen lines of Bishop's eighty-three-line poem, where the restrained attention to the 'surfaces of a world' (*GT* 105), a world of 'human attachment, grandfathers, Lucky Strikes and Christmas trees' (*GT* 106), suddenly gives way to something other, something mysterious that answers to what Heaney calls the 'knowledge-need which sets human beings apart' (*GT* 106):

> If you should dip your hand in,
> your wrist would ache immediately,
> your bones would begin to ache and your hand would burn
> as if the water were a transmutation of fire
> that feeds on stones and burns with a dark gray flame.
> If you tasted it, it would first taste bitter,
> then briny, then surely burn your tongue.
> It is like what we imagine knowledge to be:
> dark, salt, clear, moving, utterly free,
> drawn from the cold hard mouth
> of the world, derived from the rocky breasts
> forever, flowing and drawn, and since
> our knowledge is historical, flowing, and flown.[60]

Heaney emphasizes the 'truth' of these lines, but also the sense that they are 'as hallucinatory as they are accurate' (*GT* 106). What we might notice is the way that the lines assert the impossibility, or the obscurity, at least, of knowledge, knowledge not as that which is known, but instead as that which is imagined – and imagined in terms of certain piercing physical sensations 'drawn from the cold hard mouth / of the world'.[61] And knowledge is 'historical', which is to say, in the ambiguous locution that ends Bishop's poem, 'flowing, and flown'. That, then, for Heaney (or for Bishop) is poetry, lyric poetry, and the way it 'governs' the tongue in both senses: lyric poetry, like touch, is individual, unique, singular, and like touch it gives a sense of knowledge, of what we imagine knowledge to be, as historical – a sense that knowledge flows, or that it flies, or that it has 'flown'.[62]

I began this book with a discussion of Socrates' ignorance, and with a scene from *Meno* in which the Philosopher not only managed to numb his interlocutor, to make him feel as if he had been stung by a torpedo fish, but also to make Socrates himself (the man who is beginning to look like such a fish) bewildered or perplexed by the questions he is asking and failing to answer. For Socrates (at least at this point in his career), the ability to produce the kind of conceptual or intellectual torpor that is akin to the effect of being stung by a torpedo fish is itself of value. And it is significant, I think, that Seamus Heaney, our foremost lyric poet, also has recourse to the notion of torpor, to the idea of perplexity and ignorance, in relation to politics and history.

In 'A Sofa in the Forties' (from *The Spirit Level*) Heaney tells of a childhood game in which he and his siblings transformed the family sofa into an imaginary train:

> All of us on the sofa in a line, kneeling
> Behind each other, eldest down to youngest,
> Elbows going like pistons, for this was a train
>
> And between the jamb-wall and the bedroom door
> Our speed and distance were inestimable.[63]

The sofa is positioned under the radio, on which the children hear not only stories but also national and international news, history in the making: it is through the radio, therefore, that the children 'entered history and ignorance'.[64] Heaney opens his 1995 Nobel Lecture, 'Crediting Poetry', by alluding to this poem and to the domestic childhood scene of transport. In the lecture, though, he makes explicit the kind of news he must have been hearing from the radio ('the names of bombers and of cities bombed, of war fronts and army divisions, the numbers of planes lost and of prisoners taken, of casualties suffered and advances made' (*OG* 448)). As Heaney remarks, 'none of the news of these world-spasms entered me as terror':

> If there was something ominous in the newscaster's tones, there was something torpid about our understanding of what was at stake; and if there was something culpable about such political ignorance in that time and place, there was something positive about the security I inhabited as a result of it. (*OG* 448)

The child's understanding is 'torpid' in relation to the war, to history, to politics: that *is* his freedom, his play – the play and playfulness that, in the forty years between Heaney's first volume of poetry, *Death of a Naturalist* (1966), and his most recent, *District and Circle* (2006), has been integral to the subject matter as well as the procedure of his poetry.

The child's understanding, then, his political or historical understanding has something 'torpid' about it. And the adult's, the poet's? In spite of his acute sensitivity to history, and to the politics of Europe and Ireland, to the Cold War and to colonialism, and especially to the question of the 'troubles' in Northern Ireland that have dominated much of our history in the period of Heaney's writing life, there is a sense in Heaney's poems, essays and interviews of a principled resistance (call it 'evasion', call it 'reticence', call it 'irresponsibility'), even a certain torpor with regard to politics – a kind of tolerance, numbness, nescience, even, a torpedo-fish-like sense of ignorance and perplexity. It is a response of irresponsibility that is also presented, in the end, as the poet's final responsibility.

So asked by Frank Kinahan in a 1982 interview to provide one-word definitions, as T.S. Eliot had famously done, of his 'positions' with regard to literature, politics and religion (respectively classical, royalist and Anglo-Catholic for Eliot), Heaney hesitates and then answers, perhaps only half in jest: 'Jungian', he says, with regard to religion, and 'passionate' with regard to literature. And with regard to politics? He is, he declares, 'torpid'.[65]

Notes

1 For some examples and a brief engagement with this phenomenon see my *The Author* (London: Routledge, 2005), pp. 68–70.
2 Harold Bloom, *The Anxiety of Influence: A Theory of Poetry* (New York: Oxford University Press, 1973), p. 96.
3 Quoted in Christopher Ricks, *Allusion to the Poets* (Oxford: Oxford University Press, 2002), p. 5. Compare Wallace Stevens's comment in a letter to Hi Simons on 'Notes Towards a Supreme Fiction': 'There are several things in the NOTES that would stand a little annotating. For instance, the fact that the Arabian is the moon is something that the reader could not possibly know. However, I did not think that it was necessary for him to know' (*Letters of Wallace Stevens*, ed. Holly Stevens (London: Faber, 1967), p. 434: I owe this reference to Rose White). It might be said that it is precisely the question of authorial nescience and knowledge that Ricks's book elides (has to elide): for Ricks, as for other allusive critics, critics who play on the possibilities of allusion in literature, the stumbling block, the unanswerable question or indeed the governing assumption, is that of authorial intentionality or knowledge (as Garrett Stewart puts it in a review essay on Ricks's book, 'At a high pitch of intentionalism, literary writing leaves no suspicions, in Ricks's view, about the Death of the Author' ('Metallusion: The Used, the Renewed, and the Novel' (*Modern Language Quarterly* 65 (2004): 583–4)).
4 The uneasy movement in this passage from authorial to readerly ignorance is in fact suggested in a correction in which 'reader' has been substituted for 'author'.
5 T.S. Eliot, interview in *The Paris Review* 21 (1959): 8, 19. Eliot frequently refers, in fact, to what I am terming 'authorial ignorance'. In 'Tradition and

the Individual Talent', to take the most famous example, he argues that the 'business of the poet' involves a 'concentration 'of one's experiences, one 'which does not happen consciously or of deliberation': the 'bad' poet, he says, 'is usually unconscious where he ought to be conscious, and conscious where he ought to be unconscious' (Frank Kermode, ed., *Selected Prose of T.S. Eliot* (London: Faber and Faber, 1975), p. 43). See also 'The Music of Poetry' (1942): 'A Poem may appear to mean very different things to different readers, and all of these meanings may be different from what the author thought he meant ... There may be much more in a poem than the author was aware of' (ibid., p. 111). And see 'Virgil and the Christian World' (1951): 'if the word "inspiration" is to have any meaning, it must mean just this, that the speaker or writer is uttering something which he does not wholly understand – or which he may even misinterpret when the inspiration has departed from him' (*On Poetry and Poets* (London: Faber and Faber, 1957), p. 122).

6 See Georg Lukács on what he sees as the 'constitutive strength' of lyric poetry's ignorance, a strength that distinguishes such poetry from prose (*The Theory of the Novel: A Historico-Philosophical Essay on the Forms of Great Epic Literature*, trans. Anna Bostock (London: Merlin Press, 1971), p. 63). The poet Elizabeth Jennings seems to be hinting at a similarly generic sense of poetry when she remarks in an interview that 'Prose has always seemed to me an attempt to find words for something which I already know, whereas my best poems manage to say in a strict inevitable form something that I did not know before' (Clare Brown and Don Paterson, eds, *Don't Ask me What I Mean: Poets in Their Own Words* (London: Picador, 2003), p. 133).

7 In James Scully, ed., *Modern Poets on Modern Poetry* (London: Fontana, 1966) p. 149.

8 Stanley Kunitz, 'Talk with Robert Lowell' (Oct. 1982), in *Robert Lowell: Interviews and Memoirs*, ed. Jeffrey Meyers (Ann Arbor: University of Michigan Press, 1988), pp. 85–6) (I owe this reference to Stephen James).

9 Steven Ratiner, ed., *Giving Their Word: Conversations with Contemporary Poets* (Amherst: University of Massachusetts Press, 2002), pp. 97–8; see also Heaney's comment that 'I don't know what is the correct proportion between will and waiting in lyric poetry ... Every act of poetry involves some kind of strategic engagement between the passive and the active part' (ibid., p. 97). See also Frank Kirkham, 'An Interview with Seamus Heaney', *Critical Inquiry* 8 (1982): 410–11.

10 Clive Wilmer, ed., *Poets Talking* (Manchester: Carcanet, 1994), p. 111; see Wilmer's comment that, in the interviews he carried out for the book, 'Poet after poet explained, with varying degrees of patience, that the process of composition is inexplicable and largely involuntary' and that therefore 'poets are often the last people to ask about the "meaning" of what they write' (Introduction, p. xi).

11 Paul Muldoon, 'Getting Round: Notes Towards an *Ars Poetica*', *Essays in Criticism* 48 (1998): 127.
12 Brown and Paterson, eds, *Don't Ask Me What I Mean*, p. xv.
13 In each case, after quoting from the poet's statement, I have provided page references to Brown and Paterson's book and the date of the contribution.
14 Lorenzo Infantino, *Ignorance and Liberty* (London: Routledge, 2003): further references are cited in the text.
15 See also Plato's possibly (or probably) apocryphal Letter 7: 'the ills of the human race [will] never end until either those who are sincerely and true lovers of wisdom come into political power, or the rulers of our cities, by the grace of God, learn true philosophy' (*Epistles* 7, 326b).
16 José Ortega y Gasset, 'La idea de principio en Leibniz', in *Obras completas* (Madrid, 1946–83), vol. 8, p. 267 (quoted in Infantino, *Ignorance*, p. 147); see *The Idea of Principle in Leibnitz and the Evolution of Deductive Theory*, trans. Mildred Adams (New York: W.W. Norton, 1971), p. 272 (where the phrase is translated as 'primary ignorance').
17 Karl Popper, *The Open Society and Its Enemies* (London: Routledge, 2003), 1: 128.
18 The phrase is from a 1947 review of *The Open Society* by Gilbert Ryle, quoted by Infantino, *Ignorance*, p. 66.
19 Popper, *Open Society* 1: 94. For a defence of Plato, and particularly his poetic theory, against such attacks see Julius A. Elias, *Plato's Defence of Poetry* (London: Macmillan, 1984).
20 On this question see my brief discussion of the history of authorship in *The Author*, ch. 2.
21 '"The unacknowledged legislators of the world" describes the secret police, not the poets', W.H. Auden comments in 'Writing', in *The Dyer's Hand and Other Essays* (London: Faber and Faber, 1963), p. 27.
22 See Paul Bénichou, *The Consecration of the Writer, 1750–1830*, trans. Mark K. Jensen (Lincoln: University of Nebraska Press, 1999).
23 The 'performativity of writing' is, Derrida suggests, 'always more cunning and inappropriable than one thinks' (*Negotiations: Interventions and Interviews, 1971–2001*, ed. Elizabeth Rottenberg (Stanford: Stanford University Press, 2002), p. 79).
24 Jacques Derrida, *Acts of Literature*, ed. Derek Attridge (London: Routledge, 1992), p. 43: hereafter cited in the text as *AL*.
25 'Something of literature will have begun', Derrida argues in *On the Name*, 'when it is not possible to decide whether, when I speak of something, I am indeed speaking of something (of the thing itself, this one, for itself) or if I am giving an example, an example of something or an example of the fact that I can speak of something' (*On the Name*, ed. Thomas Dutoit (Stanford: Stanford University Press, 1995), pp. 142–3).
26 Ibid., p. 143.

27 *Demeure: Fiction and Testimony*, trans. Elizabeth Rottenberg (Stanford: Stanford University Press, 2000), p. 37.
28 *Dissemination*, trans. Barbara Johnson (Chicago: University of Chicago Press, 1981), p. 223.
29 *Demeure*, p. 28.
30 *On the Name*, p. 28.
31 The right is, of course, encoded as a foundation of democracy, embodied as it is in the fifth amendment in the United States, and – until very recently – in the accused's 'right to silence' in the UK.
32 'Crediting Poetry', in *Opened Ground: Poems, 1966–1996* (London: Faber and Faber, 1998), p. 451; hereafter cited as *OG*. For convenience I will use the following abbreviations for Heaney's prose collections (all published in London by Faber and Faber): *Preoccupations: Selected Prose, 1968–1978* (1980): *P*; *The Government of the Tongue: The 1986 T.S. Eliot Memorial Lecture and Other Critical Writings* (1988): *GT*; *The Redress of Poetry: Oxford Lectures* (1995): *RP*; *Finders Keepers: Selected Prose, 1971–2001* (2002): *FK*.
33 Alasdair Macrae, 'Seamus Heaney's New Voice in *Station Island*', in Robert F. Garratt, ed., *Critical Essays on Seamus Heaney* (New York: G.K. Hall, 1995), p. 57.
34 Edna Longley, '"Inner Emigré" or "Artful Voyeur"? Seamus Heaney's North', in Michael Allen, ed., *Seamus Heaney* (Basingstoke: Palgrave Macmillan, 1997), p. 32 (this is a version of an essay first published in 1982).
35 See Blake Morrison, *Seamus Heaney* (London: Methuen, 1982), p. 68, on *North* as 'speaking the language of the tribe'.
36 Ciarán Carson, 'Escaped from the Massacre?', *The Honest Ulsterman* 50 (1975): 183; quoted in Eugene O'Brien, *Seamus Heaney and the Place of Writing* (Gainesville: University Press of Florida, 2002), p. 112. See Fennell's notoriously excoriating essay, with its provocatively sarcastic title: 'Whatever You Say, Say Nothing: Why Seamus Heaney is No. 1' (*Stand* (1991): 38–65). But compare Heaney's comment that 'mystification' is 'a word I am reluctant to regard as *altogether* pejorative in poetry' (*P* 175); and see his comment in another essay that 'Poetry of any power is always deeper than its declared meaning. The secret between the words, the binding clement, is often a psychic force that is elusive, archaic and only half-apprehended by maker and audience' (*P* 186).
37 Richard Kirkland, 'Paradigms of Possibility: Seamus Heaney', in Allen, ed., *Seamus Heaney*, p. 261: here even the act of making a poem *well* is criticized.
38 James Simmons, 'The Trouble with Seamus', in Elmer Andrews, ed., *Seamus Heaney: A Collection of Critical Essays* (New York: St Martin's Press, 1992), p. 50.
39 Thomas Docherty, 'The Sign of the Cross: Review of *The Government of the Tongue*', in Allen, ed., *Seamus Heaney*, p. 149.

40 Patricia Coughlan, '"Bog Queens": The Representation of Women in the Poetry of John Montague and Seamus Heaney', in Allen, ed., *Seamus Heaney*, p. 198.
41 Kirkland, 'Paradigms of Possibility', p. 254: 'bourgeois' is itself of course a criticism in this context.
42 Elmer Andrews, Introduction', in Andrews, ed., *Seamus Heaney*, p. 3 (summarizing the position of James Simmons).
43 Simmons, 'The Trouble with Seamus', p. 61. See Eugene O'Brien's important deconstruction of such conflicting responses to Heaney's politics, in which he suggests that Heaney is seen 'either as avoiding the whole issue [of politics] or else as being mired in his own tradition's tribal identity' (*Seamus Heaney and the Place of Writing*, p. 2). O'Brien's book as a whole is one of the few responses to Heaney's work that accepts what seems to me the self-evident *complexity* of Heaney's engagement with the political: Heaney is, according to O'Brien, 'continually adjudicating between his role as part of the tribe with the attendant imperative of being "swung" by the "long tale of resentment" (*P* 30) a notion which is continually exercising a visceral attraction, and a corresponding desire to transcend that role by embracing other forms of identity, language, and culture, symbolised by his feeling "every wind that blows"' (p. 93).
44 See 'Feeling into Words', *P* 17; see also 'Incertus', from *Stations* (1975).
45 See Paul Scott Stanfield on the idea that 'Some of Heaney's best poems succeed precisely because of the exactness with which they re-create the tension' of the ambivalence with regard to a fidelity to poetry and a fidelity to his community ('Facing *North* Again: Polyphony, Contention', in Garratt, ed., *Critical Essays*, p. 97); see also Lucy McDiarmid's comment that, like Yeats, Heaney 'writes poetry out of [political or social] ambivalence and guilt' ('Heaney and the Politics of the Classroom', in ibid., p. 117); and Carolyn Meyer's comment that 'More than that of any other contemporary Irish poet, Seamus Heaney's poetic *oeuvre* has been shaped and enriched by the need to address the problem of commitment' towards which Heaney 'remains curiously ambivalent' ('Orthodoxy, Independence, and Influence in Seamus Heaney's *Station Island*', in ibid., p. 207).
46 On his 'double', 'uncertain', 'ambiguous' or 'two-minded' identity see 'Something to Write Home About' (*FK* 48–58, especially pp. 50–1), and 'Place and Displacement: Recent Poetry in Northern Ireland' (*FK* 115).
47 See Heaney's comment (in a 1974 review of Mandelstam) on the idea of 'art for art's sake' as involving 'an inadequate notion of what art can encompass' (*P* 217). For Heaney on poetry and responsibility (or for instances of the use of the word 'responsible' in this context) see also *RP* xiv, xviii, 191; *FK* 118, 240. It is significant that Heaney frequently refers approvingly in his writings to Robert Pinsky's essay 'Responsibilities of the Poet' (*Critical Inquiry*, 13 (1987): 421–33), in which Pinsky argues that the poet 'needs to feel utterly free, yet answerable' (423).

48 See also Heaney's comment on Paul Muldoon's use of language in a 1978 review of *Mules*: 'The life of the thing is in the language's potential for generating new meanings out of itself, and it is this sense of buoyancy, this delight in the trickery and lechery that words are capable of, that is the distinguishing mark of the volume as a whole' (*P* 213).
49 Seamus Heaney, *The Spirit Level* (London: Faber and Faber, 1996), p. 25.
50 Heaney does manage in fact to say something similar, although less concisely, in his Poetry Book Society introduction to *North*, where he writes that 'During the last few years there has been considerable expectation that poets from Northern Ireland should "say" something about "the situation"', but that 'in the end they will only be worth listening to if they are saying something about and to themselves' (in Brown and Paterson, eds, *Don't Ask Me*, p. 102).
51 This seems to be the sense ascribed to the lines by Ben Naparstek in 'Notes from Underground' in *The Times* (25 March 2006), for example.
52 Seamus Heaney, *North* (London: Faber and Faber, 1975), p. 53.
53 'Tolerances and Subtleties' is from *GT* xxi; the phrase is repeated (although in reverse) in Heaney's 1984 essay 'Place and Displacement', where he argues that, for his generation of Northern Irish writers, the 'subtleties and tolerances' of poetry are precisely what poetry has to 'contribute to the coarseness and intolerances of the public life' (*FK* 116) ('to set against the repetitive intolerance of public life', in *GT*).
54 Here's an example of what Heaney is talking about: 'I am neither internee nor informer', he writes in 'Exposure', but 'a wood-kerne / Escaped from the massacre', one who feels 'Every wind that blows' (*North*, p. 67): 'What massacre?', the literal-minded James Simmons asks; 'With some lamentable exceptions, you only get interned if you are sympathetic to the IRA', Simmons goes on, overly literalistic again and overlooking the negative in Heaney's line: 'Nothing in the poetry suggests a man suffering "every wind that blows"', Simmons concludes, with curious indifference to the rhetorical dimensions of poetry ('The Trouble With Seamus Heaney', p. 60).
55 'Unhappy and at Home', Seamus Heaney interview with Seamus Deane, in Mark Patrick Hederman and Richard Kearney, eds, *The Crane Bag Book of Irish Studies* (Dublin: Blackwater Press, 1982), p. 71.
56 Ibid.
57 Ibid., pp. 71–2. The question – the multiple questions – of political responsibility, and the coercive demand to speak and speak out for, or in terms of, the political, is tellingly expressed in an offhand comment on the 'public life' that Heaney made to Neil Corcoran in an interview in 1985: 'I advance and retire [he says] from any conscious or deliberate entry into that public life. I've got so much attention that my impulse is to retreat rather than to go forward at this stage. I don't know whether that's an irresponsibility or a salutary piece of survival. I just don't know; these are questions that I'm not too clear about myself' (Neil Corcoran, *The Poetry of Seamus Heaney: A Critical Study* (London: Faber and Faber, 1998), p. 262). 'I don't know';

'I just don't know'; 'these are questions that I'm not too clear about myself'. Three times Heaney insists on his ignorance in this statement, linking the poet's (ir)responsibility towards his public and an equivocation over political engagement, with nescience.

58 Sam Leith, 'Return of a Naturalist', interview with Seamus Heaney, *Daily Telegraph*, 6 April 2006.
59 See also Heaney's comment that 'I do not in fact see how poetry can survive as a category of human consciousness if it does not put poetic considerations first – expressive considerations, that is, based upon its own genetic laws which spring into operation at the moment of lyric conception', while also 'conced[ing]' the 'justice of Czesław Miłosz's rebuke to the autocracy of such romantic presumption' (*GT* 166); and see 'The Redress of Poetry' (*RP* 1–16) – an essay that can be read as a response to many of the (political) attacks on his poetry discussed above.
60 Elizabeth Bishop, *Complete Poems* (London: Chatto and Windus, 2004), pp. 65–6.
61 Michael Wood – who opens his book on literature and knowledge with a brief consideration of this poem – comments that the lines offer 'not quite an imagination of knowledge, only of what knowledge resembles' (*Literature and the Taste of Knowledge* (Cambridge: Cambridge University Press, 2005), p. 1).
62 Heaney has repeatedly asserted the knowledge-value of poetry as well as its connections with nescience: 'the role of the poet as conscience', he remarks in an essay on Robert Lowell, is as 'one who wakens us to a possible etymology of that word as meaning our capacity to know the same thing together' (*GT* 130); see also the essay on Sylvia Plath in the same volume, where one kind of poetry is described as 'that in which the poem's absolute business is an unconceding pursuit of poetic insight and poetic knowledge' (*GT* 163; see also pp. 168–9, and *RP* 8, 37, 203). But see *RP* 5, for a sense that, within W.H. Auden's terms of the 'poetic faculty' as 'making, judging, and knowing', 'the making faculty seems . . . to have a kind of free pass that enables it to range beyond the jurisdiction of the other two'.
63 Heaney, *The Spirit Level*, p. 7.
64 Ibid., p. 8. The ignorance is, not least, of the wartime symbolism of trains, where to be 'transported' ('Our only job [was] to sit, eyes straight ahead,/ And be transported and make engine noise', the poem ends) can mean to be taken to a death camp ('Ghost-train?', the older poet muses, 'Death-gondola?').
65 Kirkham, 'Interview', p. 409.

Index

Abrams, M.H. 58
aesthetics 37, 51, 62
agnoiology 17, 89, 155, 177, 216
Amis, Kingsley 229
anagnorisis 31, 124
Anderson, Quentin 104
anepistemology 16–17, 28, 89, 95, 155
Arendt, Hannah 111, 128
Aristotle 9–10, 13
    Metaphysics 27
    Poetics 31
    Problems 190
Ashbery, John
    Some Trees 197
Ashfield, Andrew 59
Auden, W.H. 101, 237, 252
author, the 37–41, 43–4, 116, 203, 204–5, 212–13, 214–15, 217–18, 222, 225, 226–33, 236–7, 246–7
autobiography 111–12, 113–15, 121, 143, 151–2, 178, 212, 221, 222
Avramides, Anita 123

Baier, Annette C. 200
Barker, George 229, 230–1
Barnard, John 47, 91
Barrett, Dorothea 127–8
Barthes, Roland
    Roland Barthes by Roland Barthes 178
Batchelor, John 143, 149
Bate, Jonathan 70, 79

Baumgarten, Alexander 37
Beardsley, Monroe C.
    'Intentional Fallacy, The' 42, 52
Beckett, Samuel 209, 218–19
    Molloy 219
Beckford, William
    Vathek 64
Belsey, Catherine 54
Bennett, Andrew 175
Benson, Hugh 25, 26
Berryman, Charles 222
Bible, The 9, 63, 65, 120, 179, 183, 196, 205, 216
Bishop, Elizabeth
    'At the Fishhouses' 243–4
Blanchot, Maurice 35–7, 116
Bloom, Harold 199, 227
Bonaparte, Felicia 103, 106
Bouissac, Paul 4, 8
Bowen, Elizabeth
    House in Paris, The 168–72, 175
Brickhouse, Thomas 13–14, 24, 25, 27
Bright, Timothie 189
Brooks, Peter
    Body Work 158–60, 173
Brown, Clare 228–9
Bruns, Gerald 56, 75
Burke, Edmund
    Philosophical Enquiry 56, 58–61, 78
Burnet, Thomas 68
Burnside, John 231
    'Otherlife' 33–4

Burrow, Colin 45
Burton, Robert
  Anatomy of Melancholy 92, 176, 177, 189, 190, 194, 198
Butler, Judith 111–113, 120, 121, 128
Byron, George Gordon (Lord)
  Cain 64, 65–6, 77
  Don Juan 77
  'Lament of Tasso, The' 176
  Manfred 64–5, 87–8, 179

Carson, Ciaran 231, 239
Caruth, Cathy 23
Cavell, Stanley 1, 7, 18, 19–20, 21, 28, 30, 32, 38, 52, 64, 102, 110, 199
Caverero, Adriana 111, 128
Chase, Cynthia 75
children 154–5, 156–62, 166–72
Christianity 25–6, 27, 65–6, 227
Cicovacki, Predrag 51
Clifford, Hugh 135
Cocker, Jarvis 178
Cockshut, A.O.J. 116–17, 121
Cohen, William 116, 117, 129
Cohn, Dorrit 124
Coleridge, Samuel Taylor 78, 97, 101, 161, 189, 196
  Biographia Literaria 175
  'Christabel' 67
  'Kubla Khan' 67
  'Rime of the Ancient Mariner, The' 67–8
Colvin, Sidney 104
composition 85–6
Conrad, Joseph 132–53
  'End of the Tether, The' 133, 135, 140, 142–8, 152, 153
  'Heart of Darkness' 133, 135, 137, 141–2, 150
  Lord Jim 132, 134–5, 137, 140
  Mirror of the Sea, The 139–40
  Nigger of the 'Narcissus', The 135
  Personal Record, A 139, 150, 151–2
  Rescue, The 136, 137, 151

  Romance 136, 149
  'Secret Sharer, The' 133, 140, 153
  'Youth' 135
Coover, Robert 148
Coughlan, Patricia 240
Cranach, Lucas 196
criticism, literary 116
Cross, John 126
Culler, Jonathan 124
Cunninghame Graham, Gabriela
  Santa Teresa 135
Cunninghame Graham, R.B. 138
  Journey in Morocco, The 135
Cunningham, Valentine 129

Dante Alighieri
  Divina Commedia 176
Davie, Donald 232
Davies, James A. 131
Deane, Seamus 243
death 161–2, 164–72
De Bolla, Peter 59, 175
Defoe, Daniel
  Robinson Crusoe 102
Deleuze, Gilles 49, 180
De Man, Paul 3, 36–7, 42, 51, 62–3, 66–7, 78
democracy 233–9, 249
Dennett, Daniel C. 124
De Quincey, Thomas 69–70, 78, 79
Derrida, Jacques 16, 39–40, 69, 179, 237–9, 241, 248
  Glas 38, 44, 45, 114
  Memoirs of the Blind 140–1, 144, 151, 152
  Of Grammatology 39
  'Time of a Thesis, The' 39
Descartes, René 11
Dickens, Charles 128–9
  Great Expectations 102–3, 113, 115–23, 129, 130–1
Dickinson, Emily 101
  'There's a certain Slant of light' 34–5
Dickinson, Patric 232

Diderot, Denis 178
Docherty, Thomas 240
Dollimore, Jonathan 221
dramatic monologue 102
Du Laurens, André 189, 190
Dunn, Douglas 230, 232

Edel, Leon 182
Edmundson, Mark 7
Elias, Julius 22, 31
Eliot, George
   'Lifted Veil, The' 126–7
   Middlemarch 102–11, 113, 125, 126, 127, 128
   'Natural History of German Life, The' 103, 128–9
Eliot, T.S. 4, 35, 36–7, 113, 226–8, 246–7
   Waste Land, The 227–8
Ellmann, Richard 126
Elton, Oliver 104
Empson, William
   Structure of Complex Words, The 57, 75
epiphenomenalism 127
epistemelancholia 180, 183–6, 189–91, 194
epistemology 16–17, 18, 19, 20, 21, 88–9, 95–6, 100, 160, 171, 172, 181, 183–4, 186–7, 189–91
epistemophilia 155, 158–60, 172, 186, 205, 216
epistemophobia 160, 186, 187, 205
ethics 13, 112–13, 120, 203, 213–14, 215
exemplarity 54, 141–2, 243

faith, religious 183–4, 235
Faust myth, the 63
Fennell, Desmond 239, 249
Ferenczi, Sándor 157, 159
Ferguson, Francis 165, 166, 173
Ferrier, James Frederick
   Institutes of Metaphysic 16–17

Foley, Richard 19
Ford, Ford Madox 132, 147
Forker, Charles 115–16, 117, 129, 130
Foucault, Michel 3
Frances, Bryan 29
Fraser, Gail 148, 149
Freud, Sigmund 23, 43, 129, 156, 158, 159, 173, 200
   Beyond the Pleasure Principle 224
   'Mourning and Melancholia' 190–1, 198
Friedman, Norman 148
Frye, Northrop 7, 36
Fry, Paul 89
Furst, Lilian 123

Garber, Marjorie 40, 52
Garnett, Edward 135–6, 137
Gasset, Ortega y 233
Gaut, Berys 45–7, 53, 172
Gentry, Marshall 210–11, 221
God 9
Gosse, Edmund 143
Gougouris, Stathis 40, 52
Graver, Lawrence 147, 153
Gravil, Richard 174
Grayling, A.C. 17, 18, 30
Greco, John 18
Grigson, Geoffrey 232
Gross, David 4
Guattari, Félix 180
Guest, Harry 232
Guillory, John 53

Hamilton, Paul 62
Hammermeister, Kai 37, 62
Hanley, Keith 174
Hardy, Barbara 104, 126
Hartman, Geoffrey 60, 75
   'Romanticism and Anti-Self-Consciousness' 57–8
   Wordsworth's Poetry 166, 175
Harvey, W.J. 105–6, 110
Hazlitt, William 79–80, 83

Heaney, Seamus 228, 239–46, 247, 249–52
  Door into the Dark 229
  'Exposure' 251
  'Flight Path, The' 241–2
  'Sofa in the Forties, A' 245, 252
  'Whatever You Say Say Nothing' 242
Heidegger, Martin 30
Hertz, Neil 76
Heyns, Michiel 186
Hill, Geoffrey
  Orchards of Syon 231
Hirsch, E.D. 38–45
Hodgson, Shadworth Holloway 127
Hofmann, Michael 229
Hollander, John 98
Hume, David 5, 18, 29, 98, 177, 190
  Treatise of Human Nature, A 191–4, 200, 201
Huxley, Thomas Henry 127

Infantino, Lorenzo 9, 233–7
intention 40–5
intertextuality 188, 199
irony, Socratic 24, 164
Irwin, William 40–1, 42
Iser, Wolfgang 227

Jackson, Stanley 194, 195
James, Alice 185–6, 188, 197, 198
James, Henry 103, 104, 177, 181–3, 186–8, 197, 199
  'Beast in the Jungle, The' 181–2, 183, 186–8, 197
  'Middle Years, The' 222
  'Spoils of Poynton, The' 149
  What Maisie Knew 160
James, Henry Sr
  Society the Redeemed Form of Man 183–4, 188, 198
  Substance and Shadow 195
James, William 177, 197
  Varieties of Religious Experience, The 182–3, 184–5, 188
Jamie, Kathleen 228–9, 230
Jamison, Kay Redfield 177, 178, 196
Jauss, Hans-Robert 227
Jay, Martin 152
Jennings, Elizabeth 230, 247

Kafka, Franz 204
Kahn, Charles 15, 27, 28
Kant, Immanuel
  Critique of Judgement 37, 51, 61–3, 76
  Critique of Pure Reason 19, 30, 38, 60, 63
Karlin, Daniel 107, 127
Kavanagh, Patrick J. 232, 243
Keats, John 45, 81–99, 178–9, 236
  Endymion 95
  'Eve of St Agnes, The' 95
  'Fall of Hyperion, The' 64, 66, 92–3, 95, 96
  'Hyperion' 64, 66, 85–6, 92–5
  'In drear nighted December' 89
  'La Belle Dame sans Merci' 49–50, 92, 93, 95
  'Lamia' 92, 95
  letters 82–6, 95–6, 97–8, 99
  'Ode on a Grecian Urn' 46–9, 90–2, 95
  'Ode on Indolence' 89–90
  'Ode to a Nightingale' 87–8, 89, 95, 96
  'Ode to Psyche' 86–7, 93, 95, 179
  'O thou whose face hath felt the winter's wind' 95
  'Sleep and Poetry' 86
  'To Homer' 86
Kennedy, X.J. 231
Kettle, Arnold 104
Kierkegaard, Søren 198
Kirkland, Richard 239–40

Klein, Melanie 156–7, 158–9, 160, 172
Klein, Peter 18
Kneale, J. Douglas 196, 197
Knowles, Owen 134
Kraut, Richard 11
Kremer, S. Lillian 222
Kristeva, Julia 177, 181, 190, 195, 199, 200
Kvanvig, Jonathan 17

Lacan, Jacques 123, 128, 161, 218
Lamarque, Peter 46, 97
Langbaum, Robert 75
Laplanche, Jean 45, 128, 156–8, 159, 160, 161, 165, 173
Larkin, Philip 158
Lawrence, D.H. 152
Lee, Hermione 208
Lehrer, Keith 18
Leibniz, Gottfried Wilhelm 51
Lemprière, John 93
Lesher, J.H. 24
Lerner, Laurence 126
Levi, Peter 230
Levinas, Emmanuel 20, 123, 161
Lewes, G.H. 126, 127
Lewis, David 18
Libet, Benjamin 127
literature 15–16, 21–4, 38, 40
Livingston, Paisley 7, 53
Lloyd, David 239–40
Locke, John
  Essay Concerning Human Understanding, An 25
Longley, Edna 239
Longley, Michael 231
Lowe, Brigid 123
Lowell, Robert 228
Luckács, Georg 247
Lukasiewicz, Julius 32
Luper, Steven 18
Lyon, John 147, 153
lyric poetry 100–1, 247

Macrae, Alasdair 239
McDiarmid, Lucy 250
McKendrick, Jamie 231
McLane, Maureen 56, 164, 174
McSweeney, Kerry 126
Maguire, Sarah 229–30
Mahon, Derek 232
Mandelstam, Osip 240
Mangan, James Clarence 188–9
Martin, Andrew 8, 25, 28, 99
Matthews, Gareth 14–15
melancholia 176–201
Melancthon, Philip 198
Mercer, Johnny
  'Dream' 217
Merleau-Ponty, Maurice 151
Mermin, W.S. 230
Meyer, Carolyn 250
Miller, J. Hillis 115
Milnes, Tim 5, 56, 72, 77, 78, 96
Miłosz Czesław 243
Milton, John
  Paradise Lost 71, 82, 98, 176, 179–80, 196–7, 205
Monk, Samuel 56
Montague, John 242
Moraes, Dom 232
Morris, Pam 123
Morrison, Blake 239
Motion, Andrew 230
Mount, Wilbert 4
Moynahan, Julian 119, 130–1
Muldoon, Paul 228, 232–3, 251
Murray, Les 228

Najder, Zdzisław 133, 140, 151, 152
Nancy, Jean-Luc 195
narrators 6–7, 102, 103, 105, 160, 214–15, 218
Nehamas, Alexander 25, 26
Nietzsche, Friedrich 9, 11, 25, 26, 31, 129
Novick, Sheldon M. 197
Nussbaum, Martha C. 124

O'Brien, Connor Cruise 239
O'Brien, Eugene 250
O'Brien, Sean 231–2
O'Connell, Michael 200
Oedpius myth 160
Olsen, Haugom 46, 97
Oswald, Alice
   Dart 230

Parrish, Timothy 210, 219–20, 224
Pascal, Blaise 89
Paterson, Don 228–9
Pawling, Sidney 143, 152
Peacock, Thomas Love
   'The Four Ages of Poetry' 70–1
Peters, John 152
Phillips, Adam 154, 155–6, 172, 173
philosophy 14–15, 16, 19, 20, 22, 23, 25, 40, 46, 48, 191–4
Pinsky, Robert 101, 250
Plato 6, 8, 13–15, 16, 22, 24, 27, 28, 31, 37, 112, 214, 234–5, 247
   Ion 22, 38
   Laws 233
   Meno 22
   Phaedrus 22
   Republic 22, 31, 234
   Theaetetus 219
   see also Socrates
Popper, Karl 8, 233, 234
Posnock, Ross 225
Pritchett, V.S. 104
Prometheus myth, the 63
psychoanalysis 155–61, 191
   see also Freud, Sigmund

queer theory 116, 129, 187–8

Rabelais, François 205, 219
Radcliffe, Ann 64
reading 35–7, 39–40, 45, 50, 116, 180, 181, 227
realism 100–3, 106, 112
Reeves, James 232

Reynolds, Oliver 229
rhizome 180, 181
Richetti, John J. 192, 200
Richardson, Alan 166, 175
Ricks, Christopher 246
Romanticism 5–6, 38, 52, 55–80, 236–7
Ronell, Avital 40, 52
Rorty, Richard 77
Roth, Philip 6, 202–25, 234
   American Pastoral 205, 206–7, 210–17, 219, 220, 222, 224–5
   Anatomy Lesson, The 204, 208, 219, 225
   Conversations with Philip Roth 203, 214, 219, 220, 222, 225
   Counterlife, The 208–9, 212, 222
   Deception 209–10, 212, 221
   Dying Animal, The 210, 221
   Exit Ghost 204
   Facts, The 212, 222
   Ghost Writer, The 204, 212, 222
   Goodbye Columbus 212
   Human Stain, The 204, 205, 212, 213, 214, 215–16, 217, 220, 221, 222–3, 224
   I Married a Communist 205, 213, 214, 217, 218, 222
   My Life as a Man 204, 212, 220, 222, 225
   Operation Shylock 204, 205, 212
   Patrimony 212, 221
   Plot Against America, The 202, 204
   Portnoy's Complaint 204, 212, 225
   Prague Orgy, The 204, 205, 225
   Reading Myself and Others 203, 204–5, 218
   Sabbath's Theatre 204, 210, 220
   Zuckerman Unbound 204
Rouse, Anne 231
Rowe, M.W. 53
Royal, Derek Parker 224
Royle, Nicholas 124, 175

Rushdie, Salman
  Satanic Verses, The 238
Ruskin, John 177
Ryle, Gilbert 234

St Augustine 155, 172
Sartre, Jean-Paul
  Nausea 177–8
scepticism, philosophical 5, 17–23, 28–9, 30, 88–9, 155, 177, 190, 191–4, 225
Schlicke, Paul 174–5
Schor, Hilary M. 119, 120–1, 130, 131
science 13, 22, 80, 103–4, 124
Sedgwick, Eve Kosofsky 116, 129
  Epistemology of the Closet 187
sex 157–60, 172, 224
Shakespeare, William 21
  Hamlet 63
  Sonnet 55 41–5
Shelley, Mary
  Frankenstein 63
Shelley, Percy Bysshe
  'Defence of Poetry, A' 31, 68–9, 70–4, 237
  Triumph of Life, The 36, 65, 66–6
short story 132–3, 148, 149
Shostak, Debra 210, 216, 220, 221, 223, 225
Simmons, James 239, 240, 251
Skelton, Robin 231
Smith, Barbara Herrnstein 7
Smith, Nicholas 13–14, 24, 25, 27
Smithson, Michael 3, 23, 28
Socrates 9, 10–16, 24–5, 26, 28, 112, 164, 191, 204, 212, 214, 234, 236
  Apology 10, 11, 22, 24
  Euthyphro 10
  Laws 11, 13, 14
  Meno 11, 12–13, 15, 27, 244–5
  Phaedo 9, 79
  Republic 13, 14, 16
  Sophist 11, 13, 14

Theaetetus 10, 11–12, 14
Timaeus 13, 27
  see also Plato
Solomon, Andrew 177, 194, 195, 197, 198, 199
Sophocles
  Oedipus Rex 63
Spender, Stephen 199
Sprinker, Michael 129
Stainer, Pauline 232
Stanfield, Paul Scott 250
Stevenson, Robert Louis 185
Stevens, Wallace 228, 246
Stewart, Garrett 246
Stroud, Barry 19, 20, 25, 28–9, 30
Strouse, Jean 197
Styron, William 176, 177, 188, 190, 195–6, 199
sublime, the 55, 56–7, 58–63
Swirski, Peter 53

Tambling, Jeremy 121, 130
Tarnas, Richard 200
Terry, Richard 78
torpedo fish 12–13, 15–16, 26–7
tragedy, 21
Tumin, Melvin 4

unconscious 156, 170
Unger, Peter 28
Updike, John 202
Usher, James
  Clio; or A Discourse on Taste 61

Vlastos, Gregory 24–5

Walcott, Derek 101
Walsh, Dorothy 97
Waters, Catherine 130
Weinstein, Philip 5, 7, 32, 124, 128
Weiskel, Thomas 56
Wells, H.G.
  Invisible Man, The 135
Wilde, Oscar 226

Williams, C.K. 233
Williams, Michael 20, 30
Willis, Thomas 189
Wilmer, Clive 247
Wimsatt, W.K.
   'Intentional Fallacy, The' 42, 52
Wittgenstein, Ludwig 23, 27, 32
Wolfson, Susan 92, 164, 173, 174
Wollaeger, Mark A. 150
Wolpert, Lewis 200
Wood, Michael
   Literature and the Taste of Knowledge 53, 252
Woodhouse, Richard 85–6
Woolf, Virginia 178
Wordsworth, William 171, 236
   'Anecdote for Fathers' 58, 164
   'Essay, Supplementary to the Preface' 79
   'Gipsies' 83
   'Idiot Boy, The' 58
   'Lines Written a Few Miles Above Tintern Abbey' 59–60, 61
   'Nutting' 197
   'Ode: Intimations of Immortality' 167, 175
   'Preface' to *Lyrical Ballads* 68
   Prelude, The 49, 55–8, 60
   'Thorn, The' 58
   'We Are Seven' 58, 161–7, 173–5

Yeats, W.B.
   'Leda and the Swan' 3
Young, Kay 125

Ziolkowski, Theodore 25–6
Žižek, Slavoj 31
Zunshine, Lisa 123–4